AF771287

THE NEW CIVIL PROCEDURE RULES

THE NEW CIVIL PROCEDURE RULES

DAVID GREENE M.Sc (London), FCI Arb
SOLICITOR OF THE SUPREME COURT, MEMBER OF THE CIVIL PROCEDURE RULES COMMITTEE AND A MEMBER OF THE WORKING PARTY ON PRACTICE DIRECTIONS

BUTTERWORTHS
LONDON, EDINBURGH, DUBLIN
1999

United Kingdom	Butterworths, a Division of Reed Elsevier (UK) Ltd, Halsbury House, 35 Chancery Lane, LONDON WC2A 1EL, and 4 Hill Street, EDINBURGH, EH2 3JZ
Australia	Butterworths, a Division of Reed International Books Australia Pty Ltd, CHATSWOOD, New South Wales
Canada	Butterworths Canada Ltd, MARKHAM, Ontario
Hong Kong	Butterworths Asia (Hong Kong), HONG KONG
India	Butterworths India, NEW DELHI
Ireland	Butterworth (Ireland) Ltd, DUBLIN
Malaysia	Malayan Law Journal Sdn Bhd, KUALA LUMPUR
New Zealand	Butterworths of New Zealand Ltd, WELLINGTON
Singapore	Butterworths Asia, SINGAPORE
South Africa	Butterworths Publishers (Pty) Ltd, DURBAN
USA	Lexix Law Publishing, CHARLOTTESVILLE, Virginia

© Reed Elsevier (UK) Ltd 1999

All rights reserved. No part of this publication may be reproduced in any material form (including photocopying or storing it in any medium by electronic means and whether or not transiently or incidentally to some other use of this publication) without the written permission of the copyright owner except in accordance with the provisions of the Copyright, Designs and Patents Act 1988 or under the terms of a licence issued by the Copyright Licensing Agency Ltd, 90 Tottenham Court Road, London, England W1P 0LP. Applications for the copyright owner's written permission to reproduce any part of this publication should be addressed to the publisher.

Warning: The doing of an unauthorised act in relation to a copyright work may result in both a civil claim for damages and criminal prosecution.

Any Crown copyright material is reproduced with the permission of the Controller of Her Majesty's Stationery Office.

A CIP Catalogue record for this book is available from the British Library.

ISBN 0 406 98379 8

Printed and bound in Great Britain by
Butler & Tanner Ltd, Frome, Somerset

Visit us at our website: http://www.butterworths.co.uk

FOREWORD

The implementation of the Civil Procedure Rules and the accompanying practice directions represents a major change in the way in which civil litigation is conducted. The many frustrations of the old-style procedure have been swept away and replaced by a fresh approach. The uncertainties and worries of mounting costs and delays, for example, are now met head on by the court's new powers to impose strict timetables to keep the progress of cases on track, and to control the amount of work done so that it is proportionate to the value and complexity of the issues at stake.

The fact that the new Rules and practice directions are written in plain English, without resorting to old-fashioned legal jargon, hopefully means that the new procedures can easily be followed. However, both for newcomers to the system and for those of us who have been using the system for any length of time, there is much to be learnt about the new approach. The publication of material such as *The New Civil Procedure Rules* is an invaluable tool in that process and I congratulate David Greene on a job well done. He and his firm Edwin Coe have been in the forefront in helping to implement the civil justice reforms.

THE RIGHT HONOURABLE THE LORD WOOLF
MASTER OF THE ROLLS

CONTENTS

CHAPTER 1
THE BACKGROUND

In 1994 the Right Honourable Lord Woolf QC, Master of the Rolls, was appointed by the then Lord Chancellor, Lord Mackay, to head an inquiry into "Access to Justice". The inquiry was to investigate the broad range of civil justice, its workings, failings and achievements. The perception at the time was that the failings outweighed the achievements particularly in relation to lower value claims.

An Interim Report was provided by the Woolf inquiry team in June 1995. In that Report Lord Woolf attempted to define what a civil justice system should deliver—

- Be *just* in the results it delivers.
- Be *fair* in the way it treats litigants.
- Offer appropriate procedures at a reasonable *cost*.
- Deal with cases with reasonable *speed*.
- Be *understandable* to those who use it.
- Be *responsive* to the needs of those who use it.
- Provide as much *certainty* as the nature of particular cases allows.
- Be *effective* meaning adequately resourced and organised.

The Report then identified problems with the pre Civil Procedure Rules ("CPR") system as five-fold—

- too *expensive* in that costs often exceeded the value of the claim.
- too *slow* in bringing cases to a conclusion.
- too *unequal* in that there was a lack of equality between the powerful, wealthy litigant and the under-resourced litigant.
- too *uncertain* with great difficulty of forecasting what litigation would cost and how long it would last.

Finally, the whole system was *incomprehensible* to many litigants.

Lord Woolf identified other organisational problems in that there was no one with clear overall responsibility for the administration of civil justice. This was met by the appointment of the Vice Chancellor, Sir Richard Scott QC, as Head of Civil Justice.

Lord Woolf also said that cases were run in too adversarial a fashion because they were controlled by the parties and not the Courts. He felt that Rules of Court were all too often ignored by the parties and in any event not enforced by the Court.

The Interim Report provided the first picture of the new landscape that Lord Woolf foresaw as tackling some of those existing problems, particularly in the lower value claims. His initial recommendations were based upon expanding the idea that for lower value claims procedures should be simpler and therefore less costly, much like the small claims procedure under the CCR. Defended civil cases would be split into three types—

- an expanded small claims jurisdiction;
- a new fast track for straightforward cases up to £10,000 with a limit on procedures, timetables and costs; and
- a new multi track for cases above £10,000 with new judicial hands-on management of the claim.

In July 1996 the Final Report of the inquiry was published. Practitioners should have regard to the Final Report because it provides the foundation for much of what has followed although in many cases ideas promulgated in the Final Report have either been further developed or changed entirely.

The Final Report consisted of a wide ranging review and recommendations of the civil justice scene, dealing in both generality and the particularity of specific areas such as the Crown Office List.

One of the main goals of the inquiry was the production of a single, simple procedural code to apply to civil litigation in the High Court and County Courts. This requirement was fulfilled by the production of a core set of rules known as the Brown Book. That book can be completely disregarded now save as an historical document.

A civil justice "landscape"

Lord Woolf wanted to establish a new civil justice "landscape" with the following features—

• Litigation will be avoided wherever possible

Court proceedings should be a last resort after using more appropriate means to resolve a dispute. Alternative dispute resolution should be encouraged, even by the grant of Legal Aid for it. Protocols would be encouraged for all areas of litigation. Failure to settle may lead to sanctions imposed by the Court.

• Litigation will be less adversarial and more co-operative

A lack of co-operation would lead to sanctions imposed by the Court. ADR would be encouraged during the course of proceedings. Experts should not become part of the adversarial tool kit¾a single expert ought to be appointed by the Court wherever possible.

• Litigation will be less complex

There should be one set of rules for both the High Court and County Court written in plain English. The claim and defence should likewise be written in plain English without technical rules as to the contents. Proceedings should be dispensed with if there is "no real prospect of success". A claimant should be able to start proceedings in any Court with an obligation on the Court itself to transfer matters to an appropriate part of the system. Discovery would be tightly controlled and reduced. Special procedures would apply to special types of proceedings such as multi party actions. The appeal system would be reviewed.

- **The timescale of litigation will be shorter and more certain**

Cases would proceed to trial in accordance with a set timetable monitored by the Court. On the fast track there would be a fixed timetable of no more than 30 weeks. Strict sanctions would be applied for failure to comply with timetables. Appeals from case management decisions would be kept to a minimum. The Court would manage the trial closely.

- **The costs of litigation will be more affordable, more predictable and more proportionate to the value and complexity of individual cases**

Costs on the fast track would be fixed. The Court would control costs either by the production of estimates by the parties or by the setting of a budget. That budget would be issued in some cases based upon guidelines compiled with the assistance of the users. There would be a new test on the taxation of costs so that the limit of costs allowed would be "such sum as is reasonable taking account of the interests of both parties to the taxation".

- **Parties of limited financial means will be able to conduct litigation on a more equal footing**

Litigants not legally represented would have assistance from advice services at the Courts. The Court would take account of the parties' financial circumstances in the allocation of the case to fast track or small claims track. Limited procedures and tight timetables would make it more difficult for costly tactical exercises by rich parties. There would be more effective sanctions against the parties including the payment of a fixed sum of costs forthwith.

- **There will be clear lines of judicial and administrative responsibility for the civil justice system**

The Head of Civil Justice would have overall responsibility for the civil justice system in England and Wales. He would be assisted by presiding Judges on each circuit who would have responsibility generally for civil work on the circuit. Again they would be assisted by a nominated Circuit Judge who would have responsibility for each Civil Trial Centre and satellite Courts. A new administrative structure would establish a partnership between the judiciary and the Court Service.

- **The structure of the Courts and the deployment of Judges will be designed to meet the needs of litigants**

Cases would generally be heard at civil trial centres but smaller local courts would deal with small claims and fast track claims. They would also deal with case management of the less complex multi track cases. The appeal system would be developed and simplified. Information technology would be used to its full. The trial would take place on the date assigned for it.

- **Judges will be deployed effectively so that they can manage litigation with the new rules and protocols**

Judges would be trained in managing cases. They would be encouraged to specialise in particular areas with cases being dealt with by the part of the Court system most appropriate. The Judges would have administrative and technological support.

- **The civil justice system will be responsive to the needs of litigants**

Systems would be developed at Courts to provide advice and assistance to litigants backed up by a readily available source of information. Court staff would help litigants with how to progress their case.

The beginnings of the new regime

As practitioners and parties become familiar with this new landscape it will be seen that many of these ideas have indeed been carried forward into the Civil Procedure Rules. Some of them, however, remain to be fulfilled. By way of example, it was intended at the time that the information technology required to support the Courts in the new system would be available on the day that the new Rules came into effect. That has not happened but remains in prospect.

The Final Report came out at a time when there were significant changes taking place in civil justice and the provision of legal services by practitioners. Legal Aid was subject to review by the then administration. Conditional fees had become lawful in personal injury and insolvency cases. Some Courts were already undertaking case management as they had done for some time prior to July 1996 - multi party actions, the Official Referee's Court (as it was then known) and the Commercial Court. Several reports had been prepared in relation to alternative dispute resolution - the Lord Chancellor's Department produced a guide: *Resolving Disputes Without Going to Court.* A pilot scheme for mediation had been commenced in the Central London County Court. The Commercial Court was particularly proactive in trying to secure settlement of as many issues in a case as possible prior to trial.

The major bar to fulfilment of Lord Woolf's desires set out in the Final Report was the question of cost. No doubt his recommendations required the commitment of funds from the Lord Chancellor's Department and the Court Service. If indeed the Court were to take a more active role in managing cases then at its simplest, further Judges would have to be appointed. This seemed to fly in the face of the Government's desire to drive down the costs to the Treasury of public service.

Notwithstanding the concern that commitment to change would involve further spending, the then Lord Chancellor supported Lord Woolf's Report by introducing the Civil Procedure Act 1997. This received Royal Assent on 31 February 1997. The relevant Sections are reproduced below.

CIVIL PROCEDURE ACT 1997

1. Civil Procedure Rules

(1) There are to be rules of court (to be called "Civil Procedure Rules") governing the practice and procedure to be followed in—

(a) the civil division of the Court of Appeal,

(b) the High Court, and

(c) county courts.

(2) Schedule 1 (which makes further provision about the extent of the power to make Civil Procedure Rules) is to have effect.

(3) The power to make Civil Procedure Rules is to be exercised with a view to securing that the civil justice system is accessible, fair and efficient.

Notes to Section 1

The new Civil Procedure Rules would replace entirely the Rules of the Supreme Court and the County Court Rules. There would be no other rules than the Civil Procedure Rules governing procedure in the County Court, the High Court and the Court of Appeal.

2. Rule Committee

(1) Civil Procedure Rules are to be made by a committee known as the Civil Procedure Rule Committee, which is to consist of—

(a) the Master of the Rolls,

(b) the Vice-Chancellor, and

(c) the persons currently appointed by the Lord Chancellor under subsection (2).

(2) The Lord Chancellor must appoint—

(a) one judge of the Supreme Court,

(b) one Circuit judge,

(c) one district judge,

(d) one person who is a Master referred to in Part II of Schedule 2 to the Supreme Court Act 1981,

(e) three persons who have a Supreme Court qualification (within the meaning of section 71 of the Courts and Legal Services Act 1990), including at least one with particular experience of practice in county courts,

(f) three persons who have been granted by an authorised body, under Part II of that Act, the right to conduct litigation in relation to all proceedings in the Supreme Court, including at least one with particular experience of practice in county courts,

(g) one person with experience in and knowledge of consumer affairs, and

(h) one person with experience in and knowledge of the lay advice sector.

(3) Before appointing a judge of the Supreme Court under subsection (2)(a), the Lord Chancellor must consult the Lord Chief Justice.

(4) Before appointing a person under paragraph (e) or (f) of subsection (2), the Lord Chancellor must consult any body which—

(a) has members who are eligible for appointment under that paragraph, and

(b) is an authorised body for the purposes of section 27 or 28 of the Courts and Legal Services Act 1990.

(5) The Lord Chancellor may reimburse the members of the Civil Procedure Rule Committee their travelling and out-of-pocket expenses.

(6) The Civil Procedure Rule Committee must, before making or amending Civil Procedure Rules—

(a) consult such persons as they consider appropriate, and

(b) meet (unless it is inexpedient to do so).

(7) The Civil Procedure Rule Committee must, when making Civil Procedure Rules, try to make rules which are both simple and simply expressed.

(8) Rules made by the Civil Procedure Rule Committee must be signed by at least eight members of the Committee and be submitted to the Lord Chancellor, who may allow or disallow them.

Notes to Section 2

The Rule Committee was appointed in July 1997. It consisted of members drawn from various professional and consumer backgrounds. It had responsibility for production of the Rules.

3. Section 2: supplementary

(1) Rules made and allowed under section 2 are to—

(a) come into force on such day as the Lord Chancellor may direct, and

(b) be contained in a statutory instrument to which the Statutory Instruments Act 1946 is to apply as if it contained rules made by a Minister of the Crown.

(2) A statutory instrument containing Civil Procedure Rules shall be subject to annulment in pursuance of a resolution of either House of Parliament.

Notes to Section 3

The initial statutory instrument signed by the Committee in December 1998 is SI 1998/3132. A further statutory instrument brought into effect further changes to fill gaps and make slight changes to the Rules prior to 26 April 1999: SI 1999/1008.

4. Power to make consequential amendments

(1) The Lord Chancellor may by order amend, repeal or revoke any enactment to the extent he considers necessary or desirable in consequence of—

(a) section 1 or 2, or

(b) Civil Procedure Rules.

(2) The Lord Chancellor may by order amend, repeal or revoke any enactment passed or made before the commencement of this section to the extent he considers necessary or desirable in order to facilitate the making of Civil Procedure Rules.

(3) Any power to make an order under this section is exercisable by statutory instrument.

(4) A statutory instrument containing an order under subsection (1) shall be subject to annulment in pursuance of a resolution of either House of Parliament.

(5) No order may be made under subsection (2) unless a draft of it has been laid before and approved by resolution of each House of Parliament.

Notes to Section 4

The modifications made to legislation under this provision were effected by the Civil Procedure (Modification of Enactments) Order 1998, SI 1998/2940.

5. Practice directions

(1) Practice directions may provide for any matter which, by virtue of paragraph 3 of Schedule 1, may be provided for by Civil Procedure Rules.

(2) After section 74 of the County Courts Act 1984 there is inserted—

"PRACTICE DIRECTIONS

74A Practice directions

(1) Directions as to the practice and procedure of county courts may be made by the Lord Chancellor.

(2) Directions as to the practice and procedure of county courts may not be made by any other person without the approval of the Lord Chancellor.

(3) The power of the Lord Chancellor to make directions under subsection (1) includes power—

(a) to vary or revoke directions made by him or any other person, and

(b) to make different provision for different cases or different areas, including different provision—

(i) for a specific court, or

(ii) for specific proceedings, or a specific jurisdiction,

specified in the directions.

(4) References in this section to the Lord Chancellor include any person authorised by him to act on his behalf."

Notes to Section 5

Well over 500 separate practice directions were identified. All of those practice directions no longer have effect after 26 April 1999. The only practice directions that will apply are those prepared for the purposes of the Civil Procedure Rules under the authority of the Head of Civil Justice (see below).

CIVIL JUSTICE COUNCIL

6. Civil Justice Council

(1) The Lord Chancellor is to establish and maintain an advisory body, to be known as the Civil Justice Council.

(2) The Council must include—

(a) members of the judiciary,
(b) members of the legal professions,
(c) civil servants concerned with the administration of the courts,
(d) persons with experience in and knowledge of consumer affairs,
(e) persons with experience in and knowledge of the lay advice sector, and
(f) persons able to represent the interests of particular kinds of litigants (for example, businesses or employees).

(3) The functions of the Council are to include—

(a) keeping the civil justice system under review,
(b) considering how to make the civil justice system more accessible, fair and efficient,
(c) advising the Lord Chancellor and the judiciary on the development of the civil justice system,
(d) referring proposals for changes in the civil justice system to the Lord Chancellor and the Civil Procedure Rule Committee, and
(e) making proposals for research.

(4) The Lord Chancellor may reimburse the members of the Council their travelling and out-of-pocket expenses.

Notes to Section 6

The Civil Justice Council was appointed during 1998.

COURT ORDERS

7. Power of courts to make orders for preserving evidence, etc

(1) The court may make an order under this section for the purpose of securing, in the case of any existing or proposed proceedings in the court—

(a) the preservation of evidence which is or may be relevant, or

(b) the preservation of property which is or may be the subject-matter of the proceedings or as to which any question arises or may arise in the proceedings.

(2) A person who is, or appears to the court likely to be, a party to proceedings in the court may make an application for such an order.

(3) Such an order may direct any person to permit any person described in the order, or secure that any person so described is permitted—

(a) to enter premises in England and Wales, and

(b) while on the premises, to take in accordance with the terms of the order any of the following steps.

(4) Those steps are—

(a) to carry out a search for or inspection of anything described in the order, and

(b) to make or obtain a copy, photograph, sample or other record of anything so described.

(5) The order may also direct the person concerned—

(a) to provide any person described in the order, or secure that any person so described is provided, with any information or article described in the order, and

(b) to allow any person described in the order, or secure that any person so described is allowed, to retain for safe keeping anything described in the order.

(6) An order under this section is to have effect subject to such conditions as are specified in the order.

(7) This section does not affect any right of a person to refuse to do anything on the ground that to do so might tend to expose him or his spouse to proceedings for an offence or for the recovery of a penalty.

(8) In this section—

"court" means the High Court, and

"premises" includes any vehicle;

and an order under this section may describe anything generally, whether by reference to a class or otherwise.

Notes to Section 7

This section gives statutory authority to the Anton Piller procedure. In accordance with the CPR such an injunction is to be known as a Search Order (see Part 25, page 135).

8. Disclosure etc of documents before action begun

(1) The Lord Chancellor may by order amend the provisions of section 33(2) of the Supreme Court Act 1981, or section 52(2) of the County Courts Act 1984 (power of court to order disclosure etc of documents where claim may be made in respect of personal injury or death), so as to extend the provisions—

(a) to circumstances where other claims may be made, or

(b) generally.

(2) The power to make an order under this section is exercisable by statutory instrument which shall be subject to annulment in pursuance of a resolution of either House of Parliament.

Notes to Section 8

This section provides specific power to the Lord Chancellor to amend Section 33(2) of the Supreme Court Act 1981 and Section 52(2) of the County Courts Act 1984. These sections provided for pre-action disclosure in actions relating to personal injury or death. The intention was to amend them to allow pre-action disclosure in all types of claims. This change has been effected by the modification order under Section 4 above (see CPR Rule 31.16).

The new administration elected in May 1997 committed itself to continuing the process of change and invoking the recommendations of the Final Report. As with the previous administration, the picture in civil justice has not stood still. As this book is prepared, the Access to Justice Bill is being studied by Parliament with a view to its provisions becoming law in late 1999.

The Rules took effect on 26 April 1999. From that day the Rules of the Supreme Court and the County Court Rules no longer have effect and all procedure is to be determined in accordance with the Civil Procedure Rules subject to the transitional provisions (see Chapter 2 post).

The structure of the new Rules

Procedure after 26 April 1999 is determined by the Civil Procedure Rules which is a collective term for all of the individual Rules. This collection is divided into individual Parts. It is further divided then into individual rules, paragraphs, sub-paragraphs, sub-sub-paragraphs and indeed on occasions sub-sub-sub-paragraphs. The various divisions of the Rules are unlikely to be used in day to day reference and will be referred to simply as a rule. By way of example, the regulation of the forms to be served with particulars of claim are contained within "Rule 7.8(1)(a), (b) and (c)".

Many of the individual Parts are supplemented by practice directions. The role of a practice direction is to complete any gaps in the Part, to provide detail not appropriate for inclusion within the Part itself and for practice guidance. The practice directions cannot provide contrary to a Part and where that may happen the Part is supreme.

The practice directions are divided into sections and paragraphs.

Civil procedure is also determined by various statutes and statutory instruments. For instance, the jurisdiction of the High Court and County Court remains regulated by the Supreme Court Act 1981, the County Courts Act 1984 and the High Court and County Courts Jurisdiction Order 1991. Reference still needs to be made to those statutes and statutory instruments although it must be remembered that they may have been amended by the Civil Procedure (Modification of Enactments) Order 1988.

Reference will also have to be made to court guides which at the time of writing are either published or being prepared. The Commercial Court Guide amends the CPR and practice directions quite substantially, deriving its empowerment to do so from Rule 49(1) and Paragraph 14 of the Practice Direction to Part 49. The Chancery Guide follows some of the guidance of Commercial Court Guide describing itself as providing additional practical information. If Chancery work is being undertaken, however, reference must be made to the Chancery Guide. The Queen's Bench is producing its own guide, as yet not on the bookshelves; so are certain county courts. Some might complain that a plethora of such guides does derogate from the concept of one set of rules for all civil procedure.

CHAPTER 2
TRANSITIONAL ARRANGEMENTS

Although there have been voices against this approach including that of the Head of Civil Justice, Sir Richard Scott, the approach of both the Lord Chancellor and Lord Woolf has been to introduce the new Rules in one "Big Bang". The alternative of drip feeding the new Rules into the system or leaving existing proceedings to run under the system pre 26 April 1999 has been rejected. For this reason quite complex transitional provisions had to be invoked.

The original intention was that details of these provisions should be contained within a Rule but this approach, regarded as too inflexible, has been rejected. Instead Part 51 of the CPR simply provides that the transitional arrangements shall be included in a practice direction.

Practice directions are made by the Head of Civil Justice under Section 5 of the Civil Procedure Act 1997 (see page 7). They provide a much more flexible method of detailing the transitional arrangements which may well have to be changed as the new Rules are introduced. In due course clearly the practice direction can be dispensed with altogether.

The **Practice Direction to Part 51** deals generally with transitional arrangements for claims issued prior to 26 April 1999 and the costs arising from them. In addition, the costs Practice Direction sets out in more detail transitional arrangements for costs. Further, the Practice Direction to the protocols also sets out transitional arrangements for the two protocols having effect from 26 April 1999; for personal injury actions and clinical disputes (see below).

Practice Direction to Part 51

The general scheme of events on or after 26 April 1999 in relation to proceedings commenced prior to that date is set out in Paragraph 2 of the Practice Direction—

(a) to apply the previous rules to undefended cases, allowing them to progress to their disposal; but

(b) to apply the CPR to defended cases so far as is practicable.

There are three situations covered by the transitional arrangements—

- Proceedings have been issued prior to 26 April 1999 (whether or not served also prior to 26 April 1999) and the Defendant has not taken any steps to respond to the claim.
- Proceedings have been issued and served prior to 26 April 1999. The Defendant has responded and pleadings have closed prior to 26 April 1999 under the rules then applying.
- Proceedings have been issued prior to 26 April 1999 (whether or not served prior to that date) and pleadings have not closed as at 26 April 1999 in accordance with the rules applying prior to that date.

These 3 situations are dealt with more fully below. Over and above these the parties can agree to the application of the CPR (see below).

Proceedings have been issued prior to 26 April (whether or not served also prior to 26 April) and the Defendant has not taken any steps to respond to the claim

The Defendant must respond to the claim which is served upon him in accordance with the RSC and CCR. Thus a Defendant served with a Writ issued in the High Court on which there is a general endorsement must acknowledge service on the form of acknowledgment served with the Writ. Similarly, in the County Court form N9 must be returned to the Court to enable the Defendant to contest the proceedings (Paragraphs 3 and 4, Practice Direction).

In addition to acknowledging service in accordance with the RSC and CCR, the Defendant must proceed thereafter in accordance with those Rules. Thus the Defence in the High Court must be served in accordance with RSC Order 18. In the County Court the Defendant must file and serve a Defence in accordance with CCR Order 9 (Paragraph 5, Practice Direction).

If no acknowledgment of service or defence is served (and in the County Court filed) in response to proceedings commenced prior to 26 April 1999, the Claimant can enter default judgment in accordance with the RSC and CCR. If an application to the Court is required on or after 26 April 1999 that application must be made in accordance with Part 23. If there remain issues to be decided by the Court upon entering default judgment such as the assessment of damages, the case will be referred to a Judge to exercise his case management powers. An application to set aside judgment will have to be made under CPR Part 23 but on that application the Court will apply not the RSC and CCR but CPR Part 13 (Paragraph 7, Practice Direction).

Proceedings have been issued and served prior to 26 April 1999. The Defendant has responded and pleadings have closed prior to 26 April 1999 under the rules then applying

If any step has been taken in such proceedings prior to 26 April 1999 it will remain valid on or after that date (Paragraph 10, Practice Direction). Similarly, if an order has been made prior to that date the parties must comply with it

(Paragraph 9, Practice Direction). If automatic directions apply (in the High Court under RSC Order 25 Rule 8 and in the County Court under CCR Order 17 Rule 11) the parties are obliged to comply with those directions on or after 26 April 1999. In the County Court if the Court has sent out the notice in relation to automatic directions (form N450) those directions still apply even if the timetable does not start until after 26 April 1999.

CCR Order 17 Rule 11(9) does not apply to any proceedings on or after 26 April 1999 (Paragraph 6, Practice Direction). Although some doubt has been expressed as to the position where an **order** has been made extending the time under Order 17 rule 11 (9).

Otherwise, subject to the application of CPR Part 1 (Overriding Objective: see Chapter 3 post) automatically to all proceedings after 26 April 1999, the Court will apply the CPR to existing proceedings (where pleadings have not closed) as soon as practicable. Thus when the proceedings come before a Judge for the first time on or after 26 April 1999 he will consider to what extent the CPR might apply to the proceedings. Although the Judge has a discretion, the impetus within the Practice Direction (Paragraph 15) is that he should apply the CPR to the proceedings as far as possible and in order to avoid that general rule he must positively dis-apply the Parts of the CPR that he feels inappropriate in the circumstances (Paragraph 15, Practice Direction).

If an application has been issued prior to 26 April 1999 but is to be heard on or after that date, again the general presumption is that the Court will apply the CPR to the order sought in such application. Thus if an application for summary judgment is issued prior to 26 April 1999 but is to be heard on or after that date, whether or not judgment will be given will be determined by CPR Part 24 and not RSC Order 14 or CCR Order 9 Rule 14. Similarly, if a trial is to be heard on or after 26 April 1999 the CPR will be applied for the purpose of conducting that trial insofar as relevant (Paragraph 15, Practice Direction).

Proceedings have been issued prior to 26 April 1999 (whether or not served prior to that date) and pleadings have not closed as at 26 April 1999 in accordance with the rules applying prior to that date

The Practice Direction provides some practical detail in relation to the application of the CPR. The general rule is that the CPR will apply to such proceedings from 26 April 1999.

Over and above these three situations the parties can irrevocably agree in writing to apply **all** the CPR under Paragraph 17 of the Practice Direction. A copy of such agreement must be filed with the court.

Paragraph 19 provides that if nothing has happened in proceedings issued prior to 26 April 1999 before 25 April 2000 the proceedings will be stayed subject to three exceptions—

- The trial is due to take place after 25 April 2000.
- Personal injury proceedings have been adjourned to determine the prognosis.

- The Court is dealing with the administration of an estate, trust or receivership.

Transitional arrangements-costs

The general rules in relation to the transitional arrangements for costs are set out in Paragraph 18 of the Practice Direction. This Paragraph needs to be read in conjunction with Section 3 of the Practice Direction to Part 48.

The general scheme is that where costs incurred prior to 26 April 1999 are to be assessed after that date they will be assessed in accordance with CPR Parts 43-48 (the costs provisions). The parties, however, should not be penalised by the application of the new Rules for work undertaken prior to 26 April 1999. If the Court would disallow costs incurred prior to 26 April 1999 under the new Rules but allow them under the old Rules then they should be allowed in any event. Although solicitors will submit bills after 26 April 1999 in accordance with the costs Practice Directions, it may be a matter of practice that solicitors prepare a bill under the old Rules for work undertaken before 26 April 1999 in order to have a ready comparison with what may have been allowed prior to that date.

Section 3 of the costs Practice Direction to Part 48 provides specifically for the application of transitional arrangements to four situations—

- **An order made prior to 26 April 1999 giving scale 1 or lower scale costs**

Where an order has been made in County Court proceedings before 26 April 1999 applying scale 1 or the lower scale then the costs will be assessed after 26 April 1999 on those scales.

- **Bills provisionally taxed before 26 April 1999**

Where costs have been provisionally taxed before 26 April 1999 the RSC and CCR determine who can request a hearing and the time limits for doing so. Otherwise the CPR govern the subsequent hearing subject to the general rule contained in Paragraph 18 of the Practice Direction.

- **Bills taxed before 26 April 1999**

Where a bill of costs has been taxed before 26 April 1999 then the RSC and CCR govern the steps which can be taken to challenge the taxation.

- **Other circumstances**

Where taxation proceedings were commenced before 26 April 1999 but not heard prior to that date, the CPR will be applied again subject to Paragraph 18 of the Part 51 of the Practice Direction. In addition, however, to the ability to appeal any subsequent order under CPR Rules 47.20 and 47.26 the party may apply for a review of that decision. That review will be treated as an appeal from an authorised Court officer under Part 47. The right to review is lost, however, if a notice is served complying with Paragraph 3.7(4) of the Practice Direction to Part 48 specifically dis-applying it.

Transitional arrangements-protocols

Paragraph 5 of the protocols Practice Direction deals with the application of the two protocols approved by it to proceedings commenced before and after 26 April 1999.

- If proceedings have been commenced prior to 26 April 1999 the pre-action protocols will have no effect. This does not mean, however, that pre-action behaviour will not be taken into account. See the decisions in *Butcher v Wolfe* (1998) Times, 9 November; and *Burrows v Vauxhall Motors Ltd* (1998) PIQR 48.
- If proceedings are commenced after 26 April 1999 as long as by commencement of the proceedings the parties have substantially achieved the object of the protocols, i.e. they have exchanged information about the claim and documentation enabling realistic negotiations to take place, parties will not be penalised for a failure to comply with the letter of the protocols or the Practice Direction (Paragraph 5.2). Further if since the protocols were published in January 1999 there has not been time to comply with these protocols e.g. because of the expiry of time limits, failure to comply will not be penalised.

  It has to be said that the Practice Direction does not provide parties with great certainty as to whether or not penalties will be imposed for failure to comply with pre-action protocols in the transitional period after 26 April 1999. Much remains within the discretion of the court. Insofar as possible it is suggested that the safest course for parties issuing proceedings after 26 April 1999 is to fulfil the protocols in entirety.

  Nothing is said in the Practice Direction about the transitional effect of Paragraph 4 of the Practice Direction which requires parties to comply with the spirit of the protocols even when one does not apply.

  The courts are already penalising parties who do not follow this "spirit" (*Butcher v Wolfe*). It is suggested therefore that before issuing proceedings within the "transitional period" after 26 April 1999 parties should comply with the "spirit" by exchanging information to allow meaningful negotiations to take place.

CHAPTER 3
PART 1—THE OVERRIDING OBJECTIVE

The adoption of an overriding or overall objective to a set of rules governing civil procedure is not an entirely new concept. Other jurisdictions have already taken this step albeit not to the extent or in the precise detail of CPR Part 1.

In developing the Civil Procedure Rules, Lord Woolf referred to the purpose of the overriding objective as follows—

- Although the Rules can offer detailed directions for the technical steps to be taken, the effectiveness of those steps depends upon the spirit in which they are carried out. That in turn depends on an understanding of the fundamental purpose of the Rules and on the underlying system of procedure.
- In order to identify that purpose at the outset, I have placed at the very beginning of the Rules a statement of their overriding objective. This is intended to govern the operation of all the Rules and in particular the choices which the Court makes in managing each case and in interpreting the Rules.
- The new Rules are deliberately not designed expressly to answer every question which could arise. Rule 1, the statement of the objective, provides a compass to guide courts and litigants and legal advisors as to their general course.

(Chapter 20 of the Final Report, pages 274-275, Paragraphs 10-12)

It is in this context that Rule 1.1(1) provides that—

> **These Rules are a new procedural code with the overriding objective of enabling the Court to deal with cases justly.**

The words **new procedural code** were added to this Rule at quite a late stage. The original Rule without them compares with similar rules in other jurisdictions.

The Federal Rules of Civil Procedure of the United States refer to the construction and administration of the Federal Rules—

> **to secure the just, speedy and inexpensive determination of every action.**

Similarly, the Federal Rules of Evidence of the United States provide that those Rules should be construed—

> **to secure fairness in administration, elimination of unjustifiable expense and delay, and promotion of growth and development of the law of evidence to the end that the truth may be ascertained and proceedings justly determined.**

Similarly, in Canada the Federal Rules provide—

> **These rules should be interpreted and applied so as to secure the just, most expeditious and least expensive determination of every proceeding on its merits.**

The underlying obligation upon the Court emanating from Rule 1.1(1) is that the Court is obliged to deal with cases justly. The Rules are simply there to enable the Court to do so. Thus they are a means to an end rather than an end in themselves. This purpose of the Rules was emphasised by the addition of the word **procedural**. They are the procedure by which the Court should seek to achieve the obligation of dealing with cases justly. What is **justly** is a matter of considerable debate. Rule 1.2 sets out some of the pragmatic elements of an interpretation of **justly** but certainly one of the overriding obligations of the Court is to try and find out the truth of the matters in issue. Rule 1.1(2) applies some pragmatic restrictions on the exercise of finding that truth (see below).

The words **new procedural code** were added rather late in the day in the drafting process at the behest of the Lord Chancellor. It was proposed that the Rules should state specifically that they acted as an exhaustive code, expressly discouraging parties from referring back to old authorities when arguing points under the new Rules. Whilst not expressly stating that the Rules are an exhaustive code, the reference **new procedural code** is intended to signify that at the very least, previous authorities should only be of persuasive effect in the understanding, construction and application of the new Rules.

It may seem somewhat ironic to refer to previous decisions when explaining the nature of a codified system. In *Bank of England v Vagliano Bros* [1891] AC 107, HL, Lord Herschell provided a judicial description of a new codified system when referring to the then new Bills of Exchange Act 1882 at pages 144, 5.

> **"I cannot bring myself to think that this [an examination of the state of the law at the time the Bills of Exchange Act was passed] is the proper way to deal with such a statute ... which was intended to be a code of the law ... I think the proper course is in the first instance to examine the language of the statute and to ask what is its natural meaning, uninfluenced by any considerations derived from the previous state of law, and not to start with enquiring how the law previously stood, and then, assuming that it was probably intended to leave itunaltered, to see if the words of the enactment will bear an interpretation in conformity with this view."**

"If a statute, intended to embody in a code a particular branch of the law, is to be treated in this fashion, it appears to me that its utility will be almost entirely destroyed, and the very object with which it was enacted will be frustrated. The purpose of such a statute surely was that on any point specifically dealt with by it, the law should be ascertained by interpreting the language used instead of, as before, by roaming over a vast number of authorities in order to discover what the law was, extracting it by a minute critical examination of the prior decisions ..."

Limitations–Rule 1.1(2)

Rule 1.1(2) sets out some examples of the manner in which the Court can meet its obligation to deal with the case justly. Put shortly, however, it might be better to describe Rule 1.1(2) as pragmatic limitations on the Court's and the parties' ability to roam widely and freely without any consideration of the costs to meet its obligation to determine the truth. It will be clear that the limitations expressed in Rule 1.1(2) are primarily financial.

Central to these limitations is the concept of **proportionality**. Lord Woolf in his Final Report described this concept as one of the core issues to the future of litigation. Its most practical aspect is that the costs incurred in relation to a claim should be proportionate to the matters in dispute (Rule 44.4, see page 359). Proportionality is also a consideration in relation to disclosure and inspection and search (Rules 31.3 and 31.7, see pages 229–242).

As the costs Practice Direction points out (see Paragraphs 3.1–3.3, Practice Direction to Part 44) the relationship between proportionality and the matters in issue in a claim is not straightforward. The value of the claim may be a guide but the issues involved in a claim of comparatively low value can very easily be more complex than the issues involved in a high value claim. It is for this reason that Rule 1.1(2)(c) includes considerations over and above the amount of money involved. The importance of the case or the complexity of the issues may be much more important considerations depending on the nature of the claim.

What is required of the Court is to exercise a balancing act between meeting its obligations to act justly and adopting a procedure with the necessary cost consequences that fits the particular claim with which it is dealing.

The other balancing act required under Rule 1.1 is adopting a procedure that does not unfairly prejudice one party against the other in terms of their financial resources and their ability to comply with any procedural requirements. Thus the Court has to ensure—

that the parties are on an equal footing

(Rule 1.1(2)(a))

and deal with the case:

> **... in ways which are proportionate ... to the financial position of each party**

(Rule 1.1(2)(c)(iv))

This is not intended to give rise to close examination of the financial standing of each party but to apply where there is an obvious financial disparity. Using this power the Court might refuse to permit a better funded party to take a step for which there is no real justification or purpose. Another example was given by Lord Woolf in his Final Report. Adopting a practice used in the procedure for the Banking Ombudsman, if one party wishes to take steps the benefit of which remains doubtful, the Court might require that that party meet the costs of the other party undertaking a similar exercise.

Proportionality will be much debated before the Courts. It is a candidate for early guidance from the Court of Appeal.

As well as an obligation to deal with a case justly, the Court is also obliged to deal with a case "fairly" (Rule 1.1(2)(d)). The use of the word **fairly** is intended to invoke a moral obligation on the part of the Court over and above that of the obligations implied in dealing with cases justly. Fairness of the Court is in any event one of its obligations under Article 6 of the European Convention for the Protection of Human Rights.

Rule 1.1(2)(e) which provides the allotment to a case an appropriate share of the Court's resources, reflects the general nature of Rule 1.1(2) by imposing economic limitations on what parties can expect the Court to provide to deal with a particular case. In particular the Court is obliged to take into account not only the parties and issues involved in the case but the call of other litigants also using the civil justice system. Thus the obligation of the Court to deal with cases justly does not extend to allow parties an unlimited call upon the Court's resources, such as the provision of a Judge to hear a case over and above a certain limited period—for example, in the fast track, one day.

Rule 1.1(2) has an overriding limit of **practicability**. Thus under Rule 1.1(2)(a) the Court is only obliged to ensure that parties are on an equal footing as far as practicable. If it is practicable it is suggested that the Court would have an obligation to ensure that the parties are on an equal footing but whether or not it is practicable in the circumstances of a particular case leaves a large area of discretion to the Court.

The occasion on which parties may expect the Court to exercise its obligations under Rule 1.1 will be at the allocation stage. For example, in performing its balancing act between the Court's and parties' resources and the obligation to deal with cases justly, the Court will require estimates of costs that have and will be incurred and may require estimates for a particular step. This information is provided in the allocation questionnaire (see page 152 post).

Exercising the Court's Discretion

Rule 1.2 invokes the use of the overriding objective by the Court when the Court:

(a) exercises any power given to it by the Rules; or
(b) interprets any Rule.

Parties' obligations

The aim of this Rule is to make it clear that the Court must use the overriding objective in two ways: firstly, as a guide in the process of exercising any discretion given to it by the Rules; and secondly, to reinforce the exhaustive nature of the Rules by providing the Court with a purposive method of interpretation of the Rules.

Rule 1.3 spells out the duty of the parties to help the Court to further the overriding objective. The obligation required has been slightly lessened in the course of re-drafting. The words **are required** have replaced the word **must**. Some concern was expressed by practitioners on a consultation that the use of **must** might impose a new professional duty on legal representatives which might conflict with the duty to the client. As finalised the Rule is intended to act as an exhortation to the parties. Accordingly the Court will expect parties to conduct litigation under the **new procedural code** so that the Court is enabled to deal with cases justly.

So in accordance with Rule 1.1(2) the parties should conduct themselves so that the case is dealt with in ways which are proportionate, expeditious and fair. This requires co-operation both between the parties and with the Court. A failure to comply with Rule 1.3 will lead to sanctions and particularly cost consequences.

Solicitors should explain to the client at the commencement of instructions exactly what will be required of them during the course of the litigation. A legal representative must be free to carry out the client's instructions but if these appear to be unreasonable in all the circumstances, the representative must warn the client of the potential consequences. For this reason it is suggested that express reference is made to Rule 1.3 in the client care letter issued by solicitors under Rule 15 of the Solicitors Practice Rules 1990 (as amended). The provisions relating to the client care letter are in any event undergoing change and fresh requirements are being made of solicitors.

Active Case Management

The final obligation established in Part 1 is the Court's duty to actively manage cases under Rule 1.4. Rule 1.4(2) sets out examples of what the Court may do when actively managing a case. Despite the obligation in Rule 1.4(1), the Court is only required to comply with Rule 1.4(2) if it is appropriate in all the circumstances. It should also be pointed out that there is no order of importance of the steps set out in Rule 1.4(2). The drafting is an attempt at a chronological order in the progress of a case through the procedure.

CHAPTER 4
PART 21—CHILDREN AND PATIENTS

Introduction

Lord Woolf did not address the issue of the representation of children and patients in the course of litigation. Thus there are no particular issues addressed in Part 21 arising from the Interim or Final Reports save for the general invocation to simplify the language of the Rules and their implementation.

The Law Commission issued a report on mental incapacity in 1995 (Law Com No 231). As yet legislation has not been introduced to bring the report into effect. If and when a statute is passed, Part 21 may need substantial change. Under the old regime, RSC Order 80 and CCR Order 10 dealt with children and patients under the old regime. The CCR provisions were drafted in more simple terms than the RSC. For this reason CCR Order 10 was used by the drafting team as the basis for the current Rules in preference to the RSC.

The most marked difference under the new regime is the renaming of the person taking the responsibility in the litigation on behalf of the child or patient, no longer a guardian ad litem or next friend but now a "**litigation friend**". This renaming was surprisingly the subject of little debate at the Committee stage. No doubt the phrase is imperfect but no one came up with anything considered better.

Because Part 21 is the result of the exercise of simply pulling together RSC Order 80 and CCR Order 10, the general changes to the regime are not substantial. Since this Part was drafted and finalised, however, the practice direction has been added to it, providing detail for the Part.

The main differences between Part 21 and RSC Order 20 are—

- the litigation friend does not have to act by a solicitor; and
- the certificate of suitability does not have to be given by a solicitor.

The differences between the CPR and CCR Order 10 are—

- CCR Order 10 Rule 3(b) provides the Court with the power to strike out proceedings if they are commenced by a child or patient without a next friend. The CPR approach is from the other way in that any step taken by the child or patient is of no effect unless the Court orders otherwise (Rule 21.3(4)).
- The appointment of a District Judge as a litigation friend has not been included in the CPR.

- Under CCR Order 10 Rule 8, a child could be allowed by the Court to defend proceedings without a litigation friend only where the claim was for a "liquidated sum". This limitation no longer applies.
- There is no specific provision as there was under the CCR (Order 10 Rule 9) that a guardian ad litem is not personally liable for costs other than those arising from misconduct or neglect. This is now generally covered by the costs provisions and the Court's general discretion under them.

Part 21 is more explicit than the old rules in some respects—

- The effect of steps taken before a litigation friend is appointed is dealt with more clearly.
- The removal of a litigation friend is dealt with expressly.
- The criteria for suitability are dealt with in greater detail.
- Part 21 sets out the procedure to be followed when the child reaches 18 or a person ceases to be a patient.
- The CPR deals more explicitly with pre-proceedings applications (Rule 21.3(2)(a)).

The general lay of the land under Part 21 is as follows—

- A child (a person under 18) and a patient (a person suffering mental disorder as defined in the Mental Health Act 1983 and incapable of managing and administering their own affairs) can only take and defend proceedings if represented by a litigation friend.
- The litigation friend of a child can either be appointed without a Court order by filing a certificate of suitability or by Court order.
- A litigation friend of a patient can be appointed in accordance with Part VII of the Mental Health Act 1983 or by Court order.
- Until the appointment of a litigation friend, any steps taken are of no effect unless the Court otherwise orders.
- The Court has the power to remove a litigation friend upon application or of its own initiative.
- The litigation friend's appointment on behalf of a child ends automatically when the child reaches 18. If a party ceases to be a patient, however, the appointment continues until it is ended by a Court order.
- Any settlement or compromise in proceedings made by or on behalf of or against a child or patient must be approved by the Court.
- If no proceedings have been commenced, that approval will be sought using the Part 8 procedure.
- The Court has the power of management of monies recovered by or on behalf of a child or patient.

In addition to the provisions of Part 21, there are other provisions in the Rules generally that apply to children and patients. Rule 6.6 deals with service upon a child, patient or litigation friend. The Practice Direction to Part 40 deals with structured settlements including those made by or on behalf of a child or patient. Rule 48.5 deals with the assessment of costs as between party and party and solicitor and client.

The Rules

Rule 21.2 provides the general regime that a patient (as defined by Rule 21.1(2)(b)) and a child (as defined by Rule 21.1(2)(a)) may only prosecute or defend proceedings through a litigation friend.

A child but not a patient may seek the Court's permission to prosecute or defend proceedings without a litigation friend. The application must be made in accordance with Part 23. Accordingly an application notice must be filed with the Court which sets out the order sought and briefly why the applicant is seeking the order. Rule 21.2(4)(a) stipulates that the application may be made by the child. It does not stipulate, however, that it may **only** be made by the child. It could, for instance, be made by a litigation friend that has previously been appointed. Similarly, it might be made by the claimant against a child defendant. This in part reflects the old CCR Order 10 Rule 8 under which a plaintiff could apply to the Court for an order that where a minor was sued for a liquidated sum, the appointment of a guardian ad litem was unnecessary. This has not been repeated but does fall within the global provisions of Rule 21.2.

On making the application, unless the application is made by the child who has no litigation friend, notice of the application must be given to the respondent to it. If the application is made by the child where a litigation friend has been previously appointed, the respondent to the application is the litigation friend.

Under Section 47 of the County Courts Act 1984, "a minor" could prosecute any action in the County Court for payment of wages. This provision has been repealed by the Civil Procedure (Modification of Enactments) Order 1998.

If at some later stage, having made an order allowing the child to conduct proceedings without a litigation friend, it appears to the Court that it would be appropriate for a litigation friend to be appointed, it can do so under Rule 21.2(5).

Rule 21.3 provides detail of at what stage in the proceedings a litigation friend becomes necessary. It is very much part of the Woolf theme that much of the work for litigation should be undertaken prior to proceedings being issued, whether under a pre-action protocol or otherwise. Under the old rules the word "proceedings" was widely interpreted. Under the CPR it is likely to be as widely, if not more, interpreted to cover pre-action steps, particularly those taken in accordance with a pre-action protocol. The position is a little unclear because there is no formal process for the appointment of a litigation friend pre-action. It might be appropriate to make an application under Part 23 pre-action or to commence proceedings under Part 8 as required for the approval of an infant settlement under Rule 21.10 (see below). Indeed, a claimant can issue and serve a claim form without the appointment of a litigation friend under Rule 21.3. However, where anyone is pursuing a claim against a child or patient or is representing a child or patient before proceedings have been commenced, they will be rightly nervous of making any commitments without a formal appointment of a litigation friend by the Court.

Settlement prior to issue

There is a formal check within the Rules as to what can be done on behalf of a child or patient prior to the commencement of proceedings (Rule 21.10). No settlement, compromise or payment (whether before or after an action has been commenced) and no acceptance of money paid into Court is valid without the approval of the Court (Rule 21.10(1)). If the action has not been commenced then the procedure for obtaining the approval of the Court is by issuing a claim form under Part 8 which should include a request to the Court for approval of the settlement or compromise (Rule 21.10(2)).

Paragraphs 6.1–6.4 of the Practice Direction to Part 21 provide further detail of what is required on such an application. If it is made in accordance with Part 8 then the claim form must also set out the terms of the settlement or compromise or have attached to it a draft consent order in practice Form N292. The Court will require the following details—

- whether and to what extent the defendant admits liability;
- the age and occupation (if any) of the child or patient;
- evidence of the litigation friend's approval of the proposed settlement or compromise; and
- generally an opinion on the merits of the settlement or compromise given by a barrister or solicitor acting for the child or patient.

In addition, in personal injury cases arising from an accident the Court will require—

- the circumstances of the accident;
- any medical reports;
- a schedule of any past and future expenses and losses claimed; and any other relevant information which is set out in Paragraphs 4.1–4.4, Practice Direction to Part 16; and
- where considerations of liability are raised—
    - any evidence or Police reports in any criminal proceedings or in an inquest; and
    - details of any prosecution brought.

If the sum to be paid under an award or settlement or compromise is to be paid by way of instalments for the remainder of the claimant's life (a structured settlement), then the Practice Direction to Part 40 sets out further information and the appropriate procedure for obtaining the Court's approval of such a settlement on behalf of a child or patient.

The costs payable by or to a child or patient are regulated by Rule 48.5 (see below).

Whilst no permission of the Court is required to issue and serve a claim form on a child or patient, permission is required if a party wishes to make an application against a child or patient before proceedings have started. This would apply, for instance, if the party sought pre-action disclosure under Rule 31.16. It is not necessary to directly refer to any such application made by a child or patient since the Court will be able to control the situation upon hearing the application itself. It is suggested that when an application is made on behalf of a child or patient before proceedings are commenced, it should be accompanied with an application for an order appointing a litigation friend.

Other than issuing and serving the claim form, the only other step that does not require the Court's permission is an application for the appointment of a litigation friend under Rule 21.6.

During the period for which there is no litigation friend, any steps taken are of no effect. This may cause some difficulties where one of the parties becomes a patient during the course of proceedings without the knowledge of the other party. In accordance with Rule 21.3(3), when that person does become a patient, no steps may be taken without the permission of the Court. If steps are taken then they are of no effect. To relieve the hardship that may follow from this Rule, however, the Court does have the discretion to validate any steps taken (Rule 21.3(4)).

Unless the Court has made an order allowing the child to conduct proceedings without a litigation friend under Rule 21.2(3), service of documents on a child or patient has to be effected in accordance with Rule 6.6. Under that Rule the Court can validate service if it is not effected in accordance with Rule 6.6 but otherwise the general picture is as follows—

- A claim form and an application for the appointment of a litigation friend where no litigation friend had previously been appointed must be served on—
    - one of the child's parents or guardians;
    - if there is no parent or guardian, the person with whom the child resides or in whose care the child is;
    - the person authorised under the Mental Health Act 1983 to conduct proceedings in the name of the patient or on his behalf; or
    - if there is no person so authorised, the person with whom the patient resides and in whose care the patient is; and
    - the patient (Rule 21.8(2)).
- Any other document will be served on the litigation friend.

Becoming a litigation friend

Rule 21.4 identifies who may become a litigation friend under the procedure by which appointment takes place without a Court order.

If the party is a patient, the Mental Health Act 1983 sets out a pecking order for those who may be authorised to act on behalf of a patient. That pecking order has not been included in the Rule because it is somewhat complex, particularly in its definition of "nearest relative" (Mental Health Act 1983 s 26). Similarly no reference to enduring powers of attorney has been included. If the authorisation includes the conduct of legal proceedings then that person so authorised is entitled to be the litigation friend of the patient in any proceedings to which the authority extends.

Otherwise, there is no limitation on who may act as a litigation friend as long as he—

- can fairly and competently conduct proceedings; and
- has no interest which is adverse to that of the child or patient (Rule 21.4(3)).

These qualifications may themselves place quite strict limitations on who can be appointed as a litigation friend. By way of example, a co-defendant would normally be barred from acting as a litigation friend.

These limitations become more important because there is no continuing requirement as there was under the RSC for a litigation friend to act by a solicitor.

In addition to these qualifications, if the child or patient is a Claimant, the litigation friend must undertake to pay any costs which the child or patient may be ordered to pay in relation to the proceedings. That undertaking can be qualified in reserving any right that the litigation friend may have to be paid from assets of the child or patient.

How to become a litigation friend

There are two methods of becoming a litigation friend, firstly by the administrative act of filing documents referred to in Rule 21.5 and secondly by obtaining a Court order in accordance with Rule 21.6.

• Becoming a litigation friend without a Court order

Rule 21.5 sets out the procedure for becoming a litigation friend through the administrative process of filing documents with the Court. More detail is provided by Paragraphs 2.3, 2.4 and 2.5 of the Practice Direction to Part 21. It must be remembered that under Rule 21.3(4) any step taken before the appointment of a litigation friend has no effect unless the Court otherwise orders. Accordingly the procedures prescribed by Rule 21.5 must be undertaken either before any step is taken or upon taking the first step.

If the child or patient is a Claimant, or presumably an applicant pre-proceedings, the appropriate documents must be filed when the claim form or any pre-action application is issued. If the child or patient is a Defendant, or a respondent to a pre-action application, then the documents must be filed when the litigation friend first takes a step in the action (Rule 21.5(4) and (5) and Paragraph 2.5 of the Practice Direction to Part 21).

The documents to be filed with the Court are as follows—

- If the party is a patient and the litigation friend is authorised under Part VII of the Mental Health Act 1983, a copy of the order or other document which provides the authorisation. The copy must be a copy certified by the office which issued the original. Thus if the authorisation was provided by order of the Court of Protection, the copy of the order filed with the Court in order to become litigation friend must be certified as a copy of the original by the Court of Protection.
- If the party is a patient but there is no one authorised to represent the patient under the Mental Health Act 1983, a person becomes a litigation friend for the patient by filing a **certificate of suitability** (Rule 21.5(3)). The prescribed form is Form N235. As with many forms, the prescribed form does not have to be used but it is suggested that the form is used simply for ease of reference. The certificate must contain—
    - The litigation friend's consent to act.
    - A statement that the litigation friend knows or believes that the Claimant/Defendant is a patient together with the grounds for his belief. If the belief is derived from medical opinion then that medical opinion or any other relevant document should be attached to the certificate. It is suggested that some care should be taken about what exactly is attached to the certificate since the file may be inspected by any party and possibly by a third party with the Court's permission.
    - A statement that the litigation friend can fairly and competently conduct proceedings on behalf of the patient and has no interests adverse to that of the patient.
    - If the patient is a Claimant, an undertaking by the litigation friend to pay any costs which the patient may be ordered to pay in relation to the proceedings (subject to any right to be repaid from the assets of the patient); and
    - The signature of the litigation friend. That signature is taken as verification of the contents of the certificate under Paragraph 2.3 of the Practice Direction to Part 21.
- There is a slightly mixed message coming out of the Rules and practice directions as to whether someone can be a litigation friend notwithstanding that someone else has been authorised under the Mental Health Act 1983 to conduct legal proceedings. On the one hand, Rule 21.4(3) provides that a person may act as a litigation friend to a patient only if nobody has been authorised under Part VII of the Mental Health Act 1983. On the other hand, Rule 21.5(6) provides that a certificate of suitability may be served on the person authorised under Part VII of the Mental Health Act 1983 on the basis that that person so authorised is not acting as litigation friend.

It is suggested that the appropriate course is that if someone wishes to become a litigation friend to a patient (notwithstanding that some other person is authorised under Part VII of the Mental Health Act 1983 to conduct legal proceedings on behalf of the patient) an application should be made under Rule 21.6 for the appointment of the litigation friend by order of the Court.

- If the party to the action is a child, the person who is to act as litigation friend must simply file a certificate of suitability as above.
- A certificate of service of the certificate of suitability (N215).

As follows from the final point above, the certificate of suitability must be served in accordance with Rule 6.6 on both persons upon whom a claim form would have to be served if it were issued. Thus for a child—

- one of the child's parents or guardians; or
- if there is no parent or guardian, the person with whom the child resides or in whose care the child is.

If the party is a patient, service has to be effected on—

- the person authorised under Part VII of the Mental Health Act 1983 to conduct the proceedings in the name of the patient or on his behalf (see above); or
- if there is no person so authorised, the person with whom the patient resides or in whose care the patient is.

- **Becoming a litigation friend by Court order**

As above, under Rule 21.6 the Court can appoint any person to be a litigation friend in appropriate circumstances even if a person has been authorised under the Mental Health Act 1983 to conduct legal proceedings in the name of the patient or whether or not a child has a parent or guardian who is not so appointed.

An application for an order appointing someone as a litigation friend is made in accordance with Part 23. It may be made either by a person who wishes to be the litigation friend or an existing party to the proceedings. The application must be supported by evidence (Rule 21.6(4)). That evidence should include matters similar to those set out in a certificate of suitability referred to above, namely—

- the consent to act;
- the statement that the litigation friend can fairly and competently conduct proceedings on behalf of the child or patient;
- confirmation that the litigation friend has no interest adverse to that of the child or patient; and
- if the child or patient is a Claimant, an undertaking by the litigation friend to pay any costs which the child or patient may be ordered to pay in relation to the proceedings subject to the right to reimbursement out of the assets of the child or patient (Paragraph 3.4, Practice Direction to Part 21).

The application notice must be served. In the case of a child, service must be effected on those persons set out in Rule 6.6, namely the child's parents or guardians or, if there is no parent or guardian, on the person with whom the child resides or in whose care the child is. In the case of a patient, service must be effected on the person authorised under Part VII of the Mental Health Act 1983 to conduct proceedings on behalf of the patient or, if there is no person so authorised, on the person with whom the patient resides or in whose care the patient is. In addition, if the application relates to a patient, the application notice must also be served on the patient unless the Court orders otherwise (Rule 21.8(2)).

As above, the application can be made by any party to the proceedings. This is likely to be most important where the child or patient is a defendant and the claimant wishes to take a step in the proceedings having issued and served a claim form or wishes to seek an order against a child or patient prior to the commencement of proceedings. In accordance with Rule 21.3(4), any step taken prior to the appointment of a litigation friend is of no effect unless the Court orders otherwise. Accordingly, even if an acknowledgment of service or a defence is filed by a child or patient, the claimant can take no consequent steps without the appointment of a litigation friend under Rule 21.5 or 21.6 unless the Court permits a child to conduct proceedings without a litigation friend under Rule 21.2(3). Similarly, if no acknowledgement or defence is filed, the claimant cannot obtain judgment in default without the appointment of a litigation friend (see Rule 21.6(3) generally).

Steps following appointment

The title to the proceedings changes following appointment. The child who is a party is thereafter referred to in the title to the proceedings as—

"AB (a child by CD his litigation friend)".

If the party is a patient then thereafter he will be referred to in the title as—

"AB (by CD his litigation friend)".

If the appointment of the litigation friend takes place by Court order, the order must be served in accordance with Rule 40.4(2) on the applicant and the respondent to the application and any other person on whom the Court orders it to be served. It is suggested that the respondents to the application include those persons on whom the application notice itself is required to be served in accordance with the Rules above. Service may be effected by the Court or by the party in accordance with Rule 6.3.

Child attaining 18 years

On a child attaining the age of 18 years, the appointment of litigation friend ceases automatically under Rule 21.9(1). When that happens the former child (now 18) must serve on the other parties to the proceedings and file with the Court a notice stating—

- that he has reached full age;
- that his litigation friend's appointment has ceased;
- an address for service; and

- whether or not he intends to carry on with or continue to defend the proceedings.

The address for service must be in compliance with Rule 6.5 and accordingly must be within the jurisdiction. The address can be that of the solicitor acting on behalf of the former child. Otherwise generally the address will be the party's residence or place of business (Rule 6.5(3)).

The liability of a litigation friend for costs continues until service of the notice. As above, the litigation friend, if representing a Claimant, will have given an undertaking to pay any costs which the child may be ordered to pay in relation to the proceedings. Clearly the litigation friend will wish to ensure that that liability ends as soon as possible. For this reason the litigation friend may also serve a notice upon the other parties to the action that the child has attained 18 years of age. The notice does not have to be in the form of the notice required to be filed and served by the former child. It simply has to state that the litigation friend's appointment has ceased (Paragraph 5.4, Practice Direction to Part 21).

After the child has attained 18 years of age and served a notice, the former child is referred to in the title to the proceedings as—

"AB (formerly a child but now of full age)".

(Paragraph 5.3, Practice Direction to Part 21).

If the former child does not serve the notice in accordance with Rule 21.9(4) within 28 days after attaining the age of 18 years, the Court is empowered under Rule 21.9(5) to strike out the claim or defence of that former child. This is not an automatic sanction but one that may be made upon application, presumably by the opposing parties. Such an application would have to be made in accordance with Part 23 and notice would have to be served on the former child. That service would have to be effected in accordance with Rule 6.5. It is suggested that it would be safest to effect service both at the address for service given by the former litigation friend and at the usual last known residence of the former child in accordance with Rule 6.5(6).

Patient upon recovery

The position is different for a patient that has recovered and is no longer incapable of managing and administering their own affairs. The appointment of the litigation friend does not terminate until an order of the Court is made. Application is made under Part 23 and may be made by—

- the former patient;
- the litigation friend; or
- a party.

The application must be supported by evidence. Under Paragraph 5.7, Practice Direction to Part 21, that evidence must include—

- a medical report indicating that the patient has recovered and is capable of managing and administering his property and affairs;

- a copy of the order or notice discharging a receiver, if any, appointed by the Court of Protection; and
- if the application is made by the patient, a statement as to whether or not he wishes to carry on with or continue to defend the proceedings.

Although not explicitly stated within the Rules, it is suggested that the respondent to such an application would only be either the former patient or the litigation friend in which event it is suggested that generally only those persons would have to be served with the application.

If and when an order is made, the former patient must serve upon the other parties to the proceedings a copy of the order. In addition, the former patient must serve on the other parties and file with the Court a notice stating—

- that his litigation friend's appointment has ceased;
- an address for service; and
- whether or not he intends to carry on with or continue to defend the proceedings (Rule 21.9(4) and Paragraph 5.8, Practice Direction to Part 21).

If that notice is not served within 28 days of the order being made, the Court may strike out the claim or defence of the former patient. It will only do so upon application under Part 23. That application will have to be served and, as above, it is suggested that service should be effected at the address for service of the former litigation friend and at the usual last known residence of the former patient.

As with a child, the liability of the litigation friend for costs, generally based upon the undertaking given if the patient is the Claimant, continues until notice that the appointment to act has ceased is served on the other parties (Rule 21.9(6)). Accordingly, as with a child, under Rule 21.9(6) the litigation friend may serve a notice on the parties that his appointment to act has ceased.

Application for change of litigation friend

Subject to cessation of the litigation friend's appointment under Rule 29.9, the Court does have the power under Rule 21.7 to—

- direct that a person may not act as a litigation friend;
- terminate a litigation friend's appointment; and
- appoint a new litigation friend in substitution for an existing one.

This power can be exercised either upon the Court's own initiative under Rule 3.3 or upon application. If an application is made then it will be made in accordance with Part 23. Following from Rule 23.6, the application notice must state what order the applicant is seeking and briefly why the applicant is seeking the order (also see Paragraph 4.2, Practice Direction to Part 21). The application must be supported by evidence. If it is proposed that a new litigation friend be appointed in substitution for an existing one, then the evidence must include the proposed litigation friend's consent to act. It must also confirm that the proposed litigation friend can fairly and competently conduct proceedings on behalf of the child or patient and has no interest adverse to that of the child or patient. If the child or patient is a Claimant then the proposed litigation friend must undertake in that evidence to pay any costs which the child or patient may be ordered to pay in relation to the proceedings subject to any right to reimbursement from the assets of the child or patient (Paragraph 3.4, Practice Direction to Part 21).

The respondents to the application are the existing litigation friend and—

- in the case of a child, one of the child's parents or guardians or, if there is no parent or guardian, the person with whom the child resides or in whose care the child is; and
- in the case of a patient, the person authorised to conduct proceedings on behalf of the patient under the Mental Health Act 1983 or, if there is no such person then the person with whom the patient resides or in whose care the patient is.

Service of the application notice must therefore be effected on those persons under Paragraph 4.4 of the Practice Direction to Part 21.

If an order is made under Rule 21.7, the authority of the litigation friend ceases upon the order being made in accordance with Rule 40.7. The former litigation friend will wish to know exactly their position in relation to costs in the proceedings if they have given an undertaking in relation to costs. It is suggested, therefore, that the order sought should specifically deal with the discharge of liability from the date that the order is made.

However the appointment of a litigation friend ceases, the authority of that litigation friend ceases at the same time and they may take no further steps on behalf of the child or patient in the proceedings. If they do so, such steps would generally be invalid and the other parties may seek appropriate recompense from the former litigation friend.

Achieving a settlement or compromise by or on behalf of a child or patient

Generally the authority of a litigation friend continues until the appointment ceases (see above). That authority extends to allow the litigation friend to take any usual step in the proceedings on behalf of the child or patient. The one thing that a litigation friend cannot do, however, is to settle or compromise any claim made by or on behalf of a child or patient or against a child or patient (Rule 21.10). Prior approval of the Court is required before such settlement or compromise becomes valid. This includes any settlement under Part 36 for which specific provision is made in Rule 36.18. Thus no Part 36 offer or Part 36 payment may be accepted without permission of the Court. Further, prior Court order is required specifically for the payment out of any sum in Court. This also applies to the payment out of monies paid in where a Defendant is relying on a defence of tender under Rule 37.3 (see also Rule 36.18(3)). There is no specific requirement that permission of the Court is required to make a Part 36 offer although effectively such an offer would be subject to the approval of the Court if settlement were to be based upon it.

If the approval of the Court is forthcoming upon application, the Court will make an appropriate order for costs consequent upon the settlement. If, however, permission is given after the trial has begun, the Court is obliged under Rule 36.18(2)(b) to deal with the whole costs of the proceedings.

It is suggested that if it is proposed to accept a Part 36 offer or Part 36 payment, appropriate advice (possibly Counsel's opinion) should be sought quickly. If as a result it is proposed to accept, an application should be issued as soon as possible but in the meantime the party making the offer or payment should be notified of the intention to make application. The application may be heard outside the 21 day limit for which the offer or payment is open for acceptance but presumably, as long as a party is notified within that 21 day limit of a proposal to make an application, the cost consequences will be the usual consequences under Part 36 (see Rule 36.13 and 36.14).

The requirement to obtain the Court's permission in order to validate a settlement or compromise on behalf of a child or patient applies equally before as after proceedings have been commenced. If the Woolf theme of avoiding litigation wherever possible is taken up by practitioners, there should be an increase in the use of the procedure for achieving settlement on behalf of a child or patient prior to commencement.

Prior to the commencement of proceedings, a litigation friend is not required but clearly someone will have to place themselves as the potential litigation friend in order to obtain the validation of the settlement when proceedings are issued for that purpose. Generally, save in very clear cases, a solicitor will have to be instructed in order to give or obtain an opinion from a barrister on the merits of the settlement or compromise (see Paragraph 6.3, Practice Direction to Part 21). For this reason, if alternative dispute resolution processes are used, particularly mediation, it is suggested that the potential litigation friend should instruct solicitors, since any outcome of negotiations will be subject effectively to approval by a solicitor or barrister before coming under the microscope of the Court.

On the flip side of the same coin, those negotiating with a potential litigation friend on behalf of a child or patient would want to ensure that those negotiations are meaningful in that the outcome will be approved, both by a solicitor or barrister and the Court.

If settlement is achieved prior to the commencement of proceedings, the validation of that settlement is obtained by issuing a claim form under Part 8. In order to seek the Court's approval of the settlement, a litigation friend must be appointed as above. The Claimant will be the child represented by the litigation friend. The Defendant will be the other party to the claim. The claim form is Form N208. Particulars of claim are not required under Part 8. The details of the claim are simply set out on the form. Within the details of claim the first item must be the statement that Part 8 applies to the claim (Rule 8.2(a)). The details of the claim must then be set out and the terms of the settlement or compromise. In the alternative to this last item, a draft consent order can be attached to the claim form in practice form N292 (Order on settlement on behalf of a child or patient) (Paragraph 6.1, Practice Direction to Part 21).

The claim form can also contain or have annexed to it the further information (as below) required by the Court. Alternatively, this information can be provided by way of separate witness statement. If it is contained within the claim form then as usual the facts will be verified by a statement of truth.

The additional information required by the Court is set out in Paragraph 6.2, Practice Direction to Part 21—

- whether and to what extent the Defendant admits liability;
- the age and occupation (if any) of the child or patient;
- the litigation friend's approval of the proposed settlement or compromise; and
- in a personal injury case arising from an accident—
  - the circumstances of the accident;
  - any medical reports;
  - where appropriate, a schedule of any past and future expenses and losses claimed; and
  - where considerations of liability are raised—
    - any evidence or Police reports in any criminal proceedings or an inquest; and
    - details of any prosecution brought.

If part of the settlement includes an award of provisional damages under Section 32A of the Supreme Court Act 1981 or Section 51 of the County Courts Act 1984 the details of the claim included on the claim form must include—

- that an award of provisional damages is being sought;
- that there is a chance that at some future time the claimant will develop some serious disease or suffer some serious deterioration in his physical and mental condition; and
- specify the disease or type of deterioration in respect of which an application may be made at a future date (Paragraph 4.4, Practice Direction to Part 16).

The Practice Directions to Part 40 set out what documents and evidence are required in relation to a structured settlement—

- Counsel's or the legal representative's opinion of the value of the claim on the basis of a conventional award;
- a report of forensic accountants setting out the effect of a structured settlement taking into account the Claimant's life expectancy and the anticipated cost of future care;
- a draft of the proposed structured agreement;
- sufficient information to satisfy the Court that—
  - enough of the agreed sum is retained as a contingency fund for anticipated future needs; and
  - the structured settlement is secure and the annuities are payable by established insurers;

- details of any assets available to the claimant other than the settlement sum; and
- where the Claimant is a patient, the approval or consent of the Court of Protection.

In addition, as above, for all cases save those which are very clear, the Court will require an opinion on the merits of the settlement or compromise given by a solicitor or barrister. For ease of reference the opinion should set out the facts which form the basis of the opinion and the instructions received. Otherwise those instructions may also need to be produced to the Court.

Any written evidence on which the claimant intends to rely must be filed with the claim form (Rule 8.5(1)). On issue a date will be given for the hearing[1] of the application for approval by the Court. The claim form must be served together with a form for acknowledgement of service. That form must be returned to the Court by the Defendant (Rule 8.3).

The hearing for approval will normally be in front of a Master or District Judge (Paragraph 6.4, Practice Direction to Part 21. If approval is not forthcoming, the Court may give appropriate directions. In extreme circumstances the Court might determine that the claim under Part 8 should henceforth proceed under Part 7 as a contested claim.

If approval is forthcoming, an order in relation to either a structured settlement or provisional damages must fulfil the requirements of the Practice Directions to Parts 40 and 41 respectively.

The Practice Direction to Part 21 sets out in some detail further provisions in relation to the control of money for and on behalf of a child or patient. Discussion of those particular Practice Directions is outside the scope of this work. Readers are reminded, however, that when considering those Practice Directions, reference should also be made to the Court Funds Rules.

1 Proceedings in relation to children should be heard in private - Paragraph 1.8, Practice Direction to Part 21. The High Court in *Beatham v Carlisle Hospitals NHS Trust* (1999) Times, 20 May said that whilst submissions of Counsel to the Court should be in private, the formal approval of the settlement should be in public.

CHAPTER 5
PART 7—COMMENCING PROCEEDINGS AND SERVICE

One of the strong recommendations of Lord Woolf in the Final Report (Chapter 12, Paragraphs 1-15) was for the simplification of the process of commencing proceedings. He described the introduction of a single claim form for every case as an important step towards achieving simplicity in civil litigation. Prior to 26 April 1999 there were four different ways of starting proceedings in the High Court (Writ, Originating Summons, Originating Motion and Petition) and another four in the County Court (Summons, Originating Application, Petition and Notice of Appeal). Different methods of commencement had different consequences, particularly in relation to the procedure to be adopted. Lord Woolf regarded this as an unnecessary complexity.

Lord Woolf was unsuccessful in his primary aim of creating simply one method of commencement. In the long term there will be two methods of commencement—commencement under Part 7 for the normal disputed claim and under Part 8 (the alternative procedure) for cases in which there is no substantial dispute as to fact. (Part 8 is dealt with in Chapter 6 at page 53.)

In the main the diversity of methods of commencement has been expunged under the CPR. There remain examples, however, of methods alternative to both Part 7 and Part 8. Certain applications under the Companies Act 1985 remain to be made by way of a Petition (an application under Section 459 of the Companies Act 1985, for example). Applications under the Housing Act 1988 relating to assured short-hold tenancies and under the Housing Act 1996 for injunctions and the exercise of powers of arrest are both made by prescribed forms.

Where to start proceedings

There are very few limits on where proceedings may be commenced under Part 7. Indeed, the previous restriction under Section 1 of the County Courts Act 1984 tying a County Court's jurisdiction to a district were removed by the Civil Procedure Act 1997 (Schedule 2). The limits that remain in the CPR are of three types; restrictions between the High Court and County Court; the choice of County Court based upon its district and the division of business within the two courts e.g. within the High Court, the Queen's Bench Division and Chancery Division.

- The general rule is that proceedings can be commenced either in the High Court or County Court at the option of the claimant (Paragraph 1, Practice Direction to Part 7). The primary restriction on commencement in the High Court is that the value of the claim (other than in personal injury) must be more than £15,000 (Paragraph 2.1). In a claim in respect of personal injuries, the value of the claim must be £50,000 or more (Paragraph 2.2). There are other restrictions on where proceedings can be commenced contained either in statute or other rules. By way of example, the County Court has exclusive jurisdiction in relation to claims for the recovery of possession in respect of dwelling houses outside Greater London (Section 21 (3) of the County Courts Act 1984 is amended by the High Court and County Courts Jurisdiction Order 1991).
- Applications for Writs of habeas corpus save those relating to the custody of a child and applications for judicial review remain the sole remit of the Queen's Bench Division in the High Court (Paragraph 2.6, Practice Direction to CPR Part 7 by reference to Paragraph 2 of Schedule 1 to the Supreme Court Act 1981). Similarly, the County Court has no jurisdiction to deal with defamation proceedings (Paragraph 2.9, Practice Direction to Part 7).
- In order to assess the value of an action for the purposes of the differentiation between the jurisdiction of the High Court and County Court - such as assessing the value for the purposes of a personal injury action - reference must be made to Article 9 High Court and County Courts Jurisdiction Order 1991. The provisions of Article 9 should be compared with and differentiated from the process of assessing the value of a claim for the purposes of allocation of the proceedings to a track (see Rule 26.8(2)).
- In the CPR there are express provisions restricting in which county court proceedings can be commenced. There is a separate Practice Direction to Part 7 which relates to claims under the Consumer Credit Act 1974. This Practice Direction also places restrictions on where a claim can be commenced. The venue for commencement is determined by the defendant's residence or place of business or, in a claim to recover goods, the situation of the goods themselves.
- Finally, the business of both the High Court and County Court may be divided into specialist divisions or lists. In this manner, for instance, any "Chancery business" as described by Paragraph 1 of Schedule 1 to the Supreme Court Act 1981 and the Chancery Guide, is either assigned to the Chancery Division in the High Court or, if issued in the County Court, has to be marked "Chancery Business". Depending on the allocation of work within the County Court it may then be allotted to a specialist Judge. For further description of Chancery Business and its procedure reference should be made to the Chancery Guide published by the Court Service.

In addition to restrictions on where proceedings can be commenced, the Court does have the power to transfer proceedings under CPR Part 30 or to order that certain parts of proceedings should be heard at a place other than the Court in which the proceedings continue.

Starting the claim – when?

Under Rule 7.2(1)—

> **Proceedings are started when the Court issues a claim form at the request of a claimant.**

and under Rule 7.2(2)—

> **the claim form is issued on the date entered on the form by the Court.**

Establishing when a claim has started can be of great significance, particularly in relation to establishing whether or not proceedings have been commenced within the limitation period dictated by the Limitation Act 1980. The Committee debated when proceedings should be started for the purposes of the CPR in the light of the provisions of the Limitation Act 1980. The statute refers to the time when proceedings are "brought" which is when the claim form in proper order is lodged with the court for issue. The Court Service could not assure the Committee that proceedings would be issued on the date of receipt by the Court. Some assurances were provided that County Courts would provide an "over the counter service" so that proceedings would be issued where necessary immediately upon personal delivery at the County Court counter on the same day. The lack of certainty about the County Court's ability to meet these requirements has led to a specific paragraph in the Practice Direction to Part 7 dealing with exactly when proceedings are started and the evidence that may be required to prove that for the purposes of the Limitation Act 1980 proceedings have been "brought". By Paragraph 4.2 of the Practice Direction the date on which the claim form is received by the Court should be recorded by date stamp on the claim form itself or on the letter that accompanies it. The Practice Direction goes so far as to suggest to parties that they should themselves be able to establish independently the date of receipt of the claim form by the Court.

In comparison the Civil Jurisdiction and Judgments Act 1982 Schedule 1, the Brussels Convention 1968, the test in particular under Articles 21–23 is when a court is "first seized" of the proceedings. As put by the European Court in *Zelger v Salinitri, Case No 129/83* [1984] ECR 2397—

> **The Courts first seized is the one before which the requirements of the full proceedings have become definitively pending are first fulfilled, such requirements to be determined in accordance with the national law of each of the Courts concerned.**

The attitude of the English Court is that a court within the jurisdiction is first seized of the proceedings upon service of the claim form (*Dresser UK Ltd v Falcongate Ltd* [1992] 2 WLR 319). Although outside the scope of this work, it is suggested that this position might change as a result of the provisions of CPR Rule 7.2. The position might also be affected by the making of a pre-action application.

The specialist proceedings listed in Part 49 and regulated by the accompanying practice directions will be assigned to specialist courts and judges.

The Claim Form

In order to commence proceedings under Part 7 the claimant must use the appropriate practice form. This is one of the rare occasions on which the use of the practice form is obligatory and no other form may be used. The form is much like the form used in the County Court prior to 26 April 1999 and indeed bears the same number—N1 or in the Claim Production Centre NI CPC.

The contents of the claim form are determined by Part 7, its Practice Direction, Part 16 and its Practice Direction.

The claim form must include—

- The name and address of the claimant.
- The name and address of the defendant.
- A concise statement of the nature of the claim.
- The remedy which the claimant seeks.
- Where the claimant is making a claim for money, a statement of value.
- Such other matters as are set out in Practice Direction (see for example the Practice Direction for the Commercial Court (Part 49) and the Commercial Court Guide and below).

The Practice Direction then provides the following (Paragraph 3)—

- Where a claim is to be served out of the jurisdiction, a statement that the Court has power under the Civil Jurisdiction and Judgments Act 1982 to deal with the claim and no proceedings based on the same claim are pending between the parties in Scotland, Northern Ireland or another territory of any contracting state to the Brussels Convention or Lugano Convention (Civil Jurisdiction and Judgments Act 1982).
- If the claim is for damages or an unspecified sum and is commenced in the High Court that
    - the claimant expects to recover more than £15,000 (or £50,000 or more if the claim is for personal injuries); or
    - some enactment provides that the claim may only be commenced in the High Court and specify that enactment; or
    - the claim is one falling within the specialist High Court Lists set out in CPR Part 49 and specify that List.
- If the claim is for damages for personal injuries and is started in the County Court, the claimant expects to recover more than £1,000 in respect of pain, suffering and loss of amenity.

- If the claim is for housing disrepair and includes a claim for an order requiring repairs or other work to be carried out by a landlord and is started in the County Court—
  - whether or not the cost of the repairs or other work is estimated to be more than £1,000; and
  - whether or not the claimant expects to recover more than £1,000 in respect of any claim for damages.
- In relation to certain types of proceedings for which provision is made in the Schedules to the CPR, there may be particular requirements of what must be included in the claim form for example.
- Under RSC Order 81 Rule 2 in a claim for libel the claim form must be endorsed with a statement giving sufficient particulars of the publications in respect of which the claim is brought to enable them to be identified.
- In a claim form which begins civil proceedings against the Crown, the claim form must include a statement of the circumstances in which the Crown's liability is alleged to have arisen and details of the Government Department and the officers of the Crown concerned (RSC Order 74 Rule 3).

The information to be provided on the front of the claim form under the heading "value" for a money claim is the value of the claim after adding statutory interest under Section 35A of the Supreme Court Act 1981 and Section 69 of the County Courts Act 1984.The figure to be inserted in the box "amount claimed" is the claim before adding statutory interest. In that same box the solicitor's costs are those set out in Tables 1 and 3 of Part 45:

TABLE 1

Fixed costs on commencement of a claim

Relevant Band	Where the claim form is served by the court or by any method other than personal service by the claimant	Where the claim form is served personally by the claimant and there is only one defendant	Where there is more than one defendant for each additional defendant personally served at separate addresses by the claimant
Where—			
the value of the claim exceeds £25 but does not exceed £500	£50	£60	£15

Relevant Band	Where the claim form is served by the court or by any method other than personal service by the claimant	Where the claim form is served personally by the claimant and there is only one defendant	Where there is more than one defendant for each additional defendant personally served at separate addresses by the claimant
Where— the value of the claim exceeds £500 but does not exceed £1,000	£70	£80	£15
Where— the value of the claim exceeds £1,000 but does not exceed £5,000; or the only claim is for delivery of goods and no value is specified or stated on the claim form	£80	£90	£15
Where— the value of the claim exceeds £5,000	£100	£110	£15

TABLE 3

Miscellaneous Fixed Costs

For service by a party of any document required to be served personally including preparing and copying a certificate of service for each individual served	£15
Where service by an alternative method is permitted by an order under Rule 6.8 for each individual served	£25

Where a document is served out of the jurisdiction—

(a) in Scotland, Northern Ireland, the Isle of Man or the Channel Islands	£65
(b) in any other place	£75

(Other rules which provide for situations where fixed costs may be allowed can be found in Schedule 1 in RSC Ord 62 and in Schedule 2 in CCR Ord 38, Appendix B).

What is to be contained within the claim form is to be differentiated from what must be included in the particulars of claim whether or not contained in the same document as the claim form or served separately. All the matters referred to above correspond to what should appear on the front page of the form N1.

The final matter which must be contained within the claim form is a statement that the particulars of claim will follow service of the claim form at some later date if the particulars of claim are not included or have not been served with the claim form (Paragraph 5.2, Practice Direction to Part 7).

As one of the examples of a statement of case (Rule 2.3(1)) the claim form must be endorsed with a statement of truth (Rule 22.1(1)(a), see page 117 post).

If the particulars of claim are served separately the statement of truth will be verifying only those facts set out in the claim form in accordance with the obligations set out above.

If the claim falls within the definition of a Consumer Credit Act claim (see Paragraph 3.1 of the Consumer Credit Act Practice Direction to CPR Rule 7.9) the particulars of claim **must** be served with the claim form.

If the claim form is drafted by a legal representative, then it must be signed either in his own name or in the name of the firm (Paragraph 2.8, Practice Direction to Part 5).

Issuing the Claim Form

When completed, the claim form together with sufficient copies for the claimant and for each of the defendant(s) should be sent or taken to the court. Most courts appear able and willing to issue forms over the counter. The fee for issue has to be paid at the time of issue, the level of which depends on the value of the claim (see the High Court Fees Order 1999 and the County Court Fees Order 1999). The court issue the claim form and provides a notice of issue (Forms N205 or N205B). If the court is to serve it will send the claim form by first class post with the response pack (Form N9). If the claimant is to serve, the court will give the claimant a response pack for service.

Particulars of Claim

What must and may be included in the particulars of claim is provided for in the main in Part 16 and the Practice Direction to it. Reference should also be made, however, to the dovetailed provisions in the Schedules to the CPR for certain types of proceedings, for example, CCR Order 6 rule 3 (recovery of land).

Paragraph 3.1 of the Practice Direction to Part 16 provides that the particulars of claim should be included on the claim form if practicable. Although the verb "must" is not used, providing an absolute obligation, parties ought to include the particulars of claim on the claim form unless there is good reason not to do so. Such good reason will usually be that the particulars of claim would be simply too long to include on the claim form. If particulars of claim are not included on the claim form then the claim form must state to that effect (Rule 16.2(2)).

Service of the particulars of claim may be effected at the time of service of the claim form or, if not, then must be effected within 14 days after service of the claim form (Rule 7.4(1)(b)). Service cannot be effected, however, later than four months after the issue of the claim form or six months where the claim form is to be served out of the jurisdiction (Rules 7.4(2), 7.5(2) and 7.5(3)). As to service, see page 50 below. In claims under the Consumer Credit Act 1974 the particulars of claim **must** be served with the claim form (Paragraph 5.2, Practice Direction to Part 7).

Where particulars of claim are served separately from a claim form they must contain (usually at the head of the document)—

- The name of the Court in which the claim is proceeding.
- The claim number.
- The title of the proceedings.
- The claimant's address for service.

(Paragraph 3.8, Practice Direction to Part 16).

In the Commercial Court there is no requirement to serve particulars of claim with the claim form. Indeed the claim form can contain a statement that the particulars will only follow filing of an acknowledgment of service (Paragraphs 3.5 and 3.6, Commercial Court Guide).

Rule 16.4 sets out the main requirements of what **must** be included in the particulars of claim—

- A **concise** statement of the facts on which the claimant relies.
- If the claimant is seeking aggravated damages or exemplary damages, a statement to that effect and his grounds for claiming them.
- If the claimant is seeking provisional damages, a statement to that effect and his grounds for claiming them.
- If a claimant is seeking interest, a statement to that effect and then appropriate details such as whether he is doing so pursuant to a contract, a statute or some other basis. If interest is claimed on a specified amount of money then the claimant must also put in the rate of interest claimed, the date from which it is claimed, the date to which it is calculated, the total amount claimed and the daily rate at which it accrues.

There are separate obligations set out in the Practice Direction to Part 16 for particular types of proceedings—

- Personal injury claims
- Fatal accident claims
- Recovery of land
- Hire purchase claims
- Defamation

The Practice Directions to Part 49 also make specific requirements in relation to the specialist proceedings to which they relate.

There are special provisions relating to Consumer Credit Act claims included within the Practice Direction to CPR Rule 7.9. In particular Paragraph 7 of that Practice Direction sets out what must be included in the particulars of claim in such an action.

Further, the dovetailed provisions appearing in the Schedules to the CPR also make provision for what must be included in the particulars of claim, for example, RSC Order 82 (defamation claims) or CCR Order 6 (particulars of claim for recovery of land).

Paragraphs 10, 11 and 12 of the Practice Direction to Part 16 set out further matters that must be included in the particulars of claim if relevant. By way of example, in a contract claim the particulars should set out by reference the details of the contract. If the contract is in writing then a copy of it should be served with the particulars of claim. If the contract is oral then the particulars should set out the contractual words used and state by whom, to whom, when and where they were spoken.

In addition to the obligations as to what must be set out in the particulars of claim, Paragraph 10.3 of the Practice Direction to Part 16 provides further items that **may** be included in the particulars of claim—

- Reference to any point of law on which the claim is based.
- The name of any witness proposed to be called.
- Reference to any document which the claimant considers necessary to the claim which document should then be attached to or served with the particulars (including any expert's report to be filed under Part 35).

The particulars of claim, if served separately from the claim form, must be verified with a statement of truth (see page 117 post).

The claim form and, if served separately, the particulars of claim must be signed by the legal representative if drafted by him either in his own name or as appropriate in the name of the firm. This is in addition to the statement of truth (Paragraph 2.8, Practice Direction to Part 5).

As Lord Woolf stated in the Final Report the intention behind the CPR is to remove the complexities of "pleading" the claim. This is an aim that does not jump out of the CPR to the reader but does follow from what **must** and **may** be included. In particular the verification of the particulars by a statement of truth indicate the manner in which evidence may be included. The particulars must however be concise. Subject to this obligation the particulars might serve a number of purposes including:

- as the claim
- as a witness statement
- as a list of documents
- as a skeleton argument

Service of the Claim Form

After the claim form has been issued, the claimant is obliged to serve it (either himself or through the court – see below) on the defendant (Rule 7.5(1)). If service is not effected, the defendant may serve notice on the claimant requiring him to serve the claim form or discontinue the proceedings within a period specified in the notice (not less than 14 days after service of the notice). If service is not then effected, the defendant can make application to the Court for a dismissal of the claim or any other order that the Court thinks just (Rule 7.7).

The claim form must be served within four months of the date of issue or six months if the claim form is to be served out of the jurisdiction. If the particulars of claim is served separately, it must be served within a like period (Rule 7.4(2)). It is suggested that the method of calculation of the period has not changed under the new Rules. A month is a calendar month (see Rule 2.10 and the Interpretation Act 1978). The rule relating to time talks only of the measurement of days by "clear days" (Rule 2.8). In like manner it is suggested that if a claim is issued on, say 30 May, it must be served on or before 30 September.

Rule 6.2 sets out how service can be effected. In general service of a claim form will be effected by either personal service or by first class post. There are special provisions of the Companies Act 1985 which provide for service upon a company.

Rule 6.4 details the manner in which personal service should be effected—

- The claim form is served personally on an individual by leaving it with that individual.
- The claim form is served personally on a company or other corporation by leaving it with a person holding a senior position within the company or corporation. Who holds a senior position is determined by Paragraph 6.2 of the Practice Direction to Part 6.
- The claim form is served personally on a partnership by leaving it with a partner or a person who, at the time of service, has the control or management of the partnership business at its principal place of business.
- If a solicitor is instructed and authorised to accept service on behalf of a party and has notified the party serving in writing that he has that authority, then service will be good if effected on the solicitor and indeed the party is obliged to serve on the solicitor in accordance with Rule 6.4(2) (Rule 6.13(2)).

If service is to be effected other than upon a solicitor then Rule 6.5 sets out details of the place at which service should be effected. Thus if service is being effected upon an individual, the place of service will be his usual or last known residence. If service is effected upon a firm then it will be the usual or last known residence of the individual proprietor or the principal or last known place of business of the firm. If service is effected upon a registered company, it should take place at the principal office of the company or any place of business of the company within the jurisdiction which has a real connection with the claim.

It will be usual to serve a claim form by post, in which case Rule 6.7 sets out details of when the claim form will be deemed to be served. This is of course subject to any evidence to the contrary. If service is effected by first class post then the deemed day of service is the second day after it was posted. There is no time limitation when service may be effected. Accordingly, even if the second day after the letter was posted is a Saturday, Sunday or Bank Holiday, service of the claim form (as distinct from any other document) will be deemed to have taken place on that day.

Rules 6.15 and 6.16 provide special rules for service by a contractually agreed method or on an agent of a principal who is overseas.

If the claim form is to be served out of the jurisdiction, the claimant should meet the obligations set out in RSC Order 11.

In accordance with Rule 6.3, the Court will serve the claim form (by first class post) unless the claimant specifies at the time of issue that he will serve the claim form or the claim is in the Commercial Court (Paragraph 5.1, Commercial Court Guide). If the Court serves then the Court will need additional copies for service. Upon service the Court will provide the claimant with a certificate of service. If the claimant serves then the claimant must file a certificate of service within seven days of service of the claim form, Form N215 (Rule 6.14). The details to be included in the certificate are set out in Rule 6.10. If the Court is effecting service but is unable to do so (for example, a letter of service is returned through the post), it will send a certificate of non-service (N216) to the claimant who can then try to effect service.

If service cannot be effected for any reason, the claimant can make an application for service by an alternative method (such as advertisements) in accordance with Rule 6.8.

If service cannot be effected within the life of the claim form then an application for extension can be made under Rule 7.6. Generally such an application has to be made within the period for serving the claim form or the extension of it previously given under Rule 7.6. The application has to be supported by evidence but can be made without notice to the other party. If the claimant applies outside the time limit, the Court is empowered to extend time but only if the Court or the claimant has been unable to serve the claim form and the claimant has acted promptly in making the application (Rule 7.6).

Service of the Particulars of Claim

If contained in the claim form or annexed as part of it the court will serve the particulars. If particulars are to follow, the party must subsequently serve them.

Documents to be served with the Particulars of Claim

As previously mentioned, the particulars of claim should be contained in the claim form where practicable. If the particulars are on the claim form or are separate but served with it, then upon service the claim form and particulars must be accompanied by—

- a form for defending the claim (form N9B or N9D);
- a form for admitting the claim (form N9A); and
- a form for acknowledging service (form N9C).

(Rule 7.8(1))

If the particulars of claim are served at another time then those three forms must be served with those particulars. They do not have to be served with the claim form.

The three forms appear as a response pack (form N9). For the defendant's response, see Parts 10, 14, and 15.

Fixed date procedure

In a claim under the Consumer Credit Act 1974 upon issue of the claim the court will fix a date for hearing (Paragraph 5.1, Practice Direction to Part 7). The defendant is not obliged to serve an acknowledgment of service or to file a defence and may simply attend on the hearing although this may subsequently prejudice his position (Paragraphs 5.3, Practice Direction to Part 7). Fourteen days' notice of the hearing date must be given, with the claim form (Paragraphs 5.6 & 5.7, Practice Direction to Part 7). At the hearing the Court will either dispose of the proceedings immediately or allocate to a track and give case management directions.

See also Part 8 for which there is a hybrid fixed date procedure (page 60 post).

CHAPTER 6
PART 8—ALTERNATIVE PROCEDURE FOR CLAIMS

Introduction

In order to simplify the procedure before the Court it was intended to replace the panoply of methods of commencement with one single method - the issue of a claim form (for instance, see the Final Report, page 5, Paragraph 9).

During the course of the work undertaken by the Civil Procedure Rule Committee it was suggested that there should be an alternative procedure for claims reflecting to a large extent the originating summons procedure in the Chancery Division of the High Court. RSC Order 5, Order 7 and Order 28 prescribed originating summons procedure. The procedure was seen to be a useful method of resolving disputes particularly, for instance, if all the Court was being required to do was interpret the terms of a contract or a statute and apply that interpretation to an agreed set of facts.

As a result of those discussions a consultation paper was issued in mid 1998.

Part 8 (the Alternative Procedure) is the result of that consultation and the further deliberations of the Civil Procedure Rule Committee.

It was intended upon consultation that the alternative procedure should only apply in the High Court because there was some concern that the County Court did not have in place the machinery for applying such a procedure to replace the existing procedure of originating application. This proposal was reversed with the result that the alternative procedure applies to both High Court and County Court.

The effect is that the originating applications procedure prescribed by CCR Order 3 Rule 4 has been replaced by the alternative procedure or, for claims not falling within that procedure, by the procedure under Part 7. Examples of proceedings commenced under Order 3 Rule 4 include applications under the Access to Health Records Act 1990, the Friendly Societies Act 1974, the Leasehold Property (Repairs) Act 1938 and the Torts (Interference with Goods) Act 1977.

Note, however, that although CCR Order 3 Rule 4 has not been retained within the dovetailed provisions, the procedure to be followed under it has been retained for housing cases which have their own special procedure prescribed by the Housing Cases Practice Direction (at the time of writing not yet published but proposed). Even housing procedure will eventually be altered to provide for a procedure in keeping with the remainder of the CPR.

The distinctive features of Part 8 procedure are:

- separate type of claim form
- no particulars of claim
- no defence
- no allocation questionnaire
- no judgment in default
- no oral evidence

The Rules

The procedure under Part 8 may be adopted by the claimant under Rule 8.1(2) only where—

- he seeks the Court's decision on a question which is unlikely to involve a substantial dispute of fact; or
- the Rule or practice direction requires or permits the use of the Part 8 procedure.

In due course whether or not there is a substantial dispute of fact is going to be decided by the Court. It may not be apparent in the first instance that there is a substantial dispute of fact. It may only become apparent when the parties have exchanged their evidence in support of and opposition to the relief claimed in the claim form.

If it became apparent that there was a substantial dispute of fact, the parties should apply to the Court for the matter to be dealt with henceforth under the Part 7 procedure or, contrary to the parties' assertions that a Part 8 procedure was appropriate, the Court could at any stage of its own initiative order that the claim continue as a claim under Part 7. If it does so, the Court will then allocate the claim to a track and give such directions as it considers appropriate (Rule 8.1(3) and Paragraph 1.6, Practice Direction to Part 8).

Types of proceedings commenced by the alternative procedure

The new Rules and practice directions set out the types of proceedings which may be commenced by the alternative procedure and those which must be commenced in that way. In the absence of such guidance it is for the claimant to determine whether there is likely to be a substantial dispute of fact. The types of claim which would certainly fall within this band include construction summonses where the Court is asked to determine the meaning of a contract or a statute.

The Practice Direction to Part 8 (March 1999) at Paragraph 1.4 sets out various types of claim for which the Part 8 procedure **may** be used—

- Child settlement (although Paragraph 6.1 of the Practice Direction to Part 21 provides that the Part 8 procedure **must** be used).
- Consent order for provisional damages agreed before the commencement of proceedings.

- Application for a deposition to be taken abroad under Part 34.
- Application for a deposition to be taken in England and Wales for use before Courts abroad.
- Claim for summary order for possession against named or unnamed defendants in occupation of land or premises without licence or consent - see RSC Order 113 and CCR Order 24.

In many cases, as indicated by Rule 8.1(6)(a), the use of the alternative procedure for claims may be obligatory. The practice direction to Part 8 (13 April 1999) sets out the types of proceedings in which the alternative procedure **must** be used in accordance with Rule 8.1 (6)(a) despite the fact that there may well be disputes of fact. Examples include mortgage claims under RSC Order 88, possession proceedings under RSC Order 113 or CCR Order 24 and claims under the Landlord and Tenant Acts 1927, 1954, 1985 and 1987. Further the CPR contains other provisions for which Part 8 must be used. In accordance with the Practice Direction relating to applications under the Companies Act 1985 (Part 49), the proceedings must be commenced using the alternative procedure. The arbitration Practice Direction (Part 49) provides to the same effect.

There is no like provision to that of RSC Order 5 Rule 3 which obliged the use of originating summons procedure in an application under any Act.

The result is that the use of Part 8 is in some aspects more restrictive than previous procedures in that there must be no substantial dispute of fact. It is, however, wider in its scope in that it is available in all cases where there is unlikely to be a substantial dispute as to fact.

How to commence proceedings

A claim using Part 8 procedure should be commenced using the practice form (N208). This form differs from the practice form for issuing a claim under Part 7 in that it contains no provision for particulars of claim. In replacement the form contains space for the "details of claim" both on the front of the form and on the reverse.

Rule 8.2 provides that the claim form must state—

(a) that this Part applies;
(b) (i) the question which the claimant wants the court to decide; or
(ii) the remedy which the claimant is seeking and the legal basis for the claim to that remedy;
(c) if the claim is being made under an enactment, what that enactment is;
(d) if the claimant is claiming in a representative capacity, what that capacity is; and
(e) if the defendant is sued in a representative capacity, what that capacity is.

In addition to the Rule, practice directions relating to certain types of proceedings may provide for other matters which should be included in the claim form. For instance,

- In a mortgage claim issued in the High Court under RSC Order 88 the claim form must have a statement showing where the mortgaged property is situated and if the claimant claims possession of the mortgaged property and it is situated outside Greater London, whether the property consists of or includes a dwelling house. The claim form must also contain a certificate that the claim is not one to which Section 141 of the Consumer Credit Act 1974 applies.

- A claim form issued in the County Court under Section 45(2) of the Matrimonial Causes Act 1973 for a declaration of legitimisation by virtue of the Legitimacy Act 1976 must state the grounds on which the claimant relies, the date and place of birth of the claimant and the maiden name of his mother and particulars of every person whose interests may be affected by the proceedings and his relationship, if any. to the claimant. (CCR Order 46)
- Proceedings commenced under the Landlord & Tenant Acs 1927, 1954, 1985 and 1987 commenced in the County Court must contain the details prescribed by CCR Order 43.

The Practice Direction to Part 21 provides what should be set out in the claim form in relation to an infant settlement. The Practice Direction for arbitration claims (Part 49) also provides specifically for the contents of the claim form.

As a statement of case (Rule 2.3(1)), the claim form must be verified by a statement of truth (Rule 22.1). If not verified, the claim may be struck out by the Court under Rule 3.3 and Rule 3.4. Until that happens, however, the claim remains effective although the contents of it may not be relied upon as evidence (Rule 22.2). As to the form of the statement of truth, who may sign it and the penalty for verifying a statement of case containing a false statement without an honest belief in its truth, see Chater 12 at page 117.

Again by analogy with Part 7 (Rule 7.3), the claimant may use the claim form under Part 8 to start all claims which can be conveniently disposed of in the same proceedings. If part of the claim, however, is likely to involve a substantial dispute of fact, it would be inappropriate for Part 8 procedure and the claim should be commenced under Part 7.

In addition to lodging the claim form with the Court for the purpose of issue, the claimant must also file any written evidence in support of the claim (Rule 8.5(1)). That written evidence should normally be in the form of a witness statement or affidavit. The claimant may rely on the matters set out in his claim form provided that it has been verified by a statement of truth (Paragraph 5.2, Practice Direction to Part 8). Other than when evidence is contained within the claim form and verified by a statement of truth, written evidence should normally be given by a witness statement and not an affidavit. A witness is entitled, however, to give evidence by affidavit if he wishes to do so (Paragraph 1.2, Practice Direction to Part 32). Part 32 and particularly the Practice Direction to it provides the layout for affidavits and witness statements and the contents.

When the claim form is served it must be accompanied with—

- The evidence in support (unless contained within the statement of case verified by a statement of truth) Rule 8.5 (2); and
- A form for acknowledgment of service (N210).

Proceedings started—when?

Although Part 8 does not specifically mention when proceedings are started, presumably by analogy with Rule 7.2, the proceedings are started when the Court issues the claim form at the request of the claimant and the claim form is issued on the date entered on the claim form by the Court. As to when the proceedings are "brought" for the purposes of the Limitation Act 1980, see page 43 above.

Proceedings started—where?

There are similar limitations on where proceedings can be started to those under Part 7—

- High Court or County Court
- A particular county court
- In accordance with a particular division of business within the court e.g. Queens Bench or Chancery in the High Court.

Part 8 claims are much more likely to be subject to such limitations because of the nature of them. Many of the claims for which Part 8 must be used in the High Court fall within the categories of Chancery Business, for example, mortgage claims (RSC Order 88) and landlord and tenant proceedings under the Landlord and Tenant Acts 1927, 1954 and 1987 (RSC Order 97). Further certain Part 8 Claims **must** be started in particular courts. These are listed in Section B Practice Direction to Part 8 (April 1999) and include claims for—

- Recovery of land
- Foreclosure or redemption of a mortgage
- Enforcing a charge or lien on land
- Recovery of moneys under a mortgage or charge on land

which must all be started in the county court for the district in which the land is situated (Practice Direction to Part 8 Paragraph B.7). Other proceedings listed must be started in the court the district in which either the defendant lives, carries on business or the subject matter of the claim is situated (Practice Direction to Part 8 Paragraph 36).

Acknowledgment of Service and Defendant's Response

Unlike Part 7 the defendant to a Part 8 claim **must** file an acknowledgment of service and serve it on the claimant and any other party unless fixed date procedure applies (see below). There is no specified time limit for service. There is, however, a time limit for filing. The period is no more than 14 days after service of the claim form. This period can be extended either by agreement under Rule 2.11 or by the Court under Rule 3.1.

Again this differs from the procedure under Part 7 in that the trigger date under that procedure is service of the particulars of claim. There are no particulars of claim under Part 8 and accordingly it has no application. Note that the obligation to serve the acknowledgment on the claimant and any other party applies whether or not that other party has itself filed and served an acknowledgment of service.

The acknowledgment of service must—

- State whether the defendant contests the claim;
- If the defendant seeks a different remedy from that set out in the claim form, state what that remedy is (Rule 8.3(2));
- Be signed by the defendant or his legal representative; and
- Include the defendant's address for service (Rule 10.5).

As to signing the acknowledgment of service and the address for service, see page 65 post.

In addition to Rule 10.5 (Contents Acknowledgment of Service), the only other Rule under Part 10 that applies to a Part 8 claim is 10.3(2). This provides that the period for filing the acknowledgment of service may not be the 14 days prescribed by Rule 8.3(1)(a) but such other period as specified in accordance with RSC Order 11 Rule 1A (Service out of the Jurisdiction) and Rule 6.16(4) (Service of a Claim Form on Agent of Principal who is Overseas).

As under Part 7, RSC Order 81 makes special provision in relation to the acknowledgment of service in a claim against a firm.

Part 11 (Disputing the Court's Jurisdiction) applies equally to a claim under Part 8 as a claim under Part 7. Under Rule 8.3(4) if the defendant wishes to dispute the Court's jurisdiction he must file an acknowledgment of service and then make the appropriate application. By filing the acknowledgment of service he does not lose any right to dispute the Court's jurisdiction (Rule 11(3)). The application must be made not more than 14 days after the end of the period for filing the acknowledgment of service. If service is effected out of the jurisdiction and RSC Order 11 applies, it would appear that the defendant wishing to dispute the Court's jurisdiction gains no further time than the 14 days prescribed by Rule 8.3(4) notwithstanding that if the claim were under Part 7 there would be further time for filing a defence. The limit is therefore fairly tight. It can be extended by written agreement of the parties in accordance with Rule 2.11.

A defendant who wishes to rely on written evidence must file and serve it when he files the acknowledgment of service. The evidence must therefore be prepared, filed and served within the 14 day period after service of the claim form. Once again this timetable is fairly tight for the defendant. This period was debated by the Civil Procedure Rule Committee and it was agreed that this period should be stipulated in the Rule.

The Practice Direction, however, specifically mentions the ability of the parties to agree an extension of the period under 2.11. Any agreement extending time must, however, be filed by the defendant at the same time as he files his acknowledgment of service and cannot extend time by more than 14 days after the defendant files the acknowledgment of service **(not 14 days after the period for filing the acknowledgment of service ends)** (Paragraph 5.6(2), Practice Direction to Part 8).

If agreement on extending the time limits under Part 8 cannot be agreed, appropriate application can be made to the Court. Such an application has to be made in accordance with Part 23. Note, however, that any application notice must be served at least three days before the Court is to deal with the application itself (Rule 23.7(1)(b)) although notwithstanding a failure to comply with this provision the Court may direct that, in the circumstances of the case, sufficient notice has been given and then hear the application. In the Queens Bench Division there are special arrangements for "time summonses".

In hearing the application the Court will be exercising its general powers of case management under Rule 3.1(2). The application can be made after the time for compliance has expired (Rule 3.1(2)(a)) but if the time has expired the Court will be exercising its powers to grant relief against sanctions for failure to comply with the Rule or practice direction. In that event the Court must have consideration of the matters set out in Rule 3.9 (Relief from Sanctions). Thus parties should try to ensure that the hearing of the application takes place within the stipulated period and that the application notice itself is issued and served in good time to comply with Rule 23.7(1)(b).

Rule 8.8 provides that if the defendant contends that Part 8 procedure is inappropriate because there is a substantial dispute of fact and Part 8 procedure is not required or permitted by Rule or practice direction, he must state his reasons for such a contention in his written evidence accompanying the acknowledgment of service. Upon receipt of such a contention (the Rule appears to suggest that the Court will review such evidence), the Court will give directions as to future management of the case and particularly whether or not the claim should continue under Part 8. If not, it can effectively direct that the claim should continue under Part 7 and give any directions it considers appropriate (Rule 8.1(3)) (see above).

If the claimant wishes to file evidence in reply to that of the defendant then he should do so and serve it within 14 days of service of the defendant's evidence on him. That period can be extended by written agreement of the parties but for a period of no more than 28 days after service of the defendant's evidence on the claimant. The period can be extended by the Court (see the comments above).

If either party wishes to put in further evidence than that allowed under Rule 8.5, the party will have to seek permission from the Court. Otherwise such evidence may not be relied on at the hearing (Rule 8).

Consequences of not filing an Acknowledgment of Service

Unlike Part 7, default judgment is not available under Part 8 (Rule 12.2(b)). Similarly judgment by request on an admission is not obtainable under Part 8 (Rule 8.9(b)(i)).

Unless fixed date procedure applies if the defendant fails to file an acknowledgment of service within the times mentioned above, the defendant may attend the hearing of the claim but may not take any part in the hearing unless the Court gives permission (Rule 8.4). In considering whether to give permission the Court will have regard to the overriding objective and particularly the obligation under Rule 1.1(2)(d) ensuring that a case is dealt with fairly (in addition to any other statutory obligations including those arising under Article 6 of the European Convention on Human Rights and of the Human Rights Act 1998 when it comes into force).

Similarly, if written evidence has not been served in accordance with the time limits set by Rule 8.5 (and presumably the Practice Direction), written evidence may not be relied upon at the hearing unless the Court gives permission.

Fixed date procedure

The Practice Direction to Part 8 sets out in Section B categories of claim for which the court will upon issue of the proceedings immediately fix a date for hearing, for example, possession proceedings under RSC Order 113 or CCR Order 24, mortgage actions and landlord and tenant proceedings under the Landlord and Tenant Acts 1937, 1952, 1985 and 1987. The claim form must be served not less than 21 days before the hearing final notice of which must be given at the same time (Paragraph B 9, Practice Direction to Part 8). For these scheduled proceedings the defendant does not have to acknowledge service (Paragraph B 12, Practice Direction to Part 8). On the hearing date the court may immediately dispose of the claim or give case management directions (Paragraph B 13, Practice Direction to Part 8). Contrary to Rule 8.9 (c) which disapplies Part 26 (case management) to Part 8 claim Paragraph B 15 re-applies it to "fixed date" claims. Accordingly such claims may be allocated to a track and appropriate directions given.

Mortgage and Landlord and Tenant Claims

A degree of confusion has arisen about certain aspects of these types of claims.

Firstly the **recovery of costs in mortgage actions**. Some Courts appear to suggest that the costs of a mortgage action are no longer recoverable in contract and equity. In simple terms this is not correct. Mortgagee's costs remain recoverable under contract and equity notwithstanding the CPR. The mortgagee does not need an order for costs to effect recovery of costs.

Secondly **landlord and tenant claims.** Unfortunately there are conflicts between Part B and CCR Order 43 (Schedule 2) which provides differing procedure between the High Court and County Court, particularly in relation to tenancy renewals. The difference may be exacerbated by court practice guides. In the High Court, for instance, in landlord and tenant renewals, the court will not fix a return date on issue of these proceedings and may also postpone the interim rent application (Chancery Division Practice Direction 4, Chancery Guide p 80). A discussion of the precise difference is outside the scope of this work but readers should be aware of it.

Case Management

A claim (save a "fixed date" claim) under Part 8 is not allocated to one of the three tracks. Part 26 therefore does not apply. It is treated, however, as though it were allocated to the multi track. Accordingly the Court might determine that a case management conference and/or a pre-trial review is appropriate to consider the future conduct of the claim and its trial.

In addition to the automatic provisions in relation to the exchange of evidence under Rule 8.5, the Court may give other directions. Indeed under Paragraph 4.1 of the Practice Direction to Part 8, the Court may give directions immediately a Part 8 claim form is issued. These directions can be given either upon the application of a party or of the Court's own initiative. A hearing date may be fixed immediately, particularly where there is no dispute such as where the Court's approval of a child settlement is sought or where there may be a dispute but it would be convenient to give a hearing date such as in claims for mortgage possession or the appointment of trustees.

If directions are not given on the issue of the claim form then they will be given as soon as practicable after the defendant has acknowledged service or the period for acknowledgment of service has expired.

Some claims, such as an application for the Court's consent under Section 38 of the Landlord & Tenant Act 1954, may not require a hearing at all since the application is made by consent.

A defendant may meet a claim issued under Part 8 by making a Part 20 claim whether by way of counterclaim or one of the other types of claims under Part 20. The Court's permission, however, is required.

The provisions of both Rule 3.4 (Power to Strike Out a Statement of Case) and Part 24 (Summary Judgment) are available in relation to a Part 8 claim. Effectively the provisions of Rule 3.4 are only available to the defendant since the application will be for the Court to strike out the claimant's claim (there being no other "statement of case" in Part 8 procedure) on the basis that it discloses no reasonable grounds for bringing it or it is an abuse of the Court's process or is otherwise likely to obstruct the just disposal of the proceedings (see page 120).

Summary judgment, however, is available to both parties on the grounds either that the claimant either has no real prospect of succeeding on the claim or issue or that the defendant has no real prospect of successfully defending a claim or issue (see page 137).

The remedy for the claimant, however, is not available without the court's permission until the acknowledgment of service is filed by the defendant (Rule 24.4(1)).

CHAPTER 7
PART 10—ACKNOWLEDGMENT OF SERVICE

The process of acknowledgment of service has been extended under the CPR to both the High Court and the County Court.

There are three separate forms for acknowledgment of service. For a Part 7 claim the form is served as part of the response pack (Form N9). In a claim under Part 8 (Alternative Procedure) the form is N210. The acknowledgment of service form for a Part 20 claim is Form 213.

Acknowledging a Part 7 claim

The acknowledgment of service for a Part 7 claim does not have to be filed until the particulars of claim are served. Save in the Commercial Court where the trigger is service of the claim form (Paragraph 37.36, Commercial Court Guide). If the particulars are not served with the claim form then time for acknowledgment does not start until the service of the particulars of claim (Rule 9.1(2)). Whether or not the particulars of claim are served with the claim form, it is the particulars of claim that must be accompanied by the response pack (Form N9), i.e. a form for defending the claim, a form for admitting the claim and a form for acknowledging service (Rule 7.8(1)).

Save in the Commercial Court where acknowledgment is obligatory (Paragraph B7.2, Commercial Court Guide), the defendant may choose whether or not to file an acknowledgment of service. Under Part 7 it is not obligatory since the defendant can simply file a defence (but see below comments on disputing the Court's jurisdiction). The filing of an acknowledgment of service, however, extends the period for filing a defence by 14 days.

Rule 15.4 provides that a defence should be filed 14 days after service of the particulars of claim or 28 days if the defendant files an acknowledgment of service under Part 10. If an acknowledgment of service is to be filed then it must be filed within 14 days after service of the particulars of claim (Rule 10.3). This is, however, subject to two exceptions.

The period for filing an acknowledgment where service is effected out of the jurisdiction is specified in accordance with RSC Order 11 Rule 1A. Further, Rule 6.16(4) (Service of Claim Form on Agent or Principal who is Overseas) provides that the Court when making an order under this Rule will state a period within which the defendant must respond to the particulars of claim.

As to service generally, and particularly when service is deemed to be effected, see Rule 6.7.

In the alternative to either filing an acknowledgment of service or a defence, the defendant may file an admission (see page 73 post).

Contents of Acknowledgment of Service

Use of Form N9 gives ready guidance as to what should be included in the acknowledgment of service. Form N9, however, is one of those forms which, although it should be used, is not absolutely obligatory. It is the contents of it which are obligatory and which must be included in any document which purports to be an acknowledgment of service—

- **The Defendant's name**
  The name should be set out in full. If the name has been incorrectly set out in the claim form, it should be correctly set out on the acknowledgment of service followed by the words **"described as N. in the claim form"** (Paragraph 5, Practice Direction to Part 10).
- **Address for service**
  The address for service must be within the jurisdiction (Rule 6.5(2)). If in the acknowledgment of service the party does not give the business address of his solicitor as his address for service but resides or carries on business within the jurisdiction, he must give his residence or place of business as his address for service (Rule 6.5(3)). Where a solicitor is acting on behalf of a party then the business address of the solicitor must be given. As to when a solicitor will be considered to be acting for a party, see Rule 42.1.
- **The Defendant's signature**
  The acknowledgment of service must be signed by the defendant or his legal representative (Paragraph 4.1, Practice Direction to Part 10). If the defendant is a company or other corporation then the acknowledgment should be signed by a person holding a senior position (as to the definition of which see Paragraphs 4.2, 4.3 Practice Direction to Part 10). If a defendant is a partnership then the acknowledgment must be signed by either any of the partners or the person having control or management of the partnership business (Paragraph 4.4, Practice Direction to Part 10). (RSC Order 81 Rule 4(1) provides specific rules in relation to acknowledging service in a claim against a firm.) If the defendant is a child or patient then they can only acknowledge service by their litigation friend (see Part 21 page 25) or the litigation friend's legal representative (Paragraph 4.5, Practice Direction to Part 10).

If two or more defendants to a claim acknowledge service of a claim through the same legal representative at the same time then only one acknowledgment of service need be used (Paragraph 5.3, Practice Direction to Part 10).

An acknowledgment of service can be amended or withdrawn but only with the Court's permission. If permission is sought then an application has to be made under Part 23 and supported by evidence (Paragraph 5.4 and 5.5, Practice Direction to Part 10).

If the defendant wishes to dispute the Court's jurisdiction under Part 11 then an acknowledgment of service must be filed (Rule 11(2)). The defendant does not thereby lose any right to dispute the Court's jurisdiction. The procedure under Part 11, however, must be followed.

Time for Acknowledgment

The acknowledgment of service must be filed within 14 days of service of the particulars of claim or such period as prescribed, for instance, in RSC Order 11 Rule 1A (Service out of the Jurisdiction). In the latter case, the application disputing the Court's jurisdiction must be made within the period for filing a defence (Rule 11(4)) (although for an exception see Acknowledging Service under Part 8 below). The period for filing a defence following service out of the jurisdiction is prescribed by RSC Order 11 Rule 1B.

If the defendant either fails to file an acknowledgment of service or fails to make an application within the appropriate period, he is treated as having accepted that the Court has jurisdiction to try the claim.

Upon filing of an acknowledgment of service, the Court will send the claimant Form N10 which gives details of the defendant's intentions, address and representation.

Acknowledging service under Part 8

The documents served with a claim initiated under Part 8 (Alternative Procedure for Claims) are a form for acknowledging service and the claimant's evidence in support of the claim.

In order to take part in the proceedings the defendant **must** file the acknowledgment of service. Form N210 should be used. Notwithstanding the obligatory nature of Rule 8.3(1)(a) which seems to stipulate that the defendant must file an acknowledgment of service in the relevant practice form, the Practice Direction reflects the Practice Direction under Part 7 in saying that the acknowledgment of service **should** be in the practice form. Unlike Part 7, however, the Practice Direction goes on to say that in the alternative, acknowledgment of service can be given in an informal document such as a letter (Paragraph 3.2, Practice Direction to Part 8).

The acknowledgment of service must be filed no more than **14 days after service of the claim form**. There are no particulars of claim with a claim under Part 8 and accordingly the trigger date is service of the claim form. Under Part 7 the only requirement is **to file** the acknowledgment of service. It is for the Court to notify the claimant when an acknowledgment of service is filed (Rule 10.4). Under Part 8, however, the acknowledgment of service must be filed and served on the claimant and any other party (Rule 8.3). It must state—

- whether the defendant contests the claim;

- whether the defendant seeks a different remedy from that set out in the claim form and, if so, that remedy has to be specified;
- an address for service of documents (see above);
- the defendant's name set out in full (see above); and
- the acknowledgment should be signed (see above).

Part 11 (Disputing the Court's Jurisdiction) applies also to a claim under Part 8 save that the references to a defence do not apply. In replacement, the time for making an application under Rule 11(4) is 14 days after the time for filing an acknowledgment of service as above (Rule 11(1) and Rule 8.3). This period of 14 days applies whether or not service has been effected out of the jurisdiction, notwithstanding the additional time given for filing a defence to a Part 7 claim under RSC Order 11 Rule 1B.

Consequences of not filing an Acknowledgment of Service (and/or a defence) in a claim under a Part 7 (Part 12)

If an acknowledgment of service is not filed in relation to a claim under Part 7 within 14 days of service of the particulars of claim (or such extended period as provided by RSC Order 11), the claimant is entitled to make application for a default judgment under Part 12. Judgment in default, however, cannot be obtained in the following proceedings—

- Where the claim is for delivery of goods subject to an agreement regulated by the Consumer Credit Act 1974.
- Where the claim is a mortgage claim made under RSC Order 88 or CCR Order 6 Rule 5 (although there will generally be issued under Part 8).
- Where the claim falls within the band of specialist proceedings under CPR Part 49 and the Practice Directions applicable to Part 49 provide that there is no requirement for an acknowledgment of service or a defence or there are special provisions about obtaining default judgment. For example, default judgment cannot be obtained on a contentious probate claim (Paragraph 6.1, Practice Direction to Part 49.1 (Contentious Probate Claims)). In the Practice Direction (Paragraph 1.3) to Part 12 it is suggested that this also applies to admiralty proceedings. This is not quite correct following publication of the Practice Direction for admiralty proceedings (Paragraph 7, Practice Direction to Part 49 (Admiralty Proceedings)). It is to be noted, however, that the corollary to the provision in the Practice Direction to Part 12 is that if there is a requirement to file an acknowledgment of service or a defence, and no special provision is made about obtaining a default judgment, Part 12 does apply to specialist proceedings under Part 49. For example, it applies to both proceedings in the Technology & Construction Court and in the Commercial Court (see Paragraph 1.2, Practice Direction to Part 12).
- Where the claim includes a claim for provisional damages (see Paragraph 5.1, Practice Direction to Part 41) although the provisional damages claim may be abandoned in which case default judgment under Part 12 would be available.

Part 12 also provides for obtaining default judgment on failure to file a defence within the requisite periods (see page 81 below in relation to a defence and to those periods). It will be remembered that the obligation to respond to the particulars of claim is to file either an acknowledgment of service or a defence within 14 days of service of the particulars of claim. If an acknowledgment of service is filed within that period then the period for filing a defence is extended by 14 days (see Parts 10 and 15). The following comments therefore refer to default judgment in relation to the failure to file an acknowledgment of service and/or a defence.

For these purposes a defence includes a purported defence, i.e. a document that describes itself as a defence but does not fulfil the requirements of the Rules – such a defence may be struck out under Rule 3.4(2((c) with the consequent availability of judgment under Part 3.

If the acknowledgment of service or the defence is not filed within the requisite period but default judgment is not obtained prior to the late filing of either document, the claimant cannot obtain judgment in default. The late filing of the acknowledgment of service, however, does not extend the time for the filing of a defence. The defence still has to be filed within 28 days of the service of the particulars of claim (see Rules 10.3, 15.4 and 12.3).

Default judgment may not be obtained if—

- The defendant has applied for summary judgment under Part 24 and that application has not been disposed of (Rule 12.3(3)(a)). An application for summary judgment cannot, however, be made before acknowledgment of service is filed save with permission from the Court (Rule 24.4(1)). If a claimant has applied for summary judgment, the period for filing a defence is extended automatically (Rule 14.4(2)).
- The defendant is satisfied the whole of the claim (including any claim for costs) on which the claimant is seeking judgment (Rule 12.3(3)(b)); or
- The claimant is seeking judgment on a claim for money and the defendant has filed or served on the claimant an admission under Rule 14.4 or 14.7 together with a request for time to pay (Rule 12.3(3)(c)).
- The claimant has not filed a certificate of service in accordance with Rule 6.14.

There are two methods of obtaining default judgment.

If the claim is for—

- a specified amount of money; and/or
- an amount of money to be decided by the Court; and/or
- delivery of goods where the claim form gives the defendant the alternative for paying their value;

the claimant may obtain default judgment by filing a request in the appropriate practice form which must be used (Forms N205A or N225 for a specified money claim or delivery of goods where the defendant will be given the alternative of paying a specified sum representing their value, or for fixed costs only; Forms N205B or N227 if the amount of money to be awarded is to be decided by the Court). Otherwise judgment in default requires an application (see below).

Deciding the amount of money in a claim for an unspecified amount

If the claim is for an unspecified amount of money, the judgment obtained in default under Rule 12.4 will be for an amount to be decided by the Court and costs (Rule 12.5(3)). Similarly, under Rule 12.5(4) where the claim is for delivery of goods and the claim form gives the defendant the alternative of paying their value, the default judgment will require the defendant to deliver the goods or, if he does not do so, pay the value of the goods as decided by the Court and to pay costs. In default judgment under Rule 12.5(3) or 12.5(4) the costs are not fixed costs but must also be decided by the Court at some point either by summary assessment or detailed costs assessment in accordance with Rule 44.7.

Having obtained judgment, the procedure for deciding the amount to be paid is provided by Rule 12.7 and the Practice Direction to Part 26 (Paragraph 12).

On entry of judgment the Court will list a disposal hearing (Paragraph 12.7 Practice Direction to Part 26). At that hearing the Court can give directions or decide the amount payable immediately. Those directions could include—

- The allocation of the claim.
- The service and filing of allocation questionnaires.
- That a date be fixed for a hearing or a further hearing.
- That the claim be stayed while the parties try to settle the case.
- Any other appropriate directions including those normally provided under general case management. Those directions may specify the level of type of Judge before whom a hearing or further hearing will take place and the nature and purpose of that hearing. It should be noted that a Master or District Judge is empowered to decide the amount payable, whatever should be the financial value of the claim (see Paragraph 12.10, Practice Direction to Part 26).

At the disposal hearing the Court will require evidence in support of the quantification of the amount payable. If the claim is not allocated to the small claims track at the disposal hearing, that evidence must be served upon the defendant at least three days before the disposal hearing (Paragraph 12.8, Practice Direction to Part 26).

Before deciding on the amount, the Court is encouraged where appropriate to allocate the claim to the small claims track. Having allocated to that track the Court may treat the disposal hearing as a final hearing in accordance with Part 27. The practical consequence is that the relatively informal procedure under Part 27 will apply and the no costs rule under Rule 27.14. The claimant will, however, already have the benefit of a costs order that was made upon the entering of default judgment. It is highly probable that the Court will summarily assess those costs at the disposal hearing. The claimant should therefore be prepared to deal with a summary assessment in accordance with the Practice Direction to Part 44.

The Court can decide the amount payable whether or not the claim is allocated to the small claims track but, as above, it will only exercise this power as long as the evidence in support of the claimant's quantification is served on the defendant at least three days before the disposal hearing.

If, as below, the default judgment has been made upon a hearing in accordance with Rule 12.10, the Judge upon that hearing will make appropriate directions in accordance with Paragraph 12.2 of the Practice Direction to Part 26. The Court will not normally allocate the claim to a track unless the value of the claim would appear to fall within the small claims track or the amount payable appears to be genuinely disputed on grounds which appear to be substantial.

If the claim would fall within the band of the small claims track then on the hearing for default judgment the Court should allocate the claim to the small claims track. It can then deal with it under the relatively informal procedure of Part 27. For instance, it could list a final hearing and give appropriate directions, if any.

Subject to the claim falling within the band of the small claims track, if there appears to be no genuine dispute then the Court can direct that a disposal hearing be listed. In preparation for that disposal hearing the claimant should serve appropriate evidence upon the defendant at least three days before the disposal hearing. It will be remembered, however, that the evidence may already be contained in the particulars of claim. If that is the case then it may be that no further evidence is required as long as the particulars of claim are verified by a statement of truth. In that event the particulars of claim will have already been served and no further service is required.

If the defendant does not respond then the Court can dispose of the claim by determining the amount payable at the disposal hearing. If, however, the defendant presents a genuine dispute, the Court may consider allocating the case and appropriate directions.

If the Court does determine the amount payable at the disposal hearing, it is likely that the Court will summarily assess the costs in accordance with Part 44. The claimant will have to be prepared to deal with summary assessment at the hearing itself. The fixed costs regime under Parts 45 and 46 has no application to the disposal of a claim at a disposal hearing. Thus, for instance, the fixed trial costs for cases allocated to the fast track have no application.

Default judgment obtained by making an application

If the claim does not fit within the categories under which default judgment can be obtained by filing a request, then an application under Part 23 for default judgment must be made. Even if the claim is of such a nature that default judgment could be obtained by filing a request, an application under Part 23 will be necessary in any event if it is sought to enter default judgment in default either of acknowledgment of service or defence against—

- a child or patient;
- in tort by one spouse against the other; or
- against the Crown.

Further, application has to be made for default judgment if the default is a failure to file an acknowledgment of service and the defendant—

- has been served with the claim out of the jurisdiction without leave under the Civil Jurisdiction and Judgments Act 1982 under RSC Order 11 Rule 1(2)(a);
- is domiciled in Scotland or Northern Ireland or in any other Convention territory;
- is a State;
- is a diplomatic agent who enjoys immunity under the Diplomatic Privileges Act 1964; or
- enjoys immunity under the International Organisations Acts 1968 and 1981.

The application notice has to comply with Part 23 and particularly has to state what order the applicant is seeking and briefly why the applicant is seeking that order (Rule 23.6). The general rule is that the application notice has to be served upon the defendant. Rule 12.11(4) provides an exception in that the application for default judgment may be made without notice if—

- the claim was served in accordance with the Civil Jurisdiction and Judgments Act 1982;
- the defendant has failed to file an acknowledgment of service; and
- notice does not need to be given under any other provision of the Rules.

The last bullet point seems to negate the purpose of this Rule since the provisions of Rule 23.7 do indeed provide to the contrary. This was clearly unintended. If the defendant is a State, even if the provisions of Rule 12.11(4) are fulfilled, the Court may on hearing the application direct that notice be served on the State.

It is not necessary to submit any further evidence upon the application than that set out in the statement of case which will be endorsed with a statement of truth. The claimant can, however, if he believes it appropriate, submit further evidence. Evidence in support of the application must, however, be filed if the claim is against a child or patient or a claim in tort between spouses.

Rule 23.7 provides the general rule that evidence in support of an application must be served with the application notice. Rule 12.11(2), however, provides to the contrary if the defendant has not filed an acknowledgment of service. Evidence does not need to be served upon him. It would have to be served if it was an application for judgment in default of defence.

As above, Rule 12.7 and the Practice Direction to Part 26 set out the procedure to be followed where the judgment obtained requires the amount of money to be paid to be decided subsequently by the Court. At the hearing at which default judgment is entered, the Court will give appropriate directions and consider allocation.

If the claim falls within the band of a small claims track claim, the Court should allocate it to that track and then deal with the claim appropriately, for instance, by listing a final hearing. If it is not a small claims track claim then the Court should only allocate it to the fast track or multi track if the amount payable appears to be genuinely disputed on grounds which appear to be substantial. If not, the Court should simply direct that there be a disposal hearing.

In a claim which would otherwise have been allocated to the fast track or multi track had it been defended, the Court will require any written evidence in support of the quantification of the monies payable to be served on the defendant at least three days before the subsequent disposal hearing. If at the disposal hearing the defendant makes out genuine grounds to dispute the amount payable, the Court may give appropriate directions which could include that allocation questionnaires be filed or that the claim be stayed while the parties try to settle it.

The consequences of not filing an Acknowledgment of Service in a claim under Part 8

In a claim under Part 8 the acknowledgment of service **must** be filed differently to the requirements of Part 7. If an acknowledgment of service is not filed, the claimant cannot obtain default judgment but, although the defendant can attend any hearing of the claim, he may not take part in it unless the Court gives specific permission.

Part 13-setting aside Default Judgment

Even if a default judgment has been entered properly, the claimant is under a duty to apply to set it aside if it subsequently comes to his notice that the particulars of claim did not reach the defendant before he entered judgment (Rule 13.5). Having learned of the non-service or late service, the claimant can take no further steps in the proceedings until the judgment has been set aside or the Court has given further directions upon application by the claimant.

Otherwise the onus is upon the defendant to apply to set aside or vary the judgment. The application has to be made in accordance with Part 23 (Form N244) and therefore must state what order the applicant is seeking and briefly why he is seeking it (Rule 23.6). The application must be supported by evidence (Rule 13.4(3)). The application must be served as soon as practicable after filing and no later than three days before the Court is to deal with the application. The application notice must be served with the evidence in support.

If it appears to the Court that the judgment was entered wrongly, that is. that the requirements of Part 12 had not been fulfilled or that the whole of the claim was satisfied before judgment was entered, the Court must set aside the judgment. Otherwise it has a discretion and will only set aside the default judgment if the defendant satisfies it that he has a real prospect of successfully defending the claim or there appears to the Court to be some other good reason why the judgment should be set aside or varied or the defendant should be allowed to defend the claim (Rule 13.3(1)).

This provision attempts to codify the case law prior to 26 April relating to the old rules concerning setting aside a default judgment. The test established by that case law and particularly *The Saudi Eagle* [1986] 2 Lloyds Reports 221, CA, is that of the "arguable" defence. The test set out in Rule 12.3—real prospect of success—is intended to be harder to satisfy.

In considering whether to set aside or vary a judgment entered in default, the Court will have regard to those matters set out in Rule 3.9 (relief from sanctions). It will take into account accordingly whether the application was made promptly, whether there was a good explanation for the failure to file an acknowledgment of service or defence or the extent to which the defendant has previously complied with any relevant pre-action protocol.

Where the claim is for a specified amount of money, the defendant is an individual and judgment was obtained in a Court which is not his home court (defined in Rule 2.3(1)) or the claim has not been transferred to another defendant's home court already, the application will be heard in the defendant's home court which for these purposes is the relevant court for the address of the defendant appearing on the last filed of—

- the application to set aside;
- the acknowledgment of service; and
- the claim form.

On hearing the application the Court may set aside the judgment but provide conditions to the order such as the requirement for a payment in (Rule 3.1(3) and 3.1(5)).

If judgment is set aside then any claims that have been abandoned in obtaining default judgment are restored.

The application to set aside the default judgment can be made by a person who is not a party but who is directly affected by the judgment (Rule 40.9).

It would be open to the Court, either upon application or of its own initiative, to strike out the claim form or particulars of claim if it appeared that either of those statements of case fell foul of Rule 3.4(2).

Consequences of not filing an Acknowledgment or Defence in a claim under Part 20

Although a Part 20 claim is treated as if it were a claim for the purposes of the Rules (Rule 20.3), there are special rules provided by Part 20 as to the consequences of failing to file either an acknowledgment of service where appropriate or a defence to a Part 20 claim.

Part 12 (default judgment) has no application to Part 20 claims unless the claim is a counterclaim (Rule 20.3(3)(a)). Even if the claim is a counterclaim, if it is the claimant that wishes to defend the counterclaim, no acknowledgment of service is required (Rule 20.4(3). Accordingly it appears default judgment cannot even be obtained in those circumstances in default of a defence because the conditions of Rule 12.3 cannot be met. It remains to be seen whether the Civil Procedure Rules Committee cures this fault. In the short term, default judgment is not available in a Part 20 claim when the Part 20 defendant is the claimant. It is available if the Part 20 defendant is not the claimant.

A party other than the claimant responding to a counterclaim would have to persuade the Court that he had a real prospect of success in defending the counterclaim under Rule 13.3(1)(a). Rule 13.3(1)(b) does allow the Court to set aside the judgment if there is some other good reason. If the claim, defence and counterclaim are closely connected then it is suggested that the Court will exercise its power under this Rule indeed to set aside so that all matters are determined at the same time. Upon such application the Court will exercise its powers under Rule 1.4.

Part 14—Admissions

In addition to the forms for acknowledgment of service and defence, the claimant in a claim made under Part 7 must also serve a form for admission as part of the response pack (Form N9A (specified amount) or N9C (unspecified amount, non-money and return of goods claims)) (Rule 7.8(1)(b)).

Although use of the allotted form is encouraged, an admission can be made in any form as long as it is in writing. Thus it can be made by letter or as part of the defence (Rule 14.1).

Part 14 directs itself towards four separate situations—

- Admission of the whole of the claim for a specified amount of money.
- Admission of part of the claim for a specified amount of money.
- Admission of liability for the whole of the claim for an unspecified amount of money.
- Admission of liability of a claim for an unspecified amount of money where the defendant offers a sum in satisfaction of the claim.

In all cases the admission must be made within 14 days of service of the claim form or particulars of claim (if served separately) (Rule 14.2(1)).

Admission of the whole of the claim for a specified amount of money—Rule 14.4

If the defendant admits the claim but does not make a request for time to pay, the claimant can apply for judgment by filing the appropriate request (Form N 205A or 225). In that request he can specify the date by which the whole of the judgment is to be paid or the times and rate at which it is to be paid by instalments. If he does not do so then judgment will be entered for the amount of the claim less any payments made and costs. The judgment will be payable immediately and not within the 14 days specified by Rule 40.11. Costs recoverable are fixed costs in accordance with Part 45. The quantification of those costs will accord with the tables provided in that Part (see page 369). If the claimant specifies that the judgment should not be paid immediately but should be paid at some future date or by instalments, the judgment will be payable accordingly.

As an alternative to admitting the claim, the defendant could make a payment of the amount claimed, plus the fixed costs, within 14 days of service of the particulars of claim. In that event nothing more than fixed costs is payable (Rule 45.3(1)).

If the defendant seeks time to pay then he should complete the statement of means included in Forms N9A and N9C. The offer of payment should be made in box number 11 on the form. The form should be served but does not have to be filed. If the claimant accepts the offer then he may apply for judgment by filing a request (Form N205A or 225). The Court will then enter judgment and the judgment will be payable in accordance with the offer of payment. Judgment will be entered for the amount of the claim and costs. Whilst the amount claimed and admitted might be payable in instalments, the cost will be payable within 14 days of the date of the judgment (Rule 44.8) unless the Court also makes an order that the costs themselves should be payable as part of the instalment process.

If on the other hand the claimant does not accept the defendant's proposals for payment, he must file the appropriate notice (Form N205A or 225). If the admission form was served direct on the claimant then the notice filed with the Court must be accompanied by the request for time to pay (Form N9A).

If the claim is no more than £50,000, a Court officer can upon receipt of the request determine the time and rate of payment. He does so not as a judicial act but as an administrative act. There is no hearing. If the claim is more than £50,000 then it must be referred to a Judge. He can then determine the time and rate of payment without a hearing. If he wishes to have a hearing then the proceedings must be transferred to the defendant's home court (for the definition of which see Rule 2.3). If the claim falls within the usual conditions that apply to the automatic transfer of defended cases under Rule 26.2, and—

- the only claim is for a specified amount of money;
- the defendant is an individual;
- the claim has not been transferred to another defendant's home court under Rule 13.4 or Rule 26.2;
- the claim was not started in the defendant's home court; and
- the claim was not started in a specialist list;

seven days' notice of the hearing must be given to both parties.

If a court officer has determined the time and rate of payment, either party may apply for the matter to be referred to the Judge within 14 days after service of the determination on the application for judgment. Although it is suggested that a Judge could then re-determine the matter without a hearing, the rule applicable (Rule 14.13) suggests by analogy with Rule 14.12 and particularly the transfer provisions under 14.13(3) that upon re-determination the Judge should hold a hearing (see below). If the Judge determined the time and rate of payment without a hearing, again either party may apply within 14 days after service of the determination upon the applicant for the decision to be re-determined by a Judge.

The same provisions relating to transfer to home court apply as in Rule 14.12(2). This seems to suggest that any re-determination will be the subject of a hearing.

Admission of part of a claim for a specified amount of money—Rule 14.5

The procedure under Rule 14.5 is much the same as that under Rule 14.4 save that in this case the defendant has to file the admission form (Form N9A and N9B). The Court will then serve a notice (Form N225A) and a form of part admission (Form N9A/N9B) on the claimant requiring him to elect between one of three choices—

- accepting the amount admitted in satisfaction of the whole of the claim;
- not accepting the amount admitted and seeking the continuance of the proceedings; or
- if the defendant has requested time to pay, accepting the amount admitted in satisfaction of the whole of the claim but not accepting the defendant's proposals for payment.

The claimant must respond to the notice (Form N225A) within 14 days following service by the Court and within that period must also serve a copy on the defendant. If it is not filed with the Court, the claim will be stayed until the notice is filed.

If on filing the notice the claimant takes the first option, the procedure is the same as though the defendant has admitted the whole of the claim. The claimant requests judgment for the admitted sum and in that request can specify the date by which the whole of the judgment is to be paid or the time and rate at which it is to be paid by instalments. Failing the provision of such detail, the judgment is payable immediately and not within the 14 days specified by Rule 40.11.

If the claimant takes the second option and the defendant has served a defence in relation to the balance of the claim which he does not admit, the balance of the claim will continue as a defended claim and the provisions of Part 26 will apply to it. Under Rule 14.3, the claimant may apply for judgment with admissions and costs in relation to the part of the claim admitted. Note that under Paragraph 7.4 of the Practice Direction to Part 26 and Paragraph 5.1 of the Practice Direction to Part 44 if the claim is in excess of the small claims track, but the admission takes it into the small claims track, the claimant can apply for judgment and costs prior to allocation, notwithstanding that upon allocation to the small claims track, the no costs rule applies (see pages 183, 184 and Paragraph 5.1(2), Practice Direction to Part 44).

The claimant that pursues the claim not having accepted the amount admitted, takes a risk on costs if the Court awards no more than the amount admitted. The claimant really ought to try and settle the case at that stage. The opportunity to settle will come following the filing of the allocation questionnaire if a request is made for a stay of the proceedings in order to attempt settlement in accordance with Rule 26.2. The Court will take this into account and possibly any subsequent negotiations under Rule 44.3 and 44.5 when making an order for costs and assessing those costs respectively.

On his part the defendant on making an admission may also make a payment into Court under Part 36. Any offer to settle a money claim requires a Part 36 payment (Rule 36.3). If a payment in (whether or not made in accordance with Part 36) is accepted by the claimant in satisfaction of the whole of the specified money claim, that payment in, having been made within 14 days of the service of the particulars of claim and having included the fixed costs stated in the claim form (i.e. all the fixed costs claimed) only fixed costs are payable (Rule 45.3).

If the claimant takes the third option of accepting the amount admitted but not accepting the defendant's proposal as to payment, the procedure under Rules 14.9, 14.10, 14.11, 14.12 and 14.13 described above will apply.

Admission of liability to pay the whole of a claim for an unspecified amount of money—Rule 14.6

If the claim is for an unspecified amount of money, such as a claim for general damages in a personal injury claim, and the defendant admits liability (usually by filing Form N9C), but does not offer a sum of money in satisfaction of the claim, the claimant can obtain judgment by filing the appropriate request (Form N226) which will be sent to the claimant by the Court together with Form N9C. The Court will then enter judgment (Form N17)for an amount to be decided by the Court and costs. The procedure then to be followed is the same as that following the entry of a default judgment for an amount to be decided by the Court and costs (see the references to Rule 12.7 and Paragraph 12 Practice Direction to Part 26). If the claimant does not file a request for judgment within 14 days, the claim is stayed until he does so.

Admission of liability to pay a claim for an unspecified amount of money where the defendant offers a sum in satisfaction of the claim—Rule 14.7

The procedure under this Rule (14.7) follows that of Rule 14.5 in that if the defendant offers a sum in satisfaction of the claim for an unspecified amount of money, the claimant has three choices which he can request in his request for judgment, namely—

- accepting the amount admitted in satisfaction of the claim;
- not accepting the amount admitted; or
- accepting the amount admitted but not accepting the defendant's proposals as to payment.

Liability is admitted by filing Form N9C with the Court which will then serve a copy on the claimant together with Form N226.

Under the first option above the claimant can obtain a final judgment which will be payable immediately and not the 14 day period specified by Rule 40.11 or at such time and rate as the claimant specifies.

If the claimant takes the second option he can request a judgment. That judgment will be for an amount to be decided by the Court and costs. The claim then follows the procedure under Paragraph 12 of the Practice Direction to Part 26.

If the claimant takes the final option, the Court will decide the time and rate of payment in accordance with Rules 14.9, 14.10, 14.11, 14.12 and 14.13.

On admitting liability and offering a sum in satisfaction of the claim, the defendant should consider making a Part 36 payment.

Fixed costs

The fixed costs regime under Part 45 on obtaining judgment in default under Rule 12.4(1) or judgment on admission under Rules 14.4(3) and 14.5(6) only applies if the claim is for a specified sum of money or the fixed date procedure applies (see Rule 7.9 and the accompanying Practice Direction) and judgment is given for the delivery of goods. The amount of fixed costs on entering judgment is set out in Table 2 to Part 45.

FIXED COSTS ON ENTRY OF JUDGMENT

	Where the amount of the judgment exceeds £25 but does not exceed £5,000	Where the amount of the judgment exceeds £5,000
Where judgment in default of an acknowledgment of service is entered under rule 12.4 (1) (entry of judgment by request on claim for money only)	£22	£30
Where judgment in default of a defence is entered under rule 12.4 (1) (entry of judgment by request on claim for money only)	£25	£35
Where judgment is entered under rule 14.4 (judgment on admission), or rule 14.5 (judgment on admission of part of claim) and claimant accepts the defendant's proposal as to the manner of payment.	£40	£55

	Where the amount of the judgment exceeds £25 but does not exceed £5,000	Where the amount of the judgment exceeds £5,000
Where judgment is entered under rule 14.4 (judgment on admission), or rule 14.5 (judgment on admission on part of claim) and court decides the date or times of payment	£55	£70
Where summary judgment is given under Part 24 or the court strikes out a defence under rule 3.4 (2)(a), in either case, on application by a party	£175	£210
Where judgment is given on a claim for delivery of goods under a regulated agreement within the meaning of the Consumer Credit Act 1974 and no other entry in this table applies	£60	£85

The figures set out in Table 2 include VAT.

In addition to these "solicitors charges", the claimant is also entitled to the fixed costs on the commencement of a claim (see Table 1 and Table 3 at pages 45–47).

Applicable RSC and CCR on staying execution of the Judgment

RSC Order 47

The Court retains the power under RSC Order 47 to stay execution by Writ of Fieri Facias in the particular circumstances set out in Rule 1 to the Order. Those circumstances are—

- that there are special circumstances which render it inexpedient to enforce the judgment or order; or
- that the applicant is unable from any cause to pay the money.

The power of the Court to stay execution is exercisable whether or not the judgment debtor has sought time to pay under Parts 12 or 14.

The judgment debtor should issue an application under CPR Part 23. The application notice together with any supporting evidence must be served no less than four clear days before the hearing. The application notice itself could of course contain the necessary evidence as long as those facts are verified by a statement of truth.

Upon the hearing of the application the Court could stay execution whilst payment by instalments is made.

Upon hearing the application the Court will have to take into account the overriding objective under Part 1 and indeed the considerations for relief from sanctions under Rule 3.9.

In accordance with Rule 50(3)(c) this power is only exercisable in the High Court.

CCR Order 22

The County Court has its own power in relation to the variation of payments under judgments. In accordance with Rule 50(4)(c) the power only relates to proceedings in the County Court. The power is contained within CCR Order 22 Rule 10.

Either party may make an application to vary the date or rate of payment under a judgment. If it is the judgment creditor making application, that application is made in writing and no notice need be served on any other party. Upon that application the Court officer is empowered to make an appropriate order unless no payment on the judgment has been made for six years before the date of the application. In that case the matter has to be referred to the District Judge. The Court officer would have to take into consideration the overriding objective under Part 1 but it is suggested that considerations under Rule 3.9 would be irrelevant.

The judgment debtor may also make application to delay payment under a judgment. That application must be made on the appropriate form (Form N245). The form should state the proposed terms, the grounds on which the application is made and a signed statement of the debtor's means. Upon receipt by the Court the Court should send a copy of the debtor's application and the statement of means to the judgment creditor. The judgment creditor then has 14 days to notify the Court if he objects to the proposals and his reasons for doing so. If he does not notify the Court accordingly then the Court officer can make an order in the terms applied for by the judgment debtor. The Court officer is empowered further to determine the issue if the judgment creditor does object to the debtor's proposals. If either party is unhappy with that decision, the proceedings are automatically transferred to the debtor's home court and the matter is then determined by a District Judge.

The judgment creditor is entitled to apply to the Court under CCR Order 22 Rule 10 for an order that the judgment should be paid at an earlier date than the date set for payment of the whole of the sum or instalments. Upon receipt of an application to this effect the Court will automatically transfer the application to the debtor's home court. A day will be fixed for the hearing of the application and no less than eight days notice of that date will be given to the parties. On that hearing the Court will make an order as seems just. The Court will take into account the considerations of the overriding objective under Part 1.

CHAPTER 8
PARTS 15, 16—DEFENCE AND REPLY

Parts 15 and 16 are the relevant Parts for the preparation and service of the defence and any reply.

The defence is a statement of case in accordance with Rule 2.3(1) and is therefore subject to all of the Rules (such as strike out under Rule 3.4) that apply to statements of case.

As with the claim form and particulars of claim, the defendant is encouraged through the Rules and Practice Direction to set out fully his defence to the claim. This carries on the "cards on the table" approach set out in Lord Woolf's Interim and Final Reports.

A defendant wishing to defend all or part of a claim must file a defence (Rule 15.2).

It should be noted that a defence is not required to respond to a claim issued in accordance with Part 8 (Alternative Procedure).

The period for filing a Defence

The defence has to be filed with the Court no later than 14 days after service of the particulars of claim or, if an acknowledgment of service has been filed, then the period is 28 days. The obligation therefore is to file the defence but not serve it within this period. The defendant is, however, required by Rule 15.6 to serve a defence even if the obligation is not time measured.

RSC Order 11 Rule 1B sets out specific periods for filing a defence where the claim is served out of the jurisdiction. Also, when service is effected upon an agent of a principal who is overseen, the Court will specify the time limit for filing a defence under Rule 6.16(4). Reference should also be made to the specified types of proceedings referred to in Part 48 for any alteration to the general procedure provided by Part 15, for example, contentious probate proceedings.

The calculation of the 14 and 28 days is determined by Rule 2.8. Days are "clear days" and do not include the day on which the period begins, i.e. in this case the date of service.

The period for filing a defence can be extended by the parties under Rule 15.5 but only up to a total period of 28 days. If agreement is reached to extend the period then the defendant must notify the Court in writing of this agreement (Rule 15.5(2)).

If agreement cannot be reached as to an extension of the time for filing a defence, an application must be made to the Court in accordance with Part 23. Parties should be warned that it is intended that Judges will no longer be lenient (if they ever were) in allowing various extensions over a period of time unless there are particularly good grounds. At the time of writing there appears to be a diversity of opinion within the judiciary as to the level of strictness to be applied by the Court in relation to such time limits and their extension. In any event, in considering such an application the Court will take into account whether or not a party has complied with any relevant pre-action protocol (Rule 3.1(4)). The court must also have consideration to the overriding objective and Rule 1.1 (2).

If a defence is not filed then judgment may be requested under Part 12 (see page 66). For these purposes a defence includes a document purporting to be a defence (Paragraph 1.1, Practice Direction to Part 12), i.e. a document which describes itself as a defence such as the return of an appropriate form but does not fulfil the requirements of the Rules (although such a defence would be liable to be struck out under Rule 3.4(2)). As previously, even if the defence is served outside the specified periods, if it is filed prior to the obtaining of default judgment by the claimant in accordance with Part 12, default judgment will not be available to the claimant.

In order to defend a claim under Part 7 (unlike Part 8), an acknowledgment of service is not required. As long as the defence is served prior to the entering of judgment it suffices to replace the acknowledgment. If there is no acknowledgment then in the defence the defendant must give an address for service (Paragraph 16.5(8), Practice Direction to Part 16).

The address given must be an address within the jurisdiction (Rule 6.5(2)). What is the jurisdiction is defined in Rule 2.3. If a party does not give the business address of his solicitor as the address for service and resides or carries on business within the jurisdiction then he must give his residence or place of business as his address for service (Rule 6.5(3)). If a solicitor is acting for the defendant then the solicitor's business address is the address for service (Rule 6.5(5) and see Rule 42.1 (Change of Solicitor)).

Contents of the Defence

The rules relating to the contents of the defence are considerably shorter than the rules relating to what must be included in the particulars of claim. They do, however, continue the encouragement and requirement of parties to include in statements of case a full explanation of what is being said in response to the claim.

The defendant may use the appropriate form (N9B or N9D) but there is no absolute requirement to do so and a defence may be contained in any document as long as it complies with the requirements as to its contents. If it is not included on the appropriate form then, although not specifically required by the Rules, it should contain the details of the parties and the case number at the head of it.

The main rule relating to the contents of the defence is Rule 16.5:

16.5 (1) In his defence, the defendant must state—

(a) which of the allegations in the particulars of claim he denies;

(b) which allegations he is unable to admit or deny, but which he requires the claimant to prove; and

(c) which allegations he admits.

(2) Where the defendant denies an allegation—

(a) he must state his reasons for doing so; and

(b) if he intends to put forward a different version of events from that given by the claimant, he must state his own version.

(3) A defendant who—

(a) fails to deal with an allegation; but

(b) has set out in his defence the nature of his case in relation to the issue to which that allegation is relevant,

shall be taken to require that allegation to be proved.

(4) Where the claim includes a money claim, a defendant shall be taken to require that any allegation relating to the amount of money claimed be proved unless he expressly admits the allegation.

(5) Subject to paragraphs (3) and (4), a defendant who fails to deal with an allegation shall be taken to admit that allegation.

(6) If the defendant disputes the claimant's statement of value under rule 16.3 he must—

(a) state why he disputes it; and

(b) if he is able, give his own statement of the value of the claim.

(7) If the defendant is defending in a representative capacity, he must state what that capacity is.

(8) If the defendant has not filed an acknowledgment of service under Part 10, he must give an address for service.

(Part 22 requires a defence to be verified by a statement of truth)

(Rule 6.5 provides that an address for service must be within the jurisdiction)

Attention is particularly drawn to Rule 16.5(5). This was a later amendment to the Rules in the process of drafting and is intended to emphasise the requirement of a defendant to deal with every allegation made by the claimant which he wishes to dispute. Accordingly, if a defendant does not deal with an allegation then he shall be taken to admit it unless generally he sets out in his defence the nature of his case in relation to the issue to which that allegation is relevant (Rule 16.5(3)). This does not apply, however, to the quantification of a money claim. Any allegation in relation to the amount of money must be proved by the claimant whether or not it is addressed in the defence, unless the defendant expressly admits the amount.

In addition to the matters set out in Rule 16.5, the Practice Direction to Part 16 (Paragraphs 14-16) contains other requirements for what must be included in the defence. Thus the defendant must give details of the expiry of any relevant limitation period relied upon (Paragraph 16.1). Paragraph 14 makes specific requirements for personal injury actions and Paragraph 15 for defamation actions. The Commercial Court Guide (Part C) and the Chancery Guide (Chapter 4) provide additionally for the defence, its contents, and accompanying documents.

In addition to those matters which must be included in a defence. Paragraph 16.3 of the Practice Direction sets out what may be included—

- Any point of law on which the defence is based.
- The name of any witness that the defendant proposes to call.
- Attached to or served with the defence a copy of any document which the defendant considers necessary to the defence including, for instance, an experts' report under Part 35.

This provision reflects the Woolf recommendations that parties shall set out their case more fully at an early stage of the proceedings. Although there is no like provision in relation to a defence, Paragraph 10.2 of the Practice Direction to Part 16 sets out various matters which the claimant must set out in the particulars of claim if he wishes to rely on them in support of his claim. Such matters include any allegations as to fraud, the fact of any illegality, or the details of any misrepresentation. It is suggested that if the defendant wishes to rely on such matters, they should be fully stated in the defence. If in the defence the defendant claims the debt is paid, the court will notify the claimant (Form N236) asking whether the claim will continue. The claimant must file the Form N236 indicating his wishes or the claim is stayed (Rule 15.10).

If the defendant is relying upon a defence of tender then a payment into Court must be made in accordance with Rule 37.3 and Paragraph 2 of the Practice Direction to Part 37.

Rule 16.6 makes special allowance for parties to claim set-off by way of defence:

16.6 Where a defendant—

(a) contends he is entitled to money from the claimant; and

(b) relies on this as a defence to the whole or part of the claim,

the contention may be included in the defence and set off against the claim, whether or not it is also a Part 20 claim.

Striking out the Defence—Rule 3.4(2)

For striking out a statement of case including a defence, see page 120 in relation to striking out the claim form or particulars of claim.

It is intended that a Court officer should review each defence as it comes in and any doubts about compliance with the Rules relating to defences should be referred to the District Judge or Master for an appropriate order if considered necessary (see Paragraph 3.1-3.5, Practice Direction to Part 3). Thus a defence which is incoherent or contains no more than a bare denial is likely to be referred to the District Judge or Master with a view to an order striking it out. There is no like provision to that relating to the particulars of claim under Paragraph 2.4 of the Practice Direction to Part 3 (claims which fall foul of Rule 3.4(2)(a) or (b)). Accordingly in exercising its power to make an order of its own initiative under Rule 3.3 striking out the defence, it is suggested that whilst the court could strike out the defence without notice normally the defendant should be given the opportunity either to make representations or to cure any defect.

In exercising a power to strike out the defence, either of its own initiative or on application by the claimant for failure to comply with the provisions of 16.5 (that is, the contents of the defence), the Court will be using the ground for striking out set out in Rule 3.4(2)—

> **that there has been a failure to comply with a Rule, Practice Direction or Court Order.**

The other grounds under 3.4(2) apply to a defence just as much as they apply to particulars of claim. Thus the defence is liable to be struck out if—

> **it discloses no reasonable grounds for defending the claim or it is an abuse of the Court's process or is otherwise likely to obstruct the just disposal of the proceedings.**

If an application is made by the Claimant to strike out the defence then the claimant should also consider making an application at the same time for summary judgment in accordance with Part 24.

If all of the defence is struck out as a result of failure to comply with an order, the claimant may obtain judgment (with costs) by filing a request for judgment. Rule 3.5(2)(b) only allows this procedure if the claim is for—

- a specified amount of money;
- an amount of money to be decided by the Court;
- delivery of goods where the claim form gives the defendant the alternative of paying their claim; or
- any combination of these remedies.

The costs concerned may be fixed costs under Part 45. In particular Rule 45.1(2)(v) applies the fixed costs regime when the Court has made an order to strike out a defence under Rule 3.4(2)(a) as disclosing no reasonable grounds for bringing or defending a claim.

As with striking out the particulars of claim, there are limits set out in Rule 3.6 and 3.9 relating to an application for relief against a striking out following a failure to comply with an order.

Statement of Truth

For statements of truth generally see Chapter 12 page 117 in their application to claim forms and particulars of claim. The form of a statement of truth on a defence will be as follows—

I believe that the facts stated in this defence are true.

If a legal representative signs it then it will read—

The claimant believes that the facts stated in this defence are true.

Just as with the claim form and particulars of claim, the defence remains effective notwithstanding that it is not verified. The Court may strike out the defence for failure to verify by statement of truth (Rule 22.2(2)) either on its own initiative under Rule 3.3 or upon application of the claimant under Part 23. Until the defence is verified by a statement of truth its contents cannot be used as evidence, for instance, in an application for summary judgment.

In addition to the statement of truth if a legal representative drafts the defence they should sign it either in their own name or where appropriate in the name of the firm (Paragraph 2.1, Practice Direction to Part 5).

Reply to Defence

The claimant is not obliged to file a reply to the defence. If no reply is filed the claimant is not taken to admit the matters raised in the defence (Rule 16.7(1)).

As with a statement of case under Rule 2.3(1) a reply has to be verified by a statement of truth.

A reply shall not be used to correct mistakes in the particulars of claim. Applications should be made to amend the particulars (Paragraph 11.2, Practice Direction to Part 16).

There are no further "statements of case" beyond a reply.

CHAPTER 9
PART 17—AMENDMENTS TO STATEMENT OF CASE

The statement of case is defined in Rule 2.3(1) as—

- a claim form;
- particulars of claim where these are not included in a claim form;
- a defence;
- a Part 20 claim or reply to defence; and
- any further information given in relation to them voluntarily or by Court Order under Rule 18.1.

The Rules in Part 17 must be read together with the Rules in Part 19 which refer to the addition and substitution of parties in the event that the amendments follow from such addition or substitution.

The word "amendment" has been retained throughout the Part although there was a proposal that the plain English alternative would have been "change". The Civil Procedure Rule Committee decided that "amendment" was a word that practitioners were familiar with and that it would be understood by the litigant in person.

Amendments to acknowledgments of service are dealt with in the Practice Direction to Part 10 (Paragraph 5.4). By this provision an acknowledgment of service may be amended or withdrawn only with the permission of the Court.

Amendments to judgments or orders in the event of accidental slip or omission are dealt with in Rule 40.12.

An admission may be withdrawn or amended but again only with the Court's permission (Rule 14.1(5)).

Amendments under the Rules of the Supreme Court were dealt with in Order 20. In the County Court the appropriate Rule was Order 15. The new Rule in some respects consolidates the differing provisions of the RSC and CCR but otherwise provides a completely new regime. This new regime fits in with the general flow of the new Rules and particularly case management.

One of the important principles under the new Rules is that when the Court allocates a case to a track under Part 26 it should have in front of it all the requisite information in relation to the claim and any allied claim such as a counterclaim to allow it to allocate the case appropriately.

The general picture under the new Rules is that a statement of case may be amended without the permission of the Court at any time before it has been served on any other party (Rule 17.1(1)) or at any time during the course of proceedings with the consent of all the other parties. If service has been effected or the written consent is not forthcoming, the permission of the Court is a necessary prerequisite. Rule 19.1, however, provides that if the amendment involves the addition, substitution or removal of any party, the permission of the Court is always necessary.

By way of example, therefore, the claimant may amend the claim form or the particulars of claim without the Court's permission or the consent of all the other parties in between the time of issue of the claim and service. Similarly the defendant may amend the defence between the filing of it in accordance with Rule 15.2 and its service under Rule 15.6.

As previously, the amendments to a statement of case take effect from the date of the original statement of case thus amended and not from the date that the amendment is effected. Further discussion of the effect of that principle is beyond the scope of this book and reference should be made to standard works such as Butterworths Civil Practice in relation to it.

If amendments are effected without the Court's permission, the Court retains the power under Rule 17.2 to disallow the amendment either upon application or of its own initiative exercising its power under Rule 3.3. An application by a party can be made whether or not that party has consented to the amendment. A party giving such consent is therefore in a position to change their mind following service of a copy of the amended statement of case itself.

The application by a party requesting the Court to disallow an amendment must be made within 14 days of service of the amended statement of case upon him. As with all periods under the Rules, this time can be extended by agreement under Rule 2.11 or by the Court under Rule 3.1(2)(a). Such an application to disallow an amendment might follow an amendment where the amendment adds or substitutes a new claim in relation to which a period of limitation may have expired under the Limitation Act 1980.

If permission from the Court is not required then the amended statement of case and the Court copy of it should be endorsed as follows—

> **"Amended Particulars of Claim, Defence (or as appropriate) under CPR Rule 17.1(1) or (2)(a) dated . . . . "**

(Paragraph 2.1, Practice Direction to Part 17.)

The manner in which an amendment should be shown on the statement of case has been a matter of much debate over the years. The Commercial Court in particular has tried to move away from the use of colours to show amendments since that procedure, on occasion adding a rich variety of colours to a pleading, is not particularly IT friendly.

The Civil Procedure Rule Committee decided that the way forward was that the amended statement of case did not have to show the manner in which amendments had been made during the course of proceedings. Accordingly the statement of case in its amended form does not have to show the original text in any fashion (Paragraph 2.2, Practice Direction to Part 17).

It should be noted that the Commercial Court has disapplied the provision (see Paragraph C5.3, Commercial Court Guide) and it remains to be seen whether any other courts follow this line insofar as they can.

If, however, the Court thinks it desirable to show both the original text and the amendments, it may direct that the amendments should be shown. The history of amendments during the course of proceedings might be of importance, for instance, in relation to costs. If the Court does direct that amendments should be shown then the old system of coloured amendments can be used with the usual order of first amendment red, second green, third violet and fourth yellow. Text deleted should be struck through in the appropriate colour and any text replacing it inserted or underlined in the same colour.

The Court may direct, however, that the amendments should be shown by use of a numerical code without the use of colour.

If the permission of the Court is required to amend then generally the parties should try and reach agreement about the amendments sought. Subject to that any application should be made in accordance with Part 23. In particular it should comply with the requirements of Rule 23.6 that the application notice must state what order the applicant is seeking and briefly why the applicant is seeking the order. There is no necessity to support the application with evidence, although if evidence is to be used on the application it may be contained in the application notice as long as that notice is endorsed with a statement of truth or by a separate witness statement. In accordance with Rule 23.7(2) any evidence in support of the application must be served with the application notice itself.

When the application notice is issued, the applicant should file with the Court in addition to the application notice, a copy of the statement of case as amended. Although the amendments do not have to be shown (as above), clearly it would be practically useful for the Court and the parties if the amendments are made clear in some fashion.

If the application to amend is made after a period of limitation has expired and the amendment requires the removal, addition or substitution of a party, reference should be made to Rule 19.4 (adding or substituting parties after the end of the relevant limitation period). Subject to that Rule the Court may allow the amendment but subject to certain limitations—

- If the amendment is to add or substitute a new claim, the Court will only allow the amendment if the new claim arises out of the same facts or substantially the same facts as the claim before amendment in relation to which a remedy has been sought.
- A mistake as to a name of a party will be allowed but only where the mistake was genuine and not one which could cause reasonable doubt as to the identity of the party in question (see Rule 19.4 below).

- The Court may allow an amendment to alter the capacity in which a party claims but only if that capacity is one which the party had when the proceedings started or has since acquired.

If the amendment is allowed then the Court will give appropriate directions such as directing the other parties to amend their statements of case consequent upon the amendment for which permission has been given.

The usual rule as to costs upon such an application will be that the applicant should pay the costs **of and arising from** the amendment.

The amended statement of case following permission should be endorsed as follows—

"Amended Particulars of Claim, Defence (or as appropriate) by order of . . . . dated . . . . ".

As to the manner in which the statement of case is amended see above.

The amended statement of case must be filed with the Court within 14 days of the date of the order or in accordance with the order. A copy of the order and the amended statement of case must be served on every other party to the proceedings or again in accordance with the Court order.

Statement of Truth

Amendments should be verified by a statement of truth (Rule 22.1 (2)) unless the court orders otherwise or the substance of the statement of case is not amended (Paragraph 1.4, Practice Direction to Part 17). Contrary to the practice direction the Commercial Court Guide specifies that **all** amendments are verified.

Part 19—Addition and substitution of parties

The permission of the Court is always required for the addition, substitution or removal of a party (Rule 19.1).

The application must be made in accordance with Part 23. The application notice must state what order the applicant is seeking and briefly why. Depending on the matters to be proved to the Court (see below), evidence in support of the application may be required. If it is then it may be contained within the application notice as long as it is verified by a statement of truth or in a separate witness statement. The evidence must be served with the application notice (Rule 27.7(3)).

The application may be made by an existing party or by any person who wishes to become a party. A person may wish to become a party if, for instance, they are likely to be affected by the outcome of the proceedings and they wish to make submissions to the Court in relation to that outcome.

If it is proposed to add or substitute a claimant then the person who will become the claimant must give their consent in writing which consent must be filed with the Court prior to the addition or substitution being made (Rule 19.3(3)). If the application is made with the intention of substituting a new party where the existing party's interest or liability has passed, the application can be made without notice but must be supported by evidence (Rule 19.3(2)).

Rule 19.1 provides for the considerations that the Court must have in mind when considering an application for the addition, substitution or removal or a party—

To add a new party

- The addition of the new party is desirable so that the Court can resolve all the matters in dispute in the proceedings; or
- There is an issue involving the new party and an existing party connected with the matters in dispute and it is desirable to add the new party so that the Court can resolve that issue.

The removal of a party

- If it is not desirable for that person to be a party to the proceedings.

A new party to be substituted for an existing one

- The existing party's interest or liability is passed to the new party; and
- It is desirable to substitute the new party so that the Court can resolve the matters in dispute in the proceedings.

There are special provisions about the addition or substitution of parties following the expiry of a limitation period (Rule 19.4). A party may be added or substituted only if the limitation period has not expired at the time that proceedings were started and the addition or substitution of a party **is necessary** (Rule 19.4(2)). Rule 19.4(3) then goes on to determine exactly what "necessary" means for these purposes—

- A new party is to be substituted for a party who was named in the claim form in mistake for the new party.
- The claim cannot properly be carried on by or against the original party unless the new party is added or substituted as a claimant or defendant; or
- The original party has died or had a bankruptcy order made against him and his interest or liability is passed to the new party.

There is a special provision for personal injury claims to the effect that the Court may add or substitute a party if it dis-applies the provisions of Section 11 or Section 12 of the Limitation Act 1980 or it leaves that question to be determined at trial.

Following the making of the Order the Court will give appropriate directions. It will usually make provision for the filing and service of both the amended statement of case (including documents referred to in it) and the order upon the other party. If the new party is a defendant then in addition to the amended statement of case the claimant will have to serve the response pack for a claim under Part 7 (Form N9) or an acknowledgment of service (Form N210) for a claim under Part 8. (Also see the reference to Part 20 below.)

The added or substituted party becomes a party from the date the order is made (Rule 40.7) but where the new party is a defendant he does not become a party to the proceedings until the amended claim form is served upon him (see *Kettleman v Hansel Properties Ltd* [1987] AC 189, HL).

The Procedure

Parties should try and agree on the removal, substitution or addition of parties and consequent amendments in which case a consent order may be sought. If agreement cannot be reached application should be made under Part 23 and comply with its provisions as to, for instance, the contents of the application notice. Notice has to be served unless the application is made under Rule 19.1/4 (substitution of a party for an existing one). If the application is to add or substitute a party as claimant the applicant should file a draft amended statement of case and the consent of the new claimant. If the consent is not available the order is not effective until consent is filed (Paragraph 2, Practice Direction to Part 19).

The Practice Direction to Part 19 sets out the orders the court may make upon the addition, substitution or removal of a party.

Practice in the High Court is that upon adding a party, the claim form must be re-issued (High Court Notes for Guidance, Published April 1999). This may also apply in other courts.

CHAPTER 10
PART 18—FURTHER INFORMATION

As originally conceived this Part of the Brown Book (then Part 35) was limited in its scope. During the course of consultation and drafting that scope has been widened considerably. For instance as initially drafted an application for an Order compelling further information was only available in the multi track. As will be seen Part 18 applies to claims in both the fast track and the multi track. It is specifically excluded in relation to the small claims track under Rule 27.2(1)(f). Further, in draft it was previously an obligation for the Court to consider whether an Order was necessary to dispose fairly of the claim or to save costs. Again that condition has been excluded but in considering whether to make an Order or not the Court must have regard to the Overriding Objective and particularly the factors to be taken into consideration under Rule 1.1(2).

In its final form Part 18 replaces entirely the provisions under the old RSC and CCR for the giving of further and better particulars of a pleading and discovery by interrogatories. The result is that the ability to obtain further information under Part 18 is a good deal wider in its scope than the former provisions. It remains to be seen what restrictions the Court imposes under Part 18 using its discretion and obligations arising from Part 1 (the Overriding Objective) and Part 3 (the Courts Case Management Powers). No doubt requests for further information could become an oppressive mechanism. It is suggested that the Court will strive to strike a balance between allowing a party requesting information to obtain such information as allows the party requesting information to see the other parties cards (taking the analogy of "cards on the table" a little further) and the potential for oppressive behaviour. The Court will also consider the general culture of the CPR and the Rules (particularly in relation to fast track) that an expeditious course towards trial should be maintained with a trial taking place as soon as practicable in multi-track or under the fast track timetable.

Information must be of matter in dispute

Subject to these considerations a request for further information under Part 18 can be made at any time during the course of the proceedings. The request for further information must direct itself towards any matter which is in dispute in the proceedings. Accordingly before making such a request the fact that a matter is in dispute must be established. It is suggested, therefore that in the absence of any other document putting the matter in dispute a defendant would have to assert the dispute. The defendant should know precisely what issues are being raised by the claimant. In accordance with Rule 16.5 the defendant's defence must deal with all allegations. Insofar as it fails to deal with an allegation then the defendant is taken to admit that allegation (Rule 16.5(5)). It is suggested therefore that to put a matter in dispute for the purposes of Part 18 does not require any particular formality. Generally the matter will be put in dispute by a defence or a witness statement but the application for an Order under Rule 18.1 could put the matter in dispute either by the evidence contained within the application notice verified by Statement of Truth or by separate witness statement.

The matter which is in dispute has to be in dispute "in the proceedings". It is suggested therefore in order to fall within Part 18 such a matter must be material to be issues to be determined by the Court. The information which may be sought is not confined simply to facts which are directly in dispute but also to facts which were relevant to the facts which are directly in dispute (see below as to "clarify").

The further information is limited in its purpose to the **clarification** of any matter in dispute in the proceedings for the giving of additional information in relation to any such matter.

Insofar as it is assists the word "clarify" is defined in the Oxford English dictionary as follows:

Text

The Practice Direction to Part 18 (Paragraph 1.2) attempts to provide some clothes for the skeleton of Rule 18.1(1) particularly in relation to the extent of clarification and additional information. The Paragraph provides that the information should be:

> **Strictly confined to matters which are reasonably necessary and proportionate to enable the first party to prepare his own case or to understand the case he has to meet.**

Subject to this limitation, however, the Court has a large amount of discretion as to whether or not the information sought will lead to a clarification.

The fact that Part 18 is intended to cover the two procedures under the old Rules of further and better particulars and interrogatories is emphasised in Rule 18.1 (1) by the fact that the matter for which clarification or additional information is sought does not have to be contained or referred to in the Statement of Case.

As above the request for information can be made at any time. It remains to be seen, however, whether the Court will apply a general Rule that insofar as it relates to any facts upon which evidence is to be given by a witness and in a witness statement the provision of further information should await the exchange of witness statements. Practice has developed to this effect in relation to Interrogatories. In order to reflect this the original draft of the Rule contained a provision of precisely to this effect. The provision was removed during the consultation and committee process because Part 18 is intended to cover the old procedures of both further and better particulars and interrogatories. Further the proposed Rule may be regarded as too rigid since request for information before service of witness statements even in relation to factual matters may well be appropriate. As above the culture under the CPR is to try and ensure that the Court and the parties know as early as possible exactly what issues have to be addressed and determined by the Court.

The request should be concise (Paragraph 1.2, Practice Direction to Part 18). As far as possible it should be contained within a single document. There is no practice form and a request can be made simply by letter. If it is made by letter then the letter should deal only with requests made under Part 18 and state that the request is made under Part 18.

Further whether or not the request is made by letter or separate document it must—

- Be headed with the name of the Court and the title and number of the claim.
- State in its heading that it is a request under Part 18, identify who is asking for further information and from whom it is sought (referred to as the first party and the second party respectively in the Practice Direction). This should also state the date on which it is made which for these purposes will be the date of despatch by the first party to the second party.
- Each request should be separately numbered.
- If the request relates to a document then it should identify the document and the relevant part.
- Finally the request should state the date on which the first party expects a response.

The Practice Direction promotes the practice adopted where such requests are made for instance in family proceedings in that the request should be listed on the left hand half of the page with space on the right hand side to put the responses. As matter of practice it would assist in providing a comprehensive document containing both the request and the further information if a floppy disk were also provided on the making of the request. In practice it is often difficult for the first party (as defined) to determine exactly how much space is needed for the further information itself to be provided by the second party.

Having served the request the first party should give the second party **reasonable time to respond**. If a response is not forthcoming or further reasonable time sought the first party may make an application to the Court. An application would have to be made in accordance with Part 23. Accordingly the application notice must state what order the Applicant is seeking and briefly why the Applicant is seeking the order (Rule 23.6). If evidence is required in support of the application (as to which see Paragraph 5.4, Practice Direction to Part 18) then it may be contained in the application notice if verified by Statement of Truth or in a separate witness statement. In addition to the requirements of Rule 23.6, the Practice Direction requires that the Applicant should explain why, if appropriate, no request was made for the information before application was made to the Court. If a request was made then the application notice or the evidence in support should describe the response, if any. The application notice should contain or have attached a draft order (paragraph 5.2).

The application notice and any witness statement must be served together upon the second party (Rule 23.7(3)). The application notice has to be served on all parties to the claim (Paragraph 5.6). Service on the second party, however, is not required if the second party has not responded to the request within the time stated in the request for the response or 14 days whichever is the later (Paragraph 5.5).

Any order made on the Part 18 application must be served on all parties to the claim including the second party whether or not they responded to the request (Paragraph 5.7).

If the Court makes an order then the second party must file and serve its response within time specified by the Court (Rule 18.1(3)).

Whether the response is given under an order or voluntarily, the Practice Direction in Paragraph 2 of the Practice Direction provides for the form of it. The response can effectively be by one of three methods: a letter, a more formal written reply or on the form of request served by the first party. Although there is no specific obligation a letter should only be used if it is made in response to a letter received from the first party. If a letter is used then it should identify itself as a response to the request under Part 18 and deal solely with the response. As with the request the letter or a more formal document should be headed with the name of the Court, the title and number of the claim. It should identify itself as a response to the request. It must set out each request and then against or under the request set out the response to it. If the request has been made using the format of setting out the request on the left hand side of the page then the second party should set out against each request the appropriate response. If any document is referred to in the response then it should be attached to the response unless the first party already has it.

Under Paragraphs 4.1 and 4.2 Practice Direction to Part 18 if the second party objects to complying with the request or part of it or is unable to do so at all within the time stated in the request then he must tell the first party **promptly** but no later than the time stated in the request. The second party should tell the first party either in a letter or a separate document. He must give his reasons for objecting or being unable to comply and in the latter case give a date by which he expects to be able to comply. If the objection is based on proportionality then the second party should raise that with the first party and explain the reasons for his grounds.

If the first party pursues the matter before the Court in seeking an order then the second party has an opportunity to present his objections to the Court or to explain his inability to comply. There is no necessity for the second party to make a specific application to the Court. The onus is on the first party to pursue the matter.

If a second or supplementary response to a request is made then it should identify itself as such in the heading.

Any further information given under Part 18 whether voluntarily or not is a Statement of Case as defined in Rule 2.3(1). Accordingly Part 22 (Statements of Truth) applies to it as much as it applies to any other Statement of Case. The further information has to be verified by the Statement of Truth (Rule 22.1). If it is not so verified then it remains effective unless struck out but a party may not rely on the further information as evidence of any of the matters set out in it (Rule 22.2(1)). The first party may make an application to the Court to strike out the further information if it is not verified by a Statement of Truth. Indeed in principle the Court has the power to do so of its own initiative under Rule 3.3. It is suggested, however, that little purpose would be served in striking out the further information under Part 18 and there may be more appropriate sanctions. The Statement of Truth must be signed either by the party or litigation friend or the legal representative (Rule 22.1(6)(a)).

CHAPTER 11
PART 20—COUNTERCLAIMS AND OTHER ADDITIONAL CLAIMS

Part 20 is one of those Parts of the CPR which underwent a metamorphosis during the process of consultation and consideration by the Civil Procedure Rule Committee. Five separate revisions to the whole of the Part were made in that process. Originally this Part of the CPR dealt with claims other than counterclaims. It was decided early on that counterclaims should be consolidated into this Part.

As ever, consideration was given as to terminology and exactly what a claim falling within the provisions of this Part should be called. The title of the Part was originally "Claims Connected to the Main Claim" (in the Brown Book). It was then changed to "Additional Claims" and, with the addition of counterclaims, it now becomes "Counterclaims and Other Additional Claims".

Such a claim was originally referred to as an "additional claim". This was regarded as somewhat confusing and in the second revision the Committee adopted the practice as with some other Parts (for example, Part 36) of adopting the descriptive title of the Part itself. Thus claims covered by Part 20 are indeed "Part 20 claims". Following on from that, a person who makes a Part 20 claim is a "Part 20 claimant" (Rule 20.2(2)).

The commonality amongst Part 20 claims is not, however, carried throughout Part 20 procedure. A counterclaim is simply made by filing particulars of the counterclaim (Rule 20.4(1)). A claim for a contribution or indemnity against another defendant is made by "notice"—presumably continuing to be termed "a contribution and/or indemnity notice". Any other Part 20 claim is made by a Part 20 claim form.

There are five broad categories of Part 20 claim—

- a counterclaim against the claimant only made by filing particulars of the counterclaim (Rule 20.4(1));
- a counterclaim against a person other than the claimant requiring an order adding that person as a defendant to the counterclaim (Rule 20.5(1));
- a claim for contribution and/or indemnity against another defendant made by filing a notice;
- a claim for contribution and/or indemnity against a person other than an existing defendant made by a Part 20 claim form;

- a claim for some other remedy against another person (whether or not already a party) made again by a Part 20 claim form.

As provided by Rule 20.1, the purpose of Part 20 is to enable the Court to manage the proceedings before it in the most convenient and effective manner. In that management the Court will have consideration for the overriding objective, the obligation to deal with cases justly subject to Rule 1.1(2), the obligation to actively manage cases under Rule 1.4 and the powers given to the Court under Part 3 (Case Management).

The purpose stated is taken into effect within the Part itself. The central core to the procedure under the CPR is the management of proceedings by the Court. The first stage in that management is the allocation of a claim to a track. At the time of allocation the Court should know exactly what issues are being put before the Court for a decision. Accordingly, if a Part 20 claim is to be made then the Court should be aware of it and manage the case accordingly.

For this reason generally a Part 20 claim can be made without the Court's permission (with exceptions) when it accompanies a defence. Thereafter the Court's permission is required.

Generally any Part 20 claim is a "claim" for the purposes of these Rules (Rule 20.3) which applies to the payment of Court fees as well. Thus a Part 20 claim form and particulars of a counterclaim and a contribution notice are statements of case for the purposes of Rule 2.3(1). They have to comply generally with Part 7 and Part 8 and are susceptible to an application for summary judgment under Part 24. This general rule, however, is subject to three general exceptions—

- Rules 7.5 and 7.6 do not apply (time within which a claim form may be served);
- Rule 16.3(5) does not apply (statement of value where claim to be issued in the High Court); and
- Part 26 does not apply (case management—preliminary stage).

In addition, other than in relation to a counterclaim, Part 12 (default judgment) has no application although special provision is made within Rule 20.11 (see below). Other than Rules 14.1(1), 14.1(2) and 14.3, Part 14 (admissions) has no application.

As dealt with in relation to the defence (see page 84 above), Rule 16.6 provides that where a defendant contends that he is entitled to money from the claimant and relies on that contention as a defence to the whole or part of the claim, it can be included in the defence and set off against the claim, whether or not the contention is also made in a counterclaim under Part 20.

In accordance with practice prior to 26 April, where a defendant to a claim serves a counterclaim, the defendant should use one document for both the defence and counterclaim with the counterclaim following on from the defence (Paragraph 6.1, Practice Direction to Part 20). The counterclaim must otherwise comply with the Practice Direction to Part 5 and particularly Paragraph 2. Thus the counterclaim must, for instance, be signed by the legal representative if drafted by him.

If the counterclaim follows on immediately from the defence, the title to the document will be at the head of the defence. As with the defence itself, it should set out the full name of each party and his status in the proceedings. Thus the normal heading will be—

AB	-	Claimant / Part 20 Defendant
CD	-	Defendant / Part 20 Claimant

If the counterclaim includes a claim against any other person other than the claimant then the documents will be headed with that other person's name as well described as the "Part 20 Defendant" (Paragraph 7.1 Practice Direction to Part 20).

Matters become complicated if there is more than one Part 20 claim—for example, if there is a counterclaim by the defendant against the claimant and the claimant then seeks a contribution or indemnity from some other person. Taking that example, the heading of the proceedings would be as follows—

AB	-	Claimant / Part 20 Defendant (First Claim) /Part 20 Claimant (Second claim)
CD	-	Defendant and Part 20 Claimant (First Claim)
EF	-	Part 20 Defendant (Second Claim)

As with any statement of case, in addition to the full name of each party and their status, the title should state the number of the proceedings and the Court or Division in which they are proceeding.

Counterclaim

In the body of a counterclaim the defendant must set out the particulars of the counterclaim (Rule 20.4). Part 7 (with the exceptions above) and Part 16 (insofar as it relates to the contents of particulars of claim) apply. Thus in accordance with Rule 16.4 the particulars must include—

- a concise statement of the facts on which the party relies;
- if the claimant is seeking interest, a statement to that effect and the details set out in Rule 16.4(2);
- if the party is seeking aggravated damages or exemplary damages, a statement to that effect and his grounds for claiming them;
- if the party is seeking provisional damages, a statement to that effect and his grounds for claiming them; and
- such other matters as set out in the practice direction.

As above (page 47), the practice direction provides extensive regulation of the particulars of claim and what must be included in them, particularly in relation to certain types of claim such as personal injury. As well as those matters which a party has to include within the counterclaim, he may also refer in the counterclaim to any point of law on which the counterclaim is based, name any witness he proposes to call and attach to or serve with the counterclaim a copy of any document which he considers necessary to the counterclaim (Paragraph 16.3 Practice Direction to Part 16).

In addition to the requirement to comply with Part 7 and Part 16, the counterclaim as a Part 20 claim must also be verified by a statement of truth.

A Part 20 claim falls within the definition of a statement of case under Rule 2.3(1) and in accordance with Rule 22.1(1) a statement of case must be verified by a statement of truth.

As with a claim which is not verified by a statement of truth, a counterclaim without verification is liable to be struck out, either upon the Court's own initiative or in more likely circumstances, upon the application of the Part 20 defendant. It remains effective unless struck out but the Part 20 claimant cannot rely upon the counterclaim as evidence of any matter set out in it. In accordance with Rule 22.1(6) the statement of truth on a counterclaim must be signed by the Part 20 claimant or his litigation friend or the legal representative on behalf of the Part 20 claimant or the litigation friend.

There seems to be no reason why the statement of truth should not cover both the defence and the counterclaim where they are contained in the same document. If that were the case the statement of truth would read—

> **I believe that the facts stated in this defence and counterclaim are true.**

If a legal representative is to sign the statement of truth then it should read as follows—

> **The defendant and Part 20 claimant believes that the facts stated in this defence and counterclaim are true.**

If the counterclaim is served separately then only it need be referred to in the statement of truth, although there will be a separate statement of truth for the defence if a defence is to be served.

As with all statements of truth, the penalty that can be imposed for not having an honest belief in the truth of the facts set out in the counterclaim, may be committal for contempt (see Rule 32.14).

The counterclaim is made when it is filed with the Court (Rule 20.4(1)). As referred to above (page 43), the Limitation Act 1980 refers to when proceedings are "brought". It is suggested that a counterclaim is brought for these purposes when the particulars of the counterclaim are filed. In accordance with the Practice Direction to Part 5, upon filing a document the Court must seal the document with a seal showing the date on which the document was filed.

If the period set by the Limitation Act 1980 is a problem then the document should be filed, as far as possible, over the counter. The Court Service has indicated that County Courts will both issue and file documents over the counter, although it remains to be seen whether this can be fulfilled at every County Court. Inquiry should be made of the County Court to ensure that they provide an over the counter service for the filing of documents at all times of the business day.

As well as filing the particulars of the counterclaim, the particulars must be served on every other party (Rule 20.8). Service will be effected by the Court or the Part 20 claimant. Service must be effected when a copy of the defence is served. Erroneously, Rule 20.8 (January 1999) refers to the service of a Part 20 claim form in relation to a counterclaim. As above, a counterclaim is not made on a Part 20 claim form but by particulars of the counterclaim.

The Rules are a little unclear as to what documents should be served with the particulars of the counterclaim. The particulars of the counterclaim are treated as a claim for the purposes of the Rules. Accordingly Rule 7.8 applies. This Rule (as above at page 52) provides that with the particulars of claim the claimant must serve—

- a form for defending the claim;
- a form for admitting the claim; and
- a form for acknowledging service.

Part 10 (Acknowledgment of Service) is specifically excluded when the claim is a counterclaim against a claimant and the form of acknowledgment does not have to be returned to to allow a claimant to defend the counterclaim – see the effect of this below (Rule 20.4(3)).

Note that service has to be effected on every other party; such as a co-defendant, whether or not they have acknowledged service or filed a defence.

As above, Part 12 applies to a counterclaim. Accordingly the Part 20 claimant could obtain judgment by default against the Part 20 defendant (but not if that Part 20 defendant is the claimant – see below) in accordance with Part 12. If the counterclaim is for—

- a specified amount of money;
- an amount of money to be decided by the Court;
- delivery of goods where the claim form gives the defendant the alternative of paying their value; or
- any combination of these remedies;

judgment may be obtained under Rule 12.4 by filing a request in the relevant practice form.

It appears that by combination of Rules 12.3 and 20.4(3) judgment in default is not available in a counterclaim against a claimant because no acknowledgment of service need be filed. This is an error in drafting but may be rectified.

In relation to any other type of claim which forms the whole or part of the counterclaim, permission from the Court must be obtained in order to enter judgment in default unless that other claim is abandoned and reliance is placed on the remaining parts of the claim which fall within the categories under Rule 12.4 above.

Service of the particulars of the counterclaim will be effected at the address given for service by the claimant. That address must be within the jurisdiction and accordingly where the counterclaim is against the claimant alone, there will be no question of seeking the Court's permission to serve out of the jurisdiction. (Where a new party is joined, see below at page 106). As to other provisions of service such as deemed service, see Part 6 (referred to at page 50 above).

Just as the particulars of the counterclaim must comply with Part 7 and Part 16, the defence served by the claimant (if any) must comply with Part 15 and Part 16. In accordance with Rule 20.3, the only exclusion from the application of these two parts to a counterclaim is Rule 16.3(5) which provides for a statement of value where the claim is to be issued in the High Court.

Accordingly, under Rule 15.5 the Part 20 claimant and the Part 20 defendant can agree an extension of time for the service of the defence to the counterclaim but only up to a further 28 days beyond the 14 days stipulated by Rule 15.4(1)(a). Any agreed extension must be notified to the Court. Otherwise the Part 20 defendant could apply to the Court for an extension of time.

Rule 15.6 provides that a defence must be served on every other party. Although it might be suggested that service on a defendant who is not party to the Part 20 claim would be unnecessary, it follows from Rule 20.8(1)(a), which provides that the counterclaim itself must be served on every other party, that the defence to the counterclaim should, too, be served on every other party.

There is no necessity to file a reply with the defence to counterclaim. As previously mentioned (page 86), if a reply is not served, the claimant/Part 20 defendant is not taken to admit the matters raised in the defence. It would be normal, however, to deal with matters raised in the defence which are relevant to the counterclaim as part of the process of defending the counterclaim itself. Even if a reply is filed but it fails to deal with a matter raised in the defence, it is taken that that matter should be proved by the defendant/Part 20 claimant. The phrase, "requiring the matter to be proved", is likened to a "non-admission" under the procedure prior to 26 April 1999.

If a reply and defence to counterclaim are served they should be contained in the one document headed as above with the reply appearing first on the document and the counterclaim appearing second (see Paragraph 3.2, Practice Direction to Part 15 and Paragraph 6.2, Practice Direction to Part 20).

If the defence to the counterclaim contains an admission, the defendant/Part 20 claimant may make application for judgment on that admission in accordance with Part 14.

If a defence is filed, the Court will determine how best to manage the case. It will be remembered that the timing of this process is that the defence to the claim and counterclaim has to be filed within 14 days of service of the particulars of claim by the claimant. It is the receipt of the defence which triggers at the Court the process of case management and in particular Part 26.

In relation to any Part 20 claim (including a counterclaim) alone, Part 26 has no application in accordance with Rule 20.3(2)(c). In relation to a counterclaim for which permission has not been required and which has thus been served with the defence, the Court will have it in front of it when it deals with the case management process under Part 26 in relation to the main claim.

In accordance with Part 26, upon receipt of the defence to the main claim (subject to the automatic transfer of the case to the "home court" in accordance with Rule 26.2) the Court will send out to the parties an allocation questionnaire. That questionnaire has to be returned to the Court within 14 days after the date when it is deemed to be served on the party in question

(Rule 26.3(6)). Unless periods have been extended, when the Court comes to allocate the case to a track, it should have in front of it the claim, the defence to the claim, the counterclaim and the defence to the counterclaim since this latter statement of case has to be filed with the Court no later than 14 days after service of the particulars of the counterclaim.

If an extension is required for the counterclaim then the defendant/Part 20 claimant must negotiate an extension for both the defence and counterclaim. Otherwise, if the defence is served, the potential Part 20 claimant will have to seek the permission of the Court before serving the particulars of counterclaim.

Note that in order to avoid the necessity for the Court's permission, the counterclaim must be filed **with the defence**. It cannot be filed either before or after the filing of the defence.

Counterclaim with permission

In relation to the making of a counterclaim, in two instances, permission of the Court is required—

- if the counterclaim is not filed with the defence; and
- if the Part 20 claimant wishes to counterclaim against a person other than the claimant.

In the former case the permission is simply to make the counterclaim. In the latter circumstances the permission is required to join a person other than the claimant as a defendant to the counterclaim—whilst the counterclaim can be made against a claimant without the Court's permission if the particulars of the counterclaim are filed with the defence a defendant to the counterclaim other than the claimant can only be joined with the Court's permission.

If permission is sought to serve a counterclaim either before or after filing a defence, an application should be made in accordance with Part 23 fulfilling all the requirements of that Part including those in Rule 23.6 that an application notice must state what order the applicant is seeking and briefly why the applicant is seeking the order. The application must be supported by evidence (Paragraph 2.1 Practice Direction to Part 20). That evidence must state—

- the stage which the action has reached;
- the nature of the claim to be made by the Part 20 claimant or details of the question or issue which needs to be decided;
- a summary of the facts on which the Part 20 claim is based; and
- the name and address of the proposed Part 20 defendant;
- if delay has been a factor, an explanation of the delay should be given in evidence.

The evidence can be contained in the application notice itself as long as it is verified by a statement of truth. Alternatively it may be contained in a witness statement. Unlike seeking permission for any other type of Part 20 claim, the application to make a counterclaim either before or after the filing of the defence must be served with the written evidence in support as soon as practicable (Rule 23.7). If the application is simply to seek permission to make a counterclaim before or after the defence is filed then the only respondent to the application will be the potential defendant to the counterclaim.

If permission is sought to add a person as a defendant to the counterclaim in accordance with Rule 20.5, the application has to made in accordance with Part 23.

Rule 20.5(2) says that the application may be made without notice. The word "notice" equates with service only and an application for permission still requires an application notice to be filed with the Court which complies with, for instance, the provisions of Rule 23.6 (referred to above).

If the Court gives permission that a person should be joined as a defendant to the counterclaim in accordance with Rule 20.5, it will give directions as to the future management of the case. It may be a little early for the Court to determine the precise management of the case because much may turn on the defence (if any) to be filed by the new Part 20 defendant joined as a result of the Court's permission.

At the hearing of the application for permission, the Court will have to consider whether it is appropriate to join the person as a defendant to the counterclaim bearing in mind the overriding objective and the Court's case management powers under Part 3. In particular the Court will consider whether it is appropriate to direct that the counterclaim be dealt with as separate proceedings in accordance with the Court's general powers of management under Rule 3.1(2)(e) or to direct a separate trial in relation to the issues raised in the counterclaim (Rule 3.1(2)(i)).

When deciding whether to give permission, the Rules provide some guidance for the Court as to what it should have regard (Rule 20.9(2))—

- the connection between the Part 20 claim and the claim made by the claimant against the defendant;
- whether the Part 20 claimant is seeking substantially the same remedy which some other party is claiming from him; and
- whether the Part 20 claimant wants the Court to decide any question in connection with the subject matter of the proceedings—
    - not only between existing parties but also between existing parties and a person not already a party; or
    - against an existing party not only in a capacity in which he is already a party but also in some further capacity.

When service is effected upon the added defendant, the particulars of the counterclaim should be accompanied with the full response pack—

- a form for defending the claim;
- a form for admitting the claim; and
- a form for acknowledging service.

The Court or the Part 20 claimant should use the Forms N9 or N213 (Acknowledgment of Service), N9A or N9C (Admission), and N9B or N9D (Defence) for this purpose.

Reference has already been made to the form and contents of the particulars of the counterclaim. There is no set form for the counterclaim which might be appropriate when a new party is becoming a defendant to the counterclaim. Thus there are no explanatory notes. At the time of writing it is intended that the Queen's Bench practice forms should be introduced within the new regime. One of those practice forms (Form 17) provides for an endorsement upon a counterclaim which gives some directions as to at least the filing of an acknowledgement of service. It remains to be seen whether such an endorsement will be recommended under the new regime but it is suggested that it would be appropriate for some form of notice to be endorsed on the counterclaim to give some direction to the added party.

In addition to the response pack, the Part 20 claimant must also serve on the new party—

- every statement of case which has already been served in the proceedings; and
- such other documents as the Court may direct.

Further in addition, in accordance with the Practice Direction to Part 5 (Paragraph 2.4(1)), the added defendant to the counterclaim is entitled to require the Part 20 claimant to supply, without charge, copies of all written evidence and any documents appended or exhibited to them which have been served in the proceedings by or upon the Part 20 claimant which relate to any issue between that party and the added defendant. If those documents are not supplied within 48 hours of the request, the added defendant may make an application under Part 23 for an order that they be supplied (Paragraph 2.4(2), Practice Direction to Part 5).

As with any counterclaim, where a party is added as a defendant to the counterclaim, he is subject to the Rules as to default judgment under Part 12. In order to avoid judgment being taken against him by default, he must serve an acknowledgement of service and/or an admission and/or a defence within the period stipulated in Parts 10, 14 and 15 respectively. (As to these Parts and Part 12, see pages 72. 73 and 81 above.)

If a defence is filed, the Court must consider the future conduct of the proceedings and give appropriate directions. Again, these directions must sit with the directions given as between the claimant and the defendant in the main claim. Indeed the Rules (Rule 20.13(2)) require the Court to ensure that the counterclaim and the main claim are managed together. This, however, is subject to the Court's obligations under Part 1 (overriding objective) and its powers under Part 3 (and particularly Rule 3.1).

The person added as a defendant to the counterclaim becomes a party to the proceedings upon service. The permission to counterclaim against an added party takes effect from the day when it is given (Rule 40.7). They do not at that point become a party. Rule 20.10(1) appears to provide that a person added as a defendant to the counterclaim only becomes a party to the proceedings upon service of the particulars of the counterclaim. This latter provision is intended to follow the House of Lords decision in *Ketteman v Hansel Properties Ltd* [1987] AC 189, HL.

Claim for Contribution and/or Indemnity against another Defendant—Rule 20.7

Note that this Rule only applies to a claim for contributions and/or indemnity against another defendant. A claim against anyone else would be a Part 20 claim under Rule 20.7 (see below).

"Contribution" is defined in the glossary as—

> **a right of someone to recover from a third person all or part of the amount which he himself is liable to pay.**

"Indemnity" is defined in the glossary as—

> **the right of someone to recover from a third party the whole amount which he himself is liable to pay.**

There is no set form of notice. Reference has been made to the Queen's Bench practice form. Again there was a practice form (Form 20) which set out the form for a notice claiming a contribution or indemnity. In the absence of a practice form under the CPR, it is suggested that the Queen's Bench practice form should be followed.

The notice is a statement of case in accordance with Rule 2.3(1). Accordingly it should be verified by a statement of truth in accordance with Part 22 (see above).

Although the discussion of these subjects is not within the scope of this work, the reader is referred to the Civil Liability (Contribution) Act 1978 which entitles a person liable in respect of any damage suffered by another person to recover a contribution from any other person liable in respect of the same damage (whether jointly with them or otherwise).

Regard should also be had to the Limitation Act 1980. This provides for special time limits for a claim in contribution. The normal time limit for bringing contribution proceedings is two years from the date of the finding, or acceptance, of liability. There are, however, further provisions for particular types of claim.

As with any statement of case, the contribution and/or indemnity notice must fulfil the requirements of Part 16 and particularly Rules 16.2 and 16.4 together with the practice direction to that Part insofar as they are relevant. It must, for instance, contain a concise statement of the facts on which the Part 20 claimant relies (Rule 16.4(1)(a). If the contribution or indemnity is based upon contract then the contract itself if in writing should be served with the notice (Paragraph 9.3, Practice Direction to Part 16). As to all of these requirements see page 48 above).

Further, as a statement of case it is potentially liable to be struck out in accordance with Rule 3.4 as, for instance, an abuse of the process. Similarly the Part 20 claimant may make application under Part 25 for an interim remedy or Part 24 for summary judgment. As to the assessment of contribution and the effect of judgment in the main proceedings, see Sections 1(5) and 2 of the Civil Liability (Contribution) Act 1978.

In accordance with Rule 20.6, the claim for a contribution or indemnity against another defendant is not made until the notice is both filed and served on the other defendant.

Judgment in default is not available to a claim for contribution or indemnity (Rule 20.3(3)(a)). Neither are the Rules in relation to admissions (Part 14) except that the Part 20 defendant may admit the truth of all or part of the notice and the Part 20 claimant may apply for judgment on that admission.

If the defendant files a defence to the notice, the Court will arrange a hearing to consider case management of the claim for contribution and/or indemnity (Paragraph 5.1, Practice Direction to Part 20). The Court has discretion to give notice of that hearing to any party that it believes will be affected by any order made at the hearing (Paragraph 5.2, Practice Direction to Part 20).

As on any such hearing the Court can make an order or directions as it believes appropriate—it can, for instance, treat the hearing as a summary judgment hearing under Part 24 (Paragraph 5.3(1)) or strike out the notice under Rule 3.4, although if the Court proposes to do that of its own initiative, regard should be had to Rule 3.3.

Subject to dealing with the notice in some summary fashion, the Court will give directions as to how the issues in the notice are to be determined. In relation to a notice issued against an existing defendant, the Court is likely to direct that the issues raised in the notice and any defence should be dealt with at or immediately after the trial. When making such directions the Court will have in mind its responsibilities to actively manage the case in accordance with Rule 1.4 and its powers under Rule 3.1.

A contribution and/or an indemnity notice can be issued both before and after judgment is obtained in the action between the claimant and the defendants subject to the limitation period referred to above. Accordingly, under Paragraph 5.4 of the Practice Direction, the Court can make case management directions either before or after any judgment in the claim.

The overall requirement of the Court on a case management conference in relation to a notice is that it must ensure that, insofar as practicable, the notice and the main claim are managed together (Rule 20.13).

Other Part 20 Claims

So far we have dealt with counterclaims against an existing party or another person and a claim for contribution or indemnity against another defendant. The remainder of Part 20 (Rules 20.7–20.13) largely deals with any other Part 20 claim. These Rules therefore provide for a claim for a contribution or indemnity against a person not a party to the proceedings or for some other remedy.

Other than a counterclaim or a contribution or indemnity against another defendant, a Part 20 claim is made by the submission to the Court and issue by it of a Part 20 claim form. This is Form N211. In its format it follows very much the Part 7 claim form (Form N1). In the same way, on the front sheet there is a space for brief details of the claim and on the second page, space for particulars of claim.

As with other Part 20 claims, the claim is treated as if it were a claim for the purposes of the Rules save for the three exceptions set out in Rule 20.3(2)—

- Rules 7.5 and 7.6 (time within which a claim form may be served);
- Rule 16.3(5) (statement of value where claim to be issued in the High Court); and
- Part 26 (case management—preliminary stage).

The Part 20 claim is "made" when the Court issues the Part 20 claim form. As with Rule 7.2(2), a Part 20 claim form is issued on the date entered on the form by the Court. This, however, may differ from the time when the proceedings are "brought" for the purpose of the Limitation Act 1980 (see page 43 above).

Notwithstanding the issue of the Part 20 claim form, the Part 20 defendant does not become a party to the proceedings (unless he is a party already) until the Part 20 claim form is served on him.

A Part 20 claim for contribution or indemnity against a person other than another defendant is differentiated from such a claim against another defendant. In the former case, a Part 20 claim form has to be used; in the latter, the Part 20 claim is made by "a notice" under Rule 20.6.

In accordance with Paragraph 7 of the practice direction to Part 20, the Part 20 claim form should include—

- the full name of each party;
- the number of the proceedings;
- the court or division in which they are proceeding;
- the status of the parties in the proceedings; thus, for instance, in relation to a claim for contribution or indemnity against a person not a party to the proceedings already, the title should read—

  AB - Claimant
  CD - Defendant / Part 20 Claimant
  EF- Part 20 Defendant

Where there is more than one Part 20 claim, the first Part 20 claim to be made should be described as the "First Claim" and any subsequent Part 20 claim numbered accordingly. Thus, for instance, if the proceedings consisted of a claim, a defence and counterclaim, and a claim for contribution or indemnity against a non-party in relation to the counterclaim, the title of the proceedings would read as follows—

AB - Claimant / Part 20 Defendant (First Claim) / Part 20 Claimant (Second Claim)
CD - Defendant and Part 20 Claimant (First Claim)
EF - Part 20 Defendant (Second Claim)

In accordance with Paragraph 7.5 of the Practice Direction to Part 20, where a party has more than one status, whilst the combined status must be included in the title to the proceedings, it may be convenient to refer to that party subsequently by name or reference. Thus, in the last example above, the

Claimant / Part 20 Defendant (First Claim) / Part 20 Claimant (Second Claim) may be referred to in the body of the statement of case as "AB".

In accordance with Rule 20.3, the Part 20 claim is treated as if it were a claim. Accordingly the Part 20 claim form must fulfil the relevant requirements of Parts 7 and 16 and their respective practice directions. Thus, for instance, in accordance with Rule 16.2(1), the Part 20 claim form must contain a concise statement of the nature of the Part 20 claim and specify the remedy which the Part 20 claimant seeks.

In relation to a Part 20 claim, the particulars must be contained in or served with the Part 20 claim form. Those particulars must comply with Part 16 and its accompanying Practice Direction. For instance, in accordance with Rule 16.4, the particulars must include a concise statement of the facts on which the claimant relies (Rule 16.4(1)(a)). In the same fashion, for instance, where the Part 20 claim is based upon a written agreement, a copy of the contract or document constituting the agreement, should be attached to or served with the particulars of the Part 20 claim and the Part 20 claim form (see page 108 above).

The Court's permission is required for the making of a Part 20 claim unless the Part 20 claim is made by a defendant and is issued before or at the same time as he files his defence (Rule 20.7(3)). This provision is slightly different from that relating to a counterclaim. As above, if the Court's permission is not to be sought to make a counterclaim, the counterclaim must be filed with the defence, not before or after it.

It is suggested that for the purposes of Rule 20.7(3), a defendant includes a defendant to a counterclaim. Thus in the example given above where the original claimant becomes a Part 20 defendant (to a counterclaim) and a Part 20 claimant (in a claim for a contribution or indemnity against a non-party), the claim for the contribution and indemnity made by that party would not need the Court's permission as long as it was issued before or at the same time as that party filed his defence to the counterclaim. There is no specific provision but by default it is suggested that if a party making a Part 20 claim is not a defendant to a claim from which the Part 20 claim arises, permission of the Court would be necessary in order to issue the Part 20 claim.

It would appear from Rule 20.7(3) that the Court's permission is not required to make a Part 20 claim if it is issued at the same time as the defence is filed, even if the defence is filed outside the period set for filing under Rule 15.4.

An application for permission to make a Part 20 claim may be made without notice unless upon hearing the application the Court provides that notice should be given (Rule 20.7(5)).

The application is made in accordance with Part 23 and must comply with the requirements of that Part. The application must be supported by evidence (Paragraph 2.1, Practice Direction to Part 20). The evidence can be contained in the application notice as long as it is verified by a statement of truth. Otherwise the evidence should be contained in a witness statement.

It is suggested that it is not sufficient simply to produce the evidence in the Part 20 claim form for which permission is being sought, even if it is endorsed with a statement of truth upon the hearing of the application. For the purposes of fulfilling what is required to be before the Court as a matter of evidence on the hearing, however, it is suggested that the proposed Part 20 claim form could be exhibited to the witness statement or application notice enclosed with a statement of truth.

Within the evidence to be presented to the Court on the hearing of the application, the following must be included—

- the stage which the action has reached;
- the nature of the claim to be made by the Part 20 claimant or details of the question or issue which needs to be decided;
- a summary of the facts on which the Part 20 claim is based; and
- the name and address of the proposed Part 20 defendant.
- If delay has been a factor leading to an application for permission (such as a defendant not issuing the Part 20 claim form before or at the same time as filing the defence), the prospective Part 20 claimant should provide an explanation of the delay.

(Paragraph 2.2, Practice Direction to Part 20).

The applicant should provide a timetable of the action to date upon the hearing of the application, although there is no specific requirement that this should be contained within the verified evidence.

The Part 20 claim form and the particulars of claim (if served separately, even though at the same time as a Part 20 claim form) must be verified by a statement of truth which will provide as follows—

I believe that the facts stated in this statement of case are true.

If a legal representative signs it on behalf of the Part 20 claimant then the statement of truth should read as follows—

The Part 20 claimant believes that the facts stated in this statement of case are true.

Rule 20.9 provides for some of the considerations the Court should have as to whether to grant permission for the making of a Part 20 claim. The alternative to granting permission would be that the Part 20 claim would be started in the usual way as a claim under Part 7. If the Court decides to give permission it may still exercise its powers under Rule 3.1(2), particularly under Rule 3.1(2)—

(e) directing that part of any proceedings be dealt with as separate proceedings;
(i) directing a separate trial of any issue; or
(g) deciding the order in which the issues are to be tried.

In considering whether to give permission, Rule 20.9(2) provides the matters to which the Court may have regard—

- the connection between the Part 20 claim and a claim made by the claimant against the defendant;

- whether the Part 20 claimant is seeking substantially the same remedy which some other party is claiming from him; and
- whether the Part 20 claimant wants the Court to decide any question connected with the subject matter of the proceedings—
  - not only between the existing parties but also between the existing parties and a person not already a party; or
  - against an existing party not only in a capacity in which he is already a party but also in some further capacity.

Where the Court gives permission to make a Part 20 claim, it will at the same time give directions as to the service of a Part 20 claim form (Rule 20.8(3)).

Upon service the Part 20 claim form must be accompanied by the forms consisting the response pack to a Part 7 claim (Form N9), namely forms for defending the claim, admitting the claim and acknowledging service.

In addition the Part 20 claimant must also serve at the same time a copy of every statement of case which has already been served in the proceedings and such other documents as the Court may direct (Rule 20.12(1)(d)).

In accordance with the Practice Direction, the defendant to a Part 20 claim is entitled to require the Part 29 claimant to supply to him without charge with copies of all statements of case, written evidence and any documents appended or exhibited to them which have been served by or upon the Part 20 claimant which relate to any issues between the Part 20 claimant and the Part 20 defendant and copies of all orders made in the proceedings.

Those documents have to be supplied within 48 hours of written request. If not so supplied, the Part 20 defendant may apply under Part 23 for an appropriate order.

As with a Part 7 claim, the defendant has 14 days after service of the Part 20 claim form and particulars of the Part 20 claim to file an acknowledgement of service or a defence. If an acknowledgement of service is filed, the Part 20 defendant has a further 14 days in which to file a defence (Rules 10.3 and 15.4). In accordance with Rule 10.5, the acknowledgement of service must be signed by the Part 20 defendant or his legal representative and include the Part 20 defendant's address for service. That address for service must be within the jurisdiction under Rule 6.5(2).

As with all claims, a Part 20 claim must be served within the jurisdiction unless leave is obtained for service out of the jurisdiction. Application for leave must be applied for in accordance with Part 23 and RSC Order 11.

A defence to a Part 20 claim must comply with Part 15 and Part 16 and the practice direction to Part 16. Thus it must state—

- which of the allegations in the particulars of the Part 20 claim the Part 20 defendant denies;
- which allegations the Part 20 defendant is unable to admit or deny but which he requires the Part 20 claimant to prove; and
- which allegations the Part 20 defendant admits.

The defence has to be verified by a statement of truth in accordance with Part 22.

Part 12 has no application to a Part 20 claim save for a counterclaim although even there it appears that Part 12 has been partially excluded by ??????? (see above). Rule 20.11, however, provides for default judgment on a Part 20 claim other than a counterclaim or a contribution or indemnity notice against another defendant. If the Part 20 defendant fails to file an acknowledgement of service or a defence, he is deemed to admit the Part 20 claim and is bound by any judgment or decision in the main proceedings insofar as it is relevant to any matter arising in the Part 20 claim (Rule 20.11(2)(a)).

If default judgment under Part 12 is given against the Part 20 claimant in the main proceedings, the Part 20 claimant may apply for judgment in respect of the Part 20 claim by filing a request in the relevant practice form but only if he has satisfied the default judgment which has been given against him or wishes to obtain judgment for a contribution or indemnity (Rule 20.11(3)). If the Court's permission is necessary then application can be made without notice.

Part 14 has no application to a Part 20 claim save for Rules 14.1(1) and (2) and 14.3. Thus under these Rules the Part 20 defendant may admit the Part 20 claimant's case in writing and the Part 20 claimant may apply for judgment on that admission.

If a Part 20 claim is defended the Court will arrange a hearing for the purpose of managing the Part 20 claim. In accordance with Rule 20.13(2) the Court must ensure that, as far as practicable, the Part 20 claim and the main claim are managed together.

Prior to the hearing the Court will give notice of it to each party likely to be affected by any order made (Paragraph 5.2, Practice Direction to Part 20).

In accordance with Paragraph 5.3 of the Practice Direction to Part 20, at the hearing the Court may—

- treat the hearing as a summary judgment hearing;
- order that the Part 20 proceedings be dismissed;
- give directions about the way any claim, question or issue set out in or arising from the Part 20 claim should be dealt with;
- give directions as to the part, if any, the Part 20 claimant will take at the trial of the claim;
- give directions about the extent to which the Part 20 defendant is to be bound by the judgment or decision made in the claim.

The Court will have to have consideration to the overriding objective and its obligations to actively manage the case. It would also have regard to its powers, particularly those contained within Rule 3.1.

There are special Rules relating to Part 20 claims against the Crown contained in CPR Sch 1 RSC Order 77. Thus, for example, a defendant may not counterclaim or claim a set off against any right or claim to repayment in respect of any taxes, duties or penalties (RSC Order 77 Rule 6). A Part 20 claim for service on the Crown where the Crown is not already a party will not be issued without the permission of the Court (RSC Order 77 Rule 10). That Rule goes on to specify that the application for permission must be served on both the claimant and the Crown and the grounds on which permission will be given.

Where a Part 20 claim (including a counterclaim) is made, it may affect the allocation of the proceedings to one of the three tracks (Rule 26.8(1)(e)). Generally proceedings will be allocated to the track having regard to the claim having the greatest financial value.

CHAPTER 12
PART 22—STATEMENTS OF TRUTH

The subject of statements of truth was during the drafting process drawn together from diverse points scattered throughout the Rules to one Part—Part 22. This Part makes general provision for statements of truth wherever required.

The documents which must be verified by a statement of truth are

- Statement of case (defined in Rule 2.3 (1))
- Claim form
- Particulars of claim
- Defence
- Part 20 claim
- Reply to defence
- Further information under Part 18
- Witness statements
- Experts reports

The claim form must be verified by a statement of truth whether or not it includes the particulars of claim. If the particulars of claim are served separately, they must also be verified by a separate statement of truth (Rule 22.1(1)(a)) by virtue of both a claim form and particulars of claim being a statement of case under Rule 2.3(1).

The statement of truth does not have to be contained in the document it verifies although this will certainly be usual practice. If the statement of truth is in a separate document **served subsequently**, it must identify the document to which it relates (Paragraph 1.5, Practice Direction to Part 22). If the statement of truth is served separately under Paragraph 1.5 of the Practice Direction to Part 22 then the document must be headed with the title of the proceedings and the claim number. It should then identify the claim form and the particulars of claim which it verifies. The Practice Direction 2.3 to Part 22 suggests that the identification should be the date on which the claim form and/or the particulars of claim were issued, although strictly particulars of claim are not "issued". They are simply served under Rule 7.4.

The form of statement of truth where the statement is signed by the party is—

> **I believe that the facts stated in this claim form/these particulars of claim are true**

(Paragraph 6.2, Practice Direction to Part 7)

If the statement of truth is signed by the legal representative of the claimant then the statement of truth should read—

> **The claimant believes that the facts stated in this claim form/these particulars of claim are true**
>
> (Paragraph 6.2, Practice Direction to Part 7)

The requirement to verify the claim form and particulars of claim by a statement of truth is an absolute under Rule 22.1(1). Accordingly, if there is no statement of truth, the Court could take peremptory action under Rule 3.4(2)(c) and strike out the statement of case. This could be done of the Court's own initiative under Rule 3.3 (see page 120 post).

It is suggested that the Court may of its own initiative fix a hearing at which it would be proposed that an order be made to the effect that unless the document is verified by a statement of truth within a certain period, it will be struck out. The alternative would be for the Court to allow the defendant to make appropriate application following service (see Paragraph 4.2, Practice Direction to Part 22).

Whilst there is no verification of the facts in a statement of case by a statement of truth, the claimant cannot rely on the contents of either the claim form or the particulars of claim as evidence (Paragraph 4.1, Practice Direction to Part 22).

Who may sign the Statement of Truth?

The statement of truth can be signed by—

- The party
- The litigation friend
- The legal representative

A legal representative for the purpose of the Rules means—

> **A barrister or a solicitor, solicitor's employee or other authorised litigator (as defined in the Courts and Legal Services Act 1990) who has been instructed to act for a party in relation to a claim**
>
> (Rule 2.3(1))

As dealt with below, if a claim form or particulars of claim contain a false statement in which the claimant did not have an honest belief in its truth, the person who signs the statement or on whose behalf it is signed may be subject to contempt proceedings under Rule 32.14. A legal representative will not primarily be liable for contempt since he signs on behalf of another. Liability might arise, however, if he knowingly aids or abets a contempt

Before signing a statement of truth the legal representative signing a statement of truth on behalf of a client should ensure that they have complied with Paragraph 3.8, Practice Direction to Part 22. Under that Paragraph the signature of the legal representative will be taken by the Court as his statement that—

- the client on whose behalf he has signed had authorised him to do so;

- before signing he had explained to the client that in signing the statement of truth he would be confirming the client's belief that the facts stated in the document were true; and
- before signing he had informed the client of the possible consequences to the client if it should subsequently appear that the client did not have an honest belief in the truth of those facts.

Accordingly legal representatives are likely to be somewhat nervous of signing statements of truth on behalf of clients. Even before the changes, however, it was common practice for solicitors to swear affidavits in support of applications for summary judgment which verified the particulars or statement of claim. It is suggested, however, that under the new regime, with particulars of claim being much more widely drawn than previously the risks for the legal representative may be greater.

In any event, if the legal representative has not fulfilled his obligations of explanation to the signatory, he may be liable to penalty by the court or an officer of the court.

Further, claimants and legal representatives should not underestimate the determination of the Court to enforce the penalty provisions of Rule 32.14 (see below).

If the claimant is a company or other corporation then the statement of truth must be signed by a person holding a senior position. For a registered company or corporation this includes a director, treasurer, secretary, chief executive, manager or other officer of the company or corporation. In respect of a corporation which is not registered, then in addition to these persons, a person holding a senior position would include the mayor, chairman, president, town clerk or other similar officer (Paragraph 3.5, Practice Direction to Part 22).

If the claimant is a partnership then the statement of truth may be signed by any of the partners or a person having control or management of the partnership business (Paragraph 3.6, Practice Direction to Part 22).

Although no express provision is made, if a sole proprietor is suing in the name of a firm, it is suggested that either the proprietor must sign the statement of truth or, if legally represented, the legal representative may sign.

Any signature to the statement of truth can be printed by computer or other mechanical means (Rule 5.3).

The individual who signs the statement of truth must print his full name clearly beneath his signature (Paragraph 3.9, Practice Direction to Part 22). If the individual signs as a person holding a senior position within a company or corporation, the individual must print his full name clearly and state the office or position he holds within the company or corporation (Paragraph 2.4).

If the legal representative signs on behalf of the claimant then he must sign in his own name and not that of his firm or employer. The capacity in which he signs and the name of his firm should also be stated below the signature if appropriate.

Part 32—False statements

32.14 provides as follows—

(1) Proceedings for contempt of Court may be brought against a person if he makes, or causes to be made, a false statement in a document verified by a statement of truth without an honest belief in its truth.

(2) Proceedings under this Rule may be brought only—

(a) by the Attorney General; or

(b) with the permission of the Court

Contempt proceedings for a false statement in a claim form or particulars of claim can be taken either in the County Court or the High Court.

If the committal application is made in existing proceedings then permission may be sought by filing an application notice in accordance with Part 23. That application notice does not have to be served on the respondent. If permission is granted, a further application notice is filed, making the substantive application for the committal. The application must be supported by an affidavit.

If the committal application is not made in existing proceedings, a Part 8 claim form must be used to commence the application. Permission to issue the claim form must initially be sought by filing an application notice under Part 23.

For these purposes "existing proceedings" means proceedings in respect of which a final judgment has not yet been given.

The committal application whether by application notice or claim form must be served personally.

The reader is referred to RSC Order 52 (Schedule 1 to the CPR) and CCR Order 29 (Schedule 2 to the CPR) and to the Practice Direction relating to committal applications.

Striking out the Claim or Particulars of Claim

As with any statement of claim the Court has the power to strike out the claim form and/or the particulars of claim or part of them under Rule 3.4

The tests on striking out are—

- That the statement of case discloses no reasonable grounds for bringing the claim;
- That the statement of case is an abuse of the Court's process or is otherwise likely to obstruct the just disposal of the proceedings; or
- That there has been a failure to comply with a Rule or Practice Direction or Court Order.

This Rule has replaced the grounds for striking out any pleading in both the High Court and County Court which were—

- it discloses no reasonable cause of action or defence, as the case may be; or
- it is scandalous, frivolous or vexatious; or
- it may prejudice, embarrass or delay the fair trial of the action; or
- it is otherwise an abuse of the process of the Court.

Paragraph 1.4 of the Practice Direction to Part 3 gives some examples of particulars of claim that may fall foul of Rule 3.4(2).

Striking out a claim means, according to the Glossary—

> **The Court ordering written material to be deleted so that it may no longer be relied upon.**

The claim form or particulars of claim may be struck out on any of the three grounds set out in Rule 3.4(2)—

(a) that the statement of case discloses no reasonable grounds for bringing the claim

As will be seen, this provision is built upon the previous Rule but with the replacement of the words "cause of action" with "grounds for bringing the claim". The replacement of "cause of action" by the word "grounds" is intended to be easier for the litigant in person to understand, although the precise meaning of the word will be the subject of judicial discretion and guidance.

Notwithstanding this particular change, there is no change to the general approach that the failure to show reasonable grounds must appear on the face of the statement of case itself. The Practice Direction gives an example in Paragraph 1.4. So, if the particulars of claim simply say, "Money owed £5,000", or are incoherent and make no sense or are coherent but even if true do not disclose any legally recognisable claim against the defendant, the particulars of claim will be struck out.

There is no express provision that evidence may not be served and filed in an application to strike out the statement of case but Paragraph 5.2 of the Practice Direction to Part 3 encourages the applicant to consider whether facts need to be proved and, if so, whether evidence in support should be filed and served. Since, as previously, the failure has to be seen on the face of the statement of case, it is unlikely that evidence will be truly relevant to an application to strike out in accordance with Rule 3.4(2)(a) alone.

Any application to strike out has to be made in accordance with Part 23. The application notice must state what order the applicant is seeking and briefly why the applicant is seeking the order (Rule 23.6). Evidence in support of the application can be contained in the application notice itself as long as it is verified by a statement of truth (Rule 22.1(3)). Otherwise the evidence will be by way of witness statement.

(b) that the statement of case is an abuse of the Court's process or is otherwise likely to obstruct the just disposal of the proceedings

This ground is a summary of the three grounds previously—

- the pleading is scandalous, frivolous or vexatious; or
- it may prejudice, embarrass or delay the fair trial of the action; or
- it is otherwise an abuse of the process of the Court.

(see Paragraph 1.5, Practice Direction to Part 3)

This sub-paragraph also codifies the court's internal jurisdiction under *Grepe v Loam* (1887) 37 Ch D 168 and *Ebert v Birch* (1999) Times, 28 April.

Grounds for striking out under this head may therefore follow much of the previously developed law. Thus, for instance, a ground for striking out may be re-litigating a matter which has already been litigated and decided.

(c) that there has been a failure to comply with a Rule, Practice Direction or Court Order

This is a new power of the Court. It is intended to strengthen the arsenal of the Court in requiring parties to comply with, for instance, time limits set by way of order or Practice Direction.

In addition to the grounds set out in Rule 3.4(2), the High Court retains its inherent jurisdiction. Further, the High Court and County Court have wide case management powers under Rule 3.1 including the general empowerment to—

take any other step or make any other order for the purpose of managing the case and furthering the overriding objective

In these case management powers, whilst the Court may not specifically be able to strike out a statement of case, it would certainly have parallel powers to ensure that the statement of case did not fall foul of Rule 3.4(2).

The Court may make an order striking out a statement of case of its own initiative. This was a matter of considerable debate in the preparation of the Rules. The general empowerment of the Court to make an order of its own initiative is contained in Rule 3.3. In exercising that power the Court must comply with Rule 3.3(2) in allowing the party the opportunity to make representations in opposition to a proposal to strike out.

Contrary to this general provision it was proposed that the Court should have a general power to strike out a clearly ridiculous statement of case of its own initiative and without giving notice. In order to deal with this situation, Paragraph 2 of the Practice Direction to Part 3 provides that before issuing the claim form the Court officer can refer the claim form to the Judge. The Judge may then on his own initiative make an appropriate order. Examples of such an order are set out in Paragraph 2.4 of the Practice Direction.

In accordance with Paragraph 2.3 the Judge may allow the claimant an opportunity to be heard before making an order but there is no obligation. Even if the Judge does not make such an order, an application could be made by the defendant at an appropriate time.

Applications to strike out should—

be made as soon as it becomes apparent that it is necessary or desirable to make it

(Paragraph 2.7, Practice Direction to Part 23)

As promoted by the Practice Direction, an application to strike out under Part 3 may be accompanied by an application for summary judgment under Part 24 (see Chapter 14 page 137 post).

If the claim form or particulars of claim are struck out following an order requiring a step to be taken in default of which the claim form or particulars of claim would be struck out, and that order is not complied with, Rule 3.5

sets out the procedure to be followed by the defendant for obtaining judgment. If the whole of the claim form or particulars of claim have been struck out then the defendant can obtain judgment with costs by simply filing a request for judgment. Otherwise the defendant must make an application under Part 23.

Rule 3.6 specifies that following the obtaining of a judgment under Rule 3.5, the party against whom the judgment has been entered may apply to set it aside but such application has to be made no more than 14 days after the judgment has been served on that party. On the application the Court will consider all the circumstances including those set out in Rule 3.9 such as whether the application for relief has been made promptly or the failure to comply was intentional.

If on an application for striking out the Court makes an order that the claim form or particulars of claim should be amended appropriately, Part 17 (Amendments to Statement of Case) will apply.

CHAPTER 13
PART 25—INTERIM REMEDIES

Introduction

As initially conceived Part 25 was in two separate parts (Parts 15 and 16 in the Brown Book). The division was generally between injunctive relief and particularly freezing and searching orders (formerly Mareva and Anton Piller) and other interim remedies particularly interim payments. Although this division has been abandoned in the final version of the Rules, the consolidation does not hide the lie of the land under Part 25 and its two principal purposes to cover injunctive relief and interim payments.

Under the old rules both the High Court and County Court interim remedies were dealt with generally under RSC Order 29. Many of its provisions found their way into Part 25 although there have been some important amendments to them in the process.

Part 25 needs to be read particularly in the light of various pieces of legislation. By way of example, the jurisdiction to grant search orders has been codified in Section 7 of the Civil Procedure Act 1997 and orders for disclosure or inspection before a claim has been made are regulated by Section 33 of the Supreme Court Act 1981 or Section 52 of the County Courts Act 1984 (see below).

Rule 25.1 sets out what interim remedies the court may grant. The list is not exclusive and if a particular relief is not within the list it may still be granted if the court has power under some other provision (Rule 25.1(3)).

The list is intended to be a guide to some well established powers. In addition, however, the list includes some powers which are not well established and break new ground. Two examples can be given.

- Rule 25.1(1)(b) places in the list **interim declarations**. The usual view would be that a declaration may only be a final remedy following a determination on the merits. The power was included at the suggestion of Lord Woolf who was concerned that the courts should be able to make an interim declaration in appropriate circumstances, which may indeed be rare. This follows through the principle of identifying issues at an early stage of the proceedings and disposing of them wherever possible.
- The second example of change is in Rule 25.1(1)(c)(v). Under RSC Order 29 Rule 4 the court could make an interim order for the sale of perishable goods. The sale of land was specifically excluded from this

provision. This restriction has not been carried through to the CPR. Indeed to the contrary land is specifically included within this power by Rule 25.1(2). The order can be made, however, only if there is good reason to sell the land quickly.

In addition to these changes the list codifies an established practice at common law. Rule 25.1(1)(g) allows enquiries as to assets in support of a freezing injunction codifying the kind of order that was considered in *Bankers Trust Company v Shapira* [1980] 3 All ER 353 and *A v C* [1980] 2 All ER 347 (as to freezing injunctions see below).

Rule 25.1(4) also codifies an established principle that the court may grant an interim remedy even if there is no claim by the party for a final remedy of the same kind. There must have been a cause of action at the time of the issue of proceedings (see *The Siskena Cargo Owners v Distos Cia Naviera* [1979] AC 210).

In addition to Part 25, if an application for an interim remedy is made, the parties should take into account other parts of the CPR—

- Part 1—the overriding objective and the principle of proportionality.
- Part 2—as to which judge can order an interim remedy (see below).
- Part 3—the court's case management powers; Rule 3.1.(5) for instance by which the court may combine an order for disclosure as an interim remedy with an order for payment in when the disclosure should have been given under a pre-action protocol.
- Part 6—service.
- Part 23—applications.
- Part 39—hearings, particularly Rule 39.1 in which hearings have to be in public.
- Part 40—judgments and orders.
- Part 49—specialist proceedings for which there may be particular procedural requirements.

When?

As previously, an application and order for an interim remedy may be given both before and after proceedings have started (Rule 25.2(1)(a)). In accordance with Rule 7.2, proceedings are started when the claim form is issued by the court, i.e. on the date entered on the form by the court. If application is made before proceedings are started, the order may only be made if the matter is urgent or the court concludes that the remedy should be granted in the interests of justice (Rule 25.2(2)(b)).

There are three instances mentioned when a claim does not have to be issued following an order granting an interim remedy—

- Section 33 of the Supreme Court Act 1981 or Section 52 of the County Courts Act 1984 and Rule 31.16 allow a party to make an application for disclosure of documents prior to the commencement of proceedings. This is a self contained procedure commenced by making an application under

Part 23. It has its own rules in relation to costs (Rule 48.1) and needs no further steps to be taken by the applicant after compliance with any order made (see Rule 25.2(4)).

- The court may make an order under Section 34 of the Supreme Court Act 1981 or Section 53 County Courts Act 1984 and Rule 31.17 for the disclosure and inspection of documents against someone not a party to the proceedings. Again this is a self contained procedure with its own rule as to costs (Rule 48.1) (see Rule 25.5).
- An interim remedy may be granted in relation to proceedings on foot in another jurisdiction under Section 25 of the Civil Jurisdiction and Judgments Act 1982. The process for obtaining such an order is set out in Rule 25.4; requiring the issue of an application in accordance with Part 23. As above it is a self contained process although there are no specified rules as to costs. Thus the general rule that costs will be in the discretion of the Court applies (Rule 43.3).

Subject to these specific exclusions, it would be usual for the court to require a party to commence proceedings forthwith after making an order before proceedings have been commenced (Rule 25.2(3). The flavour of this general rule is given by the fact that, as originally drafted, the Rule said that the court **must** give directions requiring a claim to be commenced. This was altered to "... may ..." during drafting specifically to exclude for instance, pre-action disclosure under Rule 31.16. The general principle is that the Court will require proceedings to be issued as soon as possible after making a pre-action order. Similarly in the practice direction dealing with injunctions (Paragraph 4.4(1)) the court **must** require the applicant to undertake to the court to issue a claim form immediately or the court will give directions for the commencement of the claim upon making the order for the injunction.

The court may also grant an interim remedy after judgment has been given (Rule 25.2(1)(b)). The usual circumstances in which an interim remedy is required after judgment is where a freezing order has been granted during the course of the proceedings which has effect only until judgment. Thereafter a fresh application is made for a new freezing order so that property may be preserved for the purpose of fulfilment of the judgment itself.

A **defendant** wishing to make an application for an interim remedy has one particular restriction. Under Rule 25.2(2)(c) the defendant may not seek an order for an interim remedy until an acknowledgment of service or a defence is filed. Presumably in most cases where a defendant is seeking an interim remedy it will be based upon a counterclaim.

How to make the application

The application for an interim remedy is no different from any other application to the court for an order; usually compliance with Part 23 is required. Thus an application notice is completed in accordance with Part 23 and served together with the evidence (Rule 23.7) as soon as practicable after issue but no later than three clear days before the hearing. Some parts of Part 23, however, are altered by Part 25 for the purposes of certain applications (see below).

Injunctions

Under the Rules the first matter to consider when making an application for an injunction is whether the court has appropriate jurisdiction. Jurisdiction to grant an injunction is given by a combination of the High Court and County Court Jurisdiction Order 1991 and the County Court Remedies Regulations 1991. In short, under Regulation 3 of the County Court Remedies Regulations 1991, the County Court has jurisdiction to grant an injunction save for a freezing injunction or a search order. A freezing order may only be made by the county court in certain circumstances, namely—

- In family proceedings.
- To preserve or detain property, which is or may be the subject matter of the proceedings.
- To preserve assets for the purpose of executing a County Court judgment.
- In proceedings in the Central London County Court Business List.

The County Court does not have jurisdiction to grant a search order. Application must be made to the High Court. If proceedings have been commenced in the County Court and the order is sought in support of them, the proceedings are effectively transferred to the High Court for the purpose of injunctive relief only (Regulations 4 and 5 of the County Court Remedies Regulations 1991).

Subject to this the CPR (the Practice Direction to Part 2) also make provision as to the level of judiciary that can grant injunctions. Such orders may generally only be made by a "judge" (which for these purposes does not include a master or a district judge). Search orders or freezing orders, ancillary orders and orders authorising a person to enter land to recover, inspect or sample property may only be made a judge. In similar fashion save in four specific cases, other injunctions must also be made by a judge. The four exclusions which allow a master or district judge to make an injunction are—

- if terms are agreed by the parties;
- in connection with or ancillary to charging order;
- in connection with or ancillary to an order appointing a receiver by way of equitable execution; or
- in proceedings under RSC Order 77 Rule 16 (order restraining person from receiving sum due from the Crown).

Under Paragraph 2.4 of the Practice Direction to Part 2, a master or district judge may also vary or discharge an injunction or undertaking given to the court if all parties agree to the variation or discharge.

There appears to be a slight conflict between the Practice Direction to Part 2 and that relating to Part 25 (Paragraphs 1.1–1.4) in relation to the power of master and district judges to grant injunctions. Presumably since the former

Practice Direction dates from May 1999 and the latter from January 1999, practitioners should have regard to the Practice Direction to Part 2 insofar as it is incompatible with the Practice Direction to Part 25 in this respect.

Applying for an injunction

The procedure for application for an injunction, particularly for freezing and search orders, has been increasingly regulated over the past 20 or so years, culminating in the 1994 Practice Direction (now repealed by the CPR) which provided significant detail in relation to the standard forms of order and the process of execution. The Practice Direction to Part 25 carries on much of the procedure established by the 1994 Practice Direction.

The application should be made either to the court in which the claim has been issued or, if a claim has not at the time been issued, to the court where it is likely the claim to which the application relates will be started (Rule 23.2(4)).

Unless the matter is extremely urgent an application notice must be issued.

The application notice must state—

- the order sought; and
- the date, time and place of the hearing.

(Paragraph 2.1, Practice Direction to Part 25)

In accordance with Rule 23.3(2) the court can dispense with the necessity of filing an application notice. As to giving notice to the respondent see below. Thus in very urgent cases a party could appear in front of the court without having issued an application notice to seek an injunction in appropriate circumstances.

It is not that unusual for applications to be made when the court is closed for business. Such applications might be made at the judge's home or over the telephone (see Paragraph 4.2, Practice Direction to Part 25).

The Practice Direction to Part 25 (Paragraph 4.5) sets out the procedure for making applications by telephone. The Royal Courts of Justice, the District Registries and the County Courts run a system of a duty judge who is available out of hours to deal with urgent applications. The application may be heard either in person at the judge's home or over the telephone. If the application is heard by telephone, injunctions will only be granted if the application is made by a barrister or solicitor on behalf of the applicant.

Generally, in accordance with Rule 23.4(1), notice of an application must be given to the respondent, i.e. by service of an application notice or informally (see below). In appropriate circumstances, however, the court can dispense with the notice requirements under Rule 23.4(2). Paragraph 3 of the Practice Direction to Part 23 sets out the circumstances when an application notice need not be served including, in the event of extreme urgency; to further the overriding objective and when the court permits.

If an application notice has not been issued prior to the application, the applicant should provide a form of draft order to the judge. If the application is made over the telephone this may be provided by fax. Under Paragraph 4.3(2) and Paragraph 4.3(4) of the Practice Direction to Part 25 the application notice and evidence in support must be filed with the court on the same or next working day or in accordance with any order made by the judge.

Even though an application notice is not issued unless secrecy is essential to the application, the applicant should notify the respondent as soon as practicable that an application is being made (Paragraph 4.3(3), Practice Direction to Part 25). These types of applications were previously referred to as ex parte applications on notice. In the plain English terms of the CPR presumably they will now be known as applications made without notice on notice.

Although an application notice may not have been issued there should be no reason why properly prepared evidence should not be submitted to court, although in matters of extreme urgency the court may dispense with the formalities for giving evidence. For search orders and freezing injunctions such evidence must be submitted in the form of an affidavit (Paragraph 3.1, Practice Direction to Part 25). For other interim injunctions the usual rules apply as to written evidence which may be included in a witness statement or a statement of case or application notice provided that it is certified by a statement of truth (Paragraph 3.2, Practice Direction to Part 25).

The compilation and presentation of evidence particularly in relation to search and freezing orders is of utmost importance. The Practice Direction (Paragraph 3.3) reminds parties that the evidence must include all material facts. Injunctions are quite often discharged with penal cost orders in the event that all materials facts are not disclosed to the court. The requirements become most important when an application is made without notice. Upon such an application, as well as all the material facts, the evidence must also set out the reasons for secrecy (Rule 25.3(3)).

If an application is made for a search order the evidence in support must give appropriate details of the proposed supervising solicitor. It must also give details of the address of the premises at which the search is to be conducted and indicate whether they are private or business premises (Paragraph 7.3(1), Practice Direction to Part 25). In addition the evidence (by way of affidavit as above) must deal in considerable detail with the reasons why the order is sought, detailing particularly the reason it is believed that relevant material would disappear if the order is not made (Paragraph 7.3(2)).

If time has allowed the issue of an application notice, the application can still be dealt with without service of the notice if the court believes it appropriate. The evidence in support must set out why secrecy is required (Rule 25.3(3) and Paragraph 3.4, Practice Direction to Part 25).

If the court is to serve, then the evidence in support should be filed with the application notice together with sufficient copies of service (Paragraph 2.3, Practice Direction to Part 25). As well as the application notice and evidence, the applicant should also provide the court with a draft order, preferably in hard copy and on floppy disk.

The application notice and evidence must be served in accordance with Part 23 and particularly "as soon as practicable" after issue and in any event no less than three days before the court is due to hear the application (Rule 23.7(1)). The court does have the power to abridge time both under its case management powers and particularly under Rule 23.7(4).

If the application for an injunction is made before the issue of the claim form, save in the specific exceptions referred to above, the court will require an undertaking from the applicant to issue a claim form either immediately or in accordance with appropriate directions (Rule 25.2(3) and Paragraph 4.4(1), Practice Direction to Part 25).

The Order

Notice should be taken of the provisions of Rule 23.9. This regulates the procedure if an order is made dismissing the application, notice for which has not been given to the respondent. If an order is made dismissing the application, a copy of the application notice and any evidence in support must be served on the respondent (Rule 23.9(2)). Thus if the applicant wishes to maintain the secrecy of the application in the prospect of making a further application, the court should be asked specifically to dis-apply the provisions of Rule 23.9(2).

Part 40 regulates generally the drawing up, filing, service and effect of orders (see below). If the order is an injunction, its format is regulated by Part 25 (Paragraph 5.1, Practice Direction to Part 25). Contrary to the general belief, there are no particular regulations as to what must be included in either a freezing injunction or a search order. The Practice Direction simply provides examples of the form of those orders. Clearly, however, the court will require orders to be drawn in the form of the examples.

The general requirements then for the form of injunction are that it must contain—

- an undertaking as to damages by the applicant;
- if no notice has been given, an undertaking by the applicant to serve on the respondent the application notice, evidence in support and the order as soon as practicable;
- if no notice has been given, a return date for a further hearing (of which due notice will have to be given);
- if no application notice has been filed, an undertaking to file the notice and pay the appropriate fee on the same or next working day; and
- if no claim form has been issued, an undertaking by the applicant to issue one and pay the appropriate fee on the same or next working day; alternatively the Court may give other directions as to the commencement of the claim.

All injunctions must set out clearly what the respondent must do or not do to comply with the order.

If the order is made following an application for which notice has not been given to the respondent, the order must contain a statement of the right to make an application to set aside or vary the order under Rule 23.10 (Rule 23.9(3)) (see below).

If an order is made before the issue of a claim form then there is slight change in the title endorsed on the order. The applicant will be referred to as the "claimant in an intended action". Similarly the respondent will be referred to as the "defendant in an intended action" (Paragraph 4.3(3), Practice Direction to Part 25).

Save for a search order, service of the order is regulated by Rule 40.4. The order must be served on the respondent and any other person on whom the court orders it to be served. Service may be effected by the party or the court. If the court is to serve then the applicant must provide sufficient copies for service. Service may be effected by post in accordance with Rule 6.2 although in urgent applications service is usually effected personally. If a search order is made, however, service must be effected personally by the supervising solicitor (Paragraph 7.4(1), Practice Direction to Part 25).

An order made without notice to the respondent must contain a return date for a further hearing when the respondent can be present (see above). On that occasion the respondent may apply to set aside the order or vary it (Rule 23.10(1)). A person who is not a party to the claim but who is directly affected by the order may also apply to have it set aside or varied (Rule 40.9). Such an application must be made within seven days after the date on which the order was served on that person (Rule 23.10(2)).

If an order is made for an injunction until judgment, note should be taken of the provisions of Rule 25.10 and 25.11. In the former, if the claim is stayed other than by agreement between the parties, the injunction is set aside (i.e. cancelled) unless the court orders otherwise. Remember that a claim can be stayed under the case management provisions of both Parts 3 and 26.

Under Rule 25.11, if court fees are not paid and the claim is struck out under Rule 3.7, the injunction ceases to have effect 14 days after the date that the claim is struck out unless an application is made to reinstate the claim within the 14 days. Under its case management powers the court does have the ability to extend this time period. As originally drafted, the injunction ceased to have effect immediately upon strike-out but the position has been somewhat alleviated to allow the applicant to recover his senses, pay the fee and reinstate the claim.

Executing the search order

Paragraphs 7.4, 7.5, 8.1–8.3 of the Practice Direction to Part 25 set out the procedure for service and execution of a search order. A full discussion of the procedure and effect is, at least for the time being, outside the scope of this work.

Interim Payments

Part 25 has three Practice Directions the second relating to interim payments is labelled Part 25B and the references to the Practice Direction below are to that Practice Direction

The regulation of interim payments was previously contained within RSC

Order 29. Much of what was there has been carried forward into Part 25. As previously, the procedure for application for an interim payment should be compared with the procedure for summary judgment (Part 24). Often an application for summary judgment is accompanied by an application for an interim payment as an alternative order for the court to make.

An interim payment is defined by Rule 25.1(1)(k) as—

> **an order for payment by a defendant on account of any damages, debt or other sum (except costs) which the court may hold the defendant liable to pay.**

The Application

The application is as ever made in accordance with Part 23 as slightly altered by Part 25 (see below).

Application for an interim payment cannot be made before the end of the period for filing an acknowledgment of service under Part 10. This compares with the provisions of Part 24 in relation to summary judgment. Under Rule 24.4, application for summary judgment cannot be made until an acknowledgment of service or a defence is actually filed with the court.

In accordance with Rule 23.6 the application notice must state what order the applicant is seeking and briefly why the applicant is seeking the order.

The application must be supported by evidence (Paragraph 2.1, Practice Direction to Part 25). That evidence must deal with—

- the sum of money sought by way of an interim payment;
- the items or matters in respect of which the interim payment is sought;
- the sum of money for which final judgment is likely to be given;
- the reasons for believing that the conditions set out in Rule 25.7 are satisfied (see below);
- any other relevant matters;
- in claims for personal injuries, details of special damages and past and future loss; and
- in a claim under the Fatal Accidents Act 1976, details of the persons on whose behalf the claim is made and the nature of the claim.

As is usual, any documents relied upon should be exhibited in accordance with the Practice Direction to Part 32 (Paragraphs 11.1–15.4).

The evidence may be contained in a witness statement or in the statement of case or the application notice as long as they are verified by a statement of truth.

If the application notice is to be served by the court then sufficient copies of it together with the evidence must be filed with the court for service.

The provisions in relation to service under Part 23 are amended by Part 25 reflecting the procedure in relation to an application for summary judgment under Part 24. Accordingly, under Rule 25.6, a copy of the application notice together with the evidence in support must be served upon the respondent at least 14 days before the hearing of the application. Those days are clear days but do include holidays and weekends (Rule 2.8).

If the respondent wishes to rely on written evidence then the evidence must be filed and served at least seven days before the hearing. Again this is clear days including weekends and holidays.

If the applicant wishes to respond to the evidence of the respondent then that evidence must be served and filed at least three clear days before the hearing of the application. On this occasion this period does not include weekends and holidays.

Rule 25.7 sets out the specific grounds on which the court may make an order for an interim payment:

25.7 (1) The court may make an order for an interim payment only if—

(a) the defendant against whom the order is sought has admitted liability to pay damages or some other sum of money to the claimant;

(b) the claimant has obtained judgment against that defendant for damages to be assessed or for a sum of money (other than costs) to be assessed;

(c) except where paragraph (3) applies, it is satisfied that, if the claim went to trial, the claimant would obtain judgment for a substantial amount of money (other than costs) against the defendant from whom he is seeking an order for an interim payment; or

(d) the following conditions are satisfied—

(i) the claimant is seeking an order for possession of land (whether or not any other order is also sought); and

(ii) the court is satisfied that, if the case went to trial, the defendant would be held liable (even if the claim for possession fails) to pay the claimant a sum of money for the defendant's occupation and use of the land while the claim for possession was pending.

(2) In addition, in a claim for personal injuries the court may make an order for an interim payment of damages only if—

(a) the defendant is insured in respect of the claim;

(b) the defendant's liability will be met by—

(i) an insurer under section 151 of the Road Traffic Act 1988; or

(ii) an insurer acting under the Motor Insurers Bureau Agreement, or the Motor Insurers Bureau where it is acting itself; or

(c) the defendant is a public body.

(3) In a claim for personal injuries where there are two or more defendants, the court may make an order for the interim payment of damages against any defendant if—

(a) it is satisfied that, if the claim went to trial, the claimant would obtain judgment for substantial damages against at least one of the defendants (even if the court has not yet determined which of them is liable); and

(b) paragraph (2) is satisfied in relation to each of the defendants.

(4) The court must not order an interim payment of more than a reasonable proportion of the likely amount of the final judgment.

(5) The court must take into account—

(a) contributory negligence; and

(b) any relevant set-off or counterclaim.

The claimant may make two or more applications for an interim payment as the claim proceeds (Rule 25.6(2)). On making an order the court may order that any interim payment should be paid in instalments (Rule 25.6(7)). If it does so then the order should set out—

- the total amount of the payment;
- the amount of each instalment;
- the number of instalments and the date on which each is to be paid; and
- to whom the payment should be made.

(Paragraph 3, Practice Direction to Part 25)

Under Rule 25.8 the court has the power to adjust or vary an order for an interim payment. This may be done at any stage during the course of the proceedings or (as usual) upon the trial of the action and its disposal.

When final judgment is given the court will take into account any interim payments. Indeed the order should set out in the preamble the total amount awarded by the judge disposing of the proceedings and the amounts and dates of the interim payment(s). The final amount to be paid will then be adjusted accordingly. This will mean either that there is a balance to be paid by the defendant or monies have to be repaid by the claimant from the interim payment made earlier (Paragraphs 5.1–5.6, Practice Direction to Part 25, the provisions of which are effectively repeated in Paragraphs 6.1–6.4, Practice Direction to Part 40).

If payment has to be made by the defendant to top up the interim payments the court has discretion as to the interest that it may award the claimant. If on the other hand the claimant must make a repayment to the defendant, the court may award the defendant interest on the overpaid amount from the date when he made the interim payment (Rule 25.8(5)).

Accounts and Inquiries

One of the orders that can be made under Part 25 is for accounts to be taken and inquiries to be made. If such an order is given, reference should be made to the practice direction to Part 40 which sets out the procedure then to be followed.

CHAPTER 14
PART 24—SUMMARY JUDGMENT

The number 14 has for long been synonymous with summary judgment. Even in the County Court the drafters whilst not able to provide that summary judgment should constitute Order 14, did manage to engineer it into Order 9 Rule 14.

The drafters of the Brown Book carried on the tradition and summary judgment fell under Part 14. This was not to last. When the numbers were finally allotted the Committee decided not to try and shoehorn summary judgment into Part 14 and it has become Part 24.

The two innovations in Part 24 are—

1. **the change in the test to "no real prospect of success" to reflect the same test as that applying to setting aside a default judgment; and**
2. **that either party can apply for summary judgment.**

Since the publication of the CPR some have commented that really the new test under Part 24 is little different from the old test particularly in the light of the Practice Direction (see below). Under RSC Order 14 Rule 1 the application was made by the plaintiff on the grounds that there was no defence. Order 14 Rule 3 then placed upon the defendant the burden of satisfying the Court—

> **that there is an issue or question in dispute which ought to be tried or that there ought for some other reason to be a trial of that claim or part.**

These two principles were also applied in the County Court.

This test was different from that applying upon an application to set aside judgment (RSC Order 13 Rule 9). The defining case in relation to setting aside a default judgment is *Alpine Bulk Transport Co Inc v Saudi Eagle Shipping Co Inc, The Saudi Eagle* [1986] 2 Lloyds Rep 221. In that case the Court of Appeal took a robust attitude towards the defendant seeking to set aside a full judgment. It asserted that the defendant had to go further than the requirements of Order 14 and establish not merely an arguable defence but that the defence had both "a real prospect of success" and "carried some degree of conviction".

The Court said that whilst the default was not an estoppel at law, where proceedings had been deliberately ignored, the Court should consider all the circumstances and the interest of "justice".

The approach of the Court of Appeal has been much debated. In any event, the robust approach adopted in *Saudi Eagle* has been carried into Part 13 (setting aside or varying default judgment) in that the defendant has to satisfy the Court that he has "a real prospect of successfully defending the claim" or there is some other good reason why the matter should be tried.

For summary judgment Lord Woolf recommended in the Final Report (pages 123 and 124, Chapter 12, Section III)—

> **The test for making an order would be that the Court considers that a party had no realistic prospect of succeeding at trial on the whole case or on a particular issue. A party seeking to resist such an order would have to show more than a merely arguable case; it would have to be one which he had a real prospect of winning. Exceptionally the Court could allow a case or an issue to continue although it did not satisfy this test, if it considered that there was a public interest in the matter being tried.**

In making his recommendations Lord Woolf was also carrying forward the new culture recommended in the Report that issues not requiring a full trial should be dealt with as soon as possible so that the resources of the Court Service would be available to issues and disputes requiring the full litigation process including trial. This culture finds part of its embodiment in Rule 1.1(2)(d) by which the Court is required to ensure that a case is dealt with "expeditiously and fairly".

Suffice it to say that upon Lord Woolf's recommendations, the new test for summary judgment - "no real prospect of success" - is intended to lower the hurdle for the applicant in comparison to the RSC Order 14 test and to reflect more the relevant "*Saudi Eagle*" test.

During the course of drafting the CPR comparison has been made between an application under Part 24 for summary judgment and an application under Rule 3.4 to strike out a statement of case on the grounds that it appears that it discloses no reasonable grounds for bringing or defending a claim (Rule 3.4(2)(a)). Indeed, not only have the two provisions been referred to in the same breath, but for some time the striking out provisions appeared as part of Part 24.

Even though the power to strike out a statement of case is now removed to Rule 3.4 and there are important differences between the two forms of relief, they are likely to be married as a matter of procedure on many occasions. When making an application to strike out a case under Rule 3.4, a party is also likely to seek as an alternative summary judgment under Part 24.

The main difference between the power to strike out a statement of case and to give summary judgment is that for the former the statement of case has to disclose on the face of it no reasonable grounds for bringing and defending the claim. This reflects the provisions of RSC Order 18 Rule 19 which provided that the Court could strike out a pleading on the ground that it disclosed no reasonable cause of action or defence. CCR Order 13 Rule 5 provided similarly.

What is being addressed in Rule 3.4(2)(a) is where the content of a statement of case is defective so that even if all the allegations made in it were proved, the party could still not succeed or, whatever is said in the statement of case, no matter how complete and apparently correct, the claim will fail as a matter of law.

The other difference between Rule 3.4 and Part 24 is the question of evidence. In RSC Order 18 Rule 19 evidence in support of an application to strike out, as referred to above, was generally not admissible. There is no like provision under Rule 3.4 but if an applicant is being made to strike out on the grounds that the statement of case discloses no reasonable grounds for bringing or defending the claim, evidence is unlikely to be of much relevance. On the other hand, under Part 24 the evidence is a vital part of the application.

Grounds for Summary Judgment—Rule 24.2

The grounds on which summary judgment may be obtained are dealt with above. Despite the general admonishment of reference back to previous decisions relating to the RSC and CCR, no doubt parties and practitioners will have regard to the judgment in *Saudi Eagle* when applying the test of "no real prospect of success". In that case Sir Roger Ormond said at page 224—

> **"The primary consideration is whether the defendant has merits to which the Court should pay heed, not as a rule of law but as a matter of common sense …".**

The *Saudi Eagle* decision has been commented upon in *Allen v Taylor* [1992] 1 PIQR 255 and most recently in *Day v Royal Automobile Club Motoring Services Ltd* (1998) Times, 24 November. Even if it were possible, it is not within the scope of this work to dissect what is "a real prospect of success". The Practice Direction does attempts at Paragraphs 4.1 and 4.2 to put some flesh on the bone. The problem with the Practice direction, however, is that it somewhat conflicts with the Rule (24.2). Firstly it appears to alter the burden of proof; second, the test it proffers smacks more of the old test under RSC Order 14. At the time of writing, it has been proposed that the Practice Direction may be amended or omitted altogether.

When considering the test under Part 24 and the old authorities, it is suggested that it is worth remembering the words of Lord Herschell quoted above from *Bank of England v Vagliano Bros* [1891] AC 107—

> **"… I think the proper course in the first instance is to examine the language of the statute and to ask what is its natural meaning, uninfluenced by any considerations derived from the previous state of the law, and not to start with inquiring how the law previously stood, and then, assuming that it was probably intended to leave it unaltered, to see if the words of the enactment will bear an interpretation in conformity with this view …. Law should be ascertained by interpreting the language used instead of, as before, by roaming over a vast number of authorities in order to discover what the law was,**

extracting it by a minute critical examination of the prior decisions ...".

Although the Rule is written in discretionary language so that the Court "may" give summary judgment, if the Court concludes that there is no real prospect of success and there is no other reason why the case should go forward to trial, the discretion is raised to an obligation. In accordance with Rule 1.4(2)(c) the Court is obliged to decide promptly which issues need full investigation and trial and accordingly dispose summarily of those issues that do not need full investigation and trial.

Rule 24.2(b) which provides that the Court may give summary judgment if there is no other reason why the case or issue should be disposed of at trial, is written in wide terms. It is submitted, however, that bearing in mind the directive nature of the overriding objective and the obligations of the Court, there would have to be extremely good "other reasons" as to why the matter should proceed to trial.

During the course of the drafting process, suggestions were made to exclude this ground altogether but it has been retained in order to allow a degree of flexibility to the Court where the circumstances demand.

Types of proceedings in which Summary Judgment is available

The former restrictions in relation to the types of proceedings where summary judgment could be obtained have largely been removed. These were—

- malicious prosecution;
- false imprisonment;
- libel or slander;
- misfeasance in public office; or
- an admiralty claim in rem.

The original limitations to RSC Order 14 derive in the main from Section 69 Supreme Court Act 1981 and Section 66 County Courts Act 1984. Although these provide explicitly the entitlement to a trial by jury, the view was taken in removing them that this did not in any way interfere with the ability of the Court to grant summary judgment in relation to the types of claim specified.

Rule 24.3(1) provides that the Court may give summary judgment against a claimant in any type of proceedings. Under Rule 24.3(2) it may not give summary judgment against a defendant in relation to proceedings for possession of residential premises against a tenant, a mortgagor or a person holding over after the end of his tenancy; and proceedings for an admiralty claim in rem.

In relation to proceedings for possession, reference should be made in any event to RSC Order 113 (summary proceedings for possession of land contained in Schedule 1 to the CPR) and CCR Order 24 (summary proceedings for the recovery of land contained in Schedule 2 to the CPR). Mortgage claims are dealt with under RSC Order 88 (Schedule 1 CPR). Both are subject to a fixed date procedure under Part 8 (see Paragraph 4, Practice Direction to Part 8).

Order 14 also had no application to actions for specific performance or rescission in relation to certain agreements for which provision was made under RSC Order 86. That exclusion has not been repeated and indeed RSC Order 86 does not form part of the CPR (see Paragraph 7, Practice Direction to Part 24). The application is made under Part 24. As with RSC Order 14A, an application for summary judgment can be made on a point of law and construction of a document (Paragraph 1.3, Practice Direction to Part 24).

In comparison to Part 24, an application under Rule 3(4) (strike out) has no limitations at all, although in relation to certain types of claim, the procedure under Rule 3.5 requires an application for judgment to be made in accordance with Part 23.

Procedure

Save in relation to specific performance, an application for summary judgment cannot be made prior to the filing of an acknowledgment of service by the defendant without permission of the court. Again comparison can be made with the power of the Court to strike out under Rule 3.4. A defendant may make an application to strike out prior to acknowledging service. The time for acknowledging service is not, however, automatically extended upon the filing of an application notice seeking such an order.

In Paragraph 7 of the Practice Direction to Part 24, an application under Part 24 for specific performance can be made at any time after the claim form has been served.

Rule 24.4(2) provides that if a claimant applies for summary judgment before a defence is filed, the time for filing a defence is extended until the hearing of the application takes place.

A court may make an order giving summary judgment under Part 24 without having in front of it an application seeking such an order. In accordance with Rule 1.4(2)(c), the Court is obliged to further the overriding objective by actively managing a case and under that obligation disposing summarily of issues that do not need full investigation and trial.

Under Rule 3.3 the Court can make an order of its own initiative. If it proposes to do so, however, it **may** give any person likely to be affected by the order an opportunity to make representations and if it does so, give a hearing date when those representations can be made (Rule 3.3(2)). The party being invited to make representations must be given at least three days notice of the hearing.

The Court is not obliged to allow a person the opportunity to make representations. The matter is within the discretion of the Court. This is to allow the Court either to strike out a statement of case or give summary judgment in relation to it where it is wholly ludicrous. The burden will then fall on the party affected by the order to make application to have it set aside or varied or stayed (Rule 3.3(5)).

Following the making of an order of its own initiative without notice, the order itself must contain a statement of the right of the party affected to make an application to have it set aside, varied or stayed (Rule 3.3(5)(b)). The application to set aside, vary or stay must be made within the period set by the Court or, if no period is set, no more than seven days after the date on which the order is served.

If in the allocation questionnaire a party indicates that they propose to make an application for summary judgment, the Court might proceed immediately to fix a date for the hearing of such an application even so the applicant is obliged to issue an application notice returnable on the date fixed. Whilst an application for summary judgment is pending, the Court is unlikely to allocate the case to a track. Even if allocation takes place to the small claims track, the Court may set a preliminary hearing to enable it to dispose of the claim because one or other of the parties has no real prospect of success at a final hearing or it proposes to strike out a statement of case showing no reasonable grounds for bringing or defending the claim Rule 27.6(1).

There is no like provision in relation to the fast track or multi track under Parts 28 and 29 respectively but there is no reason under the Rules why the Court should not take similar steps either at a directions hearing in the fast track or case management conference in the multi track.

Making an application for Summary Judgment

The application is made by the completion and filing of an application notice under Part 23. The application for summary judgment should be made as soon as it becomes apparent that it is necessary or desirable to make it (Paragraph 2.7, Practice Direction to Part 23).

As with all applications under Part 23, there are certain requirements for the application notice itself. It must include—

- the title of the claim;
- the reference number of the claim;
- the full name of the applicant; and
- either a request for hearing or a request that the application is dealt with without a hearing.

The practice Form N244 may be used but is not obligatory. It does, however, give an easy reference for what should be included in the notice.

In addition to the above matters, the application notice must state what order the applicant is seeking and briefly why the applicant is seeking the order (Rule 23.6). In an application for specific performance, the form of order must be attached (Paragraph 7, Practice Direction to Part 24). Further, the notice must include a statement that it is an application for summary judgment under Part 24 (Paragraph 2(2), Practice direction to Part 24). Either the written evidence or the application notice (which may be the same - see below) must also—

- identify concisely any point of law or provision in a document on which the applicant relies; and/or
- state that it is made because the applicant believes that on the evidence the respondent has no real prospect of succeeding on the claim or issue or (as

the case may be) of successfully defending the claim or issue to which the application relates;

- and in either case state that the applicant knows no other reason why the disposal of the claim or issue should await trial

(Paragraph 2(3), Practice Direction to Part 24).

The evidence in support of the application may be contained within the application notice itself. It will only be admissible, however, if the application notice is endorsed with a statement of truth (as to statements of truth see Part 22 at page 117). Otherwise any evidence should be within a witness statement. It should be made clear that a witness statement for these purposes has no relationship with a witness statement filed and served in preparation for the trial in accordance with Rule 32.4

The application notice should be filed at the Court (Rule 23.3). If it is intended that the Court should serve the application notice then sufficient copies should be lodged with the Court for this purpose. If the written evidence in support is separate it also has to be filed.

Further, although unspoken within the Rules, there is encouragement on parties to file and serve a draft of the order being sought. If the applicant has attached a draft order to the application then this must also be provided to the Court. Sufficient copies of both the written evidence and the draft order should be supplied if the Court is going to serve.

The Court will issue the application notice providing a return date in Form N244A (notice of application). If the Court is going to serve, a copy of the application notice and the notice of application will be returned to the applicant. If the applicant wishes to serve the application notice then the Court must be notified of that wish to serve. Upon the return of the issued application notice, the applicant should serve the notice together with any draft order attached to the notice and the written evidence in support.

If there is an impending hearing then an applicant should try and arrange that the application for summary judgment be heard at the same time (Paragraph 2, Practice Direction to Part 23).

The application notice must be served as soon as practicable after filing (Rule 23.7(1)(a)) and no less than 14 days prior to the date fixed for hearing (Rule 24.4(3)(a)). In accordance with Rule 23.7(7), the written evidence in support of the application and a copy of any draft order must also be served no less than 14 days prior to the hearing. Rule 24.4(3)(b) stipulates that 14 days notice must also be given of the issues which it is proposed that the Court will decide at the hearing. These issues should in any event be covered either by the application notice or by the separate written evidence in support.

In the notice of application the attention of the respondent must be drawn to the requirement of Rule 24.5(1) that if he wishes to rely on written evidence in response to that of the applicant at the hearing, he must file the written evidence and serve copies on every other party to the application at least 7 days before the hearing.

If the applicant wishes to present written evidence in reply then he must file the written evidence and serve a copy on the respondent at least 3 days before the hearing (Rule 24.5(2)).

If the summary judgment hearing is fixed by the Court of its own initiative then written evidence must be filed and served at least seven days before the date of the hearing. Any responding written evidence must be filed and served 3 days before the date of the hearing (Rule 24.5 (3)).

For all these periods, remember the measurement is of clear days (Rule 2.8(3)) and that sufficient time has to be allowed for affecting service under Rule 6.7, particularly if service is being effected in the usual way by post.

Where the remedy sought is specific performance of an agreement generally relating to land (see the specific reference at Paragraph 7.1(1)(a)), or the rescission of such an agreement or the forfeiture of return of any deposit made under such an agreement, there are particular provisions within Paragraph 7 of the Practice Direction to Part 24. (These provisions previously appeared as RSC Order 86 under the old regime.)

If a party chooses, they may give their evidence on an application under Part 24 by affidavit (Rule 32.15(2)). The form of witness statement or affidavit must comply with Part 32 and the Practice Direction which supplements it.

Parts 7 and 8 deal with what should be included in the claim form and particulars of claim but there are no provisions such as those contained within Part 32 in relation to the exhibiting of documents either to an affidavit or a witness statement. Parties should be aware that although they may serve documents referred to in the particulars of claim and/or application notice, they will still be required to be proved in front of the Court and for that purpose they should be exhibited, in the normal way, to a witness statement.

The Hearing and the Order

The hearing will normally take place before a Master or a District Judge although either may refer the matter to a High Court Judge (if that is where the case is proceeding) or a Circuit Judge (if the case is in the County Court) (Paragraph 4, Practice Direction to Part 24).

A party may apply to the Court for permission to cross examine a witness at the hearing (Rule 32.7). This would be highly unusual on an application for summary judgment since if cross examination is required, it may follow automatically that the matter really ought to go to trial.

Under Part 24 the burden of proof has been altered from that under RSC Order 14. Under Order 14 Rule 3 a plaintiff was entitled to judgment unless the defendant satisfied the Court that there was an issue or question in dispute which ought to be tried. Under Part 24 it is for the applicant to show that the respondent has no real prospect of success. Despite this the practical burden falls upon the respondent to show that he has that real prospect.

Having heard the application the Court may—

- give judgment on the claim in favour of the claimant;

- strike out or dismiss the claim in favour of the defendant;
- dismiss the application or make a conditional order.

The form of conditional order replaces the process of giving conditional leave under the RSC and CCR. Such a conditional order under the CPR would be made in accordance with the Court's power given by Rule 3.1(3). The condition to be fulfilled may be for a sum of money to be paid into Court, failing which judgment would be given on the claim or the claim would be struck out or dismissed (see Paragraph 5.2, Practice Direction to Part 24).

Paragraph 4.3 of the Practice Direction to Part 24 suggests that a conditional order may be made where it appears to the Court possible that a claim or defence may succeed but improbable that it will do so.

In accordance with Rule 40.7, a judgment or order generally takes effect from the day when it is given or made. Interest under the Judgments Act 1838 or the County Courts Act 1984 begins to run from the same date. The person against whom the judgment or order is made has 14 days within which to comply with the judgment or order unless the order made by the Court specifies a different period.

References to a claim under Part 24 are also references to a part of a claim. Accordingly the Court may give judgment on part of the claim or defence and allow the remainder to go forward to trial.

If the application for summary judgment relates to the taking of an account or an inquiry, and an order is made for an account to be taken or an inquiry to be made, the Court may at the same time give directions as to the manner in which the account is to be taken and verified or the inquiry conducted (Paragraph 1.1, Practice Direction to Part 40).

In addition to the orders the Court may make above, the Court may give directions as to the filing and service of the defence or further directions about the management of the case. The Court does have the power to dispense with the filing of a defence (Rule 6.8). It is only likely to do so if all of the issues have been raised in the written evidence before the Court on the application and a defence would not put any further issue before the Court.

If the application and order made are for damages to be assessed, the Court will give appropriate directions which may include—

- the allocation or re-allocation of the claim;
- that allocation questionnaires be filed by a specified date;
- that a date be fixed for a hearing or further hearing;
- there be a stay on the claim while the parties try to settle the case.

(Paragraph 12, Practice Direction to Part 26.)

The Court will also deal with costs upon making an order. In doing so the general rule is that costs follow the event - "loser pays". This may not be appropriate upon an application for summary judgment depending on the order that has been made. It is quite usual for the Court to make an order (using new phraseology) for "costs in the case" (possibly in favour of one party or the other) or costs reserved. In deciding whether to make an order for costs, the Court must have regard to all the circumstances set out in Rule 44.3.

If the Court does make an order for costs and the claim is for a specified sum of money, the fixed costs regime provided for under Rule 44.6 and Part 45 will apply. Under Rule 45.4, if the claimant has claimed fixed commencement costs under Rule 45.2 and judgment is entered under Part 24 in his favour, the amount to be included in the judgment in respect of the claimant's solicitor's charges is the aggregate of the fixed commencement costs and the amount shown in Table 2 to Part 45. In addition to the fixed commencement costs, where summary judgment is given under Part 24, the claimant is entitled to £175 for claims not exceeding £5,000 and £210 for claims exceeding £5,000 in respect of the claimant's solicitor's charge.

If an order for costs is made (other than "costs in case" - Paragraph 4.4(2), Practice Direction to Part 44), the Court should consider whether to make a summary assessment of those costs. The parties have to be ready for the making of such an assessment. Accordingly they must have prepared a written statement of the costs in accordance with Paragraph 4.5(2) of the Practice Direction to Part 44 and filed and served it in accordance with Paragraph 4.5(4) of the same Practice Direction. (Summary assessment is discussed at page 364 post.)

If the Court does not summarily assess the costs but makes an order in favour of one of the parties, it could exercise its power to require that there should be a payment on account by the paying party (Rule 44.3 (8) and Paragraph 4.11, Practice Direction to Part 44).

In accordance with Rule 20.3, a Part 20 claim is treated as if it were a claim for the purposes of the Rules. Part 24, therefore, applies to it and summary judgment may be obtained in relation to any Part 20 claim.

CHAPTER 15
PART 26—CASE MANAGEMENT—PRELIMINARY STAGE

The Final Report

Both in the Interim and Final Report, Lord Woolf set out the new structure for litigation with its central core being the Court's proactive management of proceedings. We have seen already in Rule 1.4 the obligation of the Court to actively manage cases. Rule 1.1(2) also requires the Court to deal with cases justly subject to certain practical limitations including those relating to proportionality under Rule 1.1(2)(c).

In addition to these obligations, the manner in which the Court will deal with proceedings is closely connected to the value of the claim or, as put in Rule 1.1(2)(c)(i), to the amount of money involved. The case management under Part 26 provides a formal procedure of allying the process between allocation and trial to, for instance, the value of the claim.

The process of case management, particularly in relation to fast track and multi track, was dealt with in Section II of the Final Report. In it Lord Woolf met many of the criticisms made by commentators. In particular, Lord Woolf dealt with various criticisms of APIL in relation to the fast track and the concept of proportionality.

In the Interim Report, Lord Woolf first floated the idea that there should be different procedures to be followed for different types of case. He categorised cases into three "tracks" - a track for small claims, a track for somewhat larger and more complex claims and finally a track for everything else. For want of better descriptions these were described as and retain the descriptions of the small claims track, the fast track and the multi track.

The idea of dividing cases for the purpose of procedural requirements is nothing new. The small claims procedure has been with us for some time and has provided a simplified procedure for smaller value claims.

Whilst not necessarily ascribing a set procedure to claims of a certain value, there has been for some time a process of case management in certain courts. The Commercial Court has always been proud of its procedure for a hands-on approach to the management of cases before it. Similarly, the Technology & Construction Court (formerly the Official Referee's Court) has required the involvement of Judges in every stage of the proceedings allowing them to take a proactive role in the management up to trial.

In addition, in the preparation of his Reports, Lord Woolf had the opportunity of seeing the process in other jurisdictions and particularly the more recent innovations in the court management of civil litigation procedure. Other common law jurisdictions including the United States, Canada and Australia have experimented with case management to meet the self same problems as those identified by Lord Woolf. The opposition to changes in all common law jurisdictions remains the perceived conflict between judicial case management and the adversarial system of justice. The result of the imposition of case management in other common law systems has been somewhat mixed. These experiments have been most advanced in the United States. Indeed, some commentators have referred to the civil procedure reforms in England as the Americanisation of English procedure.

Lord Woolf was not shy either in the Interim or Final Report of addressing these potential criticisms and indeed has not been shy to meet them since. Lord Woolf has remained committed to judicial case management. The case management process under Part 26, however, does not of itself oblige the Courts to take a proactive approach to case management. This truly derives from the Court's obligations under Part 1.

At its heart Part 26 simply provides initially for the transfer of particular claims to the defendant's home court and, subject to that, the process for the division of claims into appropriate tracks which then determines the complexity of the procedure to be followed by the Court between allocation and trial. The detail of those tracks is set out in the following Parts, namely Parts 27 (small claims track), 28 (fast track) and 29 (multi track).

For all this, the initial stage of case management under Part 26 may be a hotly contested issue bearing in mind the effect upon subsequent procedure resulting from allocation to a particular track. Since allocation is largely determined by the value of the claim the question of that value may give rise to considerable argument.

Anyone wishing to follow the course of the debate concerning case management will need to refer not only to the Interim and Final Reports but also to the case management working paper which was published following publication of the Brown Book. The working paper proposed substantive changes to the Brown Book. One of those changes was the retention of automatic transfer for County Court cases (as it was then drafted). It should be noted that Part 26 has been disapplied in the Commercial Court and reference should be made to the Commercial Court Guide.

Automatic transfer

Practitioners are always somewhat fearful of the physical transfer process because, although the evidence be anecdotal, it has been known for either the transfer process to take considerable time or for files to be lost in that process. Until such time as the Courts have a paperless file system, the potential for these problems remains.

In any event, akin to the practice upon transfer under Part 30 and its practice direction, the transferring court will send a notice of the transfer to the receiving court and that notice will contain the name of the case and the number of the case. At the same time the transferring court will notify the parties of the transfer. No order is made and therefore there is no set machinery (unlike Part 30) for applying to set aside or appealing against the transfer itself. It is suggested that one method of reopening the issue of automatic transfer would be to make an application to the transferee court for a transfer under Part 30.

As with the whole of Part 26, the automatic transfer provision in Rule 26.2 only applies to defended cases (in accordance with Rule 24.2(1)). The filing of the defence is therefore a pre-condition to transfer. The question of what is a defence may be closely debated. The practice in many County Courts under the old Rules appeared to be that upon filing the then form N9B, the Court would automatically transfer the proceedings to the defendant's home court whatever form of defence was tendered, even if it did not amount to a proper defence. Under the new Rules and particularly Parts 15 and 16, the matters which must be addressed in the defence are more closely regulated. In particular, a simple denial of the claim is not generally a sufficient defence for the purposes of the Rules.

One of Lord Woolf's express desires is that County Courts will review defences when they are filed so that those that do not comply with Parts 15 and 16 will be referred to the District Judge to consider making an appropriate order such as striking out the defence of the Court's own initiative under Part 3. The only matter militating against such a step being taken before the proceedings are transferred to the defendant's home court is that one of the principles behind automatic transfer is to enable the defendant to have physical access to the Court for any hearing in relation to it. If a hearing is necessary for the question of striking out a defence, it might be thought appropriate that that hearing take place in the defendant's home court following automatic transfer.

It is to be noted on the one hand that the reference to a defence which triggers automatic transfer in Rule 26.2(3) is not qualified as a defence "complying with the CPR". On the other hand, it refers to a defence rather than simply the form of defence which remains form N9B.

Comparison should be made with obtaining judgment in default of defence which is not available on the filing of a defence or a document purporting to be a defence (Paragraph 1.1, Practice Direction to Part 12).

If the defendant admits part of the claim in accordance with Rule 14.5 and, presumably, with the effect that the remaining part of the claim is defended, there is no immediate automatic transfer. Under Rule 14.5(3) the Court will serve a notice on the claimant requiring him to notify the Court whether—

- he accepts the amount admitted in satisfaction of the claim;
- he does not accept the amount admitted by the defendant and wishes the proceedings to continue; or

- if the defendant has requested time to pay, he accepts the amount admitted in satisfaction of the claim, but not the defendant's proposals as to payment.

If the claimant does not notify the Court within 14 days, the proceedings will be stayed. If the amount admitted is accepted in satisfaction for the whole of the claim then the claimant can make an application for judgment. If it is not accepted, the matter will then be transferred to the defendant's home court in accordance with Rule 26.2. If the only argument is about the timing of payment, then there is no automatic transfer, and that matter will be dealt with by the Court in which the proceedings were issued.

Similarly, if in the defence the defendant states that the money claimed has been paid, the Court will send a notice to the claimant asking him to state whether he wishes the proceedings to continue under Rule 15.10. If he responds positively, only then will the proceedings be automatically transferred in accordance with Rule 26.2. If he does not respond at all to the Court within 28 days, the claim would simply be stayed (Rule 15.10(3)).

Subject to these exceptions and the preconditions set out below, the claim will be transferred to the defendant's home court whether the claim is issued in the High Court or the County Court as long as—

- the claim is for a **debt**, i.e. for a specified amount of money;
- the claim was commenced in a court which is not the defendant's home court;
- the claim has not already been transferred to another defendant's home court under Rule 13.4 or Rule 14.12 (see below); and
- the defendant is an **individual**.

In accordance with the definition of what is the "defendant's home court", if the proceedings are issued in the High Court then automatic transfer under Rule 26.2 takes place only within the High Court system, that is, between District Registries or between the Royal Courts of Justice and a District Registry. In that event the defendant's home court as defined by Rule 2.3, is the District Registry for the district in which the defendant's address for service, as shown on the defence, is situated, or, if there is no such District Registry, the Royal Courts of Justice.

If the claim is proceeding in a County Court then the defendant's home court is the County Court for the district in which the defendant's address for service as shown on the defence is situated.

It is to be noted that the reference is the address for service shown on the defence. The defendant is not required, however, to put an address for service on the defence if he has filed an acknowledgement of service. If the defence does not have an address, it is suggested that the appropriate address for automatic transfer would be the address in the acknowledgement of service and not, for instance, the address set out in the claim form.

It is to be noted further that in accordance with the definition of home court, the reference is to the address for service rather than any other address such as the defendant's residential address. Accordingly, in accordance with Rule 6.5(3), the appropriate address for determining a home court may be—

- the defendant's solicitor's address;
- the defendant's place of business;
- the defendant's residence.

Which of these will be appropriate will depend, as above, on the defendant nominating one of them as the address for service under Rule 6.5.

In addition to the powers conferred by Part 30, in accordance with Sections 40, 41 and 42 of the County Courts Act 1984, the Court does have certain powers to order transfer of proceedings between the High Court and County Court. Such an order can be made upon the Court's own initiative in accordance with those Sections and Rule 3.3.

If proceedings are commenced in a specialist list then there is no automatic transfer even though the other conditions of Rule 26.2 are fulfilled. Those specialist proceedings are set out in Part 49 broadly as follows—

- Admiralty proceedings
- Arbitration proceedings
- Commercial and Mercantile actions
- Patents Court business
- Technology and Construction Court business
- Proceedings under the Companies Acts
- Contentious Probate proceedings

In relation to such proceedings, however, the Court does have the power to effect transfer in accordance with Part 30 and Sections 40, 41 and 42 of the County Courts Act 1984.

Much debate in the Civil Procedure Rules Committee surrounded the question of proceedings in which there is more than one defendant. As finalised, the position is that if the defendant who files his defence first is an individual, the proceedings will be automatically transferred to the home court of that defendant. This applies whether or not the co-defendants are all individuals or a mixture of individuals and, for instance, companies. If one of the co-defendants is a company and it files its defence first then automatic transfer will not apply although of course the Court may be willing to consider a transfer under Part 30. The automatic transfer should not take place in any event until allocation questionnaires are served (see below).

The Summons Production Centre has slightly different rules. These are contained within the practice direction to Part 7 dated 1 April 1999. Under Paragraph 5.2 of that Practice Direction, if the defendant files a defence to all or part of the claim issued by the Summons Production Centre in Northampton, the Court will serve a notice on the claimant requiring him to notify the Centre within 28 days whether he wishes the claim to proceed. Only on receiving notification to that effect will the Court transfer to the defendant's home court under Rule 26.2. Otherwise the proceedings will be stayed.

In discussion at Committee it was proposed that for the Summons Production Centre the requirement that the defendant had to be an individual as precondition for automatic transfer would not apply. This provision does not appear to have been included in the practice direction although as a matter of practice the Summons Production Centre might put it into effect, thus transferring all cases to the defendant's home court whether or not an individual.

Before effecting the transfer under Rule 26.2, the transferring court will send out to the parties the allocation questionnaire. In accordance with Rule 26.3 it is assumed that where there are two or more defendants the Court will wait until all the defendants have filed a defence or the period for filing the last defence has expired before sending out the allocation questionnaire. The effect of this is that where there are two or more defendants, the transfer to the defendant's home court will not occur until such time as all the defendants have filed a defence or the period for filing the last defence has expired (but see Rule 26.3(5) below).

Allocation Questionnaire

Upon receipt of the defence, the Court will send out to each of the parties an allocation questionnaire (Rule 26.3(1)) unless under Rule 14.5 (admission of part of the claim) a notice has been sent to the claimant requesting him to state whether—

- he accepts the amount admitted in satisfaction of the claim;
- he does not accept the amount admitted by the defendant and wishes the proceedings to continue; or
- if the defendant has requested time to pay, he accepts the amount admitted in satisfaction of the claim but not the defendant's proposal as to payment.

The allocation questionnaire will then only be sent out if the claimant files the notice indicating that he wishes the claim to continue. Similarly, no allocation questionnaire will be sent out if the defendant claims that he has paid the debt and the Court sends out a notice to this effect requiring the claimant to elect whether or not he wishes the proceedings to continue. The allocation questionnaire will only be sent out to the parties if that notice is returned indicating that it does wish the proceedings to continue.

The Court is not obliged to send out allocation questionnaires, retaining the power to dispense with them under Rule 26.3(b). The circumstances in which it might dispense with them include, for instance, if an application for summary judgment has been made which fails, the Court could both dispense with the need for a defence and give immediate case management directions.

If there are two or more defendants, the allocation questionnaire will not be sent out to the parties until such time as—

- all defendants have filed a defence; or

- when the period for filing the last defence has expired;

whichever is the sooner (Rule 26.3(2)).

The effect of this is that if a claimant has difficulty serving one of the defendants or that defendant is out of the jurisdiction, it may be a little time before allocation questionnaires are sent out by the Court. Unless the Court is serving the claim form, the Court's knowledge of when the period for filing the last defence expires will be dependent on the filing of certificates of service under Part 6 by the claimant. Until those certificates of service are filed with the Court, the Court will not send out allocation questionnaires.

The practical aspects of this provision (Rule 26.3(2)) were much debated in the Civil Procedure Rule Committee. The rationale for adopting the approach in the Rules is that allocation questionnaires are sent out to all of the parties at the same time. If the trigger date for that event were to be anything other than when all defences have been filed or the period for filing the last defence has expired, a defendant might receive the allocation questionnaire before the proceedings are served.

In accordance with Rule 15.5, the parties can agree to extend the time for defence by up to 28 days but the defendant is obliged to notify the Court in writing of extensions of time agreed. If the Court is not notified, it will send out the allocation questionnaires upon expiry of the time for defence without the extension.

If the trigger event is the expiry of the period for filing the last defence, the claimant may be able to make an application for a default judgment against the defaulting defendant. If the allocation questionnaire is sent out to the defaulting defendant, it does not in any way interfere with the claimant's right to seek default judgment under Part 12.

Because the provisions of Rule 26.3(2) might cause unnecessary delay in the process, the claimant may apply to the Court to serve allocation questionnaires earlier than it would under Rule 26.3(2). Such an application would be made in accordance with Part 23.

Fee

A fee of £80 is payable by the claimant upon filing the allocation questionnaire. Obviously quite a substantial fee for the smaller claims. If the fee is not paid, the procedure under Rule 3.7 will be adopted by the Court and the claim will be automatically struck out if payment is not made.

The form of questionnaire

The specified form for the questionnaire is form N150. The form is colour coded. It bears the Court seal and apparently the form that is issued by the Court and served on the parties must be completed and returned to the Court although at the moment practice appears to differ from court to court.

It raises ten categories of questions.

A SETTLEMENT

Do you wish there to be a one month stay to attempt to settle the case?

The question is simple as is the answer. The effect, however, of answering one way or the other may not be. In accordance with Rule 26.4, if both parties request a stay, the Court will direct that the proceedings be stayed for one month. If less than all the parties request a stay, the Court can still order a stay if it believes it would be appropriate (Rule 26.4(2)(b)). If a stay is ordered, there would be a positive obligation on the parties to attempt to settle the case. It must be remembered that the conduct of the parties in attempting to settle will be one of the considerations of the Court when it makes its order for costs under Rule 44.3(4) and when the Court decides the amount of any costs awarded under Rule 44.5(3). In that last aspect Rule 44.5(3)(a)(ii) specifically mentions **the efforts made, if any, before and during the proceedings in order to try to resolve the dispute.**

The period of stay that was initially proposed to the Committee was three months. This was considered to be too long and the period of one month has been specified. The Court does, however, have the power to extend the stay as it considers appropriate under Rule 26.4(3). As with the original period, an extension for a stay should only be made if there is a realistic possibility of settling the case in that period.

Rule 26.4(1) refers to attempts to settle the case by alternative dispute resolution or other means. Alternative dispute resolution is one of the explained terms in the glossary. Its place within Rule 26.4(1) is not in any way intended to be mandatory and there is absolutely no reason why attempts to settle the case should not be undertaken in usual negotiations between the parties or their solicitors.

The stay by the Court does provide a useful opportunity for the parties. Often negotiations are difficult to commence because neither party wishes to display any weakness by making the first move. Since the obligation of the party to try and settle the case is emphasised within the Rules generally and particularly by the costs provisions, this shyness to commence negotiation should be removed. Indeed parties might wish to appear to be seen as the most reasonable in attempting to negotiate a settlement.

If settlement is reached during the course of this stage then the claimant is obliged to tell the Court (Rule 26.4(4)).

If the Court is not informed of settlement, the stay will end automatically and the Court will give appropriate case management directions. Prior to the end of the stay the Court will hold back from making case management directions.

B TRACK

Which track do you consider is most suitable for your case?

If you think your case is suitable for a specialist list, say which.

If you have indicated a track which would not be the normal track for the case, please give brief reasons for your choice.

There are notes at the back of the allocation questionnaire which explain the three tracks. There is also available a separate leaflet of explanation. As indicated in the notes to the form, the principal measure for allocation is the money value of the claim.

In short the three tracks are—

- Small Claims Track - claims valued at £5,000 or less unless they include a claim for personal injury (i.e. claims for compensation for pain, suffering and loss of amenity) worth over £1,000; or a claim for housing disrepair where the costs or repairs or other work is more than £1,000 and any other claim for damages is more than £1,000.
- Fast Track - claims valued at no more than £15,000 or above the other limits at the small claims track above.
- Multi Track - claims over £15,000.

The money value of the claim which pre-determines the "normal" track, however, is not the only matter to which the Court will have regard when allocating to a track. Other considerations set out in Rule 26.8 such as the nature of the remedy sought; the likely complexity or the number of parties.

Thus what is the normal track for the case is likely to be determined primarily by the financial value of the claim but when a party completes the questions within Section B of the allocation questionnaire, they may consider the criteria under Rule 26.8 in determining what they consider to be the most suitable track for the case. If they indicate a track which is different from the "normal track" as determined by the financial value, the allocation questionnaire raises the question of why they have chosen that different track and ask that brief reasons be given for the choice. Bearing in mind that these reasons have to be set out briefly, the parties should concentrate on the aspects of the case which might affect allocation in accordance with Rule 26.8. The Practice Direction (Paragraph 2.2) provides for further information to be given to the Court relevant to allocation or case management. That further information will be taken into account by the Court as long as it is agreed with the other parties or the document containing it (i.e. usually the allocation questionnaire) has been delivered to the other parties. The practice direction gives examples of information that may assist the

Court. The defendant, for instance, may indicate that they are proposing to issue (with the permission of the Court) a Part 20 claim or will seek to add another party.

Rule 26.8 is directive in that the Court "shall" have regard to the matters set out in it. One of those matters is the views expressed by the parties. If the proceedings have been commenced in a specialist list as set out in Part 49, there may be either no allocation questionnaire (such as in the Commercial Court) or the allocation questionnaire is modified (such as in the Technology & Construction Court). Modified forms are annexed to the practice directions to Part 49. If a case is not proceeding in the specialist list set out in Part 49 and the party believes that it should be, then it must indicate to that effect on the allocation questionnaire in Section B.

C PRE-ACTION PROTOCOLS

Have you complied with any pre-action protocol applicable to your claim?

If Yes, please say which protocol.

If No, please explain to what extent and for what reason it has not been complied with.

Failure to comply with a pre-action protocol may have costs and other consequences. One of the reasons for failure to comply may well be the impending expiry of a limitation period. In that event the Court might consider staying the proceedings, exercising its power under Rule 3.1(2)(f) to allow the parties time to comply with the procedure set out in the applicable pre-action protocol.

Whatever be the reasons for failure to comply, they will have to be set out in Section C of the allocation questionnaire.

D APPLICATIONS

If you have not already sent the court an application for summary judgment, do you intend to do so?

If you have not already issued a claim in the case against someone not yet a party, do you intend to apply for the court's permission to do so?

In either case, if Yes, please give details.

The first question addresses the intention of either of the parties to make an application for summary judgment (see Chapter 14). Such an application is specifically mentioned as one of the points at which the Court should be informed under the Practice Direction to Part 26 (Paragraph 2.2(3)(a)). As well as an application for summary judgment, the Court should be informed also of any other applications that might dispose of the case, reduce the amount in dispute or the number of issues remaining to be decided - such as an application to strike out all or part of the statement of case under Rule 3.4. If either party indicates an intention to make such an application but has not done so at the time of filing the allocation questionnaire, the Court will usually direct that an allocation hearing be listed. The application may then be heard at that hearing as long as an application notice is issued and served in sufficient time (Paragraph 5.3, Practice Direction to Part 26).

In similar vein, if a party indicates in response to the second question that they are proposing to issue a claim in a case against someone not yet a party, the Court will usually set an allocation hearing and the application will be heard at it as long as the application notice is issued and, if necessary, served within sufficient time.

E WITNESSES OF FACT

So far as you know at this stage, what witnesses of fact do you intend to call at the hearing?

One of the factors to be taken into account by the Court in allocation is the amount of oral evidence that may be required for the hearing or trial. The questionnaire requires some detail as to names of witnesses and the facts to which they will give evidence. The requirement emphasises the necessity for early preparation of cases to the extent of early identification of witnesses.

The amount of oral evidence will be an important determining factor as to the appropriate track, particularly in the determination between fast track and multi track. In the former the trial can take no longer than one business day of the Court's time.

F EXPERT EVIDENCE

Do you wish to use expert evidence at the hearing?

Have you already copied any experts' report(s) to the other party(ies)?

The question of whether experts will be needed for the claim should be closely considered at this stage. In accordance with Rule 35.4, no party may call an expert or put in evidence an expert's report without the

Court's permission. That permission will be considered upon allocation of the trial to a track and in the giving of directions consequent upon that allocation.

There is a differentiation made in the questionnaire as to expert evidence which will be in writing under Rule 35.5 and any oral testimony given at trial which will require the Court's further express permission. In the small claims track it will be unusual for the Court to allow any expert evidence whether written or oral; in the fast track expert evidence will usually be in writing only; and in the multi track expert evidence will initially be in writing but may then be given orally at the hearing subject to appropriate permission. In addition parties will have to give consideration as to whether the Court will make an order (particularly in the fast track) that there should be a single jointly instructed expert in accordance with Rule 35.7.

G LOCATION OF TRIAL

Is there any reason why your case needs to be heard at a particular court?

If Yes, give reasons (e.g. Particular facilities required, convenience of witnesses, etc.)

And specify the court.

The trial of a claim will usually take place at the Court which has conduct of the proceedings or the relevant trial centre for that Court. There may be reasons related to the circumstances of one of the parties such as a disability that might sway the Court to consider holding the trial at another Court or trial centre. The power of the Court to do so derives from its general powers of case management under Rule 3.1. In exercising that power the Court will give consideration to the overriding objective, particularly Rule 1.1(2), by which, for instance, the Court has to ensure that the parties are on an equal footing. This may lead the Court to directing that the trial or final hearing should take place on premises other than that Court or trial centre.

The alternative to relocating the final hearing or trial would be to transfer the whole of the case under Part 30 to another Court in order to meet the representation in relation to location. Such a transfer could be promoted by the party by making an appropriate application under Part 30.

H REPRESENTATION AND ESTIMATE OF HEARING / TRIAL TIME

Do you expect to be represented by a solicitor or counsel at the hearing/trial?

How long do you estimate it will take to put your case to the court at the hearing/trial?

If there are any days when you, your representative, expert, or an essential witness will not be able to attend court, give details.

The likely length of the trial could have a substantial effect upon the allocation to a track. In particular it may make the difference between the allocation of a claim between fast track and multi track. In fast track cases the trial can last no longer than a day. If the Court accepts that the trial is going to last longer than a day then the case must be allocated to the multi track. The Court does not have to accept the representations as to the estimates of trial time and it is likely that the Court will impose the fast track on parties notwithstanding their representations as to the length of the trial.

This section of the allocation questionnaire also deals with the availability of representatives, experts and essential witnesses. In practice the fixing of dates for experts to attend Court is always difficult. Experts whom often give evidence to the Court will have limited availability for long periods of time. The Court will take the availability of experts into account in fixing dates for trial. It must be remembered, however, that generally expert evidence will not be allowed in claims in the small claims track. Even if expert evidence is permitted, it is highly unlikely that the Court will allow an expert witness to give oral evidence at the final hearing. Similarly in fast track expert evidence will be allowed in writing but there will be restrictions on experts giving oral evidence. Further in relation to fast track cases, the Court will be exercising its power under Rule 35.7 to appoint single and jointly instructed experts (see above).

I COSTS

What is your estimate of costs incurred to date, excluding disbursements, VAT and court fees?

What do you estimate the overall costs are likely to be, excluding disbursements, VAT and court fees?

The provision by legal representatives of estimates of costs during the course of the proceedings was a relatively late insertion in the Rules and

Practice Directions. In the autumn of 1998 the Committee discussed an "issues paper" which raised the question of legal representatives providing such estimates. It was suggested that in certain circumstances those estimates would be binding on the legal representatives. A consultation paper was proposed. In the event there was no consultation prior to 26 April 1999 and the changes to the Rules and Practice Directions in relation to the provision of estimates were inserted without further public consultation. In the short term they are not, however, as extensive as proposed and there is no provision that those estimates are binding upon the legal representative as to the recoverable costs. The relevant part of the Rules and Practice Directions is Section 4 of the Practice Direction to Part 43.

Neither Section I of the allocation questionnaire nor the notes for completing it indicate whether the estimate for costs is based on what might be expected to be recovered from the other party or what might be expected to be recovered between solicitor and client. Paragraph 4.2 of the Practice Direction, however, indicates that in Section 4 the estimate to be provided relates to the costs which a party, if successful, would seek to recover from any other party under an order for costs. It is a little unclear from Section 4 whether the reference to the estimate in Paragraph 4.2 is to the estimate given in the allocation questionnaire or to a separate statement. It is suggested that whether or not it is a reference to a separate statement (see below), the figures to be inserted in the allocation questionnaire are indeed costs recoverable party and party rather than between the solicitor and client.

Paragraph 4.5 of the Practice Direction requires that—

When a party to a claim which is outside the financial scope of the small claims track files an allocation questionnaire, he must also file an estimate of costs and serve a copy of it on every other party unless the Court otherwise directs.

This appears to require serving of a separate estimate of costs over and above the figures contained within the allocation questionnaire. Under Paragraph 4.4 of the same Practice Direction an estimate of costs is to find as a form of a statement of costs as illustrated in form one of the schedule of costs form. That form is the form used for summary assessment and gives relatively detailed breakdown of the costs. The estimate broken down in this way, relates not only to costs incurred to date but also to the overall costs likely to be incurred.

It is a little unclear between the allocation questionnaire and the Practice Direction as to what costs have to be included in the estimate. The allocation questionnaire specifically asks that the party exclude disbursements, VAT and court fees from the estimate. The Practice Direction by its reference to Costs Form One requires the inclusion of disbursements, VAT and court fees since these are included in the breakdown in Costs Form One. It is suggested that the two figures will simply have to differ although it is difficult to see the rationale for this difference.

One of the other slight conflicts between the allocation questionnaire and the Practice Direction is that the allocation questionnaire does not suggest that estimates of costs should not be given for claims outside the financial scope of the small claims track but Paragraph 4.5 (1) (as above) provides specifically to that effect. One can see that the reason for the Practice Direction is that the question of recovery of costs may be largely academic in a small claims track case although some limited costs are recoverable in accordance with Rule 27.14.

What then is the reason for the provision of estimates of costs in relation to the general management of the case by the Court? The overall rationale to add a greater degree of predictability to the process of costs is that parties can measure the likely outcome of the case as it proceeds. Under Paragraph 4.1 of the Practice Direction the provision of estimates is stated to have two reasons—

- to keep other parties informed about their potential liability in respect of costs; and
- to assist the Court to decide what, if any, order to make that costs and the bad case management.

Solicitors will have to be careful about the estimate of costs they give on the basis of the first reason for providing them. Solicitors must ensure that the estimates that are given are rational and as far as possible accurate. Providing highly inaccurate figures would undermine the Rules for giving them. Inaccuracy might be used at some subsequent point by the other party in relation to either orders for costs or the quantification.

The manner in which the estimates are likely to affect case management, for example, would be that if the Court felt that costs were in some way going beyond what was reasonable and proportionate, the further steps to be taken by the parties may be limited to try and ensure that costs remain within the band of reasonableness and proportionality.

As a matter of practice, therefore, the solicitor will have to complete the allocation questionnaire and provide a separate statement of estimates for costs in the form of the costs form one.

J OTHER INFORMATION

Have you attached documents you wish the judge to take into account when allocating the case?

Have they been served on the other parties?

If Yes, say when.

Have the other parties agreed their content?

Have you attached a list of the directions you think appropriate for the management of your case?

Are they agreed with the other parties?

Are there any other facts which might affect the timetable the court will set? If so, please state.

This is the section of the allocation questionnaire in which the party can provide the Court with extra information that he believes may affect its decision about the allocation or case management. The manner in which this is done is set out in the Practice Direction to Part 26 (Paragraph 2.2). Some of this information will already have been dealt with - for instance, whether or not a party intends to make an application to the Court.

In relation to any other information the Practice Direction (Paragraph 2.2) provides that generally it will only be taken into account if —

- all parties have agreed the information and that it should be before the Court; or
- the additional information has been supplied to all other parties.

As a result of the other information, the Court may decide that it is desirable to have an allocation hearing or a hearing on which case management directions would be given (Paragraph 2.2(3)(f), Practice Direction to Part 26).

This section of the allocation questionnaire also asks whether the party has proposals for directions and whether these have been agreed with the other parties. Paragraph 2.3 of the Practice Direction encourages the parties to consult with one another and to co-operate in completing the allocation questionnaire and giving other information to the Court. In particular the parties are encouraged to try and degree case management directions which they believe appropriate for the Court to make. In both fast track (Part 28) and multi track (Part 29) the parties are further encouraged to try and agree directions. Paragraph 3.5 of the Practice Direction to Part 28 provides that—

If:

(1) the parties have filed agreed directions for the management of the case, and

(2) the court considers that the proposals are suitable, it may approve them and give directions in the terms proposed.

Paragraph 3.6 provides specific directions that should be agreed.

- Timetable for the taking of steps for the preparation of the case.
- Date or a period (no more than 3 weeks) when it is proposed the trial will take place. That date or period can be no later than 30 weeks after the directions order is made.
- Provide appropriately for disclosure of documents whether or not by list.

- The provision and exchange of expert evidence (if any) which could specifically deal with the appointment of a single joint expert.
- The provision and exchange of factual evidence.
- The filing and service of any further statements of case including amendments.
- Questions to experts under Rule 35.6.

The Court is not obliged to accept the agreed directions but will take them into account when giving directions (Paragraph 3.8, Practice Direction to Part 28).

Rule 29.4 and paragraphs 4.6, 4.7 and 4.8 of the Practice Direction to Part 29 provide in similar fashion for multi track cases. In the multi track there is no requirement for setting of a trial date or trial period within the 30 week period mentioned above.

The allocation questionnaire has to be returned to the Court no later than the date specified within it which must be at least 14 days upon the date on which it is deemed to be served by the Court to the party in question (Rule 26.3(6)). A fee of £80 is payable by the claimant on the filing of the questionnaire. If this fee is not paid, the claim may be struck out under Rule 3.7.

If a party fails to return the allocation questionnaire within the time, the Court file will be referred to a Judge for directions. Those directions will usually be to the effect that unless an allocation questionnaire is filed within three days from service of the order, the claim and any counterclaim will be struck out (Paragraph 2.5(1), Practice Direction to Part 26).

If less than all the parties file allocation questionnaire the Court can proceed immediately to allocate the claim to a track or list a hearing and require the parties to attend (Paragraph 2.5(2), Practice Direction to Part 26).

Allocation cannot take place until—

every defendant has filed an allocation questionnaire; or

the period for filing the allocation questionnaire has expired

whichever is sooner unless proceedings were stayed under Rule 26.4 (see above) or the Court has dispensed with the need for allocation questionnaires.

If a party does not file an allocation questionnaire and the Court does set a date for a hearing, the defaulting parties may be ordered to pay the costs of any other party attending on an indemnity basis. Those costs will be summarily assessed and payable within 14 days under Rule 44.8. The Court may also order that if the party does not pay the costs within the time stated, his statement of case will be struck out (Paragraph 6.6(2), Practice Direction Part 26). If at the allocation hearing fixed as a result of the default the party in default has still not filed the allocation questionnaire and does not attend the hearing, the Court will usually make an "unless order" to the effect that if an allocation questionnaire is not filed within a certain period, his statement of case will be struck out (Paragraph 6.6(3) Practice Direction Part 26).

Before allocation the Court can require the parties to give further information (Rule 26.5(3)). It might be required, for instance, to justify any statement of value that they have given in relation to the claim. If that information is not given by the party, a hearing can be fixed for which the defaulting party may be required to pay the costs of any other party attending on an indemnity basis. Again these will be summarily assessed and payable within 14 days failing which (subject to order) the statement of case may be struck out. If at such a hearing the information has still not been provided, the Court will usually make an unless order requiring the provision of the information by a certain date failing which the statement of case may be struck out (Paragraph 6.6, Practice Direction to Part 26).

The process of allocation will have to await the termination of any period of a stay given under Rule 26.4. At the end of such a period the Court will usually deal with allocation.

Allocation following an "interim" judgment

Paragraph 12 of the Practice Direction to Part 26 sets out the procedure for allocating a claim to a track and the giving of directions following the making of a "relevant order". A relevant order for these purposes is an order for an amount of damages or interest to be decided, an order for the taking of an account or the making of an enquiry as to any sum due or any similar order (Paragraph 12.1(3), Practice Direction to Part 26) which is made on—

- judgment in default under Part 12;
- judgment on an admission under Part 14;
- the striking out of a statement of case under Part 3;
- summary judgment under Part 24;
- the determination of a preliminary issue or a trial as to liability; or
- a trial.

Often such orders will follow a judicial hearing. Upon making such an order at such a hearing the Court should consider allocation and directions.

Under Part 24, for instance, this is provided in Rule 24.6. Under Part 12 it is provided in Rule 12.7 and in Part 14 in Rule 14.8. The claim may already have been allocated to a track in which case the Court could consider reallocating the claim. If it has not been allocated then the Court could consider allocating but before doing so require that allocation questionnaires should be filed with the Court (Paragraph 12.2(1)).

Paragraph 12.3, however, suggests—

> **Where a claim has not been allocated to a track at the time the relevant order is made, the Court will not normally consider it to be appropriate to allocate it to a track (other than the small claims track) unless the amount payable appears to be genuinely disputed on grounds which appear to be substantial. It may instead direct that a disposal hearing (referred to in Paragraph 12.8) be listed.**

Under both paragraphs 12.6 and 12.7 of the Practice Direction the Court is firstly encouraged to list a disposal hearing where judgment is entered on admissions without a hearing under Part 14 and **required** to list such a disposal hearing if a judgment is entered in default under Part 12 without a hearing.

Allocation

As above, when either every **defendant** has filed an allocation questionnaire or the period for filing the allocation questionnaire has expired, the Court will allocate the claim to a track subject to obtaining any further necessary information (as above) requested either by writing or at an allocation hearing (Rule 26.5).

Rule 26.8 sets out the considerations relevant to the allocation to a track. In its original form this was partly lifted from the list in article 7 of the High Court and County Courts Jurisdiction Order 1991. The Practice Direction then provides a little more assistance as to those matters.

- Financial value, if any, of the claim.

The question of the financial value of the claim maybe a hotly contested issue since it will be the pre-determinant factor to be taken into account when allocating to a track. Under Rule 26.8(2) it is for the Court to assess the financial value of the claim. In doing that it will disregard—

- any amount not in dispute;
- any claim for interest;
- costs;
- any contributory negligence.

The first matter to be disregarded is causing some concern. It is considered that a defendant could tactically admit part of the claim to take it below, for instance, the threshold for the small claims track and thereby have the matter dealt with in that track with the consequent effect that there will be severe limits on recoverable costs in accordance with Rule 27.14. Rule 44.9 provides that after a claim is allocated to a particular track, the special Rules relating to costs generally applies to the period before, as well as after, allocation.

If part of the claim is admitted in accordance with Part 14 then the claimant can, before allocation, apply for judgment with costs on the amount of the claim that has been admitted (see Paragraph 7.4, Practice Direction Part 26).

Further, by Paragraph 5.1(3) of the Practice Direction to Part 44, if a claim is issued for a sum in excess of the normal financial scope of the small claims track, it is allocated to that track following an admission of part of the claim by the defendant on entering judgment for the admitted part the Court may allow costs in respect of the proceedings down to that date.

It is suggested that this does not meet fully the concern that practitioners have of tactical admissions of part of the claim but goes some way to do so. In many cases it may be that an admission of part of the claim, in any event, opens the way for a claim to obtain summary judgment or other early disposal. In that event an application for summary judgment for the amount in dispute should be made prior to allocation. If then an order is made giving summary judgment for (by way of example) damages to be assessed, the case may not be allocated (as above) and proceed quickly to a disposal hearing. Then costs would be an open issue.

The reference to disregarding interest under Rule26.8(2)(b) does not include capitalised interest included in the claim.

It will be noted that the reference in Rule 26.8(1)(a) is to the financial value of the claim. This includes not only the amount of damages that may be claimed but also other measures of value. For instance, in an intellectual property claim the damages might be limited but the overall value of the claim could be very substantial.

If there are two or more claims in the proceedings and each claimant has a claim against the defendant separate from the other claims, the Court considers each of them separately when it assesses its financial value (Rule 26.8(3)). If there are two or more claims, this may be a relevant factor for the Court to take into consideration on allocation in any event. The effect of this provision is that where there is more than one claimant in a claim and each claimant has a separate cause of action claims should not be aggregated for the purposes of allocation. Thus if four claimants each had a claim for £4,000 based upon separate causes of action although the defendant would be facing a total claim of £16,000 the Court would still be empowered to allocate the claim to the small claims track. This would not limit the ability of the Court upon, say, the application of the defendant to allocate to a different track if it thought it appropriate. In these circumstances the appropriate track may be the multi track if only because the trial may be likely to last more than a day.

If there is only one claimant and his claim is based upon two or more courses of action the financial value of those claims will be aggregated for the purposes of allocation.

If a claim has no financial value the Court will allocate to the track which it considers most suitable having regard to the remaining factors set out in Rule 26.8(1) (26.7(2)).

As above the Court has discretion in assessing the value of the claim under Rule 26.8(2). In that assessment it may ask for further information under Rule 26.5(3) and indeed as mentioned in the Practice Direction (Paragraph 7.3(2)) either party may be required to justify the value that they placed on the claim. It will be remembered that under Rule 16.3 the claimant has to put to a statement of value in the claim form and under Rule 16.5(6) if the defendant disputes the claimant's statement of value then they must state why they dispute it and give their own statement of value of the claim. If there is a remaining dispute which bears upon allocation to a track the Court could fix an allocation hearing for the dispute to be resolved.

Note that the exaggeration of a claim is one of the express factors to be taken into account in relation to costs under Rule 44.3(5)(d).

Having assessed the financial value of the claim the Court will also consider the remaining factors listed in Rule 26.8(1). Subject to those (see below) the Court will allocate the claim to a track in accordance with the scope of those tracks under Rule 26.6:

26.6 (1) The small claims track is the normal track for—

(a) any claim for personal injuries where—

(i) the financial value of the claim is not more than £5,000; and

(ii) the financial value of any claim for damages for personal injuries is not more than £1,000;

(b) any claim which includes a claim by a tenant of residential premises against his landlord where—

(i) the tenant is seeking an order requiring the landlord to carry out repairs or other work to the premises (whether or not the tenant is also seeking some other remedy);

(ii) the cost of the repairs or other work to the premises is estimated to be not more than £1,000; and

(iii) the financial value of any other claim for damages is not more than £1,000.

(Rule 2.3 defines "claim for personal injuries" as proceedings in which there is a claim for damages in respect of personal injuries to the claimant or any other person or in respect of a person's death)

(2) For the purposes of paragraph (1) "damages for personal injuries" means damages claimed as compensation for pain, suffering, and loss of amenity and does not include any other damages which are claimed.

(3) Subject to paragraph (1), the small claims track is the normal track for any claim which has a financial value of not more than £5,000.

(Rule 26.7 (4) provides that the court will not allocate to the small claims track certain claims in respect of harassment or unlawful eviction)

(4) Subject to paragraph (5), the fast track is the normal track for any claim—

(a) for which the small claims track is not the normal track; and

(b) which has a financial value of not more than £15,000.

(5) The fast track is the normal track for the claims referred to in paragraph (4) only if the court considers that—

(a) the trial is likely to last for no longer than one day; and

(b) oral expert evidence at trial will be limited to—

(i) one expert per party in relation to any expert field; and

(ii) expert evidence in two expert fields.

(6) The multi-track is the normal track for any claim for which the small claims track or the fast track is not the normal track.

Thus the financial value of the claim as assessed by the Court determines what is the "normal" track. Under Rule 26.7(3) once the Court has assessed the value and determined what would be the normal track for the claim it cannot allocate it to any lower track without the consent of the parties. Thus if a claim is assessed at £6,000 the Court cannot, whatever other factors apply allocate the claim to a small claims track without the consent of the parties. If the normal track would have been the fast track but the parties consent to the claim proceeding in the small claims track Rule 27.14(5) provides that the no costs Rule under Part 27 (Small Claims Track) is dis-applied and subject to certain limitations the parties can recover costs as though the claim proceeded in the fast track. It should be noted that there is no similar provision as between the multi track and fast track.

Although the Court cannot allocate a claim to a track which is not the normal track it can design and apply appropriate directions which would be more simplified version of the directions it would normally have given for that particular track.

Both the terms "a claim for personal injuries" and "damages for personal injuries" are defined (in the former case by reference back to Rule 2.3) within Rule 26.6. It is important to understand the interplay between the two definitions. Under the definition for a claim for personal injuries any proceedings in which there is included a claim for personal injuries becomes a claim for personal injuries for these purposes. The definition of damages for personal injuries specifically limited to general damages for pain, suffering and loss of amenity. It does not include consequential losses (eg, loss of earnings). The rationale behind this limitation is that if one included consequential losses within general damages for these purposes claims would be even more rarely under £1,000. Although practitioners differ in their view the reason for providing a special limit for personal injury claim arises from the more complex nature of and the requirement of specialist evidence for the claim for pain and suffering and loss of amenity.

Thus looking at the financial value of the claim as a whole one takes into account not only the claim relating to the personal injuries, but for instance, the claim relating to damage to a vehicle in a road traffic accident if that be the nature of the claim. If the claim arises from a road traffic accident and the claims relating to the personal injuries including general damages for pain suffering and loss of amenity and consequential losses is less than £5,000, but when aggregated with a claim relating to damage to the vehicle takes the claim over £5,000 as assessed by the Court the small claims track would not be the normal track. If that aggregate is less than £5,000 but any claim for pain suffering and loss of amenity is itself in excess of £1,000 the normal track will, again, not be the small claims track.

The value of the claim may predetermine whether the action proceeds in the County Court or High Court. No proceedings for a value of no more than £15,000 can be issued in the High Court and it is likely that any claims above that value but with a value of less than £50,000 will be transferred out of the High Court to the County Court. The reader is also referred to the High Court and County Courts Jurisdiction Order 1991 and the County Court Remedies Regulations 1991.

If the claim has no financial value then the Court will allocate to the track **which it considers most suitable having regard to the matters mentioned in Rule 26.8(1) and Rule 26.7(2). The list is not exclusive however and the Court could take into account any other relevant factors.**

The nature of the remedy sought

There is one specific limitation which predetermines that a claim cannot be allocated to the small claims track based upon the nature of the remedy. This is contained in Rule 26.7(4) and provides—

(4) The court will not allocate a claim to the small claims track, if it includes a claim by a tenant of residential premises against his landlord for a remedy in respect of harassment or unlawful eviction.

The reference in this Rule is to the nature of the remedy sought but the Court may also wish to take into account the nature of the claim and the issues to be decided within it. The nature of the claim may in any event predetermine that it should proceed in the specialists lists such as the Technology and Construction Court or the Commercial Court. This will have a knock on effect both on where the proceedings are issued and its allocation to a track. Subject to the question of whether a claim falls within specialist proceedings there is a specific example given in the Practice Direction as to when the nature of the claim and the issues to be decided does have an effect upon allocation. Paragraph 8.1(1)(d) of the Practice Direction (Part 26) provides that where a case involves a disputed allegation of dishonesty the small claims track will not usually be the suitable track. Paragraph 8.1 of the Practice Direction goes on to give examples of cases which are generally suitable for the small claims track (subject to the financial limitations above)—

- consumer disputes
- accident claims
- disputes about the ownership of goods
- most disputes between a landlord and tenant other than those for possession

Although the nature of the remedy is an important factor in allocation under Rule 27.3 the Court may grant any final remedy (not an interim remedy save an injunction) in relation to a claim proceeding in the small claims track (Rule 27.3).

The nature of the remedy sought, the issues involved (and as above) the value of the claim may predetermine the Court in which the matter proceeds. The reader is referred to the High Court and County Court Jurisdiction Order 1991 and the County Court Remedies Regulations 1991.

The number of parties or likely parties

At the time of writing special Rules in relation to multi party actions are in contemplation. It is likely that these will be finalised to come into effect some time in 2000.

The value of any Counterclaim or other Part 20 Claim and the complexity of any matters relating to it

Rule 20.3(2)(c) specifically excludes Part 26 from Part 20 claims. Thus there was no provision for "normal" track for Part 20 claim under Rule 26.6. Rule 26.8(1) fills the gap and allows the Court to take into consideration the Part 20 claim including a counterclaim. Rule 26.8(1) (e) refers specifically to its value or the complexity of any matters relating to it. The Court may also take into account other factors under Rule 26.8(1) when considering the Part 20 claim such as the nature of the remedy sought.

As indicated under Paragraph 7.7 of the Practice Direction Part 26 when the Court is considering thc counterclaim or other Part 20 claim it will not generally aggregate claims but deal with them separately. Factors relating to the Part 20 claim may determine allocation. For instance if the value of the counterclaim is larger than the claim generally the Court will allocate to a track in accordance with that value. Similarly if the counterclaim gives rise to greater complexity of facts, law or evidence these may determine the appropriate track. This is, however, not a hard and fast Rule and one of the reasons why Part 20 claims have been excluded from the more formal process of allocation is to give some discretion to the Court to ensure that a claim is not hi-jacked from one track to another by a defendant and Part 20 claimant. Thus if a claimant issues a claim which would normally be allocated to the small claims track the Court could still allocate to the small claims track whatever the value of any Part 20 claim. Whatever track to which the claim and, on its coat tails, the Part 20 claim are allocated the Court retains a discretion in relation to the case management directions and could manage the Counterclaim in appropriate fashion bearing in mind its value or complexity. It may, for instance, provide for more extensive disclosure and inspection of documents than usually apply in the small claims track. Otherwise upon allocation the Rules that relate specifically to the track will apply to both the claim and the Part 20 claim including, for instance, those relating to costs.

The views expressed by the parties

The parties in fulfilment of their obligation to co-operate under the Rules could express common view that the claim should be allocated to a particular track. As above whilst the Court is not entitled to allocate to a lower track than that which would be the normal track for a claim of a particular financial value the parties could consent to that allocation to a lower track.

The parties may also express a common or individual issue as to allocation to a higher track. As Paragraph 7.5 of the Practice Direction indicates although the Court will take expressed views into account it is not bound by them.

The circumstances of the parties

This provision within Rule 26.8(1)(i) touches upon (but not only) the financial position of the parties. This factor must be taken into account in any event under the overriding objective in fulfilment of the Courts obligation to deal with cases justly (Rule 1.1(2)). Thus the Court is obliged to ensure that so far as practicable the parties are on an equal footing and that the case is dealt with in ways which are proportionate to the financial position of each party. It must be remembered however, that whatever the financial position of each of the parties the Court cannot allocate a claim to a lower track than the normal track having assessed the financial value whatever be the financial circumstances of the parties. The Court can, however, deal with case management in an appropriate fashion which may take into account the financial circumstances of the parties under Rule 1.1(2).

Other circumstances that the Court may wish to take into account could be a disability which would make the small claims track inappropriate as the party affected may have difficulty conducting their own case. It may in the circumstances serve the overriding objective that they should be allowed greater freedom to obtain legal representation with the opportunity of recovery of the costs of it.

The overriding objective

Subject to the limitation of the Courts power to allocate to a lower track without the consent of the parties the Court will have in mind the overriding objective when exercising its discretion on allocation as it was required to do under Rule 1.2. Thus proportionality will be a major consideration. The Court will also take into account under Rule 1.1(2)(e) the allotment of an appropriate share of the Courts resources to the claim whilst taking into account the need to allot resources to other cases. If, for example, the normal track for the claim would be the fast track with its limitation of one day for trial but the parties either individually or in common express the view that the trial will last more than one day the Court may consider allocating the claim to the fast track limiting the length of trial to one day notwithstanding the representations of the parties.

Even if the Court is obliged to allocate to the normal track it must take into account the overriding objective in exercising its powers and discretion relating to case management.

Notice of allocation and reallocation

Upon allocating to a track the Court will complete and serve a notice of allocation on every party. The notice is in Forms N154 (fast track), N155 (multi-track) or N157–160 (small claims).

Unless the Court has allocated in accordance with the expressed wishes of all the parties filing allocation questionnaires it will, in the notice of allocation, give brief reasons for the allocation decision (Paragraph 4.2(4), Practice Direction Part 26).

Together with the notice of allocation the Court will also send to the parties copies of the allocation questionnaire filed by the other parties together with copies of other information provided by the parties either voluntarily or upon the Courts request. There is no obligation on the parties to serve the responses to the allocation questionnaires on other parties although in completing the questionnaires the parties should consult with one another and co-operate (Paragraph 2.3(1), Practice Direction Part 26). It may well be the case, therefore, that the first time that a party will see the other party's responses to the allocation questionnaire will be when they are served by the Court. If the Court has decided upon allocation based upon a particular factor set out in one of the questionnaires a party would want the opportunity to object to allocation on that factor if it felt it to be inaccurate. The allocation could be appealed to a Judge. Undercurrent appeal procedure such an appeal is a rehearing. This means that the Judge can exercise afresh the Courts discretion on allocation.

The alternative is for an application to be made in accordance with Part 23 for reallocation to a different track.

In either case it has to be said that the Court will not encourage satellite litigation over the question of allocation.

CHAPTER 16
PART 27—SMALL CLAIMS TRACK

Introduction

The small claims track did not receive much attention from Lord Woolf in his Final Report but he did cover some aspects of it in the Interim Report. The rationale behind this lack of consideration for small claims lay with the perceived success of the small claims procedure in the County Court under the then existing arbitration process.

Lord Woolf's recommendations in the Interim Report were to enhance the system and take its apparent success forward. He recommended that the limit of small claims should be raised to £3,000 from the then £1,000 and subsequently to £5,000 after monitoring the results. This resulted in the increase in the limit for small claims to £3,000 in January 1996.

Lord Woolf was not without some criticism of the system and particularly the lack of consistency from court to court when District Judges sat as arbitrators under the small claims procedure. The result was that a protocol for the conduct of small claims arbitrations was developed by the Judicial Studies Board and the Association of District Judges.

Lord Woolf made a number of recommendations which had not been implemented at the time that his Final Report was published in July 1996 and he repeated them as recommendations numbered 274-280 at page 324 of the Final Report.

In the event the Rules for the small claims track have developed into a final form which excludes some of the ideas that Lord Woolf had for the track. In particular, the small claims track is no longer likened to an arbitration process as was originally suggested. All references to arbitration have been excluded since although the word was used to give an air of informality to the process, it has few of the essential characteristics of true arbitrations such as those to which the Arbitration Act 1996 applies. Until quite late in the day the only continuing reference to arbitration was contained in a draft rule concerning the power of the Court to appoint an outside arbitrator to determine issues. Although the Court retains this power under Section 64 of the County Courts Act 1984, there is no continuing reference to it within the Rules relating to the small claims track.

It is vitally important to remember that a claim is not a small claim for the purposes of Part 27 until after allocation to the small claims track. Accordingly the restrictions on procedure and costs contained within the small claims track do not apply to any proceedings whatever their value until such time as the claim is allocated to the small claims track. Prior to that date, for instance, interim remedies can be sought from the Court under Part 25. Similarly, further information may be sought by one party against another under Part 18.

Whether or not the Court makes such orders in relation to a claim (the value of which would normally determine that it will be allocated to the small claims track) must, however, be in some doubt. The Court will certainly have consideration to the overriding objective and such applications and orders may well be considered inappropriate being disproportionate to, for instance, the amount of money involved in the case under Rule 1.1(2)(c)(i). Although the Parts in question are not excluded until allocation, the Court will certainly take into account the fact that they would be excluded following allocation when considering applications for such orders.

As detailed in Part 26, the Court will not allocate a claim to a track whilst it remains possible that some of the issues apparently in contention may be decided summarily. The allocation questionnaire raises directly the question of whether the parties intend to make an application, for instance, for summary judgment. If that question is answered in the positive, the Court will set a date for hearing and the potential applicant will have to issue an application returnable on that date and comply generally with Part 24.

Allocation

The considerations the Court will take into account when allocating a claim to a track under Rule 26.8 have been dealt with at length in the chapter relating to Part 26. In allocation to the small claims track the primary consideration is going to be the financial value of the claim. The Court will have consideration, however, for the other factors set out in Rule 26.8(1).

Bearing in mind the simplified nature of the procedure, the specific requirement that the hearing should be informal and the no costs rule may make the small claims track inappropriate for many claims in which it would otherwise be the normal track based upon the financial value. It may be inappropriate, for instance, in relation to a claim which is of significant public interest or a claim the resolution of which would have a wide ranging effect upon persons who are not parties (such as a test case).

The circumstances of the parties may also make the small claims track inappropriate. The service of the obligations under the overriding objective in Part 1 (and particularly ensuring that the parties are on an equal footing) might lead the Court to conclude that a party with a disability should have the greatest opportunity to obtain legal assistance that the potential for recovery of costs might give.

Readers are reminded of the elements of a claim which a Court will disregard when assessing its financial value—

- any amount not in dispute;
- any claim for interest;

- costs; and
- any contributory negligence.

As detailed in the previous chapter, the deduction from the financial value of amounts admitted by a defendant could allow tactical admissions by a defendant to reduce the claim to a figure below £5,000, thus taking advantage of the no costs rule under Part 27. As detailed previously, some measures towards defeating this tactical move have been taken within the Rules themselves. Readers are referred to Paragraph 7.4 (Practice Direction to Part 26) and Paragraph 5.1(3) (Practice Direction to Part 44), the combination of which could allow the Court to make an order entering judgment for the amount admitted and all the costs in respect of the proceedings - to the date of such judgment.

Further, the Court is bound to have some view of tactical admissions. Upon sight of such tactics the Court retains the discretion to allocate the claim to the fast track notwithstanding that the normal track would be the small claims track.

Scope of the Small Claims Track

Rule 26.6(1), (2) and (3) sets out the criteria based upon the financial value of the claim for the small claims track.

26.6 (1) The small claims track is the normal track for—

(a) any claim for personal injuries where—

(i) the financial value of the claim is not more than £5,000; and

(ii) the financial value of any claim for damages for personal injuries is not more than £1,000;

(b) any claim which includes a claim by a tenant of residential premises against his landlord where—

(i) the tenant is seeking an order requiring the landlord to carry out repairs or other work to the premises (whether or not the tenant is also seeking some other remedy);

(ii) the cost of the repairs or other work to the premises is estimated to be not more than £1,000; and

(iii) the financial value of any other claim for damages is not more than £1,000.

(Rule 2.3 defines "claim for personal injuries" as proceedings in which there is a claim for damages in respect of personal injuries to the claimant or any other person or in respect of a person's death)

(2) For the purposes of paragraph (1) "damages for personal injuries" means damages claimed as compensation for pain, suffering, and loss of amenity and does not include any other damages which are claimed.

(3) Subject to paragraph (1), the small claims track is the normal track for any claim which has a financial value of not more than £5,000.

(Rule 26.7 (4) provides that the court will not allocate to the small claims track certain claims in respect of harassment or unlawful eviction.)

The differentiation of personal injury claims and repair claims by tenants of residential premises from all other claims arises from a debate that started under the small claims procedure dictated by the County Court Rules, continued through Lord Woolf's Interim and Final Reports and in the drafting and finalisation of the Rules by the Civil Procedure Rule Committee. The nature of this debate was summarised in a consultation paper issued by the Lord Chancellor's Department in November 1997 relating to the small claims procedure.

In personal injury cases the broad argument in giving them special treatment is that the level of damages for pain, suffering and loss of amenity has a knock-on effect upon the degree of investigation required and resultant argument in front of the Court. These matters were aired by the Court of Appeal in *Afzal v Ford Motor Company Limited* [1994] All ER 720.

Similarly, in housing disrepair claims it is argued that such cases are unsuited to the small claims track because of—

- the complexity of the facts and law involved;
- the inequality of the means of the parties;
- the fact that some claimants may be illiterate or otherwise incapable of conducting their case;
- the difficulty in identifying and collecting the evidence required; and
- the requirement for expert evidence.

These matters were reviewed under the old Rules by the Court of Appeal in *Joyce v Liverpool City Council* [1995] 3 All ER 110.

As detailed in Chapter 15 (Part 26), a personal injury claim for the purposes of Rule 26.6 is proceedings which include a claim for damages in respect of personal injuries to the claimant or any other person or in respect of a person's death (defined by Rule 2.3). Thus a mixed claim for damages arising both from personal injuries and otherwise would be, for the purposes of the Rules, a claim for personal injuries and in particular for Rule 26.6. In assessing the value of the claim and particularly whether it is more than £5,000, the claimant will include both the damages arising from the personal injuries and any other damages sought by the claimant.

Further, in assessing the value of £5,000, the Court will take into account any damages arising from the personal injuries including pain, suffering, loss of amenity and any consequential losses. For the purposes of Rule 26.6(1)(a)(ii) and whether or not the financial value of any claim for damages for personal injuries is not more than £1,000, the Court only takes into account compensation for pain, suffering and loss of amenity.

If a claim has no financial value, the Court has greater discretion since there is no prescribed normal track. The Court will have regard to the matters set out in Rule 26.8(1) save that in relation to a claim by a tenant of residential premises against his landlord which includes a claim for remedy in respect of harassment for unlawful eviction, the Court cannot allocate the claim to the small claims track (Rule 26.7(4)).

The Court is discouraged from allocation to the small claims track where a case involves a disputed allegation of dishonesty (Paragraph 8.1(1)(d), Practice Direction to Part 26).

In both *Joyce v Liverpool City Council* and *Afzal v Ford Motor Company Limited*, the Court of Appeal described the small claims arbitration procedure under the County Court Rules as, "… no more, and no less, than a procedure for resolving low value claims … with a minimum of formality and expense" (Sir Thomas Bingham MR in *Joyce v Liverpool City Council*) and a procedure getting away " …from the rigid rituals which characterise ordinary litigation" (Beldan LJ in *Afzal v Ford Motor Company Limited*). These descriptions are in a fashion repeated in the practice direction to Part 26 which describes the small claims track as—

> **A proportionate procedure by which most straightforward claims with a financial value of not more than £5,000 can be decided, without the need for substantial pre-hearing preparing and the formalities of a traditional trial, and without incurring large legal costs …**
>
> **The procedure laid down in Part 27 for the preparation of the case and the conduct of the hearing are designed to make it possible for a litigant to conduct his own case without legal representation if he wishes.**
>
> **Cases generally suitable for the small claims track will include consumer disputes, accident claims, disputes about the ownership of goods and most disputes between a landlord and tenant other than those for possession.**

Case Management

Upon allocation the Court will consider whether it should hold a preliminary hearing under Rule 27.6. Generally it will not hold a preliminary hearing since the costs incurred in attendance (which would be generally irrecoverable) would be contrary to the spirit of the small claims track which is designed specifically to limit expenses and costs incurred.

There are in any event specific limits on when the Court may hold a preliminary hearing—

- The Court considers that something other than standard directions ("special directions") are necessary to ensure a fair hearing and the Court believes that an explanation at a preliminary hearing needs to be given to a party to ensure that he understands what he must do to comply with the special directions.
- To enable the Court to dispose of the claim summarily under Part 24 on the basis that one or other of the parties has no real prospect of success at a formal hearing; or

- To enable the Court to deal with the case summarily by striking out all or part of the statement of case under Rule 3.4 in that the statement of case discloses no reasonable grounds for bringing or defending the claim.

The Court could treat any allocation hearing as a preliminary hearing for these purposes although there are differing periods for service of notice of hearing upon the parties by the Court - seven days for an allocation hearing (Paragraph 6.2(1), Practice Direction to Part 26) and 14 days for a preliminary hearing (Rule 27.6(3)).

The Court may consider it appropriate to hold the hearing over the telephone.

Whilst the question of special directions is peculiar to Part 27, the Court may consider giving either summary judgment under Part 24 or an order striking out all or part of the statement of case under Rule 3.4 of its own initiative either side of the allocation process. If the Court is considering making such an order at the time of allocation, it would seem an unnecessary expense to proceed through the allocation process and then to set a preliminary hearing of which 14 days notice must be given. The alternative would be for the Court to exercise its power under Rule 3.3 by setting a hearing to deal with these issues prior to allocation. If the claim continues thereafter the claim can be allocated and directions given.

The one advantage of a preliminary hearing is that under Rule 27.6(4) it can be converted into a final hearing if all the parties agree.

If the claim continues after the preliminary hearing under Rule 27.6(5) the Court will—

- fix the date for the final hearing of which at least 21 days notice must be given unless the parties agree on less notice;
- tell the parties how much time will be allowed for the final hearing; and
- give any appropriate directions.

If, as will be usual, there is no preliminary hearing, the Court will give directions immediately upon allocation. These directions would either be standard directions or special directions. Precedents for standard directions in relation to four categories of claim are included in the practice direction—

- Form B - road accidents;
- Form C - building disputes, vehicle repairs and similar contractual claims;
- Form D - tenants' claims for the return of deposit / landlords' claims for damage caused; and
- Form E - holiday and wedding claims.

Form A, however, sets out the usual "standard directions" that will be given by the Court in accordance with Rule 27.4(3)(a). These provide very simply—

- Each party deliver to every other party and to the Court office copies of all documents (including any expert's report) on which he intends to rely at the hearing no later than 14 days before the hearing.

- The original documents should be brought to the hearing.
- The hearing will take place on X with the time allowed being X.
- The Court to be informed immediately if the case is settled by agreement before the hearing date.

If the Court concludes that there should be some special directions over and above the "standard directions", Form F gives some examples. For instance, if the hearing is to take place other than at the Court, the place of the hearing will be specified; if experts' evidence is necessary then special directions will be given concerning it.

The case management directions should ensure that the case is dealt with in as short a time as possible. Accordingly, as suggested by Paragraph 8.1(2)(d) (Practice Direction to Part 27), the Court might consider giving directions of a kind not usually seen in small claims cases, for example, for Scott Schedules setting out the contradicting views of the parties in relation to issues in dispute.

When it gives directions the Court will either fix a date for a final hearing or put that decision off for no more than 28 days following the giving of any special directions (Rule 27.4(1)). Whenever it does fix the date for the hearing it must give at least 21 days notice to the parties unless they agree to accept less notice and at the same time tell them how much time has been allowed for the final hearing (Rule 27.4(2)). The Court will not normally allow more than one day for the hearing of a claim in the small claims track (Paragraph 8.1(2)(c), Practice Direction to Part 26).

In the alternative, the Court could put it to the parties that the claim should be resolved without a hearing under Rule 27.10. It can only proceed without a hearing, however, if all parties agree. Accordingly, when it gives notice of its proposal to the parties, it must invite them to notify the Court by a specified date if they agree (Rule 27.4(1)(e)). If there is agreement, the Court could make a decision on written submissions only.

Having given directions the Court is empowered to add to, vary or revoke them under Rule 27.7.

Certain parts of the Rules are specifically dis-applied to the small claims track (i.e. following allocation) under Rule 27.2(1).

27.2 (1) The following Parts of these Rules do not apply to small claims—
(a) Part 25 (interim remedies) except as it relates to interim injunctions;
(b) Part 31 (disclosure and inspection);
(c) Part 32 (evidence) except rule 32.1 (power of court to control evidence);
(d) Part 33 (miscellaneous rules about evidence);
(e) Part 35 (experts and assessors) except rules 35.1 (duty to restrict expert evidence), 35.3 (experts—overriding duty to the court) and 35.8 (instructions to a single joint expert);
(f) Part 18 (further information);
(g) Part 36 (offers to settle and payments into court); and
(h) Part 39 (hearings) except rule 39.2 (general rule—hearing to be in public).

As to experts, Rule 27.5 provides that expert evidence may not be submitted at a hearing without permission of the Court. This reflects, in any event, Rule 35.4(1) that either written or oral evidence of an expert cannot be called without the Court's permission. Although Part 35 is largely excluded from Part 27, if the Court is considering allowing expert evidence in the small claims track, it will have consideration for many of the factors contained in Part 35. Thus if one of the parties submits that expert evidence should be allowed, the Court is likely to require identification of the field of expert required and the name of the expert where possible. It is suggested, however, that the giving of expert evidence in the small claims track should be avoided wherever possible. If expert evidence is allowed, Rule 27.14 provides for the recovery of the expert's fees which are limited to £200 by Paragraph 7.3(2), Practice Direction to Part 27.

The Hearing

Rule 27.8 provides generally for the manner in which the hearing should be conducted. The basic consideration is that the method of proceeding in the hearing must be fair (Rule 27.8(1)).

The remainder of Rule 27.8 provides—

- the hearings will be informal;
- strict rules of evidence do not apply;
- the Court need not take evidence on oath; and
- the Court may limit cross examination (but not dispose of it altogether) and the Court must give reasons for its decision.

The practice direction goes into some more detail (Paragraph 4.3, Practice Direction to Part 27) in providing that a Judge may—

- ask questions of any witness himself before allowing any other person to do so;
- ask questions of any or all of the witnesses himself before allowing any other person to ask questions of any witnesses;
- refuse to allow cross examination of any witnesses until all the witnesses have given evidence in chief; and
- limit cross examination of a witness to a fixed time or to a particular subject or issue or both.

As above, in exercising this power the Court must have consideration to what is a fair procedure.

Under Paragraph 4.1, Practice Direction to Part 27, the general rule is that a hearing in the small claims track will be in public. This reflects the provisions of Part 39 (miscellaneous provisions relating to hearings) which Part (save for Rule 39.2) is otherwise excluded from the small claims track.

The hearing can be in private if the parties agree or (under Rule 39.2)—

- publicity would defeat the object of the hearing;
- the hearing involves matters relating to national security;
- the hearing involves confidential information (including information relating to personal financial matters) and publicity would damage that confidentiality;

- a private hearing is necessary to protect the interests of any child or patient; or
- the Court considers a private hearing to be necessary in the interests of justice.

Generally hearings will take place in front of a District Judge, although a Circuit Judge can conduct the hearing (Paragraph 1, Practice Direction to Part 27). As under the old arbitration procedure, the hearing will usually take place in the Judge's room. Under the old Rules this would have been referred to as a hearing in chambers. For this purpose the word "chambers" had two meanings, firstly that the hearing was in private, and secondly, that it was in a small room. Under the new Rules a hearing in a Judge's room simply means that it is in a smaller room than the usual Court and the layout is somewhat different. The District Judge, however, can adjourn the hearing into a courtroom. This may be appropriate if there are sufficient members of the public wanting to attend the hearing to make the accommodation provided in the Judge's room insufficient.

Paragraph 3.2 of the Practice Direction provides guidance as to the presentation of the case at hearing. A party may of course present their own case. If that party is a corporation then any of its officers or employees can present the case for it. Alternatively, either a lawyer (barrister, solicitor or legal executive employed by a solicitor) or a lay representative (anyone else) may present the case for the party. As to the rights of lay representatives, see Section 11 of the Courts and Legal Services Act 1990; the Lay Representatives (Rights of Audience) Order 1992 and Section 60 of the County Courts Act 1984. Under Paragraph 3.2 of the Practice Direction, a lay representative may only present the case if the party is present at the hearing or, if not present, the representative is that party's employee or otherwise the Court gives permission.

Paragraph 5 of the Practice Direction (Part 27) sets out the requirements as to the recording of evidence. Basically, either the Court will tape record the proceedings or the Judge will take a note of the central points of oral evidence.

Having heard the parties, the Judge is encouraged to determine the issues there and then and give a judgment orally at the hearing. Unless he tape records his judgment, he should make a note of the central reasons for his judgment. The parties are entitled to a copy of that note.

Although normally the Judge will give judgment and the reasons immediately, he can adjourn the hearing to give his judgment and/or reasons later in writing or at another hearing.

If there is no hearing under Rule 27.10 or a party does not attend the hearing having given notice under Rule 27.9(1), the Judge will prepare a note of his reasons and a copy will be sent to each of the parties.

Rule 27.9 makes special provision in the event that either one or both parties does not attend the final hearing and either does or does not give notice of that non-attendance.

27.9 (1) If a party who does not attend a final hearing—

(a) has given the court written notice at least 7 days before the date of the hearing that he will not attend; and

(b) has, in that notice, requested the court to decide the claim in his absence,

the court will take into account that party's statement of case and any other documents he has filed when it decides the claim.

(2) If a claimant does not—

(a) attend the hearing; and

(b) give the notice referred to in paragraph (1)

the court may strike out the claim.

(3) If—

(a) a defendant does not

(i) attend the hearing; or

(ii) give the notice referred to in paragraph (1); and

(b) the claimant either—

(i) does attend the hearing; or

(ii) gives the notice referred to in paragraph (1),

the court may decide the claim on the basis of the evidence of the claimant alone.

(4) If neither party attends or gives the notice referred to in paragraph (1), the court may strike out the claim and any defence and counterclaim.

Under Rule 27.11, if a party does not attend or is not represented at the final hearing and has not given notice under Rule 27.9(1), he may apply for an order that any judgment given consequent upon the hearing should be set aside and the claim re-heard. If he wishes to make such an application then he must do so no more than 14 days after notice of the judgment was served on him. The application must comply with Part 23 and, no doubt, would have to be supported by evidence. The applicant must make out to the Court that he had a good reason for not attending or being represented or for his failure to give written notice under Rule 27.9(1). He must also satisfy the Court that he has a reasonable prospect of success at any re-hearing. If judgment is set aside then the Court can either fix a new hearing date for some time in the future or proceed immediately to re-hear the claim.

These provisions do not apply, however, if the Court dealt with the claim without a hearing under Rule 27.10.

Judgment and Appeal

The judgment or order made at the final hearing will be drawn up by the Court. Part 40 which relates to judgments and orders generally has not been excluded from Part 27 and therefore applies. The judgment takes effect from the day when it is given (Rule 40.7). Any interest under the Judgments Act 1838 or Section 74 of the County Courts Act 1984 begins to run from the date that judgment is given (Rule 40.8). If the judgment is the payment of an amount of money then payment is due within 14 days of the date of the judgment (Rule 40.11).

The appeal process under Part 27 is very different from the process following the final hearing that previously applied under the County Court Rules. There is now no review of the hearing.

An appeal is made from the District Judge to the Circuit Judge. The grounds for appeal are limited by Rule 27.12(1) to—

- a serious irregularity affecting the proceedings; or
- the Court made a mistake of law.

The appeal is made by filing a notice of appeal not more than 14 days after the date on which notice of the order or judgment is served on the appellant (Rule 27.13(1)). The notice of appeal must set out the particulars of the serious irregularity or mistake of law relied upon (Paragraph 8.3, Practice Direction to Part 27). The Court will serve a copy of the notice on all the parties (Paragraph 8.5, Practice Direction to Part 27).

Upon receipt of the notice it will be put before the Circuit Judge together with the file as soon as possible. The Circuit Judge can immediately dismiss the appeal without a hearing if no sufficient ground is shown on the notice of appeal or order that the appeal be listed for hearing (Paragraph 8.6, Practice Direction to Part 27). If the appeal is dismissed, the order for dismissal should contain brief reasons for the decision.

If the appeal is to be listed, the Court can give any directions including any necessary directions in relation to the filing of evidence or the supply of copies of documents which may be relevant to the appeal (such as the notes of the District Judge) (Paragraph 8.7, Practice Direction to Part 27).

Seven days notice of the hearing of the appeal has to be given to the parties (Paragraph 8.9, Practice Direction to Part 27). If the appeal is allowed the Circuit Judge could move straight on to disposing with the case (Paragraph 8.10).

Costs

As ever the question of costs and the small claims track has been a matter of some debate. The die was cast early to the effect that the general no costs rules relating to arbitration in the County Court Rules would be carried through to the small claims track notwithstanding the increase in the limits and concerns expressed by various consultees in the consultation process.

The general rule is that following allocation to the small claim track, a party will not be able to recover costs from another party. The costs in question include representation by a lawyer or a lay representative (Rule 27.14(4)). The no costs rule does not apply when a claim in which the normal track would have been the fast track has been allocated to the small claims track with the agreement of the parties under Rule 26.7(3), save that the trial costs can be lower but no higher than the amount that could have been awarded in the fast track based upon the amount awarded. It must be remembered that before allocation the special rules in relation to costs do not apply but after allocation the special rules apply to work done before as well as after allocation save to the extent (if any) an order for costs in respect of that work was made before allocation (Rule 44.9(2) and Paragraph 5.1(2), Practice Direction to Part 44).

If the claim exceeded the small claims track limit and is only allocated because of an admission judgment, the admitted amount should be requested before allocation and costs up to allocation will then be payable (Paragraph 5.1(3), Practice Direction to Part 44, and Paragraph 7.4, Practice Direction to Part 26).

Rule 27.14 provides some limited exceptions to the general rule and the Court may order one party to pay another party—

- Paragraph 1.2 of the Practice Direction to Part 45 provides that fixed costs under 27.14(2)(a) are the sum of the fixed costs set out in Table 1 and the appropriate Court fee or fee paid by the claimant.
- The fixed costs payable under Part 45 (or which would be payable if Part 45 applied) relating to the issuing of the claim. These fixed costs are set out in Table 1 in Rule 45.2 and apply whether or not the conditions in Rule 45.1(2) are met.

TABLE 1

FIXED COSTS ON COMMENCEMENT OF A CLAIM

Relevant Band	Where the claim form is served by the court or by any method other than personal service by the claimant	Where the claim form is served personally by the claimant; and there is only one defendant	Where there is more than one defendant, for each additional defendant personally served at separate addresses by the claimant
Where— the value of the claim exceeds £25 but does not exceed £500	£50	£60	£15
Where— the value of the claim exceeds £500 but does not exceed £1,000	£70	£80	£15

Relevant Band	Where the claim form is served by the court or by any method other than personal service by the claimant	Where the claim form is served personally by the claimant; and there is only one defendant	Where there is more than one defendant, for each additional defendant personally served at separate addresses by the claimant
Where— the value of the claim exceeds £1,000 but does not exceed £5,000; or the only claim is for delivery of goods and no value is specified or stated on the claim form	£80	£90	£15
Where— the value of the claim exceeds £5,000	£100	£110	£15

- A sum of £260 for legal advice and assistance in proceedings which included a claim for an injunction or an order for specific performance (Rule 27.14(2)(b) and Paragraph 7.2, Practice Direction to Part 27).
- Costs assessed by the summary procedure in relation to an appeal under Rule 27.12 (Rule 27.14(2)(c)).
- Any further costs the Court may consider appropriate to order against a party who has **behaved unreasonably**. Such costs will be summarily assessed. The term "unreasonable behaviour" replaces the term that was used in the County Court Rules - "unreasonable conduct". There are no guidelines in the Rules as to what unreasonable behaviour means. It is suggested that unreasonable behaviour may be a different animal in the post Woolf world from unreasonable conduct before it. Trying to categorise what is unreasonable behaviour would be merely speculative but placing it within the context of the costs rules and particularly Rule 44.3(5) and Rule 44.5(3), the behaviour to be considered would be before as well as during the proceedings.

Further, it might include whether a party had made any efforts to try to settle the case or complied with any pre-action protocol. In that respect we have already seen the Court taking a strong line in *Burrows v Vauxhaull Motors Limited* [1997] 141 Sol Jo LB 237, (1997) Times 17 December, CA; and *Butcher v Wolfe* (1998) Times, 9 November, CA. The obligation of the Court is to assess the costs summarily. Parties should therefore be prepared for that summary assessment. Although all the relevant Paragraphs of the Practice Direction to Part 44 (Paragraphs 4.3-4.10) may not have direct application to summary assessment on the small claims track, it is suggested that if a party proposes to make an application for the award of costs resulting from unreasonable behaviour, they should prepare a statement of costs in Form 1 costs form. Although it may be appropriate to serve such a statement on the other party and lodge a copy with the Court prior to the hearing, it is suggested that this not be used in an overbearing fashion or it would be quite contrary to the spirit of the small claims track.

In addition to these costs, under Rule 27.14 the Court may also order a party to pay all or part of—

- any Court fees paid by another party;
- expenses paid by a party or witness travelling to and from a hearing or in staying away from home (i.e. overnight expenses) to attend the hearing;
- loss of earnings of a party or witness arising from attending the hearing (limited to £50 per day for each person) (Paragraph 7.3(1), Practice Direction to Part 27);
- no more than £200 for experts' fees (Paragraph 7.3(2), Practice Direction to Part 27).

As generally applies to allocation and reallocation, the Rules relating to the small claims track only apply to a claim whilst it is within that track and ceases to apply if the claim is reallocated to another track. This cessation, however, does not have retrospective effect (unlike the original allocation). In particular the no costs rules continue to apply up to re-allocation.

CHAPTER 17
PART 28—THE FAST TRACK

Introduction

In both his Interim and Final Reports, Lord Woolf developed the idea of a special procedure for claims larger than small claims but not of such substance as to justify substantial costs being incurred. It was within this band identified initially as between £3,000 and £10,000 that Lord Woolf saw the civil justice system failing both claimants and defendants. For such moderate claims the procedure under the RSC and CCR was too complex and particularly too costly to put into effect.

Lord Irvine summarises some of these criticisms in a speech to the Solicitors Annual Conference at Cardiff in October 1997—

> **Civil justice today is too expensive and too exclusive. The very rich and the very poor have access but middle income Britain is left out in the cold - and middle income Britain is the overwhelming majority of people in this country. They cannot litigate because the lawyer's fees are so high and because they cannot afford the risk of losing and having to pay their opponent's lawyer's fees as well.**
>
> **Not only is civil justice far too expensive for people to afford because of the scale of the costs: they are deterred from pursuing good cases because they cannot make any rational assessment of how much it will cost them in the end. These and the level of costs are the biggest bars to access to justice.**

Much time and energy has therefore been spent in developing the fast track. Three chapters of the Final Report are devoted to it. Research projects have been undertaken such as that conducted by the Institute of Advanced Legal Studies published in June 1998 (Costing Fast Track Procedures through Hypothetical Studies, LCD Research Series No 4/98).

Lord Woolf's concept of a system to deal with middling claims was a set procedure with the trial date being established at the commencement and recoverable costs being limited in all aspects. Broadly the result follows these lines albeit that Lord Woolf's proposals in relation to recoverable costs have not been followed in detail by the Committee, drawing partly upon the research of the Institute of Advanced Legal Studies and a consultation paper that was issued by the LCD as a result of it ("Justice at the Right Price").

The resultant Rules and practice directions are relatively short and concise. Broadly the system is as follows—

- The fast track is the normal track for claims with a financial value above £5,000 and equal to or below £15,000.
- Upon allocation the Court will give appropriate directions either in accordance with those agreed by the parties or of its own making.
- The Court will upon allocation further fix a trial date or a period not exceeding three weeks within which the trial is to take place. That period should be no more than 30 weeks after the giving of directions.
- The trial will take no longer than a day. A calendar day will be allotted to it and the parties will be notified of the precise date no later than three weeks before the date fixed.
- Recoverable costs should be broadly proportionate to the matters in issue save in respect of the limited fixed costs relating to the trial of the action.

The Lord Chancellor has recently announced that fixed fast track costs for the whole process remains a short term goal.

Allocation

The reader is referred to page 165 in relation to allocation under Part 26 particularly in relation to the filling in of the allocation questionnaire, the fee, and estimates of costs.

Part 26 sets out the procedure for allocation of claims to one of the three tracks. Rule 26.6 sets out the scopes of each track. In relation to the fast track—

(4) Subject to paragraph (5), the fast track is the normal track for any claim—
(a) for which the small claims track is not the normal track; and
(b) which has a financial value of not more than £15,000.

(5) The fast track is the normal track for the claims referred to in paragraph (4) only if the court considers that—
(a) the trial is likely to last for no longer than one day; and
(b) oral expert evidence at trial will be limited to—
(i) one expert per party in relation to any expert field; and
(ii) expert evidence in two expert fields.

As with the other two tracks, the primary measure of whether a case should be allocated to a track is its financial value. Rule 26.8, however, provides other factors that the Court should take into account in undertaking the allocation exercise, such as the nature of the remedy sought, the complexity of the law involved or the circumstances of the parties (for discussion on these aspects see page 165).

It is suggested that the fast track will be the repository for many of those claims for which the financial value would make the small claims track the normal track but other factors determine the small claims track as inappropriate. For example, if the circumstances of the parties (which make the ability to obtain legal advice more important) determine that the claim should not be allocated to the small claims track, the fast track would allow the recovery of costs for legal representation.

One of the factors to be taken into account by the Court specifically relating to the fast track is whether the trial is likely to last for no longer than one day. This does not place an absolute limit on the trial length since clearly matters arise during the course of a trial which may cause the length of the trial to be extended. Even if in prospect at the time of allocation the Court considers that the trial might last longer than one day, this is not an absolutely conclusive factor predetermining that the matter should be allocated to the multi track (Paragraph 9.1(3)(c), Practice Direction to Part 26). It is simply one of the factors that the Court should take into account.

In the allocation process the Court will have consideration for the overriding objective and particularly the factors set out in Rule 1.1(2). The general direction to the Court in relation to allocation to the fast track is that if the fast track would be the normal track based upon a financial value of the claim, the Court will allocate the claim to the fast track unless it believes that it cannot be dealt with justly on that track (Paragraph 9.1(1), Practice Direction to Part 26). In that exercise the practice direction goes further to suggest that the matters the Court should take into account in assessing whether the case can be dealt with justly are the limits placed on disclosure, the extent to which expert evidence may be necessary and whether the trial is likely to last more than a day (Paragraph 9.1(2)).

For the purposes of the small claims track and allocation, the reference to one day equates to a period of five hours (Paragraph 9.1(3)(a), Practice Direction to Part 26). The same practice direction requires the Court to consider whether that is likely to be a sufficient time for the case to be heard taking into account the case management directions that are likely to be given and the Court's powers to control evidence and to limit cross examination.

The period of five hours might look something like this—

- Judge's reading time 30 minutes (although Judges are encouraged to read before commencement).
- Opening speech 10 minutes.
- Cross examination and re-examination of claimant's witnesses 90 minutes.
- Cross examination and re-examination of defendant's witnesses 90 minutes.
- Defendant's submissions 15 minutes.
- Claimant's submissions 15 minutes.
- Judge's consideration and judgment 30 minutes.
- Costs and other orders 20 minutes (including the period for summary assessment of the costs).

The parties are requested to estimate the length of trial in their responses to the allocation questionnaire. Similarly they are required to give their views as to the appropriate track. Neither the estimate nor the views, however, are in any way binding upon the Court. It seems likely that the Court will impose the fast track upon parties notwithstanding that estimates are given for length of trial beyond one day. The Court will have in mind its obligations under Part 1 and particularly the appropriate allocation of the resources of the Court.

When completing the allocation questionnaire the parties should consider in advance whether it is likely that the claim will be allocated to the fast track. With that in mind they should consult one another and co-operate in completing the questionnaire and try to agree case management directions (see Paragraph 2.3, Practice Direction to Part 26).

Case Management

Directions for the claim will normally be given on only two occasions - at allocation and subsequently on the filing of listing questionnaires. Both allocation and the giving of case management directions may otherwise be given on the disposal of an application to strike out under Rule 3.4 or for summary judgment under Part 24.

As above, the directions may be agreed between the parties upon filing the allocation questionnaire. The Court is not bound to follow those directions and it will not do so unless they comply with Paragraph 3.6 of the Practice Direction to Part 28. The directions must—

- Set out a timetable by reference to calendar dates for the taking of steps for the preparation of the case (presumably on a rough estimate of when the order will be made).
- Include a date or a period (the trial period) when it is proposed that the trial will take place which must be no later than 30 weeks from the date the directions order is made. The trial period must be no longer than three weeks.
- Include provision about disclosure of documents which could limit the extent of or the procedure for disclosure or dispense with it altogether.
- Include provision about both factual and expert evidence which could be to the effect that no expert evidence is required or that there should be a single joint expert.
- The directions agreed by the parties should also, where appropriate, provide for—
    - the filing of any reply or amended statement of case that may be required;
    - dates for the service of request for further information under Part 18 or questions to experts under Rule 35.6 and the timing of responses;
    - the disclosure of evidence;
    - the use of a single joint expert or where each party has an expert, the exchange and agreement of expert evidence and discussions between the experts.

The process of agreeing directions should be dealt with as quickly as possible bearing in mind the limitation on the period in which allocation questionnaires have to be returned to the Court. The process could be useful particularly in agreeing appropriate dates for experts reports and the trial so that it can be ensured that the dates are convenient for parties and witnesses.

The parties could do no better than complete a form for fast track standard directions in accordance with the appendix to the practice direction to Part 28. As far as the writer is aware, there is no practice form available to the parties containing these directions and it is suggested that unless a form is provided by the Court with the allocation questionnaire (which some Courts are doing) practitioners might produce their own as a standard form.

If the Court does not approve of the directions agreed between the parties it will take them into account when making its own directions. There may in particular be difficulties over the question of experts. The use of a single jointly instructed expert under Rule 35.7 is to be strongly promoted in the fast track and the prospect is that the Court will impose a single expert even though the parties have already agreed and instructed separate experts. This encouragement is reinforced by the practice direction to Part 28 (Paragraph 3.9(4)) where the general approach in relation to experts is for the appointment of a single joint expert unless there is good reason not to do so.

If directions are made by the Court of its own initiative they will generally follow a standard form set out in the practice direction. With the guideline of timing included, those directions will be—

- The filing and service of any further information required to clarify either party's case (presumably in 2 weeks).
- Standard disclosure of documents between the parties—four weeks.
- Simultaneous exchange of witness statements—ten weeks.
- The filing of the single expert's report or the exchange of experts' reports—14 weeks.
- If separate experts are to be instructed, directions as to the discussion between them under Rule 35.12(1) and the preparation of a report on those discussions under Rule 35.12(3).
- The sending of listing questionnaires by the Court—20 weeks.
- Filing of completed listing questionnaires—22 weeks.
- Trial—30 weeks.

All periods run from the date of notice of allocation.

The Court is not obliged in any way to follow these suggested directions. It may, for instance, omit or add to them as appropriate.

Allocation/Directions Hearing

If the Court needs further information in relation to allocation or in order to assist it to give appropriate directions, it may hold a hearing. It is likely that if an allocation hearing is fixed it will also deal with directions. The parties may apply for the listing of a directions hearing if there are particular matters that should be raised with the Court. As with the Court, however, the parties should be discouraged from doing so, particularly bearing in mind the potential limit on recoverable costs. If a hearing is fixed the parties are under a specific obligation to co-operate in trying to agree directions beforehand and to make any application to the Court that may be appropriate to deal with at the hearing (Paragraph 2.5, Practice Direction to Part 28). The parties will be given at least three days notice of any hearing fixed by the Court. Any application to be made by a party would have to be made in accordance with Part 23.

Variation of Directions

If a party is dissatisfied with any directions given by the Court it may either appeal the decision or seek the Court's review of it. Appeals should only be made if the direction was given at a hearing (Paragraph 4.3(2), Practice Direction to Part 28). Otherwise the applicant should ask that the Court reconsider its decision. Such an application to reconsider should be made within 14 days of service of the order containing the directions (Paragraph 4.2(2), Practice Direction to Part 28).

The application will usually be heard by the judge who gave the directions, or another judge of the same level (Paragraph 4.3(4)(a), Practice Direction to Part 28). The Court will take into account how quickly the application has been made following service. If not made within the 14 day period mentioned above, there will be an assumption that the applicant was content with the directions and they were correct in the circumstances then existing (Paragraph 4.2(2), Practice Direction to Part 28). Three days notice of the hearing will be given by the Court and at the hearing the Court can either confirm its decision or make a different order (Paragraph 4.3(4)(b) and (c), Practice Direction to Part 28). In considering whether to vary any directions the Court will take into account any change in the circumstances since the order was made (Paragraph 4.4, Practice Direction to Part 28).

Under Rule 2.11 the parties are free to vary the timetable by written agreement. Further, the parties can dispense with or limit the procedure for or the extent of standard disclosure (Rules 31.5, 31.10(8) and 31.13). The freedom of the parties to vary dates set by the Court, however, is limited by Rule 28.4. Whilst dates may be varied the dates for—

- the return of the listing questionnaire under Rule 28.5,
- the trial, or
- the trial period,

cannot be varied. Indeed other dates cannot be varied if they would have a knock-on effect upon those milestone dates. If it is desired to change the milestone date or other dates having effect upon them, application must be made to the Court. This can either be done by consent or on a contested basis. If the application is made by consent the parties are obliged to file a draft of the order sought and an agreed statement of the reasons why a variation is sought (Paragraph 4.5(2)(b), Practice Direction to Part 28). Upon the application the Court can either fix a hearing or make an order either in accordance with the agreed terms or in other terms without a hearing (Paragraph 4.5(2)(c), Practice Direction to Part 28).

Failure to comply with Directions

One of the criticisms of Lord Woolf of the system under the Rules of the Supreme Court and County Court Rules was that rules were often ignored both by the Court and by the parties and that sanctions were rarely imposed. Over the past few years the Courts have become much tighter in their control of litigation and the imposition of time limits upon the parties. Practitioners may expect that this control will tighten under the Civil Procedure Rules. There appears to be debate amongst the judiciary as to exactly how hard time limits will be imposed. Since the matter is entirely within the discretion of the Court, practice may change from Court to Court and from judge to judge.

The Practice Direction to Part 28 places the emphasis on the non-defaulting party to take steps to enforce compliance or for the imposition of a sanction (Paragraph 5.1). Under Paragraph 5.2 the party intending to make such an application should warn the other party but make the application without delay. If the applicant has delayed this may be taken into account in the order that is made by the Court (Paragraph 5.3). If a sanction has been imposed for a failure to comply with any rule, practice direction or court order, the rule practice direction or court order has effect unless the party in default applies for and obtains relief from the sanction (Rule 3.8). Whilst as above parties are free to vary the timetable for directions in the fast track, they cannot extend a time limit which has with it a specified consequence (for example, striking out a statement of case) of a failure to comply with the time limit set. That time may only be extended by the Court.

On an application for relief from any sanction imposed by a rule, practice direction or court order the Court will take into account the factors set out in Rule 3.9 such as whether the application for relief has been made promptly or the failure to comply was intentional.

Upon the hearing of an application to enforce compliance after the imposition of a sanction, the Court will have in mind that the trial date or trial period should only be varied as a last resort (Paragraph 5.4). With this in mind the Court will impose very tight timetables with sanctions to ensure that the parties are ready for trial. Alternatively the Court might limit the issues to be dealt with upon trial with appropriate costs sanctions on any further hearing necessary as a result. If there is no option but to postpone the whole trial, the legal representatives of the parties may be required to attend to explain a failure to comply with the timetable set by the Court. In postponing the trial the Court will try to list it as soon as possible with appropriate directions.

Disclosure in the Fast Track

Disclosure will be limited to standard disclosure as defined in Part 31. As provided within that Part, the parties can agree to limit the extent or procedure of disclosure as can the Court (Rule 28.3(2)).

The Court has the discretion to make an order for specific disclosure or specific inspection under Rule 31.12(1) but a court will rarely do so in the fast track since on both timing and costs this would lend itself to defeating the purpose of fast track procedure. Indeed it is a precursor to allocation to the fast track that the Court takes into account the limits likely to be placed on disclosure within the track (Paragraph 9.1(2), Practice Direction to Part 26).

Experts in the Fast Track

As provided in Rule 26.6(5), the fast track is the normal track for claims with a financial value of not more than £15,000 only if the Court considers that—

oral expert evidence at trial will be limited to—
(i) one expert per party in relation to any expert field; and
(ii) expert evidence in two expert fields.

Upon making a decision between the fast track and multi track the Court must take into consideration the extent to which expert evidence may be necessary (Paragraph 9.1(2), Practice Direction to Part 26).

When giving directions in the fast track the Court should direct that there be a single joint expert **unless there is good reason not to do so** (Paragraph 3.9(4), Practice Direction to Part 28). The parties should bear this in mind when attempting to achieve a consensus in relation to experts. Under the pre-action protocols (particularly of the personal injury pre-action protocol) there is specific encouragement to try and agree the identification of a single expert. Clearly if the parties wish to have their own experts on a particular issue they will have to convince the Court that it is appropriate in the circumstances.

A direction giving permission to use expert evidence will say whether it gives permission for oral evidence or written reports or both and will name the experts concerned (Paragraph 7.3, Practice Direction to Part 28). An expert will only be able to give oral evidence at trial if the Court believes it necessary in the interests of justice. The difficulty for the Court and the parties is trying to fit in expert evidence in addition to the witnesses of fact in the allocated time of five hours. If expert oral evidence is to be permitted, both the Court and the parties will want to ensure that the issues to which such evidence relate are closely delineated. The Court will be keen to ensure that the experts do their utmost to limit the issues that may be in dispute between them. Accordingly, if no meeting for this purpose has taken place, the Court may make its permission for an expert to give oral evidence conditional on such a discussion taking place and a report of that discussion being filed before trial (Paragraph 7.2(4)(c), Practice Direction to Part 28).

Listing Questionnaires and Listing

The listing questionnaire is in Form N170. The time for filing of completed listing questionnaires will be part of the directions. The listing questionnaires should be sent out in good time for the parties to comply with the date for return. Whilst the listing questionnaire is similar in its format to the allocation questionnaire, it bears no seal of the Court. The form is colour coded. Practice tends to differ from court to court as to whether the form that is sent by the Court has to be the form that is returned duly completed.

The listing questionnaire is divided into five sections—

A Directions complied with—

- Have the parties complied with the directions; if not, why not.
- If further directions are required, give details with reasons.

B Experts

There are a range of questions as to what has happened so far in relation to experts. Further, in the listing questionnaire the parties have to seek the Court's permission to call an expert at the trial giving reasons.

C Other witnesses

There are a range of questions in relation to witnesses of fact.

D Legal representation

The parties must state who will be presenting the case.

E Other matters

This includes the estimate of length of trial and the number of pages of evidence to be included in the trial bundle. Most importantly for fast track cases, the parties can indicate whether they are willing to accept a period of notice for the trial of less than the three weeks that would normally be given.

The Court does ask the parties to indicate in the listing questionnaire any dates that are inconvenient for the witnesses or the advocate.

As with the allocation questionnaire, the parties should consult with each other on completing it and particularly in relation to any further directions that are required in preparation for the trial.

In addition to Form N170 the Court will also serve a form N171 which details the date on which the listing questionnaire must be returned to the Court. When all listing questionnaires have been filed or the time for filing them has expired, the Court file will be passed to the Judge for directions (Paragraph 6.1(3), Practice Direction to Part 28). If no party files a listing questionnaire the Court will usually make an order that the listing questionnaires must be filed within three days from service of such order. If filing does not take place then the claim and any counterclaim will be struck out (Paragraph 6.5(1), Practice Direction to Part 28). If only one party files a listing questionnaire the Court would normally give listing directions but clearly this must depend on it having sufficient information. It is more likely to proceed upon receipt only of the claimant's listing questionnaire rather than the defendant's.

A fee is payable on the listing questionnaire. This fee in the fast track is £200. If the fee is not paid the Court will serve a notice on the claimant requiring payment of the fee and the date by which payment must be made. If the claimant does not pay the fee the claim will be struck out and the claimant will be liable for the costs which the defendant has incurred unless the Court orders otherwise (Rule 3.7). Rule 44.12 provides for the basis of assessment where a right to costs arises under Rule 3.7. The claim can be reinstated upon application under Rule 3.9 (Relief from Sanctions) but the relief granted will be conditional on a claimant paying a fee (Rule 3.7(7)). In the fast track, whether relief is granted or not will depend on whether the striking out has in any way affected the trial date. The defaulting claimant will have to be prompt in making the application for relief. Left too late and the trial date may have been vacated in which event the Court will be much more guarded in granting the claimant relief. Rule 3.7 provides the only circumstances akin to Order 17 Rule 11(9) CCR in which a claim will be struck out automatically by the Court. For this reason there was much debate in the Committee in relation to Rule 3.7 which was introduced at a late stage in the process of finalising the Rules.

The Court will usually give appropriate directions without the necessity of a hearing. However, under Rule 28.5(3) if—

- a party fails to file the completed questionnaire by the date specified;
- a party has failed to give all the information requested by the listing questionnaire; or
- the Court considers that a hearing is necessary to enable it to decide what directions to give in order to complete preparation of the case for trial;

the Court may fix a listing hearing. This will be held as early as possible and the parties will be given at least three days notice of the date which will be contained in Form N153 (Paragraph 6.3, Practice Direction to Part 28).

Listing Directions

In accordance with Rule 28.6 the Court will fix the date for trial as soon as practicable after the date specified for filing a completed listing questionnaire unless it has already done so in which case it will simply confirm the date. Notice of that fixing or confirmation will be given to the parties no less than three weeks before the hearing unless the parties have agreed to accept shorter notice which they can do in the listing questionnaire or the Court authorises shorter notice under Rule 28.6(2) "… in exceptional circumstances …". The notice of the hearing is in Form N172. The date that is fixed for the trial will be a calendar day (Paragraph 7.1(1), Practice Direction to Part 28). This is quite an important provision for practitioners. Thus the trial should commence at or near the beginning of the day and end some five hours later excluding the lunch break. If the parties attend at Court on the day of trial and the Court fails to comply with its obligations the parties might be entitled to compensation (at the time of writing the compensation scheme has yet to be finalised).

As well as fixing the trial date the Court will give appropriate directions. These may be in accordance with the directions agreed between the parties. These will deal with—

- the evidence to be produced at the trial, both oral and written, including expert evidence;
- a trial timetable and time estimate;
- the preparation of the trial bundle;

- any other matter needed to prepare the case for trial (Paragraph 7.2, Practice Direction to Part 28).

The appendix to the Practice Direction to Part 28 contains some standard directions following the filing of the listing questionnaire dealing with the matters above.

One of the directions that the Court may give is that a case summary not exceeding 250 words outlining the matters still in issue should be lodged with the bundle of papers for the Judge to read. As to the nature of a case summary some guidance is given in the practice direction to Part 29 (multi track). This provides—

5.7 (1) A case summary:

(a) should be designed to assist the court to understand and deal with the questions before it,

(b) should set out a brief chronology of the claim, the issues of fact which are agreed or in dispute and the evidence needed to decide them,

(c) should not normally exceed 500 (in the multi track) words in length, and

(d) should be prepared by the claimant and agreed with the other parties if possible.

Trial

The trial will take place on the date fixed by the Court. As above, this will be a calendar day. As a matter of Court management the Court will be listing a number of fast track cases to be heard on the same day on the basis that many will fall away by way of settlement. The County Courts do not usually list in this way and clearly there will be a learning curve for all involved. The process needs some flexibility on the part of the provision of Judges and this is likely to lead to a greater reliance upon Civil Trial Centres rather than individual courts with limited resources. The Court can postpone the trial prior to the day of hearing. If, however, the parties turn up at Court for the hearing and they do not get the appropriate time of the Court that day they may seek compensation, the scheme for which has yet to be finalised. The division of the five hours allotted to the parties is detailed above. As indicated, the Judge may have to read the papers prior to the commencement of the hearing. He may also dispense with an opening address from the parties' advocates (Paragraph 8.2, Practice Direction to part 28).

Generally the judge hearing the matter should comply with the trial timetable that has been set on listing although he is not strictly bound by it.

If the trial is not finished on the day for which it is listed, it should continue the next business day. In the past this has been a problem for practitioners with cases before the County Court being adjourned to dates considerably far ahead. A few County Courts have run a rolling list system but it is intended that this should be introduced for all County Courts.

Practitioners should expect judges to be relatively tight on the control of the trial and the time given to the parties to present their case and witnesses. As with previous practice, a witness statement will usually stand as evidence in chief. Permission is necessary from the Court for a party to amplify the witness statement or give evidence in relation to new matters which have arisen since the witness statement was served (Rule 32.5(3)). Under Rule 32.1(3) whilst the Court cannot dispense with cross examination altogether (which may lead to Article 6 problems), it can limit cross examination.

As above, the judiciary are encouraged to give the parties a decision on the day of trial. This should be followed immediately by the making of any consequential orders such as costs and summary assessment of those costs.

Costs in the Fast Track

Lord Woolf proposed an extensive limitation on the costs recoverable in the fast track. He estimated that the costs in relation to a claim of £10,000 should be no more than £2,500 excluding VAT and disbursements. He proposed three bands of recoverable costs based upon the value of the case. At that time the upper limit on fast track was proposed to be £10,000. In order to take this idea forward and to test it, the Institute of Advanced Legal Studies was commissioned by the Lord Chancellor's Department to undertake research using hypothetical case studies. Their report was published in June 1998. The result of the case study was that it was simply not possible to produce a framework for a fixed costs scheme because of the very differing views of practitioners as to the amount of work they thought necessary for different types of claim. The Institute advised that it was not able to determine a cost matrix based on the amount of work required. Instead it recommended that the question of cost in the fast track should be approached from the other end in that final quantification of costs would lead to a figure for recoverable costs which was proportionate to the value in dispute.

The Lord Chancellor's Department issued a consultation paper as a result in which it was proposed that pre-trial costs would be capped at 50% of the award (if in favour of the claimant) or the claim (if in favour of the defendant). Trial costs would be limited to a scale dependent upon the value again either of the award (of the claimant) or the claim (for the defendant).

As a result of the consultation the Committee considered rules to codify the Lord Chancellor's recommendations.

Fixed Trial Costs

Part 46 is the source of the regulation of fast track trial costs. In a manner it is suggested that the length and complexity of this Part evidences the difficulty in trying to place a rigid framework into a system in which there are many outcomes, making regulation difficult.

The broad scheme of things is that the successful party will be able to recover only a fixed amount for the fees of the advocate for the preparation and attendance on the trial. If a party's legal representative attends the trial with the advocate then the Court may award an additional sum in respect of that attendance.

The Rules

The question of quantification of the recoverable costs in the fast track may arise either upon summary assessment after the trial or in detailed costs assessment at some subsequent point. As below, the Court is encouraged to summarily assess costs immediately after the trial wherever possible. Subject to certain exceptions contained in Rule 46.3, if the Court has made an order for costs in favour of one of the parties which order covers the trial, the Court must award to the receiving party a figure for the trial costs (a defined term) on the scale set out in Rule 46.2(1).

46.2 (1) The following table shows the amount of fast track trial costs which the court may award (whether by summary or detailed assessment).

Value of the claim	Amount of fast track trial costs which the court may award
Up to £3,000	£350
More than £3,000 but not more than £10,000	£500
More than £10,000	£750

The exceptions are set out in Rule 46.3 (see below). When making an order for costs the Court has a general power to apportion costs. This is also reflected in Part 36 in that the Court may apportion the scale costs between the parties to reflect respective degrees of success on the issues at trial (Rule 46.2(2)).

The work included within the "trial cost" is the cost (excluding VAT and other disbursements) of an advocate (a person exercising a right of audience as a representative of, or on behalf of, a party) for preparing for and appearing at the trial (which includes a hearing for the assessment of damages following default judgment or judgment on admission but excludes the hearing of an application for summary judgment or a hearing for the Court's approval of a settlement or other compromise on behalf of or against a child or patient)—see Rule 46.1.

Although the fixed trial costs do not apply to a "disposal hearing" at which the amount to be paid under a judgment or order is to be decided by the Court (Paragraph 1.3(6), Practice Direction to Part 26).

The question addressed by Rule 46.2 is how to value the claim. There are differing regimes for the claimant and the defendant. If the order is made in favour of the claimant then the value of the claim is based upon the total amount of the judgment taking into account any reduction for contributory negligence but excluding interest and costs (Rule 46.2(3)(a)). If the order is made in favour of the defendant the value of the claim is the value of the claim specified in the claim form (Rule 46.2(3)(b)(i) and (ii)). If the claimant stated in the claim form that he could not reasonably say how much he expected to recover, the maximum scale costs are payable, i.e. £750 (Rule 46.2(3)(b)(iii)).

If the claimant sought only a remedy other than the payment of money the value of the claim for assessing recoverable costs for either the claimant or the defendant is deemed to be the middle band, i.e. recoverable costs are £500 (Rule 46.2(4)).

If the claim is a hybrid for both the payment of money and some other remedy the value of the claim is for these purposes deemed to be the higher of—

- the value of the money claimed decided in accordance with Rule 46.2(3); or
- the deemed value of the other remedy decided in accordance with Rule 46.2(4);

unless the Court orders otherwise.

As with all of the Rules a Part 20 claim including a counterclaim is treated as a separate claim (Rule 20.3). If there is a counterclaim which has a higher value than the claim, if the claimant succeeds at trial both on the claim and the counterclaim the value of the counterclaim is the appropriate value for assessing the cost to be awarded to the claimant (Rule 46.2(6)). Rule 46.3(6) deals with the situation in which the defendant makes a counterclaim against the claimant and the claimant succeeds on his claim and the defendant succeeds on the counterclaim. In that event the Court quantifies the amount of the claim (with no regard to the counterclaim) and quantifies the counterclaim (again with no regard to the claim). It then assesses the award of costs that would be made on the basis of those values and deducts the lower from the higher. The party that was entitled to the higher award of costs receives the difference between the two. Thus if a claim has a value of, say £3,000, and the counterclaim has a value of £10,000, the resultant award to the Part 20 claimant for the trial costs would be £150 (the difference between £350 and £500). Subject to dividing the scale costs between the parties to reflect degrees of success, the Court does not have a discretion to award more or less than the scale costs save for those circumstances set out in Rule 46.3.

Rule 46.3(2) provides that a legal representative (defined in Rule 2.3) attending the trial is entitled to an additional award of £250. The Court will have to be persuaded, however, that it was necessary for the legal representative to attend to assist the advocate. This may not always be easy but will certainly be a contentious issue. The Court will have regard to the overriding objective and particularly the question of proportionality. On the other hand it is suggested that a legal representative may be necessary to deal with questions of settlement of the claim or costs bearing in mind that the Court is going to make a summary assessment of them. Whilst the Court has a discretion about making the award of the additional costs, it has no discretion as to the quantification of it. If the award is made, the figure is fixed at £250. As with the trial costs the figure of £250 is not affected by the length of trial. Whether it lasts for five minutes or a day, the figure of £250 is fixed although clearly the length of the trial may have some bearing on whether the Court considers it necessary for a legal representative to attend. Again the figure of £250 is not affected by the level of legal representative attending and it remains the same whether it be a solicitor or a trainee. Again, however, the level of person attending is likely to affect the Court's consideration of whether it was necessary for anyone to attend.

Split trials may be dealt with on the fast track (Paragraph 9.1(3)(d), Practice Direction to Part 26). If a separate trial is directed by the Court then the Court can award an additional amount in respect of the separate trial but that award cannot exceed two-thirds of the amount awarded for the first trial subject to a minimum award of £350. Thus if the value of the claim as measured by Rule 46.2(3) for the claimant is more than £10,000 the costs which may be awarded will be £750 on the first trial and £500 on the separate trial (Rule 46.3(3) and (4)).

Rule 46.3(5) deals with the costs to be awarded to a litigant in person. Generally recoverable costs for litigants in person are dealt with in Rule 48.6 (see page 396). If the litigant in person can prove financial loss then the Court will award him two-thirds of the amount that would have been awarded had that person been represented by an advocate. In order to prove financial loss the litigant in person must produce to the Court any written evidence he relies on to support that claim and serve a copy of that evidence on any party against whom he seeks costs at least 24 hours before the hearing at which the question may be decided (Paragraph 1.4, Practice Direction to Part 48). If he cannot prove financial loss then the Court will award him £9.25 per hour (see Paragraph 1.6, Practice Direction to Part 48) for the time spent reasonably doing the work, i.e. preparing for the trial and attending upon it.

When the Court is considering the question of awarding the trial costs it can take into account unreasonable or improper behaviour on the part of either party. If it considers that the receiving party has behaved unreasonably or improperly **during the trial** it may reduce the amount awarded. If the paying party has behaved improperly, again, during the trial, an additional amount could be added to the costs awarded. Note that this only applies to the fast track trial costs as defined, i.e. the costs of the advocate and not any additional award for the legal representative's attendance.

Costs where there is more than one Claimant or Defendant

The final provision under Part 46 deals with the situation where there is more than one claimant or defendant.

Rule 46.4(1)(ii) and (iii) deals with the situation where there is more than one claimant. If one advocate acts for more than one party, those parties can only recover jointly one award. If the claim against the defendant is a joint claim amongst the claimants, then the value of the claim is assessed against the value of that joint claim. If, however, they have separate claims the value is determined in accordance with Rule 46.4(3)—

- if the only claim of each claimant is for a payment of money and the award is in favour of the claimants, the value of the claim is the aggregate of the judgment made in favour of all the claimants jointly represented by the advocate;

- if the only claim of each claimant is for the payment of money and the award is made in favour of the defendant, the value of the claim is the aggregate amount claimed by the claimants;
- if the claim of each claimant is for a remedy other than the payment of money then the value of the claim is the middle band for claims of more than £3,000 but not more than £10,000;
- if the claims of the claimants' are hybrid claims for money and other remedies then the value is again either deemed to be the middle band of the scale or based on the total aggregate of the money claims calculated as above dependent on whether the award is in favour of the claimants or the defendants;

If there is more than one claimant and a single defendant and the award is made in favour of the defendant then the defendant can receive only one award for which the claimants are jointly and severally liable (Rule 46.4(5));

If there is more than one defendant and any or all of the defendants are separately represented, each of those separately represented is entitled to an award of the scale costs if the Court makes an order for costs in their favour.

Pre-Trial costs

Other than the fixed trial costs under Part 46, fast track costs will be assessed in the usual way. If an award is made in favour of a party under Rule 44.3, the costs will be assessed either on the standard basis or on the indemnity basis under Rule 44.4. On the standard basis the important qualification is that the Court will only allow costs which are proportionate to the matters in issue (Rule 44.4(2)(a)). This question of proportionality is raised initially in the overriding objective but is likely to have its greatest force in this small provision within the costs rules. In the consultation paper referred to above, the Lord Chancellor referred to proportionality meaning a cap of 50% of the claim. This question was much debated in the Civil Procedure Rule Committee. It was agreed particularly that the concept of proportionality adopted by the Committee and included within the Rules did not equate with a fixed cap. This debate emanated from anecdotal evidence that some courts were considering setting fixed caps for recoverable costs both on the fast track and multi track. The result of the ensuing debate was Paragraphs 3.1, 3.2 and 3.3 of the Practice Direction to Part 44. These Paragraphs are worth repeating in full.

> *3.1 In applying the test of proportionality the court will have regard to rule 1.1(2)(c). The relationship between the total of the costs incurred and the financial value of the claim may not be a reliable guide. A fixed percentage cannot be applied in all cases to the value of the claim in order to ascertain whether or not the costs are proportionate.*
>
> *3.2 In any proceedings there will be costs which will inevitably be incurred and which are necessary for the successful conduct of the case. Solicitors are not required to conduct litigation at rates which are uneconomic. Thus in a modest claim the proportion of costs is likely to be higher than in a large claim, and may even equal or possibly exceed the amount in dispute.*

3.3 Where a trial takes place, the time taken by the court in dealing with a particular issue may not be an accurate guide to the amount of time properly spent by the legal or other representatives in preparation for the trial of that issue.

The consultation paper referred to the quantification of costs on the basis of valuing the claim rather than applying simple measurement of the time that has been spent on the case. This attitude is reflected in Rule 44.5(3) which sets out the matters to which the Court is to have regard when quantifying the costs. The matters are set out in order of priority. Most important is the conduct of the parties before as well as during the proceedings and the efforts made to try to resolve the dispute. Secondly, the Court will look at the amount or value of any money or property involved. The time spent on the case is consigned to the penultimate item. This consignment does not, however, sit well with the process of assessment whether it be by summary assessment (see below) or detailed costs assessment. In both cases the parties submit details of the costs based upon hourly charges and time spent. It is suggested that in practice the Court will look at time spent on the case initially and then apply the principles of proportionality based upon the value of the claim.

The Lord Chancellor has recently announced that his Department is still intent on imposing a fixed scale of costs for the whole fast track procedure. Until then the test of proportionality will be the main limiting factor.

Procedure for assessing the costs

The Court can assess costs either summarily or by a detailed costs assessment. The Court is encouraged to make a summary assessment of costs at the conclusion of a trial on the fast track (see Paragraph 4.4, Practice Direction to Part 44). Accordingly the parties must be ready to deal with costs at the conclusion of a fast track trial. The procedure is set out in Paragraph 4.5 of the Practice Direction to Part 44. A written statement of the costs should be prepared in the form of the statement of the costs which is Form 1 of the cost forms. That statement must be filed at Court and copies must be served on any party against whom an order for payment of those costs is intended to be sought as soon as possible and in any event not less than 24 hours before the date fixed for the hearing. If a party does not comply with that obligation the Court will take that failure into account when deciding on the appropriate amount. If costs result from the failure they may be awarded against the defaulting party. There are some limitations on summary assessment set out in Paragraph 4.9 of the Practice Direction to Part 44—

- There can be no summary assessment of the costs of a receiving party who is an assisted person within the meaning of the Legal Aid Act 1988.
- Whilst the Court can summarily assess the costs payable by an assisted person, that assessment is not itself a determination of the assisted person's liability to pay those costs.
- The Court can only make a summary assessment of the costs if the receiving party is a child or patient (see Part 21) if the solicitor acting for the child or patient has waived the right to further costs.

CHAPTER 18
PART 29—MULTI TRACK

Scope of the Track

In accordance with Rule 26.6(6)—

> **The multi track is the normal track for any claim for which the small claims track or the fast track is not the normal track.**

By the process of exclusion therefore, the multi track is the normal track for anything with a financial value of more than £15,000 or if under that value (applying Rule 26.6(5)) it is likely to last for longer than one day and/or it will be necessary (taking into account the overriding objective) for oral expert evidence at trial to exceed one expert per party in relation to any expert field and expert evidence in more than two expert fields.

Lord Woolf's Recommendations

The small claims track took up the existing small claims procedure under the CCR and developed it. The fast track was new. It forms, however, a central part of the Woolf landscape for litigation. The multi track received less attention than the fast track but at its core is one of the main Woolf recommendations which has been carried forward into the Rules—case management.

This is not to suggest that claims over £15,000 should be regarded as outside Lord Woolf's landscape—they are very much part of it. Practitioners, however, will find the least change from previous practice for claims proceeding in the multi track. This general view, however, should not be taken to suggest that the practice for claims over £15,000 does not change.

Lord Woolf made a number of recommendations in relation to multi track cases—

- The procedural judge should undertake an initial scrutiny when the defence is received with a view to doing one or more of the following—
- fixing a case management conference;
- issuing directions in writing for the preparation of a case;
- fixing a date for the trial;
- specifying a period within which it is intended that the trial should take place;
- fixing a pre-trial review.
- The allocation questionnaire will assist the judge in his work.

- The objective of the case management conference is to set the agenda for the case before significant costs have been incurred and too much time has elapsed. At a case management conference the procedural judge will narrow the issues, decide on the appropriate future work and case management required, set a trial date and a timetable for the case, and consider ADR and the question of costs.
- Parties should file statements of issues, if possible agreed beforehand, for the conference.
- Where a party has refused unreasonably a proposal by the Court that ADR should be attempted, or has acted uncooperatively in the course of ADR, the Court should be able to take that into account in deciding what order to make as to costs.
- The dates of the case management conference, the pre-trial review and the trial cannot be changed except with the permission of the Court. Parties would be able to agree other changes to the timetable subject to the overriding power of the Court to intervene if appropriate and any such agreement should be notified to the Court, with the proposed new timetable.
- Application to vary the timetable must be made within the relevant time limit. If that time has passed, a sanction will apply automatically, unless relief is applied for.
- A listing questionnaire should be sent out by the Court at a time specified in the initial directions to establish whether directions have been complied with and to inform the decision on hearing time.
- At a pre-trial review about eight to ten weeks before the hearing the judge will settle the statement of issues to be tried and set a programme for trial.
- A general streamlined procedure should be developed for the assistance of judges and practitioners for more straightforward cases on the multi track. This should involve limited disclosure and expert evidence, a short timetable and limited trial time and a system of controlled costs which, while less restrictive than in the fast track, would provide many of the same benefits to parties.

These recommendations are repeated here because they describe quite well the system that is now provided by Part 29.

Allocation

Part 26 deals with the allocation of cases to a particular track and the reader is referred to page 152 Part 26 which covers the subject of the allocation questionnaire. The scope of the multi track is set out above. If a claim has a financial value and that financial value assessed by the Court exceeds the limit for fast track, the claim cannot be allocated to the fast track unless the parties consent (Rule 26.7(3)). The parties may be a little shy of agreeing that a claim which would normally proceed in the multi track should be allocated to the fast track bearing in mind some of the limitations specifically imposed or likely to be imposed in the fast track.

It should be remembered, however, that the Court will be quite free to impose similar restrictions upon a claim in the multi track. Indeed, as recommended by Lord Woolf, for the simpler types of case just in excess of the fast track limit, the Court might give directions mirroring those in the fast track. It would certainly be within the discretion of the Court to limit the trial to one day and to award limited recoverable costs.

There is no provision relating to the fast track and the multi track by which if the parties agree to the allocation to the fast track of a claim that would normally proceed in the multi track, the multi track regime in costs applies to the proceedings notwithstanding the allocation by consent to the fast track. (This is unlike the provision under Rule 27.14(5) which relates to allocation between the fast track and the small claims track). The reason for the absence of such a provision between the fast track and multi track is that the automatic regime applying in the fast track under Part 28 may be applied in any event to a multi track case just above the fast track limit under Part 29.

As with the other two tracks, if the claim has a financial value the Court should also consider the factors set out in Rule 26.8(1) in deciding on the appropriate track. If the claim has no financial value then the Court should allocate it to the track which it considers most suitable having regard to the matters set out in Rule 26.8(1)(b)-(i) (Rule 26.7(3)). The factors set out in Rule 26.8(1) have previously been discussed (see page 165). One point that is mentioned in the Practice Direction (Paragraph 9.1(e), Practice Direction to Part 26) is that if as a result of a counterclaim or other Part 20 claim the trial will last more than a day, the Court may not allocate it to the fast track.

In certain cases the hands of the Court are tied—

- If a claim is issued under the alternative procedure (Part 8) it is treated as being allocated to the multi track although there is no formal allocation. Part 26 is specifically dis-applied by Rule 8.9(c).
- Certain specialist proceedings must be allocated to multi track, for instance, proceedings before the Technology & Construction Court or before the Commercial Court.

The parties are obliged to co-operate in all matters before the Court but particularly in relation to completion of the allocation questionnaire. If the parties are considering allocation to a particular track then they should liaise over their submissions to the Court although, as ever, the Court is not bound by them but will take them into account.

As to the timing of allocation, notification to the parties and application for re-allocation or appeal, see page 165.

Case Management Directions

The parties are obliged to co-operate with each other in relation to the management of the case, subject to the Court's agreement to their proposals. Under Rule 29.4 (supported by Paragraph 4.6, Practice Direction to Part 29) the parties should try to agree proposals for the management of proceedings (including a proposed trial date or period in which the trial is to take place). If the Court finds the proposals suitable, it may approve them and give directions in the terms proposed.

The Practice Direction sets out the matters which should be included in any proposals made by the parties (Paragraph 4.7 and 4.8). The directions **must**—

- Set out a timetable by reference to calendar dates for the taking of steps for the preparation of the case.
- Include a date or a period (the trial period) when it is proposed that the trial will take place (which date or period must be no later than is reasonably necessary).
- Include provision about disclosure of documents which, as with fast track could—
- limit disclosure to standard disclosure or less than that; and/or
- direct that disclosure will only take place by the supply of copy documents without a list accompanied by a disclosure statement unless the parties specifically agree to dispense with the statement.
- Include provision about factual and expert evidence including its disclosure. The agreement might reflect that no expert evidence is required or that there should only be a single joint expert. If parties are to have separate expert evidence then there should be provision within the agreement as to the exchange of such evidence and subsequent discussion.

In addition to these requirements, the agreed directions could provide also for—

- the filing of any reply or amended statement of case that may be required; and
- the date for service of request for further information and answers under Part 18 and of questions to and responses from experts under Rule 35.6.

Unlike the small claims track and the fast track, there are no standard directions for multi track contained in the Practice Direction. For guidance, however, particularly in relatively straightforward multi track cases, parties might have regard to the appendix to the Practice Direction to Part 28 (fast track) when attempting to agree directions on the filing of the allocation questionnaire.

The Court has a discretion in relation to the directions it gives and does not have to follow those agreed between the parties but it should take them into account in deciding what directions to give (Paragraph 4.9, Practice Direction to Part 29).

If directions are given of the Court's own initiative without holding a case management conference, there will be generally set standard directions. Again these will follow the form of directions listed in the appendix to the Practice Direction to Part 28. In particular the Court will deal with—

- Filing and service of any further information required to clarify either party's case.
- Standard disclosure of documents.
- The disclosure of witness statements by way of simultaneous exchange.
- The appointment of a single joint expert on any appropriate issue **unless there is good reason not to do so**. Note, however, that the Court

cannot make an order under Rule 35.7 directing that evidence on a particular issue is to be given by a single expert without holding a case management conference unless the parties consent in writing. Similarly, if the Court is proposing to appoint an assessor under Rule 35.15, a case management conference must be held unless the parties consent in writing (Paragraph 4.13, Practice Direction to Part 29).

- If the parties are to have separate experts, the disclosure of experts' reports either by way of a sequential or simultaneous exchange. Paragraph 4.11 of the Practice Direction to Part 29 provides that if expert evidence is required both on issues of liability and on the amount of damages, the Court may direct that the exchange of reports relating to liability should be simultaneous but that those relating to quantification be sequential. Subject to this the usual direction will be for simultaneous exchange.
- If experts' reports are not agreed, the discussion between experts under Rule 35.12 and the preparation of their report to the Court under Rule 35.12(3).
- The listing of a case management conference/pre-trial review, usually after the time for the direction has expired.
- The trial date or trial period.

Case Management in the Royal Courts of Justice

The Practice Direction to Part 29 (Paragraphs 2.1-2.7) makes specific rules relating to cases in the Royal Courts of Justice (whether in the Queen's Bench or Chancery Divisions). Generally claims with an estimated value of less than £50,000 will be transferred to a County Court although the Court has the discretion to transfer cases of higher value. The transfer is effected in accordance with Section 40 County Courts Act 1984 and Part 30 CPR. The Court can act of its own volition under Rule 3.3. There is no requirement for a hearing but in that event the parties do have the opportunity to return to the Court to seek to overturn the order.

The transfer will not take place, usually, if either party is proposing to make an application to strike out a statement of case or for summary judgment under Part 24 or some interim remedy under Part 25 (Paragraph 2.5, Practice Direction to Part 29).

Whatever the value of the claim, particularly in relation to claims below or around £50,000, the parties should state in their allocation questionnaire whether they claim that the matter should remain in the Royal Courts of Justice. Paragraph 2.6 of the Practice Direction to Part 29 sets out the types of claims that would be suitable for the Royal Courts of Justice such as professional negligence or defamation.

Case Management Conference

If the Court concludes that it really needs to discuss directions with the parties rather than making directions in accordance with an agreement between the parties or of its own initiative, it will fix a case management conference. Lord

Woolf at page 62 (Paragraph 11) of the Final Report set out some aims for the procedural judge at the case management conference—

- to identify the key issues;
- to earmark issues for summary disposal;
- to explore the scope for ADR or settlement;
- to give directions as to witness statements, experts' reports and the disclosure of documents, including setting a limit where appropriate;
- to set a timetable for the case;
- to consider the trial date or trial period, the date when the listing questionnaire should be sent out;
- whether there should be a pre-trial review and the estimated length of the trial;
- to find out what costs have been incurred to date and to control likely future costs.

In the Royal Courts of Justice the case management conference will usually take place in front of a Master. This may change, particularly in relation to specialist proceedings. For example, in both the Technology & Construction Court and in the Commercial Court, case management is dealt with by the Judge. In a District Registry or County Court, case management will generally be dealt with by a District Judge. In the County Court, however, the Circuit Judge might deal with case management particularly if, for instance, it is allocated to a business list.

The parties need to prepare for a case management conference. In particular the Court may require that a case summary should be filed with the Court. This is a document which will generally be prepared by a claimant and agreed with the other parties. It should not exceed 500 words in length. It should include a brief chronology of the claim, the issues of fact which are agreed or in dispute and the evidence needed to decide them. Generally a case summary should be able to assist the Court to understand and deal with the questions before it on the case management conference (Paragraph 5.7, Practice Direction to Part 29).

The parties should consider whether they want an order that would not usually be made at the case management conference. If an order is sought then the party should issue and serve an application specifying the order (complying with Part 23) in good time for it to be heard at the case management conference. If a party believes that the time allowed for the case management conference is insufficient then it should inform the Court. As ever, if an adjournment is required, the Court could impose a cost sanction.

In further preparation for the case management conference the party should—

- ensure that all documents that the Court is likely to ask to see (including witness statements and experts reports) are brought to the hearing;
- consider whether the parties should attend;
- consider whether a case summary would be useful; and
- consider what orders each party wishes to be made and give notice of them to the other party.

(Paragraph 5.6, Practice Direction to Part 29)

Under Rule 29.3(2) if a party has a legal representative, the person who attends the case management conference must be familiar with the case and be able to deal with any issues that are likely to arise. The Practice Direction takes the point a little further in Paragraph 5.2(2) by suggesting that the person who attends must be personally involved in the conduct of the case. It is suggested, however, that this will not always be practicable. Solicitors often use agents to attend hearings in front of courts local to the agent but far distant from the instructing solicitor. The instructing of an agent makes economic sense from everyone's point of view. It may be doubted that an agent is personally involved in the conduct of the case. However, to require solicitors or their employees to travel long distances to attend case management conferences does not with respect make much sense. No doubt the agent must have the authority and information to deal with any matter which may reasonably be expected to be dealt with at a case management conference including the fixing of the timetable, the identification of issues and matters of evidence (Paragraph 5.2(2), Practice Direction to Part 29).

As well as the requirement that the legal representative attending should be familiar with the case and have appropriate authority, the Court can also require the parties themselves to attend, exercising the general powers of management under Rule 3.1(2)(c). Lord Woolf saw this as a critical part of the case management process, particularly with a view to encouraging the parties to try to settle the case at that stage. Lord Woolf put it this way—

> **The conference is a significant opportunity to take important decisions about a case, including the possibility of settlement or referring the dispute to ADR, and to consider the cost so far and the estimate of the future costs. The client must be enabled to know what has happened and be involved in the decisions about the future of the action. The litigation is his responsibility. He has both an interest in being involved and a duty to be involved. The presence of the parties will ensure that the lawyers take the event seriously and prepare for it properly.**

Lord Woolf strongly recommended that parties should almost always be required to attend the case management conference when one is fixed—

> **To ensure the effectiveness and emphasise the importance of case management conferences ... I believe that it is essential for the lay client to attend, or for someone to attend on his behalf, unless this is very difficult to arrange. Exhortation is not enough. The onus must be on the parties, before the conference, to give very good reasons to the Court why they are not attending.**

It remains to be seen how far the courts put Lord Woolf's encouragement into effect. There has been much debate about whether it is really appropriate to order the parties to attend when it may well be that the parties have little or no interest in the continuing proceedings with an insurance company picking up the tab. The power of the Court is, however, limited to a requirement that the party attend. If that requirement is made, presumably the Court will be flexible if, taking the example above, a representative of the insurance company attends effectively as a representative of the party.

Paragraph 5.3 of the Practice Direction to Part 29 sets out the topics which the Court is likely to consider at the case management conference.

5.3 The topics the court will consider at a case management conference are likely to include:

(1) whether the claimant has made clear the claim he is bringing, in particular the amount he is claiming, so that the other party can understand the case he has to meet,

(2) whether any amendments are required to the claim, a statement of case or any other document,

(3) what disclosure of documents, if any, is necessary,

(4) what expert evidence is reasonably required in accordance with rule 35.1 and how and when that evidence should be obtained and disclosed,

(5) what factual evidence should be disclosed,

(6) what arrangements should be made about the giving of clarification or further information and the putting of questions to experts, and

(7) whether it will be just and will save costs to order a split trial or the trial of one or more preliminary issues.

Other matters which the Court may consider at the case management conference would include the location of trial, the level of judge that should hear the claim and whether the claim should be transferred to another court or into a specialist list.

Variation of Directions

The Practice Direction to Part 29 contains a like provision to that in the fast track as to the variation of directions following the making of them either at a case management conference or without a hearing. If there has been no hearing and a party is dissatisfied with a direction then they should make an application to vary the directions. That application should be made within 14 days of service of the order containing the directions. If made later, the Court may take that into account when making an appropriate order. The application to vary will usually be heard by the same judge who gave the directions or a judge of the same level.

If a party is dissatisfied with the case management directions given at a case management conference, they should appeal in the usual way to the judge on the next level or as appropriate.

Under Rule 2.11 the parties can vary the dates set by the Court for particular steps included in the directions. Under Rule 29.5, however, the parties are not entitled to vary dates for—

- a case management conference;
- a pre-trial review;
- the return of the listing questionnaire under Rule 29.6;
- the trial; or
- the trial period.

Neither can they vary any dates, the knock-on effect of which would be to interfere with the dates mentioned above. Subject to that limitation, if dates are varied there is no requirement to notify the Court of that variation.

Similarly the parties can agree to limit the extent or procedure for disclosure and inspection under Part 31. Again, any agreement to this effect does not have to be notified to the Court.

If the Court's permission is necessary to vary the milestone dates as above then the parties must apply for an appropriate order. That order may be by consent. Unless there are good reasons it is unlikely that the Court will allow a variation of the trial date or trial period, particularly if variation is sought late in the day.

Failure to comply with the Directions

As detailed previously, there appears to be a debate amongst the judiciary as to exactly what happens when a party fails to comply with an order that requires a step to be taken on or before a certain date. It is suggested by some that that party would need to apply for relief from the Court in order to extend the period in which that act can be done. On the face of it that application would be made under Rule 3.9. The alternative view is reflected in the practice directions for both Part 28 (fast track) and Part 29 (multi track). Paragraph 7.1 of the Practice Direction to Part 29 stipulates that when a party fails to comply with a direction given by the Court, any other party should apply without delay for an order requiring a compliance and/or for the imposition of a sanction. Before making such an application, the applicant should notify the other party of their intention to do so (Paragraph 7.2). The court may, however, stipulate in advance that failure to comply with certain directions will automatically lead to the imposition of sanctions. It is suggested that this will be rare in practice.

The warning in relation to interfering with the trial date following a failure to comply with the order for directions is driven home by Paragraph 7.4 of the Practice Direction to Part 29. Where there has been a failure to comply, the Court will not adjourn the trial unless there are very good reasons for doing so. Where those reasons exist, the Court should first consider whether it can avoid the problem by any means including limiting what issues will be decided by the Court at the trial. In that event any defaulting party may be made liable to pay the costs wasted by the necessity for any further hearing. If adjournment of the trial is inevitable, the Court will postpone it for the shortest possible time and give appropriate directions.

At any hearing required to consider these issues, the Court is encouraged in the Practice Direction (Paragraph 7.4(6)) to require the attendance of solicitors and the parties themselves.

Listing Questionnaires and Listing

One of the directions given by the Court is the date on which completed listing questionnaires must be returned to the Court following service by it.

That service will take place in good time and should be no less than 14 days before the date specified for the return of completed questionnaires. The Rules do not require the parties to serve allocation questionnaires on each other but the Practice Direction (Paragraph 8.1(5), Practice Direction) does encourage the parties to exchange them so that any differences between them are ironed out before the completed questionnaires are submitted to the Court.

If neither party files a listing questionnaire the Court will normally make an unless order of its own initiative to the effect that unless the listing questionnaire is filed by any of the parties within three days from service of the order, the claim and any counterclaim will be struck out.

There is a fee on the filing of the listing questionnaire. It is £300 in the multi track. If the fee is not paid the Court will issue a notice under Rule 3.7 specifying the date by which the claimant must pay the fee. If payment is not made by that date, the claim will be struck out automatically under Rule 3.7.

Upon filing the listing questionnaire the parties are required to provide the Court with an estimate of costs already incurred and costs to be incurred which he intends to seek to recover from any other party under an order for costs. Unlike the allocation questionnaire, there is no space for the estimate. The parties must comply with Section 4 of the Practice Direction to Part 43. This requires that the estimate should be substantially in the form of a statement of costs as illustrated in Form 1 of the cost forms. Paragraph 4.5(3) provides further that the party compiling the statement of costs must show separately the costs which have already been incurred and those which will be incurred if the case proceeds to trial.

If only one of the parties files a listing questionnaire the Court will fix a listing hearing. This slightly differs from the provisions under Part 28 in which the Court will usually give listing directions based upon the one or more questionnaires completed and filed. At least three days notice of the listing hearing will be given to the parties (Paragraph 8.4). At the hearing the Court will normally fix or confirm the trial date and make other appropriate orders. In completing the listing questionnaires the parties should co-operate to determine whether or not they can agree directions. If so, when returning the completed listing questionnaires they could also file an agreed draft order. Those directions should deal with—

- evidence, especially expert evidence;
- a trial timetable and time estimate;
- the preparation of a trial bundle; and
- any other matter needed to prepare the case for trial.

Again, reference back to the standard directions on the fast track appearing as an appendix to the Practice Direction to Part 28, will give parties some idea of what is expected.

At this stage the Court may decide that it wants to hold a listing hearing or a pre-trial review. Indeed, in the original directions upon allocation or at the case management conference, the Court may have fixed the date for a pre-trial review. A listing hearing will be held if the Court considers that a hearing is necessary in order to enable it to decide what direction to give in order to complete preparation of the case for trial (Rule 29.6(3)(c)). The parties will be given at least three days notice of the hearing (Paragraph 9.4, Practice Direction to Part 29).

A pre-trial review might be held at the same time as a listing hearing or at some later point in the process to ensure, for instance, that the parties have complied with the directions given on listing. If a pre-trial review is to be held then the Court must give at least seven days notice (Rule 29.7). If a pre-trial review was fixed at some earlier stage and is then cancelled, again the Court must give seven days notice of that cancellation.

Both a listing hearing and a pre-trial review would be used by the Court in much the same way as the case management conference to consider with the parties what issues need to be addressed at trial, what evidence is required and whether the claim can be settled by agreement. For this purpose once again the legal representative attending should be familiar with the case and able to make decisions in relation to it. It may be appropriate that the trial advocate should attend. Further, the Court might require the parties to attend, exercising its power under Rule 3.1(2)(c).

If the parties have not agreed directions then either at a listing hearing or of its own initiative the Court will make appropriate directions. These will follow very much those referred to above including the fixing of the trial date or a trial week (Rule 29.8(ii)). The trial week is defined as the week within which the trial is to begin. If the trial date or trial week has already been fixed then the Court will simply confirm the date to the parties.

In addition to fixing the date, the Court will set a timetable for the trial unless a timetable has already been fixed or the Court considers that it would be inappropriate to do so (Rule 29.8(i)).

As with case management directions, the parties are entitled to vary the date for compliance with directions given on listing or at the pre-trial review. They cannot interfere, however, without the Court's permission with the trial date. Again, if there has been a failure on a party to comply with an order and this has a knock-on effect upon the trial date, the Court will adjourn the trial only as a last resort with appropriate orders as to costs.

The Trial

A trial in the multi track is less regulated by the Rules and the practice directions than trials in either of the other tracks. Lord Woolf recommended, however, that in partnership with the parties, the Court should lay down in advance exactly what will happen at the trial—

> **An important task of the pre-trial review is to determine the timetable of the trial ... periods for examination and cross examination of witnesses are fixed in advance. Disruption to the parties' and witnesses' business is reduced and Counsel prepare**

their questions and argument on a concentrated and specific basis. Listing by the Court will then be able to be more accurate and precise.

If a timetable has been set, the Court will usually try and follow it but the judge has the discretion to vary it appropriately. If there is no timetable set then the judge may set one of his own initiative at the beginning of the trial.

Unlike the fast track there is no requirement on the Court to provide a calendar day for hearings. If, however, a trial does not take place when it is fixed to take place, the parties may be able to claim compensation subject to a new scheme being introduced at the time of writing.

Certain trial management issues are mentioned in the Practice Direction to Part 29 to emphasise them, in particular, those dealing with evidence under Part 32. Upon giving judgment the Court will deal in the usual way with costs. Although the costs Practice Direction (Paragraph 4.4, Practice Direction to Part 24) mentions specifically summary assessment for fast track cases, the Court may make a summary assessment of costs in multi track cases (see Paragraph 10.5, Practice Direction to Part 29). The parties will have filed estimates of costs in accordance with Section 4, Practice Direction to Part 43. In preparation for a potential summary assessment of costs the parties should have ready for the Court (and possibly served and filed beforehand) schedules of costs in the form of Form 1 of the costs forms.

Trials will usually take place at a Civil Trial Centre. As mentioned in relation to fast track, the Court needs the flexibility of resources (i.e. judges) to deal with the new listing process under the CPR. Obviously the drawback is the requirement to travel to a Civil Trial Centre. On the other hand, the advantage is that cases should come on for hearing on the day fixed and the Court will be able to maintain a rolling list, i.e. if a case is not finished at the end of the business day, it will continue on the next business day and so on until it is concluded (Paragraph 10.6 Practice Direction to Part 29).

CHAPTER 19
PART 30—TRANSFER

Introduction

One of the logical conclusions to be drawn from these forms is that there is no particular necessity to maintain the High Court and County Court as separate jurisdictions. As the jurisdiction of the County Court has been increased over the years, the rationale behind the division has become less acute. The only remaining issue is the assignment of a particular claim to a judge of certain experience and standing. This does not require a division between the High Court and County Court but simply some hierarchical system for judges and their assignment to particular cases. We may well see ultimately the combination of the High Court and County Court into a simple civil court system.

Until that happens there are some important differences. Proceedings in the High Court are regulated by the Supreme Court Act 1981 and in the County Court by the County Courts Act 1984. The County Court is a specifically statutory body and derives all its powers from the statute. If a power is not given by statute then the County Court does not have it. The High Court, however, has its own inherent jurisdiction which it uses regularly. It provides the High Court with a degree of flexibility not enjoyed by the County Court.

Part 30 of the CPR which deals with the transfer of proceedings between County Courts, between the High Court and the County Courts, the Royal Courts of Justice and the District Registries and between District Registries reflects some of the loosening of the jurisdictional limits of the Courts.

Section 1 of the County Courts Act 1984 divided England and Wales into various districts and appointed courts for those districts. This placed jurisdictional limits on the County Courts. These have been removed by Section 10, Schedule 2 paragraph 2(1), (4) to the Civil Procedure Act 1997.

Otherwise, the jurisdiction of County Courts and High Courts is determined by a whole range of statutes and regulations, for instance, the Courts and Legal Services Act 1990, the County Courts Act 1984, the Supreme Court Act 1981, the High Court and County Courts Jurisdiction Order 1991 and the County Court Remedies Regulations 1991. This list is not intended to be exhaustive since a detailed discussion of the differing jurisdiction between the County Courts and High Courts is outside the scope of this work. In considering the new Rules in relation to transfer under Part 30, however, readers should have in mind the remaining jurisdictional limits which are particularly important in relation to proceedings for the possession of premises.

Of the old rules, RSC Order 107 Rule 2, RSC Order 78, RSC Order 4 and CCR Order 16 dealt with questions of transfer and other related matters. Whilst these old rules have been repealed in entirety (save CCR Order 16 Rule 7 which deals with interpleader proceedings under execution), Sections 40, 41 and 42 of the County Courts Act 1984 have not been repealed despite an intention to do so and provide the regulatory framework of transfer to and from the High Court.

The General Scheme

The combination of Sections 40, 41 and 42 of the County Courts Act 1984, CPR Part 30 and Rule 26.2 give a general picture as follows—

- If a claim is for a specified amount of money and the defendant is an individual, the claim will be automatically transferred to the defendant's "home court" upon the filing of a defence under Rule 26.2.
- The High Court can make an order transferring proceedings to a County Court (Section 40 of the County Courts Act 1984).
- The High Court can transfer proceedings in a County Court to the High Court (Section 41 of the County Courts Act 1984).
- The County Court can order the transfer of proceedings to the High Court (Section 42 of the County Courts Act 1984).
- County Courts can order the transfer of proceedings between County Courts (Rule 30.2).
- A judge at the Royal Courts of Justice ("RCJ") can transfer proceedings to a District Registry and a judge at a District Registry can transfer proceedings to the RCJ or another District Registry (Rule 30.2(4)).

The Court in considering transfer has to take into consideration certain factors under Rule 30.3(2).

In addition to the power of transfer the Court has its case management powers set out in Part 3.

The Rules

Automatic transfer

The provisions of Rule 26.2 have already been covered in Chapter 15 at page 149. In short, when a defendant files a defence the Court will automatically transfer the proceedings to the defendant's home court if the claim is for a specified amount of money and the defendant is an individual. Rule 2.3 defines "defendant's home court". This is not a provision that is repeated within Part 30 although clearly it will be an important factor in determining the appropriate County Court for any order of transfer. By Rule 2.3 the defendant's home court means—

- If the claim is proceeding in a County Court, the County Court for the district in which the defendant's address for service, as shown on the defence, is situated; or
- If the claim is proceeding in the High Court, the District Registry for the district in which the defendant's address for service, as shown on the defence, is situated or, if there is no such District Registry, the Royal Courts of Justice.

Since the reference is to the address for service, the relevant district will not necessarily be tied to the defendant's residential or business address but could be tied to the defendant's solicitor's business address.

Transfer between County Courts

Under Rule 30.2 transfer of proceedings between County Courts may be effected under an obligation or in accordance with the Court's discretion.

Although the restrictions on where proceedings can be commenced have been much loosened over the years, there are still certain restrictions particularly in relation to possession proceedings. CCR Order 4 (included in Schedule 2 of the CPR) provides that any mortgage proceedings or proceedings otherwise for the recovery of land can only be commenced in the court for the district in which the land or any part of the land is situated. There are similar restrictions in Consumer Credit Act claims provided for in the Practice Direction to Part 7.

If the proceedings are started in the wrong County Court, the Court has a choice. The Judge may—

- transfer the proceedings to the County Court in which they ought to have been started;
- allow the proceedings to continue in the County Court in which they have been started; or
- strike the proceedings out under Rule 30.2(2)).

This discretion, however, is limited in the event of a restriction on venue being imposed by a statute over and above the provisions of the Rules. If there is such a restriction to the proceedings then the proceedings must be transferred to the correct County Court or struck out altogether (Rule 30.2(7)).

The reference to **a judge** in Rule 30.2(2) means that the jurisdiction in relation to proceedings commenced in the wrong County Court may only be exercised by a judge, a district judge or any person authorised to act as such (see the definition in Rule 2.3(1)).

If the Court concludes of its own initiative that the proceedings ought to have been commenced in another Court then it could make an order for transfer of its own initiative under Rule 3.3. Although the Court is not obliged to hold a hearing or to give the parties an opportunity to make representations (Rule 3.3(4)), it will usually give advance warning that it is proposing to make an order of transfer to allow the parties to make representation in advance.

If the order is not made of the Court's own initiative then it will be made following an application. The application should be made in accordance with Part 23 and comply with the requirements of that Part and the Practice Direction. The application must be made to the Court where the claim is proceeding (Rule 30.2(3)).

Rule 30.2(1) provides the general power of the Court to transfer from one County Court to another. Again, if this power is exercised upon application, the application must be made to the Court in which the claim is proceeding (Rule 30.2(3)).

Under Rule 30.2(1)—

> **a County Court may order proceedings before that Court, or any part of them (such as a counterclaim or an application made in the proceedings), to be transferred to another County Court if it is satisfied that an order should be made having regard to the criteria in Rule 30.3.**

Unlike Rule 30.2(2) where proceedings are commenced in the wrong Court, it is specifically stated in Rule 30.2(1) that the Court's discretion may only be exercised in relation to proceedings before that Court.

The criteria set out in Rule 30.3(2) (which are not exclusive) are as follows—

- **The financial value of the claim and the amount in dispute, if different.**

Like the other criteria under Rule 30.3(2) this element reflects the criteria for allocation under Rule 26.8. As with Part 26 it is for the Court to assess the financial value of the claim. Similarly, the amount in dispute if different can also be taken into account. For determining what is in dispute see page 165 and Paragraph 7.4, Practice Direction to Part 26. This element of the criteria will have more importance as to transfers between the High Court and the County Court rather than transfers between County Courts.

- **Whether it be more convenient or fair for hearings (including the trial) to be held in some other Court.**

It is not necessary for the proceedings to be transferred in order for a hearing or the trial to take place in another location. By Rule 30.6 the Court may specify the place where the trial or some other hearing is to be held. Although this may be effected by transferring the proceedings altogether, it is not an absolute prerequisite and the proceedings do not have to be transferred for this purpose.

One of the considerations the Court will have is the requirement under Rule 1.1(2)(a) that insofar as practicable the Court should ensure that the parties are on an equal footing. Clearly the cost of and ability to travel might be taken into account in that balancing act.

- **The availability of a judge specialising in the type of claim in question.**

Certain County Courts will retain specialist judges. For instance, the Central London County Court has the Business List. Some County Courts have judges specialising in patents, others have judges specialising in Chancery business.

Whilst this does not necessarily require the transfer of the case, it may do if it is more convenient for case management purposes. By way of example, case management in the Central London County Court Business List is often undertaken by the trial judges themselves and it would be appropriate that there should be a transfer so that they can fulfil that role.

- **Whether the facts, legal issues, remedies or procedures involved are simple or complex.**

This criteria is likely to be more important in relation to a transfer of proceedings between the County Court and the High Court. Again these elements reflect the provisions of Rule 26.8 in relation to allocation.

- **The importance of the outcome of the claim to the public in general.**

This also reflects Rule 26.8(1)(g) and will be more important in relation to transfers between the High Court and County Court.

- **The facilities available at the Court where the claim is being dealt with and whether they may be inadequate because of any disabilities of a party or potential witness.**

Again, this element does not necessarily require a transfer of the proceedings. Rule 30.6 could be relied upon and the order could be made that the hearing take place in an appropriate County Court. Otherwise the provision is self explanatory and relates to matters such as wheelchair access to the Court.

The discretion of the Court under Rule 30.2(1)(a) is limited by Rule 30.2(7) in that the Court cannot order the transfer of proceedings to a Court which is not the Court in which those proceedings should have been started resulting from any restrictions as to venue either under the Rules or by statute, for example, possession proceedings.

The Court is also empowered to order transfer of proceedings under Rule 30.2(1) if those proceedings are for—

- the detailed assessment of costs; or
- the enforcement of a judgment or order.

This discretion has a limit and can only be invoked if the judge concludes that those proceedings could be more conveniently or fairly taken in another County Court (Rule 30.2(1)(b)).

As far as detailed assessment is concerned, Rule 47.4 deals with the appropriate venue for detailed assessment proceedings. The venue is "the appropriate office". For these purposes under Paragraph 1.4(1), Practice Direction to Part 47 the appropriate office means—

> **the County Court in which the case was being dealt with when the judgment or order was made or the event occurred which gave rise to the right to assessment, or to which it has subsequently been transferred.**

Under Rule 47.4(3) the County Court may, without necessarily transferring proceedings, direct that another County Court is to be the appropriate office. A transfer is only likely to take place if the detailed assessment proceedings are defended, i.e. the paying party serves a notice of dispute.

As to enforcement it is to be noted that the reference is to "proceedings for enforcement". This does not include the issue of a warrant of execution. CCR Order 25 (retained in CPR Schedule 2) provides for the transfer of proceedings for enforcement. It has particular application to—

- an oral examination;
- an application for a charging order under Section 1 Charging of the Orders Act 1979;
- an application for an attachment of earnings order; or
- the issue of a judgment summons.

Although Rule 30.2(1)(b)(ii) is written in discretionary terms, CCR Order 25 gives rise to an obligation to transfer in the event of the judgment creditor making a request in writing for the transfer of the proceedings to the other Court (CCR Order 25 Rule 2). If an obligation does not arise under CCR Order 25 then the Court has a discretion. Such discretion might be exercised, for instance, in relation to garnishee proceedings. The Court may think it more convenient and/or fair for the proceedings to be transferred to the garnishee's local court.

Transfers within the High Court

As with the County Courts the High Court may order proceedings (or part of them) in the RCJ or District Registry to be transferred from the RCJ to a District Registry or from a District Registry to the RCJ or to another District Registry. The Court should take into account the factors set out in Rule 30.3(2) referred to above. Again, some of the criteria set out in that Rule will not be of significant influence in determining where within the High Court a case should proceed.

This power to transfer within the High Court is supplemented by Rule 30.5 which gives the High Court the power to transfer proceedings between divisions of the High Court or to or from a specialist list.

As with transfers between County Courts, the Court could make an order of its own initiative or upon application. If application is made then it must be made to the Court in which the case is proceeding (Rule 30.2(6)). If the application is for the transfer of proceedings to or from a specialist list then it must be made to a judge dealing with claims in that list (Rule 30.5(3)). Probate proceedings may only be transferred to the Chancery Division at the RCJ or to one of the Chancery District Registries (Rule 30.2(8)).

As with the County Courts, a District Registry may order proceedings for detailed costs assessment to be transferred to another District Registry if it believes that they could be more conveniently or fairly dealt with in that other District Registry (Rule 30.2(5)).

Transfer under the County Courts Act 1984

The relevant sections of the County Courts Act 1984 relating to transfer are—

- Section 40—Transfer of proceedings from the High Court to the County Court.
- Section 41—Transfer to the High Court by order of the High Court.
- Section 42—Transfer to the High Court by order of a County Court.

Annotations to these Sections can be seen at page 2074 and following Butterworths Civil Practice (The Green Book).

The general picture is that under Section 40(1) the High Court will transfer proceedings to the County Court if those proceedings should have been issued in the County Court in the first place, either under Section 1 of the Courts and Legal Services Act 1990 or by any other enactment. If, however, the Court concludes that the claimant knew or ought to have known that the proceedings should have been started in a County Court, it may order them to be struck out.

Otherwise under Section 40(2) the High Court has a discretion to order the transfer of any proceedings before it to a County Court. In exercising that discretion the Court should take into account the convenience of the parties and that of any other persons likely to be affected and the state of business in the Courts concerned.

The transfer could take place at any stage of the proceedings. It could be for the purpose of the trial or simply for proceedings for the enforcement of a High Court judgment or order. Since the repeal of Section 105 of the County Courts Act 1984 it is usually necessary to transfer proceedings for the purpose of enforcement of a judgment save that the special procedure under CCR Order 25 Rule 11 (retained in CPR Schedule 2) can be used for enforcement by charging order, attachment or earnings or by judgment summons.

Under Section 41(1) the High Court can make an order transferring proceedings or part of them from the County Court to the High Court.

Under Section 42(1) if a County Court concludes that proceedings before it should have been started in the High Court it will order the transfer of them to the High Court or if it is satisfied that the claimant knew or ought to have known of the requirement to commence in the High Court, it may strike the proceedings out. Under Section 42(2) the County Court also has a residual discretion to transfer any proceedings to the High Court where it thinks it appropriate.

These provisions are now supplemented by Rule 30.3(2) in that when either the High Court or County Court come to consider exercising the discretionary power to transfer, they must take into account the matters set out in Rule 30.3(2) (and see the High Court and County Courts Jurisdiction Order below). These are referred to above in relation to transfers within the two parts of the Court system. Some of the criteria become more important to determine whether proceedings should be transferred between the two parts of the Court system. For example, under Rule 30.3(2)(a) the Court has to take into account the financial value of the claim and the amount in dispute. This condition reflects the similar test in the allocation exercise under Rule 26.8. Indeed the transfer from High Court to County Court might follow automatically from the determination of the financial value of the claim by the

Court upon allocation. Thus if, contrary to the claim, the High Court assesses the financial value of the claim to be less than £15,000 the claim would be allocated to the fast track and transferred to a County Court.

The reader is also referred to the Practice Direction to Part 29 which deals with case management in the Royal Courts of Justice (Paragraphs 2.1–2-6). If a claim in the Royal Courts of Justice has an estimated value of less than £50,000 it will generally be transferred to a County Court. Parties are encouraged to address the question of transfer in the allocation questionnaire and to justify why a claim should continue in the Royal Courts of Justice.

Article 7(5) of the High Court and County Courts Jurisdiction Order 1991 provides for the criteria to be taken into account when dealing with a transfer under the relevant sections of the County Courts Act 1984. These reflect very much the criteria set out in Rule 30.3(2) but they are not mirror images and reference should be made to both provisions.

Multi Party Actions

In the Final Report Lord Woolf addressed the question of multi party actions and the manner in which they might be consolidated under one system and court. The Court does have the power under Rule 3.1(2)(g) to consolidate proceedings. Transfer may follow from that consolidation. There are other Rules which bear upon multi party actions such as the provisions relating to representative actions in both the High Court and the County Court (RSC Order 15 Rule 12 and CCR Order 5 Rule 5) but as yet there is no machinery provided by the Rules designed specifically for multi party actions and their issue and transfer into one court.

A consultation paper was issued by the Lord Chancellor's Department late in 1997 suggesting new procedures but as yet no rules have been produced. The prospect at the time of writing is that these will be discussed by the Civil Procedure Rule Committee during the course of 1999 and come into effect some time in the year 2000. In the meantime those involved in multi party actions must rely upon the ad hoc use of the current rules for consolidation and transfer.

The Transfer

When the Court makes an order for transfer it takes effect immediately. Thus although the machinery for transfer including the physical transfer of the file has not been effected, the transferee court immediately obtains jurisdiction over the proceedings when the order for transfer is made by the transferor court. From that time on, any application in the proceedings must be made to the transferee court under Rule 23.2(2) save in relation to an application to set aside the order of transfer which should be made to the transferor court.

The notice of transfer will be sent to the transferee court and the parties (Rule 30.4(1)).

Setting aside and appealing against Orders of Transfer

When an order for transfer is made a party to the proceedings may apply to set it aside if empowered under a particular provision of the Rules. For instance, if the application for transfer was not served on a party they may apply to set aside the order (Rule 23.10). Similarly, if the Court has made an order of its own volition without hearing the parties, a party may apply to set the order aside. Any application to set aside must be made to the Court which made the original order and not the Court receiving the transfer (Paragraph 6.1, Practice Direction to Part 30).

If a party seeks to appeal the order of transfer, Paragraph 5.1 of the Practice Direction to Part 30 sets out to which Court the appeal should be made—

- If the order was made by a Master or District Judge in the High Court then the appeal should be to a Judge in the High Court. That appeal should be commenced by an ordinary application notice under Part 23.
- If the order was made by a Judge in the High Court then the appeal is to the Court of Appeal (See CPR Sch 1, RSC Order 59).
- If the order was made by a District Judge in the County Court for transfer to another County Court, the appeal should be to a Judge in the receiving court. Such an appeal is commenced by an application notice under Part 23.
- If the order was made by a Circuit Judge in the County Court the appeal should be made to the Court of Appeal under RSC Order 59.

Parties cannot expect much encouragement from the Court to appeal orders for transfer particularly when such appeals have to be made to the Court of Appeal. Permission would be needed and it is unlikely to be forthcoming on many occasions.

The new Rules do not deal specifically with appeals against other orders made prior to transfer. Section 40(7) and 42(6) of the County Courts Act 1984 contain provisions relating to appeals and the powers of any court to set aside, correct, vary or quash a judgment or order made prior to transfer. Generally those powers are unaffected by the transfer.

In *Kings Quality Homes Ltd v AJ Paints Ltd* [1997] 3 All ER 267, CA, the Court of Appeal determined that a county Court Judge had jurisdiction to hear an appeal from an order made by a District Judge of the High Court which predated the transfer.

CHAPTER 20
PART 31—DISCLOSURE AND INSPECTION OF DOCUMENTS

Background

The question of disclosure and inspection of documents received especial attention from Lord Woolf in both the Interim Report and the Final Report (Chapter 21 and Chapter 12 respectively.).

As with many commentators on the common law system, Lord Woolf was critical of the current state of the process for discovery of documents, the manner in which it was carried out and its extent. He referred to it as being "monumentally inefficient". Indeed, he suggested that the more conscientiously the process is carried out by a party, the more inefficient it is.

Lord Woolf's principal recommendations in relation to "discovery" were to place limits upon it under the new Rules and to enforce those limits through the Court.

Similar comments have been made in relation to the process for disclosure of documents in the United States of America. Amendments were made to the Federal Rules of Civil Procedure in 1993 and, at the time of writing, further amendments are proposed to limit the scope of initial disclosure to documents directly supporting the claims of the disclosing parties or adverse to their position. It is proposed that any further disclosure of documents will be controlled by the Court, particularly in relation to documents "relevant to the subject matter involved in the action".

It is a difficult balancing act for the Rules and the Court between ensuring that "all the cards are on the table" and not allowing over-burdensome and disproportionate requirements for disclosure. In *Davies v Eli Lilly & Co* [1987] 1 WLR 428, Sir John Donaldson MR in referring to "discovery" said—

> **In plain language, litigation in this country is conducted "cards face up on the table" ... litigation is not a war or even a game. It is designed to do real justice between opposing parties and, if the Court does not have all the relevant information, it cannot achieve this object.**

Lord Woolf did not in any way disagree with this approach in either the Interim or Final Report. His concerns, however, were that modern day discovery had gone way beyond what was truly necessary for the Court to achieve the object of doing real justice. This question of achieving justice was of course primarily addressed in both the Interim and Final Reports and is the subject of the overriding objective in Part 1.

Under the RSC and CCR, the broad category of documents to be disclosed were those that, "... are or have been in [the party's] possession, custody or power relating to any matter in question in the proceedings ...". In *Compagnie Financiere du Pacifique v Peruvian Guano Company* [1882] 11 QBD 55, Brett LJ (later to become Lord Esher MR) laid down four categories of documents falling within the definition of "relating to any matter in question in the proceedings"—

1. The party's own documents, which they rely upon in support of their contentions in the proceedings.
2. Adverse documents of which a party is aware and which to a material extent adversely affect his own case or support another party's case.
3. Documents which do not fall within categories 1 or 2 but are part of the "story" or background including documents which, though relevant, may not be necessary for the fair disposal of the case.
4. Train of inquiry documents. These are documents which may lead to a train of inquiry enabling the party to advance his own case or damage that of his opponent
   (as quoted in the Final Report).

Whilst accepting entirely the necessity for disclosure of documents falling within categories 1 and 2, Lord Woolf questioned the necessity to extend disclosure to documents under category 3 and particularly category 4. Rather, as now proposed in the United States, Lord Woolf recommended that disclosure (referred to as standard disclosure) should be given save in lower value claims but anything further than standard disclosure ("specific disclosure") broadly of categories 1 and 2 should be limited to higher value claims in the multi track subject even then to very precise control by the Court.

In both his Interim and Final Reports, Lord Woolf went further in trying to limit the steps that a party had to take in giving disclosure. As he put it in his Final Report (Chapter 12, Paragraph 41)—

> **It is no use, limiting the categories of document which a party has to disclose, if he still has to search through all the documents to identify those in categories 1 and 2.**

He recommended that initial disclosure should apply only to relevant documents of which a party was aware at the time when the obligation to disclose arose. As he recognised, the test of awareness is particularly difficult. In practice few would remember exactly what a document said and whether it fell within categories 1 and 2 unless they actually read it again in preparation for disclosure. Further, a culture of wilful non-awareness might develop.

Accordingly, in the process of drafting, the Civil Procedure Rule Committee abandoned awareness as a test for disclosure and moved towards an obligation upon a party to undertake a reasonable search for documents falling within the new categorisation of "standard disclosure".

New Disclosure "landscape"

The general landscape of disclosure is as follows—

1. In the small claims track Part 31 has no application and the standard requirement is that a party will only disclose documents on which they rely (see page 237).
2. In the fast track only standard or less disclosure will be given (Rule 28.3) (see page 237).
3. In the multi track only standard disclosure will be given in the first instance but an application for specific disclosure can be made (Rule 29.2 and Rule 31.12).
4. When an order for disclosure is made, the party must undertake a reasonable search for documents on which he relies; and documents which—
   (a) adversely affect his own case;
   (b) adversely affect another party's case; or
   (c) support another party's case; and

   the documents which he is required to disclose by a relevant practice direction. Such documents are limited to those which are or have been in his control (Rule 31.8).
5. Having identified the documents, they have to be listed in the list of documents and a disclosure statement has to be signed by the disclosing party (Rule 31.10). The list then has to be served in accordance with the order.
6. The disclosing party then has to give inspection of the documents (Rule 31.15).

The question of proportionality is at the heart of the disclosure process. Rule 31.7 talks of the reasonableness of search. Rule 31.3 specifically mentions proportionality in relation to the giving of inspection of documents. Most importantly, reference must be made to the overriding objective and Rule 1.1(2)(c) which requires that insofar as practicable, the Court must deal with the case in ways which are proportionate to—

- the amount of money involved;
- the importance of the case;
- the complexity of the issues; and
- the financial position of each party.

Subject to the Court's control, the question of reasonableness or proportionality is very much in the hands of the disclosing party. For this reason, checks (see below) have been put into the Rules to ensure that where they exercise that judgement in restricting either a search for documents or inspection, the restrictions must be stated within the disclosure statement.

It is interesting to note that the Commercial Court Guide which at the time of writing has recently been published, gives a general guidance of disclosure in Commercial Court cases as follows—

> **Documents are often of particular importance in a commercial case, and of particular assistance in enabling the Court to deal**

with cases justly. Parties to litigation in the Commercial Court can expect that disclosure beyond standard disclosure may be required either in the case as a whole or on particular issues in a case.

It might be said that the Commercial Court Guide goes beyond what had been suggested by Lord Woolf and the deliberations of the Committee in the production of the final Rules. On the other hand the Commercial Court will be dealing only with cases on the multi track and usually cases of considerable complexity. Certainly the Commercial Court Guide reinforces the process of disclosure being undertaken in "waves" as recommended by Lord Woolf in the Final Report (Chapter 1, Paragraph 32). Thus initial disclosure may be simply standard disclosure followed by further disclosure as the case proceeds. The Guide suggests specifically that the issues of disclosure should be addressed in the case management conference.

Rule 31.2—Meaning of Disclosure

31.2 A party discloses a document[1] by stating that the document exists or has existed.

Rule 31.2 was inserted to differentiate disclosure of the document from inspection of it. The "discovery" process covers both disclosure and inspection but also covers other steps taken in proceedings such as the old procedure of interrogatories now replaced by further information under Part 18. The normal way of disclosing a document under Rule 31.2 will be by way of list prepared and served in accordance with Rule 31.10. A document, however, may be disclosed in many other ways. In particular, if a document is referred to in one of the documents set out in Rule 31.14, for instance a statement of case or an expert's report (see page 234), the document is disclosed for the purposes of Rule 31.2 and a right to inspect arises under Rule 31.14. A document may, of course be disclosed inadvertently. Even there, following disclosure, an automatic right to inspection arises subject to the exceptions set out in Rule 31.3.

The interplay between Rules 31.2, 31.3 (right of inspection of a disclosed document) and 31.6 (standard disclosure—what documents are to be disclosed), is that whilst a party is only obliged to give only limited disclosure under Rule 31.6, if documents are disclosed beyond the limits set out there then the automatic right to inspect those documents so disclosed arises (see below).

Rule 31.3—The right of Inspection

Rule 31.3 provides the second leg of the "discovery of documents" process. Upon stating that a document exists or has existed in accordance with Rule 31.2, the other party is entitled automatically to inspection of that document subject to the exceptions set out in Rule 31.3(1)(a), (b) and (c). The process of inspection is undertaken in accordance with Rule 31.15. Thus, although the right automatically arises, notice must be given of a wish to inspect and compliance with that notice is required within seven days. In conjunction with the right to inspect, a party is also entitled to copies of documents, again in accordance with Rule 31.15. As long as the requesting party undertakes to pay the disclosing party's reasonable costs, copies of documents must be supplied within seven days of a request (Rule 31.15(c)).

The automatic right to inspect is, however, subject to certain limitations set out in Rule 31.3. Those limitations are where—

- the document is no longer in the control of the party who disclosed it;
- the party disclosing the document has a right or duty to withhold inspection of it; or
- the party disclosing the document asserts that inspection of it would be disproportionate to the issues in the case.

The use of the word "**control**" in the new Rules replaces the phrase used in the RSC and CCR, "possession, custody or power". The word control is almost a reversion to the provisions of the Evidence Act 1851 which gave rise to inspection at common law. That statute referred to "the custody or under the control". The reversion to the word control is intended to cover exactly the same category of documents as previously under the RSC and CCR. It was felt that the word "control" encapsulated each of them and it was not necessary to retain the old expression. The meaning of the word "control" is set out in Rule 31.8(2) (see below).

The combination of Rules 31.2, 31.3(1)(a) and 31.8 is to differentiate between a right to disclosure and a right to inspect. The right to disclosure arises whether or not at the time of disclosure the disclosing party actually has physical control of the document disclosed. Inspection, however, is dependent upon physical control. Thus the party receiving disclosure does not have a right to inspect documents unless they are in the physical possession of the disclosing party or that party has a right to possession of the document or has a right to inspect or take copies of them. Naturally there may be many subjective arguments as to whether a document is truly within a party's control (as to which see Rule 31.8 below).

Rule 31.3(1)(b) text re-emphasises the difference between disclosure and inspection. Subject to the limitations of Rule 31.6, disclosure is still required of documents even though those documents are, for instance, privileged. It is the right to see those documents, i.e. inspect them, which is restricted under this Rule. No mention is made here specifically of "privilege" but clearly the main band of documents that will be covered by the limitation in Rule 31.3 (1)(b) will be legal professional privilege as a right to withhold inspection. The Rule goes a little further in referring to a duty to withhold inspection. Such a duty might arise, for instance, in relation to documents the inspection of which may be injurious to public interest. The scope of this work does not include a general discussion about a right or duty to withhold inspection but see the notes to Rule 31 in the Green Book.

Under Rule 31.3(2) a party is not required to permit inspection of documents where that party considers that it would be **disproportionate** to the issues in the case to permit inspection of documents which have been disclosed. Rule 31.3 (2) should be viewed in combination with Rule 31.7 under which a party in giving disclosure only has to make a **reasonable** search for documents (see below).

The limitation of proportionality relating to "discovery" was a relatively late insertion during the deliberations of the Civil Procedure Rule Committee. Rule 31.3(2) re-emphasises the requirements of the overriding objective and particularly the provisions of Rule 1.1(2)(c) obliging the Court to deal with cases in ways which are proportionate to—

- the amount of money involved;
- the importance of the case;
- the complexity of the issues; and
- the financial position of each party.

Whilst proportionality is of primary relevance throughout the Rules, the measure of proportionality within Rule 31.3(2) is in relation to "the issues in the case". This reflects a similar provision within Rule 44.4(2)(a) by which the amount of costs to be assessed under the standard basis of assessment must be proportionate to the matters in issue.

Within the test of proportionality under Rule 44.4, reference is made in the Practice Direction to Part 44 (Paragraph 3) to Rule 1.1(2)(c) (proportionality tested against the financial resources of the parties. Whilst this reference should also apply to Rule 31.3(2), the reference in Rule 31.3(2) to the "issues in the case" might on first blush appear to exclude the proportionality test under Rule 1.1(2)(c) as to the financial position of each party. If, however, a party were to state in his disclosure statement that he were not allowing inspection of the documents because "he could not afford it", the Court would be able to exercise its discretion under Rule 1.1(2)(a) by limiting inspection in this way, thus "ensuring that the parties are on an equal footing".

Further, using this discretion, if the party to whom inspection is being provided should pursue the point, the Court could provide that that party pay the costs of inspection of those documents to which objection is taken.

It is to be noted that Rule 31.3(2) refers to a category or class of documents as opposed to documents which are listed individually. Paragraph 3.2 of the Practice Direction to Part 31 refers to categories of documents by providing that—

> **where there is a large number of documents all falling into a particular category the disclosing party may list those documents as a category rather than individually.**

The Practice Direction goes on to provide an example of a series of bank statements which could be listed as a category rather than individually. The Practice Direction also gives an example of letters passing between one party and another which again could be listed by way of category rather than individually. The reference to "a class" in Rule 31.3(2)is also intended to cover such a practice of listing "classes" of documents within the list of documents.

In this way it is hoped that some flavour of what was intended within this provision by the Committee becomes apparent. The easiest example is to carry on the example given within the Practice Direction in relation to bank statements. Say, for instance, those bank statements are required to be disclosed in accordance with Rule 31.6 as supporting another party's case. The manner in which they support it, however, relates only to its quantification and will affect that quantification in a very small degree. On the other hand the disclosing party no longer has the documents in his possession but he can obtain copies and thus they are within his control at, however, some considerable cost. In those circumstances the disclosing party may object to the inspection of the documents on the basis that the cost of providing that inspection would be disproportionate to the issues in the case.

Proportionality, however, is a subjective test and must be measured against all the circumstances of the case before the Court. It is difficult to make hard and fast rules when so much discretion lies initially with the parties and subsequently with the Court.

The check within the Rules to ensure that the discretion given to the disclosing party under Rule 31.3 (2) is not abused, is that they must state in their disclosure statement (as to which see Rule 31.10(5) below) that although a category or class of document as detailed is disclosed, inspection of them will not be permitted because the disclosing party considers that to do so would be disproportionate to the issues in the case.

The disclosure statement appears on the front of the list of documents in its standard form (N265). Within that standard form is a statement—

> **I have not permitted inspection of documents within the category or class of documents (as set out below) required to be disclosed under Rule 31(6)(b) or (c) on the grounds that to do so would be disproportionate to the issues in the case.**

Appearing immediately below that statement is a box in which it is intended that such category or class of documents should be detailed. Presumably within that box specific reference can be made to the section within the remaining part of the list of documents in which the party has to indicate that whilst disclosure of documents is made, objection to inspecting them is taken.

The only requirement of the disclosing party is to set out the categories or class of documents to which objection to inspection is taken. They do not have to set out within the list of documents the grounds for taking that objection. This compares with a claim that a party disclosing the document has a right or a duty to withhold inspection under Rule 31.3(1)(b). In that case the party withholding inspection must state the grounds on which he claims that right or duty (Rule 31.19(3)). Thus a party wishing to challenge the withholding of inspection in accordance with Rule 31.3(2) may be somewhat in the dark before making the application as to exactly the grounds for considering that inspection would be disproportionate.

On the other hand, it is suggested that the disclosing party should let the other party know of the grounds for the objection in accordance with their duty under Rule 1.3 to assist the Court to further the overriding objective and particularly to co-operate with each other as promoted by Rule 1.4(2)(a).

Two very minor points arise from this provision within the disclosure statement. Firstly, it talks about inspection in the past tense where it should truly speak of it in the future tense. Secondly, it refers to Rule 31(6)(c) whereas in fact the documents to which that sub-Rule refer—those to be disclosed in accordance with the relevant practice direction—do not automatically fall within the category or class of documents to which objection to inspection can be taken under Rule 31.3(2). Those categories or class of documents must fall within Rule 31.6(b).

In the event of the party to whom disclosure is being made taking objection to the refusal to permit inspection under Rule 31.3(2), that party can make an application for specific inspection in accordance with Rule 31.12(3). It will be borne in mind in relation to such an application that the disclosing party has already accepted by disclosing the category or class of document that those documents are required to be disclosed in accordance with Rule 31.6(b). The only question before the Court therefore will be whether to permit inspection would be disproportionate to the issues in the case.

Such an application must be made in accordance with Part 23. In particular the application notice must state what order the applicant is seeking and briefly why the applicant is seeking the order in accordance with Rule 23.6. Any written evidence may be included within the application notice and used as evidence on the hearing as long as it is verified by a statement of truth. Alternatively, evidence may be provided by way of witness statement.

The objection to permitting inspection on the basis of disproportionality to the issues in the case can be directly compared with a refusal to undertake a search for particular documents and thus whether they are disclosed at all under Rule 31.7. The duty to search is limited by the measure of "reasonableness". The Practice Direction to Part 31 and particularly Paragraph 4.2(2) appears to liken the test of reasonableness with that of proportionality. Certainly in setting out the factors relevant in deciding the reasonableness of a search, Rule 31.7(2) includes factors which would be relevant to the test of proportionality in relation to inspection, namely—

- the number of documents involved;
- the nature and complexity of the proceedings;
- the ease and expense of retrieval of any particular document; and
- the significance of any document (to which objection to inspection is taken).

In the Commercial Court Guide it is suggested that at the case management conference any limitation intended to be placed upon the duty of search under Rule 31.7 by a party should be disclosed and discussed at the case management conference. Although the matter may not have become apparent at that stage of the case management conference, there appears to be no reason why a similar discussion should not take place in relation to any proposed limitations as to inspection in accordance with Rule 31.3(2).

Document and copy defined

Rule 31.4 defines what is meant by the words "document" and "copy" within Part 31.

> **31.4 In this Part—**
>
> **"document" means anything in which information of any description is recorded; and**

"copy", in relation to a document, means anything onto which information recorded in the document has been copied, by whatever means and whether directly or indirectly.

These definitions are directly lifted from Section 13 of the Civil Evidence Act 1995.

Order for Disclosure

It is part of the case management philosophy that the process of disclosure should be under the control of the Court. One of the effects of this philosophy of case management is that the automatic process for disclosure previously applied by RSC Order 24 Rule 2 and in relation to default and fixed date actions in the County Court CCR 17 Rule 11(3)(a) has been excluded from the CPR. Whilst it may be a duty under the overriding objective for the parties to co-operate with each other, they cannot do so to override the intention that the Court should have complete control over the disclosure process. In each of the three tracks there will be fairly automatic directions applying in most cases. Whilst they may be regarded as relatively automatic, they still require a positive step by the Court to make the appropriate order even if it be by consent. Part 31 has no application to the **small claims track** in which, as above, rather than a requirement to give standard disclosure, the only requirement will be for a party to disclose the documents on which they rely. In the **fast track** the Court will give directions under Rule 28.3 as to the disclosure of documents. The direction for disclosure will be limited to standard disclosure in accordance with Paragraph 3.9, Practice Direction to Part 28 (which is also reflected in the fast track standard directions included within the Practice Direction to Part 28). This approach is also reflected in the Practice Direction to Part 29 (**multi track**). Again, when the Court is giving directions for a multi track case, its general approach will be to direct standard disclosure. As above, however, disclosure may be considered at the case management conference in multi track cases in which questions of proportionality and reasonableness in relation to the duty to search and the right to inspection may be considered. The directions given in both fast track and multi track are based upon the general premise set out in Rule 31.5(1) that—

an order to give disclosure is an order to give standard disclosure unless the Court directs otherwise.

The Court is able to make an order that something more than standard disclosure should be given but it is discouraged from doing so at least in the first instance. In the Commercial Court Guide, however, some indication is given that bearing mind the nature of the business before that Court, to which documents are a very important aspect, something beyond standard disclosure might be given if grounds can be made out at the case management conference. It is highly unlikely that an order going beyond standard disclosure will ever be made in the first instance, if at all, in fast track cases. Going beyond standard disclosure would be venturing into the last two categories of documents referred to in the *Peruvian Guano* case referred to above, namely relevant documents and train of inquiry documents. It is these two categories of documents which Lord Woolf was specifically trying to avoid by the limitations placed upon standard disclosure.

In addition to the power of the Court to go beyond standard disclosure, notwithstanding the limiting intentions of the Rules, Rule 31.5(2) expressly provides that the Court can dispense with or limit standard disclosure if it believes it appropriate. Where it has the capacity and inclination to do so, the Court may consider that disclosure should be made in "waves". This is likely to apply only in multi track cases because to provide for disclosure in stages in a fast track case may lead to delays in bringing the matter on for trial. In a multi-track case, however, on considering the issues to be decided by the Court at the case management conference, the Court may consider it appropriate to provide for disclosure in relation to a limited number of the issues before giving any further order for disclosure.

In addition to the Court's power to dispense with or limit standard disclosure, the parties may also dispense with or limit standard disclosure by agreement in writing. The Practice Directions to both the fast track (Part 28) and multi track (Part 29) encourage the parties to agree directions to be made by the Court. In those directions in accordance with Rule 31.5(3) the parties could agree to dispense with or limit standard disclosure as they thought appropriate. Any agreement in writing to limit or dispense with standard disclosure must be lodged with the Court in accordance with Paragraph 1.4 of the Practice Direction to Part 31. In addition to limiting or dispensing with standard disclosure, the parties can agree in writing or the Court may direct that disclosure should take place in stages (also applies to inspection).

Any agreement between the parties is, of course, subject to the Court's approval in accordance with the Practice Directions. Under the old rules what the parties may have done is extend disclosure beyond standard disclosure simply to avoid argument. It was noted by Lord Woolf in both his Interim and Final Reports that an assiduous party acting under the old Rules may give "discovery" far and beyond that that was necessary for the disposal of the proceedings. There was a tendency for parties to provide too much discovery, possibly either to avoid any arguments about its extent at some future point or in order to "bury" important documents within a great mass of documents disclosed. Lord Woolf was particularly keen to avoid this happening under the CPR.

To a certain extent the giving of too much by way of disclosure is not easy to police. The sanctions that can be imposed will tend to be after the event, namely in relation to costs. It has already become a practice that where a great mass of documents is produced to the Court at trial in the trial bundle to which the Court has little or no reference, the Court may disallow the costs of preparation of that part of the bundle which it found to be irrelevant. Giving too much discovery would be one of those circumstances to be taken into account by the Court in exercising its discretion as to costs under Rule 44.3 or upon deciding the amount of costs under Rule 44.5.

Standard Disclosure

Having established under Rule 31.5 that standard disclosure will be the normal extent of disclosure in most cases, Rule 31.6 goes on to define what standard disclosure is—

31.6 Standard disclosure requires a party to disclose only—
(a) the documents on which he relies; and
(b) the documents which—
(i) adversely affect his own case;
(ii) adversely affect another party's case; or
(iii) support another party's case; and
(c) the documents which he is required to disclose by a relevant practice direction.

This provision follows the recommendation of Lord Woolf in his Final Report (Chapter 12 Paragraph 39 page 124) that the documents which should form the base for standard disclosure should be only those falling within the first two categories set out in *Peruvian Guano*, namely—

- the parties own documents which they rely upon in support of their contentions in the proceedings;
- adverse documents of which the party is aware and which to a material extent adversely affect his own case or support another party's case.

What is excluded are the second two categories of documents under *Peruvian Guano*, namely—

- documents which do not fall within the categories above but are part of the "story" or background including documents which, although relevant, may not be necessary for the fair disposal of the case; and
- train of inquiry documents: documents which may lead to a train of inquiry enabling a party to advance his own case or damage that of his opponent.

The Rule itself has gone through important changes during the course of its drafting and finalisation by the Civil Procedure Rule Committee. Initially, as above, one of the tests to be applied under the specific recommendation of Lord Woolf was that of "awareness" of the disclosing party of the document. As above, many commenting believed that that test was inappropriate. This view was accepted and the test of awareness was deleted. At one point, however, during the course of the Committee's deliberations attempts were made to broaden the scope of Rule 31.6 but upon reconsideration it was restored to its limited scope as now applies. The limit of that scope is emphasised by the addition of the word "only" in the first line of the Rule.

The test for what documents should be disclosed under Rule 31.6 may appear to the practitioner to be too limited in its scope, thus leaving this important part of the adversarial process open to abuse. Lord Woolf addressed the potential criticism in his Final Report (Chapter 12 Paragraph 45) with the response that limiting standard disclosure to documents falling within categories 1 and 2 of the *Peruvian Guano* categories was a better alternative to either dispensing with disclosure entirely as in the Continental systems or to limit initial disclosure to documents upon which a party intends to rely. Both these alternatives Lord Woolf regarded as going too far in their limitation.

There are in any event two checks within the Rules themselves. Firstly, specific disclosure under Rule 31.12 and the continuing obligation to provide disclosure during the proceedings under Rule 31.11 (see below).

The duty of search

Rule 31.7 sets out the obligation on the disclosing party to undertake a **reasonable search for documents which should be disclosed in accordance with Rule 31.6.** This obligation does not specifically extend to documents falling within Rule 31.6(a) (the documents on which the party relies) but insofar as disclosure (or inspection) is not given of such documents, the party may not rely on that document unless the Court gives permission.

The obligation to search is both independent of and dependent upon the categories of documents set out in Rule 31.6. Initially in compiling the documents to be disclosed, a search as such may not be required because the whereabouts of the documents falling within Rule 31.6(b) and (c) will be well known to the disclosing party. To a certain extent Lord Woolf's test of "awareness" is the relevant factor here. If a party is aware of documents falling under Rule 31.6 without conducting a search then as long as those documents are or have been in his control (Rule 31.8) they have to be disclosed. The second stage is that a party has an obligation under Rule 31.7 to make themselves aware of documents that fall within Rule 31.6 by the process of a search. The obligation to search is subject to the substantial restriction of reasonableness. What is reasonable is very much dependent upon the circumstances in the litigation and otherwise but Rule 31.7(2) gives some indication of the factors as to the measure of reasonableness—

- the number of documents involved;
- the nature and complexity of the proceedings;
- the ease and expense of retrieval of any particular document; and
- the significance of any document which is likely to be located during the search.

Thus the disclosing party is required to consider reasonableness before undertaking the search itself. Bearing in mind the time limitations on the process of disclosure, consideration as to these factors should be given at an early stage. Very usefully the Commercial Court Guide suggests that this might be a matter which is discussed at the case management conference.

No hard and fast examples can be given of reasonableness. The very subjectivity of the test, it is suggested, might be displayed in a building dispute. One small item of claim might give rise to a wide ranging search which might be regarded as unreasonable bearing in mind the quantification of that particular item and its relationship with the whole claim. On the other hand the small item might be of crucial importance to the whole claim, for instance, in relation to establishing the "critical path of events".

In a document of explanation prepared by the Lord Chancellor's Department, the drafting team explained the test as one that can be applied looking both forwards by the party and backwards by the Court.

> **A party or his lawyer, looking at the thing reasonably, has to ask himself whether, in the light of what he proposes to look for and disclose, a Court will subsequently make an order for specific disclosure and what view it would take of that party's conduct in limiting its original search. The significance of the haul produced in response to an application for specific disclosure will give the Court a reasonable indication of whether a party has "wilfully" held back or had made a justifiable decision to do so (even where the subsequent material is of some relevance).**

The Practice Direction at Paragraph 2 provides broad examples of the categories of documents for which it would be reasonable to decide not to search;

- documents coming into the existence for some particular date;
- documents in some particular place or places;
- documents falling into particular categories.

The test of reasonableness is very much tied up with the test of proportionality. The latter test is not mentioned in Rule 31.7 but is mentioned in the Practice Direction (Paragraph 2). In assessing reasonableness the parties are encouraged to consider the overriding principle of proportionality under Rule 1.1(2)(c). Thus the disclosing party must consider the proportionality of a search in relation to—

- the amount of money involved;
- the importance of the case;
- the complexity of the issues; and
- the financial position of each party.

Rule 31.7(3) provides the check upon the abuse of the discretion for the disclosing party.

> **(3) Where a party has not searched for a category or class of document on the grounds that to do so would be unreasonable, he must state this in his disclosure statement and identify the category or class of document.**

Rule 31.10(6) provides that in making the disclosure statement the disclosing party must set out the extent of the search that has been made to locate documents which he is required to disclose. The Practice Direction at Paragraph 4.2(2) provides that—

> **(2) in setting out the extent of the search (see rule 31.10 (6)) draw attention to any particular limitations on the extent of the search which were adopted for proportionality reasons and give the reasons why the limitations were adopted, e.g. the difficulty or expense that a search not subject to those limitations would have entailed or the marginal relevance of categories of documents omitted from the search.**

The standard form for the list of documents (N265) specifically ties reasonableness and proportionality in the disclosure required under Rule 31.7.

The standard form provides—

> **I state that I have carried out a reasonable and proportionate search to locate all the documents which I am required to disclose under the order made by the Court on ____________.**
>
> **I did not search for documents -**
>
> **1. Pre-dating ______________**
>
> **2. Located elsewhere than _____________**
>
> **3. In categories other than ______________**

The duty of search and the measure of reasonableness is also associated with the question of proportionality in relation to the giving of inspection. The combination of Rules 31.7 and 31.3 contemplates circumstances in which it may be reasonable to carry out a search and locate documents but then not be reasonable to provide inspection on the grounds of proportionality.

Parties will often look to their legal advisors as to the measure of reasonableness under Rule 31.7 and indeed in relation to the general concept of proportionality or disclosure and inspection. The legal representative has an obligation to ensure that the party, for instance, starting the search process, is fully aware of their obligations of the type of documents to which a search is to be effected and the obligation to conduct a reasonable search for them.

It is suggested that this is not any easy task and may involve a much closer involvement than previously by the legal representative in both the disclosure and inspection process.

As the duty of disclosure continues until the proceedings are concluded (Rule 31.11) it is suggested that if having given standard disclosure a party becomes aware of a location at which documents falling within Rule 31.6 could be found if a reasonable search were undertaken, the disclosing party would be under a continuing obligation to conduct such a reasonable search until the proceedings have been concluded.

If the party to whom disclosure is being given objects to the limitations placed upon it by the disclosing party then an application can be made under Rule 31.12 for specific disclosure. Upon such an application which would be made in accordance with Part 23, the Court could require a party to extend the search generally or specifically beyond the limitations set by the disclosing party upon the application of the test of reasonableness. The order would also require the party to disclose any documents located as a result of that search (Rule 31.12(2)(b) and (c)) (see below).

There may be physical restrictions on the ability to carry out a search but in accordance with Rule 31.8 the search extends to documents which are or have been in the control of the disclosing party. Thus in accordance with Rule 31.8(2)(b) and (c), a search extends to documents of which a party has or has had a right to possession or has or has had a right to inspect or take copies. Thus part of the search process may be to request third parties to give up possession of a document to the disclosing party so that the disclosing party can meet his obligations under Rule 31.6. That obligation to seek possession, inspection or copies from a third party is subject to the test of reasonableness under Rule 31.7 and proportionality under Part 1.

Subject thereto disclosure is limited to documents which are or have been in a party's control (Rule 31.8(1)). Control is defined in Rule 31.8(2) as—

- physical possession;
- a right to possession;
- a right to inspect or take copies.

The word "control" replaces the previous phrase of "possession, custody or power" as detailed above.

The list

Having identified the documents to be disclosed, a list of documents is prepared in accordance with Rule 31.10. The list is in a standard form N265.

As will be seen, the front page consists mainly of the disclosure statement and the reverse is divided into three sections replacing the two schedules to the form under the RSC and CCR. The three categories are self explanatory.

As to the manner in which a party should set out the documents within any of those three categories, the Practice Direction gives some guidance at Paragraph 3.2.

> **3.2 In order to comply with rule 31.10 (3) it will normally be necessary to list the documents in date order, to number them consecutively and to give each a concise description (e.g. letter, claimant to defendant). Where there is a large number of documents all falling into a particular category the disclosing party may list those documents as a category rather than individually e.g. 50 bank statements relating to account number ... at .... Bank ....19/20... to ....19/20... or, 35 letters passing between ....and .... between ....19/20... and ....19/20... .**

As provided, the description of any documents has to be concise. The description does not have to describe the contents particularly where a right or duty to withhold inspection is being claimed in accordance with Rule 31.3(1)(b).

The disclosing party is not required to list within the list more than one copy of the document unless the copy is in some way altered from the original and the altered copy is a document falling within the tests of Rule 31.6 and thus the alterations are such that the disclosing party wishes to rely on them or they adversely affect his own case, adversely affect another party's case or support another party's case (Rule 31.9). As to what is a copy, see Rule 31.4 referred to above.

Disclosure statement

The list of documents must contain a disclosure statement. The text of the disclosure statement is set out on form N265 above. The disclosure statement must always be signed by an individual even where the disclosing party is a company, firm, association or other organisation. In that event the disclosure statement must identify the person making the statement and explain why he is considered an appropriate person to make the statement. In accordance with the Practice Direction (Paragraph 4.3) that person must include his name and address and the office or position he holds in the disclosing party. There is no like provision, however, to that concerning the signing of the statement of truth that the disclosure statement must be signed by a person holding a senior position in, for instance, a registered company. Thus the limitations on the person who signs on behalf of, for instance, a registered company is only that they are the appropriate person in accordance with Rule 31.10(7)(b). The person signing on behalf of a company, firm, association or other organisation will wish to ensure that upon making the disclosure statement, all those persons having responsibility for particular documents within the company, for instance, are aware of the party's obligations and that they individually have complied with them.

These provisions reflect the recommendations of Lord Woolf (Paragraph 41, Chapter 12, Final Report) that effectively an organisation nominates a supervising officer whose task is to collate the documents for disclosure. The further recommendation of Lord Woolf, however, has not been put into effect, namely that that "supervising officer" should identify the individuals within the organisation of whom inquiries have been made in relation to the document. To a large extent this recommendation has been overtaken by the new obligation to search under Rule 31.7.

A legal representative is not entitled to sign a disclosure statement on behalf of a party. He does, however, have a significant obligation to ensure that the person who does sign the disclosure statement understands the duty of disclosure under Rule 31 (Paragraph 4.4, Practice Direction to Part 31). This obligation on solicitors within a practice direction is in addition to the general obligation on solicitors as officers of the Court to ensure that a party complies with their duty to give disclosure and, for instance, ensure that documents are preserved for the purposes of disclosure.

There is no specific policing provision in relation to the disclosure statement. This compares with a statement of truth which has a specific policing provision under Rule 32.14 by which proceedings for contempt of Court may be brought in relation to a false statement in a document verified within a statement of truth. It is not within the scope of this work to discuss whether the process of a disclosure statement could be enforced by like means. If proper disclosure has not been given in accordance with Part 31, the party giving disclosure would be in breach of the order for disclosure. If the individual signing the disclosure statement on behalf of, for instance, a company, does not honestly believe that the company has complied with its obligations but certifies that it has within the disclosure statement, such action may be regarded as calculated to prejudice the due administration of justice for which contempt proceedings may follow.

It should be noted that where the Court has some doubt about disclosure there is no specific requirement as there was under the RSC (Order 24 Rule 2(7)) for a party to apply that a list of documents be verified by affidavit. It was considered that the disclosure statement was sufficient for these purposes and no separate provision was required. The Commercial Court Guide, however, talks of requiring parties to verify lists of documents either by witness statement or affidavit. This would appear to revert to the former position under the RSC and CCR although there is no specific provision within Part 31 to this effect.

Specific Disclosure or Specific Inspection

The application of Rule 31.12 which provides that the Court can make an order for specific disclosure or specific inspection might arise in four circumstances—

- Where a party in the disclosure statement has indicated that they have limited the search for documents on the stated ground of reasonableness/proportionality, the other party may seek an order from the Court that the search should be extended beyond the limit adopted.
- If the applicant believes that the disclosure given is inadequate in that it does not include all of the documents which would fall within the categories set out in Rule 31.6.
- If the applicant believes that it would be appropriate for further documents to be disclosed beyond those that have been disclosed, whether or not they fall within the categories of documents under Rule 31.6.
- The only ground for specific inspection mentioned in Rule 31.12 is where inspection is withheld on the grounds of proportionality under Rule 31.3(2) and the applicant believes that inspection should be given of those documents withheld.

Although not an application specifically made in accordance with Rule 31.12, there may be further argument about inspection arising from the withholding of inspection on the grounds set out in Rule 31.3(1)(a) and (b), namely that the party no longer has control over a document or that there is a right or duty to withhold inspection of it. Similarly there may be argument concerning a claim to withhold inspection under Rule 31.19 on the grounds of public interest. Rule 31.19 also applies to the giving of discovery and the withholding of it in the public interest (see below).

In addition to "specific disclosure" under Rule 31.12, the Commercial Court Guide refers to an order for disclosure to be known as a "Special Disclosure Order". This appears to take Rule 31.12 somewhat further. Without limiting when a special disclosure order would be appropriate, the Guide gives as examples cases in which fraud, dishonesty or misrepresentation is alleged or where knowledge or lack of knowledge or disclosure or non-disclosure is in issue.

In those circumstances when a special disclosure order is made, the suggested order would be as follows—

> **On or before ______________, each party shall carry out a thorough search for all documents relevant to the issues listed in the schedule to this order/the issues in the case including (for the avoidance of doubt) all documents which may lead to a**

train of inquiry enabling a party to advance his own case or damage that of his opponent.

Whilst Commercial Court cases may indeed be document reliant, the Guide might give a lead in other Courts that where, for instance, fraud or misrepresentation is alleged, discovery should be given of train of inquiry documents (i.e. fourth category of documents from *Peruvian Guano*).

As detailed above, the Guide suggests that in relation to specific disclosure under Rule 31.12 and "special disclosure", the Court might require verification by witness statement or affidavit.

The order for specific disclosure or specific inspection can be given of the Court's own initiative under Rule 3.3. It will usually, however, result from an application by the other party. Such an application would have to comply with the provisions of Part 23. Accordingly the application notice must state what order the applicant is seeking and briefly why the applicant is seeking the order (Rule 23.16 and Paragraphs 5.2 and 5.3, Practice Direction to Part 31). The application must be supported by evidence (Paragraph 5.2). That evidence can be contained within the application notice itself as long as it is verified by a statement of truth or in a separate witness statement.

An order for specific disclosure is defined under Rule 31.12(2) as an order requiring a party to—

- disclose documents or classes of documents specified in the order;
- carry out a search to the extent stated in the order;
- disclose any documents located as a result of that search.

In deciding whether to make such an order, the Court is bound to have regard to the issue of proportionality and the other issues raised in the overriding objective.

In the Final Report Lord Woolf said that where ordering specific disclosure the court would have to be satisfied not only that it was necessary to do justice but that the cost of such disclosure would not be disproportionate to the benefit to be achieved and that a party's ability to continue the litigation would not be impaired by an order for specific disclosure against him (Page 125 Paragraph 4).

Even taking this into account, however, if a party has not complied with their obligation to give disclosure under an order that has been made, then the Court will make such order as is necessary to ensure that those obligations are properly complied with (Paragraph 5.4, Practice Direction to Part 31).

Documents referred to in Statements of Case etc

Rule 31.14 reflects broadly the previous Rules, and in particular Order 24 Rule 10 RSC, to the effect that any document **mentioned** in—

- a statement of case;
- a witness statement;
- a witness summary;
- an affidavit; or
- an expert's report

may be inspected. Thus in effect following Rule 31.2 a party discloses the document simply by mentioning it within one of the documents referred to under Rule 31.14. Nothing in Rule 31.14 gives an entitlement to withhold inspection either on the ground of control of the document or that a party has a right or duty to withhold inspection. If inspection, however, is not given of such a document in compliance with Rule 31.15, and the person claims the right or duty to withhold inspection he must notify the person seeking inspection that he has such a right or duty and the grounds on which he claims it (Rule 31.19(3) and (4)). If the party seeking inspection does not accept the claim then an application can be made to the Court for an appropriate Order. The Court would then have a discretion as to whether to make the order or not.

For the right to inspection to arise, the document must be **mentioned** in the appropriate document. The previous rules used the word "referred". Often argument surrounded the inspection of documents that were referred to in some manner indirectly. It is suggested that the word "mention" is much more tightly drawn, requiring a positive "mention".

A statement of case is defined in Rule 2.3 as a claim form, particulars of claim, defence, Part 20 claim, reply to defence or any information given under Rule 18.

A witness statement is either a signed written statement which is prepared and served in advance of the trial or a signed written statement which is prepared and served for use as evidence at a hearing other than trial (Part 32).

Rule 32.9 provides for witness summaries. These are unsigned summaries of the evidence that an intended witness (such as one obliged to attend the trial as a result of the service of a witness summons) will give at trial.

An expert's report is one prepared and served in accordance with Part 35. In accordance with Rule 35.10(4), a party cannot claim privilege in relation to any instructions given to the expert but despite this the Court will not order "disclosure" of any specific document. There is a slight conflict between Rule 35.10(4) and Rule 31.14 in relation to this question since one refers to disclosure and the other to inspection but the intention is clear (see the reference to Rule 35.10 in the chapter dealing with experts).

Inspection

When the right to inspect has arisen in accordance with Rule 31.3 either, for instance, under Rule 31.14 or by the more formal method of giving disclosure under Rule 31.10, the party must give inspection of the document so disclosed upon receiving a notice from the other party expressing a wish to inspect (Rule 31.15(a) and (b)). Inspection must be given no more than seven days after the date on which the notice requiring inspection is served. This entitlement to inspect is, however, restricted to those documents for which there is no claim by the disclosing party that he no longer has control of them, he has a right or duty to withhold inspection or inspection is withheld on the grounds of proportionality in accordance with Rule 31.3.

In practice, although parties really should conduct inspection of originals, often the right to inspect is taken by seeking copies of the documents. This practice is codified into Rule 31.15(c) to the effect that if the party seeking inspection undertakes to pay reasonable copying costs, he may request copies of documents. The disclosing party then has to provide those copies within seven days after receiving the request.

Disclosure before proceedings start

One of the recommendations made by Lord Woolf in the Final Report was that the limits on pre-action disclosure under Section 33 of the Supreme Court Act 1981 and Section 52 of the County Courts Act 1984 should be lifted. Pre-action disclosure prior to 26 April was limited to potential claims in respect of personal injury or death. At Paragraph 47, Chapter 12, page 127 of the Final Report, Lord Woolf said—

> **an important part of my thinking is the need for parties to adopt a sensible and co-operative approach from the earliest stages at which a potential claim begins to materialise.**

and at Paragraph 48—

> **in support of this strategy, I recommend that parties should be able to make pre-action applications for disclosure against potential defendants in all cases.**

The extension of pre-action disclosure is intended to take place within the context of the recommendation that litigation should be avoided wherever possible. On the back of this recommendation Lord Woolf promoted pre-action protocols and their development within the scheme of things legislated for in the Civil Procedure Rules. Although at the time of writing there are only two approved pre-action protocols which ironically both relate to personal injury, others are being developed and as stated previously, Paragraph 4 of the Practice Direction to the pre-action protocols states specifically that parties should adopt the spirit of the protocols in all litigation—

> **to act reasonably in exchanging information and documents relevant to the claim and generally in trying to avoid the necessity for the start of proceedings.**

Section 8 of the Civil Procedure Act 1997 empowered the Lord Chancellor to amend the Supreme Court Act and the County Courts Act to remove the limits and the change was then effected, by the Civil Procedure (Modification of Enactments) Order 1998, to Section 33 of the Supreme Court Act 1981 and Section 52 of the County Courts Act 1984.

The procedure in seeking pre-action disclosure may be started automatically in accordance with a pre-action protocol. Paragraph 3.10 of the protocol relating to personal injury provides that the prospective defendant should—

> **Enclose with a letter of reply, documents in his possession which are material to the issues between the parties, and which would be likely to be ordered to be disclosed by the Court,**

either on an application for pre-action disclosure or on disclosure during proceedings.

Annex B to the protocol provides a specimen list of those documents.

Paragraph 3.18 of the protocol for clinical disputes provides similarly, although in this case it is the potential claimant who should provide copies of documents with the letter of claim.

If documents are not produced in accordance with the protocols then an application should be made to the Court in accordance with Rule 31.16.

In accordance with the spirit of the protocols, parties in other types of litigation are encouraged to provide documents voluntarily under Paragraph 4 of the Practice Direction referred to above. There will undoubtedly be many arguments about pre-action disclosure, the obligations arising and the extent of them. If disclosure and inspection is not given voluntarily then the party seeking it may make an application to the Court under Rule 31.16. Under the old Rules the application was made by originating summons. Under the CPR it is made by an ordinary application under Part 23. Whilst Rule 23.6 provides that the application notice must state what order the applicant is seeking and briefly why the applicant is seeking the order, Rule 31.16(4) effectively also provides that the applicant must specify the documents or the classes of documents which the respondent must disclose. This additional requirement could be included in the application notice or in a separate witness statement. The application must be supported by evidence (Rule 31.16(2)) but that evidence again may be included in the application notice as long as it is verified by a statement of truth.

Although the discretion of the Court is wide, there are limitations. Firstly, it is clear that the applicant must make out a prima facie case against the proposed respondent since the Rules specifically provide that the respondent is likely to be a party to subsequent proceedings and the applicant is also likely to be a party to those proceedings (Rule 31.16(3)(a) and (b)).

The documents, disclosure of which is sought, must be documents which the respondent would have a duty to disclose by way of standard disclosure if the proceedings based upon the applicant's prima facie case had commenced. To determine that question the Court must examine the prima facie case and determine whether the documents sought would fall to be disclosed in accordance with Rule 31.6. The Court cannot make an order for disclosure before proceedings have started in relation to any documents that fall outside Rule 31.6. even though they may normally be the subject of an order for specific disclosure under Rule 31.12. The other preconditions to an order for disclosure before proceedings have started are set out in Rule 31.16(3)(d).

(d) disclosure before proceedings have started is desirable in order to—

(i) dispose fairly of the anticipated proceedings;

(ii) assist the dispute to be resolved without proceedings; or

(iii) save costs.

These additional preconditions are written in fairly wide terms. Lord Woolf made it clear that he was aware of concerns that might arise from the opening up of pre-action disclosure to a wide range of potential defendants. It may be said that such a provision licenses "fishing expeditions" for documents so that the potential claimant can dip into the potential defendant's documents to establish whether or not they have either the prima facie case made out to the Court or any other claim. On the other hand, bearing in mind that the applicant has to make out a prima facie case and the documents would be discoverable during the course of proceedings, the potential defendant may not be losing anything by providing early disclosure save a potential tactical advantage. If the documents were to be disclosed in any event during the course of proceedings, it could be argued that to foreshorten the procedure is of advantage to all involved. As Lord Woolf put it, this may fulfil his express desire that litigation should be avoided by early resolution wherever possible.

One of the unspoken but most important considerations that the Court will have when exercising its power under Rule 31.16 will be its obligations under Part 1. In particular, in considering the general principle of disclosure or its extent, the Court will have in mind the question of proportionality. The party from whom disclosure and inspection is sought will have to raise these questions before the Court on the application.

Rule 31.16 refers to disclosure before proceedings have started rather than inspection. No indication is given in the Rule or the Practice Direction as to the manner in which documents are disclosed. There is no specific requirement for the service of a list and presumably disclosure can be made simply in a written form such as a letter. In any event, the order made by the Court should specify the document or class of documents which the respondent must disclose (Rule 31.16(4)). Further, when making that disclosure, the order should require the respondent to specify any of those documents which are no longer in his control or in respect of which he claims a right or duty to withhold inspection.

On the face of it therefore it is no ground for objection to an order for pre-action disclosure that, for instance, the documents for which the application is made are privileged. This would be a ground for objection only to inspection. It is unlikely, however, that the Court would make an order if the purpose of it, i.e. disclosure and inspection was unlikely to be achieved because of proper objection to inspection being taken.

Specifically, however, it would be a proper objection to the giving of disclosure if either disclosure or inspection would be injurious to public interest (Section 35(1) of the Supreme Court Act 1981 and Section 54(1) of the County Courts Act 1984). Such objection could be made without notice in accordance with Rule 31.19(1).

When making the order for disclosure, the Court may under Rule 31.16(5) order the time and place of disclosure and inspection. The relevant sections of the two Acts (s 33 SCA and s 52 CCA) provide that the order can require the respondent to give inspection (subject to appropriate conditions) to—

- the applicant;
- the applicant's legal advisors;
- the applicant's legal advisors and any medical or other professional advisor of the applicant; or
- if the applicant has no legal advisor, to any medical or other professional advisor of the applicant.

Rule 31.17—Disclosure by a non-party

One of the recommendations made by Lord Woolf was that pre-action disclosure in personal injury and death cases should include disclosure by a respondent who is not likely to become a party to any subsequent proceedings. This recommendation has not found its way into the Rules although there are statutory rights to certain documents such as medical records, and the principles established in *Norwich Pharmacal* still apply (see below). Rule 31.17 which provides for disclosure by a person who is not a party to proceedings only applies after the proceedings have been commenced. Prior to 26 April the power to make an order against a person not a party extended only to personal injury and death cases (Section 34 of the Supreme Court Act 1981 and Section 53 of the County Courts Act 1984). These limitations, however, have been lifted by the Civil Procedure (Modification of Enactments) Order 1998. Accordingly the power to make such an order is now extended to any types of proceedings.

The application will be made in accordance with Part 23. Accordingly the notice must not only state what order the applicant is seeking (and in this case specify the document) but also briefly why the applicant is seeking the order. The respondent to the application will be the person against whom an order is sought.

The application must be supported by evidence (Rule 31.17(2)). That evidence may be contained within the application notice as long as it is verified by a statement of truth.

Not only will the applicant have to identify the documents, the disclosure of which is sought, but also make out the grounds on which the Court will make an order under Rule 31.17(3). The Court's discretion to make an order for disclosure by a non-party can only be exercised where—

- the documents of which disclosure is sought are likely to support the case of the applicant or adversely affect the case of one of the other parties to the proceedings; and
- disclosure is necessary in order to dispose fairly of the claim or to save costs.

When considering whether to make such an order the Court will have in mind its obligations under Part 1 of the Rules and principally the question of proportionality.

The Court will also have in mind other procedures available to the applicant to seek disclosure, namely by the issuing of a witness summons under Part 34 and particularly Rule 34.2 (witness summons to produce documents to the

Court). As dealt with in relation to Part 34, the Court can set a date for the production of documents to the Court at any time and not simply at the beginning of the trial (Rule 34.2(4)). Alternatively, the Court can make an order for evidence to be taken by deposition under Rule 34.8. The order made may require the production of documents for the purposes of the examination (Rule 34.8(4)).

It will be interesting to see how the Courts combine these different remedies and the extent to which Courts will be willing to make disclosure orders under Rule 31.17. Such an order is not without other difficulties such as potential problems with the European Convention for the Protection of Human Rights, the Human Rights Act 1998 and indeed the Brussels Convention on enforcement of such orders in other jurisdictions.

As with disclosure under Rule 31.16, any objections that the respondent has to providing disclosure should be voiced before or upon the hearing of the application. Specifically, objection to disclosure can be taken under Section 35(1) of the Supreme Court Act 1981 or Section 54(1) of the County Courts Act 1984 if disclosure would be injurious to public interest. That objection may be taken by the respondent upon application to the Court without notice. Whilst other objections to the making of an order relate to inspection, the Court is unlikely to make an order if disclosure were effectively to be neutered by a successful claims, for instance, to privilege in relation to the documents disclosed.

One of the objections that may be taken by the respondent to the application would be that the necessary search for the documents and any subsequent inspection would be disproportionate to the advantage to be gained by the applicant. Certainly the Court will have this in mind in any event in accordance with its obligations under Part 1.

If the Court does make an order then under Rule 31.17(4) the order must—

- specify the documents or the classes of documents which the respondent must disclose; and
- require the respondent, when making disclosure, to specify any of those documents—
    - which are no longer in his control; or
    - in respect of which he claims a right or duty to withhold inspection.

The limitations as to what documents may be disclosed reflect the limitations under Rule 31.6.

It is likely that the order will specify how and when disclosure and inspection is to be given. There is no set procedure for the mechanism of giving disclosure. Presumably it could be given by letter. Since the order will be stating specific documents that have to be disclosed, a disclosure statement would not necessarily be required although the Court may feel it appropriate in particular circumstances that the respondent should be required to verify that they have given effect to the order made.

The order is also likely to provide how inspection is to be given (Rule 31.17(5)(b)).

Finally, the order may require the respondent to indicate what has happened to any documents which are no longer in his control.

Costs under Rules 31.16 and 31.17

Part 48 makes specific provision for costs in relation to pre-commencement disclosure and orders for disclosure against a non-party. Under Rule 48.1(2) the general rule is that the respondent to the application will be entitled to their costs of the application and the costs of complying with any order. The Court has a general discretion in relation to costs and in exercising it the Court will take into account whether it was reasonable for the respondent to resist the application or whether the parties to the application (pre-action disclosure only) have complied with a pre-action protocol (Rule 48.2(3)). In relation to pre-action disclosure the Court may wish to consider whether the respondent has complied with the spirit of a pre-action protocol even though there is no specific protocol applying to the type of proceedings in question. The respondent to any application under 31.16 and 31.17 should therefore carefully consider whether they are acting reasonably in refusing to give disclosure. Certainly in making that refusal it cannot be automatically assumed that the Court will make an order for costs in their favour. On the other hand it may seem reasonable that in seeking pre-action disclosure or disclosure by a non-party, the applicant should undertake to meet the reasonable costs of compliance.

Other powers

Rules 31.16 and 31.17 are specifically stated to be without prejudice to any powers that the Court may have generally to order disclosure before proceedings have started or disclosure against a person who is not a party to the proceedings. This was intended particularly to ensure that other powers were unaffected including—

- The powers to order the inspection, preservation and detention of property in accordance with Sections 33(1) and Section 34(3) of the Supreme Court Act 1981 and Sections 52(1) and 53(3) of the County Courts Act 1984 in relation to which there is specific provision within Rule 25.5. This jurisdiction includes the now statutory jurisdiction under Section 7 of the Civil Procedure Act 1997 (formerly an "Anton Piller Order" and now a "Search Order" in accordance with Rule 25.5).
- The *Norwich Pharmacal* jurisdiction under *Norwich Pharmacal v Customs & Excise Commissioners* [1974] AC 133, [1973] 2 All ER 943, HL.
- The Court's powers under RSC Order 48 (examination of judgment debtor etc) or CCR Order 25 Rule 3 (oral examination of the debtor).

Inspection of a privileged document given inadvertently

It is outside the scope of this work to discuss generally privilege and when it may be claimed. In particular, the question of waiving any privilege is not discussed. Insofar as privilege has not been waived by, for instance, the giving of disclosure, Rule 31.20 that if **inspection** is given of a privileged document, the document or its contents may only be used with the express permission of the Court.

Subsequent use of disclosed documents

Rule 31.22 reflects the previous rules in relation to the subsequent use of disclosed documents, namely RSC Order 24 Rule 14A and CCR Order 14 Rule 8A. These were introduced following an undertaking given by the Government to the European Commission for the Protection of Human Rights in the *Harman* case, i.e.—

> **To seek to change the law so that it will no longer be a contempt of Court to make public material contained in documents compulsorily disclosed in civil proceedings, once those documents have been read out in open Court.**

Rule 31.22 therefore provides that the general rule that a document, disclosure of which is made during the course of proceedings, can only be used for the purposes of those proceedings applies save where—

- the document has been read to or by the Court, or referred to, at a hearing which has been held in public;
- the Court gives permission; or
- the party who disclosed the document and the person to whom the document belongs agrees.

The Court has an overriding discretion to allow a party to use a document otherwise or under Rule 31.22(2) restrict the use of a document that would otherwise be open for use as falling within one of the heads under 31.22(1) above. The application for an order restricting the use of the document can be made either by a party to the proceedings or by any person to whom the document belongs (Rule 31.22(3)).

CHAPTER 21
PART 35—EXPERTS AND ASSESSORS

Background

One of Lord Woolf's major concerns about the conduct of litigation is the use of, or in his view, misuse of, expert evidence. Indeed he was extremely condemnatory of both experts and legal practitioners in his Final Report in relation to the use and calling of expert evidence. It is worth repeating what he said—

> **It was a basic contention in my Interim Report that two of the major generators of unnecessary cost in civil litigation are uncontrolled discovery and expert evidence. No one has seriously challenged that contention.**
>
> **A large litigation support industry generating a multi-million pound fee income has grown up among professions such as accountants, architects and others, and new professions have developed such as accident, reconstruction and care experts. This goes against all principles of proportionality and access to justice. In my view its most damaging effect is that it has created an ethos of what is acceptable which has in turn filtered down to smaller cases. Many potential litigants do not even start litigation because of the advice they are given about cost and in my view this is as great a social ill as the actual cost of pursuing litigation.**
>
> **In my Interim Report I recommended that the calling of expert evidence should be under the complete control of the Court. Within that framework, I argued for a wider use of single or neutral experts that would be jointly selected and instructed by the parties or, if the parties could not agree on a single expert, appointed by the Court. I also put forward a number of other recommendations designed to achieve more economical use of expert evidence in cases where opposing experts were involved by narrowing the issues between them as early as possible.**

The Report goes on to list the perceived problems—

- the partiality of experts as compared to the impartiality required by the Court and justice;
- delay incurred through experts;
- the unnecessary attendance at trial of great numbers of experts; and
- the excessive or inappropriate use of experts.

Lord Woolf therefore recommended—

1. The calling of expert evidence to be subject to the complete control of the Court.
2. That the Court should have a discretion with or without the agreement or the parties to appoint an expert to report to them and to give evidence to the Court.
3. The Court should have wide power to appoint assessors.
4. Experts should be given clear guidance that when preparing their evidence or actually giving evidence to the Court, their first responsibility is to the Court and not to their client.
5. Any report prepared for the purposes of giving evidence to the Court should be addressed to the Court.
6. Such a report should end with a declaration that it has included everything which the expert regards as being relevant to the opinion that he has expressed in his report and that he has drawn to the attention of the Court any matter which would affect the validity of that opinion.
7. If experts instructed by the parties meet at the direction of the Court it should be unprofessional conduct for an expert to be given or to accept instructions not to reach agreement. If the experts cannot reach agreement on an issue they should specify their reasons for being unable to do so.
8. Once an expert has been instructed to prepare a report for the use of the Court, any communication between the expert and the client or his advisors should no longer be the subject of legal privilege.
9. Codes of practice providing guidance as to the practice in relation to experts should be drawn up jointly by the appropriate professional bodies representing the experts and the legal profession.
10. Unless the claimant is relying on the doctor by whom he is being treated, the defendant should be told whom the claimant intends to instruct and be invited to make any comments as to the proposed instructions.
11. Before a doctor reports on behalf of a claimant or a defendant, the opposing party should have the opportunity to give instructions to that doctor.
12. If more than one doctor is to be instructed in a case on the fast track, the doctors should be instructed at the same time with a view to producing a draft report.
13. Every effort should be made by the Court to avoid doctors having to attend Court or if they have to attend Court to reduce the inconvenience this involves. Video technology should be used for this purpose.

The issues were much debated within the Civil Procedure Rule Committee. The product is Part 35. Not all Lord Woolf's recommendations have been carried into effect but the general spirit of his proposals is very much part and parcel of the new Rules.

Part 35

The general scheme under Part 35 is—

- The Court has ultimate control over expert evidence which will be limited to that reasonably necessary to resolve proceedings.
- There is a direct relationship between the expert and the Court which overrides any relationship between the expert and the party to whom they are contracted. Accordingly the first duty of the expert is to assist the Court in relation to matters within the expert's discipline.
- The general requirement that an expert should be **impartial** is emphasised although not specifically provided.
- Wherever possible there should be a single jointly instructed expert, particularly in lower value claims.
- The expert/s will report in writing. There will be no automatic provision that an expert should give oral evidence particularly in lower value claims.
- The written report is closely regulated. In particular the expert has to set out material instructions which do not enjoy privilege.
- Questions arising from the reports may be put to the expert who should then answer to the parties posing the questions.
- The experts should meet to try and limit the issues in debate. Again, the meeting is closely regulated with the Court requiring a report direct to it of matters agreed or which remain in issue with reasons.
- Only insofar as necessary experts will give oral evidence but again this will be closely regulated by the Court both in preparation for the trial and at the trial.

Pre-Action instruction of Experts

It is of course routine for experts to be instructed prior to the commencement of proceedings to advise the respective parties. Indeed, in relation to personal injury actions, there is a standard requirement that a medical report should be annexed to the particulars of claim.

The existing pre-action protocols relating to personal injury and clinical disputes regulate the fashion in which experts should be selected and instructed. In particular the protocol for personal injury requires the parties at Paragraphs 3.14–3.18 to achieve a consensus about the identification of an expert or, where appropriate, experts. The personal injury protocol is specifically directed towards fast track cases which in personal injury range between claims for sums in excess of £5,000 (or a lesser sum if within that sum the general damages exceed £1,000).

The parties to a potential fast track case are therefore encouraged to appoint a single expert between them to be separately instructed. This ties in with the provisions of Part 35 and particularly Rule 35.7 in which the Court may require that expert evidence is to be given by a single joint expert after proceedings have commenced.

If the requirements of the protocol are ignored by either party, sanctions may be subsequently imposed including costs. If consensus cannot be reached, parties take the risk that at some later point the Court will decide that there will only be one expert in which event the costs of the parties instructing their own experts may be irrecoverable.

The encouragement therefore is for the parties to try and reach a consensus on the identification of a single jointly instructed expert prior to the commencement of proceedings.

The letter of the pre-action protocol in personal injury does not apply to multi track cases but undoubtedly cases should follow the practice established within the protocol in relation to experts. Although the general picture is that the appointment of single experts is geared towards fast track cases, the Court has the power to apply it by sanctions, to all cases whatever the value of the claim. Accordingly in lower value multi track cases it might be expected that the Court will be seeking a consensus between the parties as to the appointment of a single expert.

The Practice Direction to the pre-action protocol also encourages the parties to adopt the spirit of the pre-action protocol in all litigation. Paragraph 4 of the Practice Direction makes no specific mention of trying to agree experts prior to commencement of proceedings although again it would be very much in the spirit of the Woolf reforms if parties were to consult about the appointment of experts before instructing them.

Small Claims Track

Part 35 has no application to a case allocated to the small claims track (Rule 27.2(e)) save Rules 35.1 (duty to restrict expert evidence), 35.3 (experts—overriding duty to the Court) and 35.8 (instructions to a single joint expert).

Specifically Rule 27.5 provides that no experts may give evidence, whether written or oral, at a hearing without the permission of the Court. If permission is given for an expert then the recoverable fees are closely regulated. The Practice Direction to Part 27 applied by Rule 27.14(d) provides that the recoverable amount for an expert's fees is no more than £200 (Paragraph 7.3(2), Practice Direction to Part 27).

Although a small claim does not fall into the small claims track until it is allocated, when it is allocated, the Rules relating to recoverable costs have retrospective effect prior to allocation (Paragraph 5.1(2), Practice direction to Part 44).

The Practice Direction to Part 27 gives an indication of the type of order the Court might make if it believes that expert evidence should be given—

> **It appears to the Court that expert evidence is necessary on the issue of __________ and that that evidence should be given by a single expert N. to be instructed by the parties jointly. If the parties cannot agree about who to choose and what arrangements to make about paying his fee, either party may apply to the Court for further directions.**

The Rules under Part 35

In accordance with Rule 35.2, Part 35 only applies to an expert who has been instructed to give or prepare evidence for the purpose of Court proceedings. Accordingly a party can instruct an expert without having a view to that expert giving or preparing evidence but simply for the purpose of giving an opinion to the party instructing him. In that event such an expert will not be regulated by Part 35. Of course it will be difficult to justify the taking of such an opinion for the purpose of recovering costs at the end of the day.

All material instructions, whether or written or oral, on the basis of which the expert gives a written report, do not enjoy privilege (Rule 35.10(3)). Accordingly if instructions are given for the expert to give an opinion rather than to give or prepare evidence as referred to in Rule 35.2, although initially privileged, the instructions for the opinion will still be material instructions for the purposes of Rule 35.10(3) if the expert subsequently gives a written report for the purpose of the proceedings and the report is based upon those instructions.

Under Rule 35.4 the Court exerts control over the calling of expert evidence. Specifically under Rule 35.4(1) no party may call an expert or rely upon an expert's report without the Court's permission.

In applying for that permission the party must identify the field or discipline in which he submits expert evidence should be given and if possible name the particular expert.

The question of whether expert evidence may be called is likely to be dealt with when the Court gives directions on allocation. The allocation questionnaire itself in Section F seeks information in relation to the calling of expert evidence. Under both Part 28 (the fast track) and Part 29 (the multi track) the parties can agree directions with a view to putting them to the Court for approval. This would include directions relating to expert evidence. The Court might of its own initiative give directions which again would deal with expert evidence. As a final alternative the Court under fast track or multi track may hold a hearing to determine the directions including those relating to experts. This will be more likely in multi track cases in which such a hearing is referred to as a case management conference. At that hearing the parties may be required to attend but where legal representatives attend they should ensure that they are familiar with the case and able to deal with substantive matters relating to the case such as experts.

When considering whether to allow parties to submit expert evidence, the Court is required to restrict that evidence to that which is reasonably required to resolve the proceedings (Rule 35.1). The Court will also have in mind the overriding objective. Accordingly the Court will have to consider its obligations under Rule 1.1(2)—

- To ensure that the parties are on an equal footing.
- To save expense.
- To deal with a case in ways which are proportionate to the—
    - amount of money involved
    - importance of the case

- complexity of the issues
- financial position of each party

- To ensure that the case is dealt with expeditiously and fairly.

If the Court gives permission then it will limit it to a named expert or an expert from a particular field/discipline.

When making an order in relation to experts the Court can prescribe the amount of fees and expenses of the expert that one party may recover from the other dependent naturally on securing an appropriate order for costs in the proceedings (Rule 35.4(4)).

Single joint Expert

When considering what order to make in relation to expert evidence the Court will turn its mind to the question of whether the parties should call separate experts or a single jointly instructed expert should be the only expert allowed to give evidence. This provision within the Rules (Rule 35.7) was one of the principal recommendations of Lord Woolf in his Final Report following on from the Interim Report.

Lord Woolf identified that the opposition to his proposal for a neutral single expert was particularly strong from those "... who are reluctant to give up their adversarial weapons".

Lord Woolf did not see that in some fashion there was thereby a shift towards an inquisitorial process. He saw the single expert as very much part of the adversarial process in that the expert would be subject to thorough cross examination on behalf of the parties. Lord Woolf accepted that a single expert was inappropriate to large complex and strongly contested cases "... where the full adversarial system, including oral cross examination of opposing experts on particular issues, is the best way of producing a just result".

He went on to recommend—

> **As a general principle, I believe that single experts should be used wherever the case (or the issue) is concerned with a substantially established area of knowledge and where it is not necessary for the Court directly to sample a range of opinions.**

In conclusion Lord Woolf said—

> **Given the strength of opposition to my proposals, it would not be realistic to expect a significant shift towards single experts in the short term. What is needed to initiate such a shift is a clear statement of principle in the Rules, coupled with procedures to ensure that parties and procedural judges always consider whether a single expert could be appointed in a particular case (or to deal with a particular issue); and, if this is not considered appropriate, that they indicate why not.**

As with the pre-action protocols, Rule 35.7 promotes consensus between the parties to try and agree a single expert or at least a list from which the Court could choose. If consensus is not possible then the Court can direct the method by which the expert should be selected. As with commercial arbitration, it may well be that the Court retains lists of appropriate experts or it directs that an expert be selected by, for instance, the president for the time being of some professional body.

One of the main criticisms of Lord Woolf's proposals was and remains that if a single expert is "appointed" by the Court, the parties will wish to retain their own expert in relation to whom Part 35 will have no application, for instance, to feed the advocate with questions for cross examination. The single expert will only add to the costs rather than diminish them. The parties will have to consider, however, that the cost of their own expert will be irrecoverable against the other party when it comes to the assessment of costs.

Experts duty to the Court

Whether or not a single expert is "appointed" by the Court, all experts have an overriding duty to the Court to help it on the matters within their expertise (Rule 35.3(1)). That duty overrides any obligation that the expert owes to the person from whom he has received instructions or by whom he is paid (Rule 35.3(2)). This specific obligation of the expert to the Court emphasises the direct relationship under Part 35 between the Court and the expert. As produced in the Brown Book, the similar draft rule specifically mentioned the duty of impartiality on the part of an expert. This has been a matter of considerable debate in recent years. Cresswell J. set out in *National Justice Compania Naviera P.A. v Prudential Assurance Co. Ltd (Ikarian Reefer)* [1993] 2 Lloyd's Rep 68 the standards and duties of an expert in proceedings.

1. **Expert evidence presented to the Court should be, and should be seen to be, the independent product of the expert uninfluenced as to form or content by the exigencies of litigation (*Whitehouse v Jordan* [1981] 1 WLR 246, per Lord Wilberforce).**
2. **An expert witness should provide independent assistance to the Court by way of objective unbiased opinion in relation to matters within his expertise (see *Polivitte Ltd v Commercial Union Assurance Co plc* [1987] 1 Lloyd's Rep 379 at 286 per Garland J and *Re J* [1990] FCR 193 per Cazalet J). An expert witness in the High Court should never assume the role of an advocate.**
3. **An expert witness should state the facts or assumptions upon which has opinion is based. He should not omit to consider material facts which could detract from his concluded opinion (*Re J* above).**
4. **An expert witness should make it clear when a particular question or issue falls outside his expertise.**
5. **If an expert's opinion is not properly researched because he considers that insufficient data is available, then this must be stated with an indication that the opinion is no more than a provisional one (*Re J* above). In cases where an expert witness who has prepared a report could not assert that the report contained the truth, the whole truth and nothing but the truth without some**

qualification, that qualification should be stated in the report (*Derby v Weldon* (1990) Times, 9 November per Staughton LJ).

6. **If, after exchange of reports, an expert witness changes his view on a material matter having read the other side's expert's report or for any other reason, such change of view should be communicated (through legal representatives) to the other side without delay and when appropriate to the Court.**
7. **Where expert evidence refers to photographs, plans, calculations, analyses, measurements, survey reports or other similar documents, these must be provided to the opposite party at the same time as the exchange of reports.**

The codification of an overriding duty of the expert is intended to strengthen the obligations of the expert in line with Cresswell J's direction.

In the course of reviewing the Brown Book draft, the word "impartially" which appeared in Rule 35.3(1) was omitted because it was felt that it was an unnecessary test upon an expert's evidence taking no further the obligation that the expert owes to the Court. Its omission, however, does not in any way lessen the obligations nor does it in any way derogate from the standards that Cresswell J attempted to set in *Ikarian Reefer.*

When preparing the expert's report, each expert has to specify that they understand the obligation to the Court and they have complied with it (Rule 35.10(2)).

Instructions

When instructing an expert each party will have to consider that those instructions will not enjoy privilege. In other respects there are no changes to the practice of giving instructions from the previous rules save if the expert is a single joint expert "appointed" by the Court under Rule 35.7. A single joint expert is instructed separately by each of the parties (Rule 35.8(1)). A copy of the instructions must be sent to the other instructing parties (Rule 35.8(2)). Other than the relationship established between the Court and the expert under Part 35, the contractual position between a party and the expert remains the same. The expert will be entitled to be paid in accordance with that contract whatever limits the Court should place upon recoverable fees. When the Court "appoints" a single joint expert, it can give directions about the payment of the expert's fees and expenses and indeed direct that the instructing parties pay an appropriate amount into Court, effectively by way of security for those fees (Rule 35.8(4)). Unless the Court stipulates to the contrary, the instructing parties are automatically jointly and severally liable for the fees and expenses of the single joint expert (Rule 35.8(5)).

Paragraph 5 of the Practice Direction relating to single experts provides that if the Court makes an order under Rule 35.7 for the "appointment" of a single expert, in relation to a claim where a number of disciplines might be relevant to an issue, the Court should appoint a leading expert in the dominant discipline as the single joint expert. That expert will then prepare the general part of the report and be responsible for annexing or incorporating the contents of any reports from experts in other disciplines which are allowed by the Court.

It has been a matter of much debate that with the growth of conditional fee encouraged by the government experts fees might be some way be made conditional. It is said, however, that whatever the difficulties for the solicitor working under a conditional fee agreement to tie the experts fees to the outcome of the case will impair his "impartiality". For the time being solicitors and experts should not enter into conditional fee agreements although agreement can be reached to defer payment, although some would even criticise that type of arrangement.

The Expert's Report

The evidence of the expert will initially be given in a written report (Rule 35.5(1)). Indeed, in the fast track the general rule is that an expert will not give oral evidence "... unless it is necessary to do so in the interests of justice" (Rule 35.5(2)). In determining whether it is appropriate the Court will have to consider its obligations under the overriding objective and the necessity to deal with cases justly.

Rule 35.10 and the Practice Direction set out the matters which must be included within the expert's report. Reference should also be made to the Law Society's protocol on experts and current guidance from the Academy of Experts and the Expert Witness Institute. An experts protocol is being developed but at the time of writing awaits finalisation.

By way of reminder of the direct relationship between the expert and the Court, Paragraph 1.1 of the Practice Direction to Part 35 invokes the expert to address the report to the Court and not to the instructing party.

There are a number of requirements for exactly what should be included in the expert's report—

- Details of the expert's qualifications.
- Details of any literature or other material which the expert has relied upon in making the report.
- Details of who has carried out any test or experiment which has been referred to in the report and whether or not that test or experiment has been carried out under the expert's supervision.
- The qualifications of any person who carried out any such test or experiment.
- Where there is a range of opinion on the matters dealt with in the report, summarise the range of opinion and give reasons for his own opinion.
- A summary of the conclusions reached by the expert.
- A statement that the expert understands his duty to the Court under Rule 35.3 and that he has complied with it.
- The substance of all material instructions (whether written or oral) together with a summary of the facts and instructions given to the expert which are material to his conclusions and opinions expressed in the report.

In accordance with Rule 35.10(4) the material instructions do not enjoy privilege against disclosure. This removal of privilege, however, is somewhat limited and follows very much the example of assessment of costs in which a solicitor's file is available to the Court but not necessarily to the opposing party. On cross-examination of the expert, the opposing party is not entitled to cross examine on the contents of the instructions, nor will those instructions be available to the opposing party unless the Court orders to that effect having been satisfied that there are reasonable grounds to consider that the statement in the report of the substance of the instructions is inaccurate or incomplete. Even then the Court will have regard to the overriding objective and its obligation to deal with cases justly in releasing documents to the other side or allowing cross examination (refer to Rule 35.10 and the Practice Direction to Part 35).

Paragraph 1.3 and 1.4 of the Practice Direction to Part 35 require that the experts report should be verified by a statement of truth as well as the statement as to the recognition of the obligation to the Court and its performance. The prescribed statement of truth should read as follows—

> **I believe that the facts I have stated in this report are true and that the opinions I have expressed are correct.**

If it were to appear subsequently that the expert did not have an honest belief in the facts stated or the opinions, he may be susceptible to an application for contempt under Rule 32.14. To this writer whilst the addition of the statement of truth re-emphasises the obligations of the expert to the Court, it is difficult to see what further is added by the statement of truth. Suffice it to say that experts may have some concern as to exactly what they are letting themselves in for when signing the statement of truth.

Experts should be careful about exactly what documents are "mentioned" within the experts report since (subject to the restrictions relating to material instructions) those documents may be inspected by the other party upon giving notice in accordance with Rule 31.14.

Under Rule 35.13, if a party does not "disclose" an experts report then they may not rely upon it unless the Court gives permission. The use of the word "disclose" is somewhat odd in the circumstances. Presumably it is not intended to reflect the provisions under Part 31 relating to disclosure by which under Rule 31.2 a party discloses a document by stating that the document exists or has existed. It is suggested that the word "disclose" in Rule 35.13 means that it is served in accordance with an order of the Court. Under Rule 35.11 where a party has "disclosed" an experts report, any party may use the report as evidence at the trial. Again it is suggested that the word "disclose" means served in accordance with the order of the Court.

Neither Part 35 nor its Practice Direction give any directions about the manner in which the reports should be either exchanged or served. This is left to the discretion of the Court. The Practice Directions to Parts 28 (fast track) and 29 (multi track) refer to both the simultaneous exchange and, as an alternative, to sequential exchange. This will be a matter for the discretion of the Court.

Written questions to Experts

The pre-action protocol for personal injury provides specifically for the putting of questions to the expert in relation to their report. Rule 35.6 also provides in a similar fashion in relation to a report served following the commencement of proceedings and in accordance with the order of the Court. There are, however, some limitations—

- Questions can only be put once.
- They must be put within 28 days of service of the experts report.
- They must be for the purpose only of clarification of the report unless the parties agree to the contrary or the Court gives permission.

If the expert does not answer those questions, the other party may make an application to the Court for an order that the answers be provided subject to the condition that if they are not so provided the party may not rely on the evidence of that expert or the party may not recover the fees and expenses of that expert from any other party.

The Chancery Guide reminds parties that questions to experts should not be used oppressively or in a manner intended to restrict the exchange of opinion between experts (Chapter 6, Paragraph 19, Chancery Guide).

The answers when given are treated as part of the experts report and thus are subject to the overriding obligation of the expert and the statement of truth. Any document mentioned in the answers may be inspected by the other party under Rule 31.14.

Experts' request for Directions

The potential for conflict between the obligations of the expert to the Court and their position as an expert instructed by one of the parties is well recognised. Lord Woolf in his Final Report (Paragraph 25, Chapter 13, page 143) referred to an article in the May 1996 issue of *The Psychologist*. This report apparently evidenced improper pressure on experts from solicitors found in a survey of clinical and educational psychologists. Rule 35.14 provides the relief from such impropriety by which the expert may seek the assistance of the Court by filing a written request for directions to assist him in carrying out his function as an expert (Rule 35.14(1)).

This request can be made without giving notice. As originally conceived, the expert could serve the request on all of the parties together with any supporting evidence. As finalised the Rule does not specifically provide for the giving of notice although on the other hand it does not in any way restrict the expert from taking any action that he believes appropriate.

The Commercial Court Guide suggests that in the Commercial Court only 7 days before making a written request to the court for directions the expert should send a copy of the request to the party instructing him and then 4 days before making this request the expert should provide a copy of the request to all other parties (Commercial Court Guide H2.16).

It may be wholly inappropriate for an expert to serve such a request on all the other parties (save the instructing party), particularly if it is suggested that a solicitor or a party has imposed some improper pressure. When the Court deals with a request it may direct that a party be served with any order it makes and a copy of the expert's written request for directions upon which it acts.

In making a request the expert must be careful not to breach the solicitor/client privilege by, for instance, disclosing to the Court any without prejudice discussions.

Discussions between Experts

Again, the direct control that the Court has in relation to experts is emphasised under Rule 35.12. Meetings between experts took place under the old procedure but it was felt that those meetings were restricted, either by direct instructions from parties to their experts or by the experts' perception of their duty to the instructing client.

Under the new regime (Rule 35.12) the Court can direct that the experts meet to discuss the issues relevant to their own expertise in the proceedings (which may be identified by the Court in advance) and, where possible, to reach agreement on issues (Rule 35.12(1) and (2)).

The Commercial Court Guide puts the purpose of this meeting "to decide, with the benefit of that discussion, on which expert issues they share or can come to agree the same expert opinion and on which expert issues there remains a difference of opinion between them (and what that difference is) (Commercial Court Guide H2.20).

As to the course of the meeting the Rule gives no further guide. The Commercial Court Guide provides that the procedure to be adopted at the meeting is a matter for the experts and not the parties or the lawyers (Paragraph H2.22). It goes on to reflect Lord Woolf's views that—

Neither the parties nor their legal representatives should seek to restrict the freedom of experts to identify and acknowledge the expert issues on which they agree (i.e. on which they share the same expert opinion) at (or following further consideration after) meetings of experts.

When the Court makes an order for a meeting to take place, it can also require that a report is prepared by the expert identifying the issues on which they agree and those issues on which they disagree with a summary of their reasons for disagreeing (Rule 35.12(3)). This requirement is automatic in the Commercial Court (Paragraph H2.24). It is suggested that parties may want the expert to provide a short supplemental report relating to the issues remaining in dispute as to why the expert maintains his views notwithstanding the opposing view.

If an expert changes his views after the meeting (or at any time) the other side should be told without delay (Commercial Court Guide App 12).

The discussion remains without prejudice unless the parties agree to the contrary. Accordingly it cannot be referred to at the trial. Even if the experts reach agreement, that agreement does not bind the parties unless they expressly agree to be bound.

Assessors

Section 70 of the Supreme Court Act 1981 and Section 63 of the County Courts Act 1984 provide the authority for the High Court and the County Court respectively to appoint assessors. RSC Order 40 and CCR Order 13 Rule 11 provided for the appointment of assessors or "court experts". Rule 35.15 re-codifies the old provisions. The Court can make an appointment of an assessor either upon application of a party or of its own initiative exercising its power under Rule 3.3.

When appointed the assessor is very much the creature of the Court with the specific intention that the expert should assist the Court without deposing the Judge's role to decide the case on its merits and the law. Primarily, therefore, the assessors advises the Court rather than the parties. This is a system which is often used on the Continent in inquisitorial process. It may be regarded as less relevant to the adversarial process in which the parties seek a right to examine and cross examine an expert whose opinion may influence the decision made by the Court.

If the Court proposes to make an appointment it must give 21 days notice to the parties with the name of the proposed assessor, details of the matter in respect of which the assistance of the assessor will be sought and the qualifications of the assessor to give that assistance (Paragraph 6.1, Practice Direction to Part 35). If a party objects then notice of objection must be filed with the Court within seven days of receipt of the Court's notice. The Court will then decide whether or not to make the appointment taking into account the observations of the objecting party or parties (Paragraph 6.3, Practice Direction to Part 35).

The Court will make appropriate directions upon the appointment. It may direct that the assessor should prepare a report and/or attend the Court on the whole or any part of the trial to advise it on any identified matter (Rule 35.15(3)). If a report is prepared prior to the trial then the Court will send a copy to each of the parties and the parties may use it at the trial (Rule 35.15(4)). The assessor will not, however, give oral evidence or be open to cross examination or questioning (Paragraph 6.4, Practice Direction to Part 35).

When making the appointment the Court may set the remuneration to be paid to the assessor. It may also require the parties to lodge monies as security for those fees. If it so requires, the assessor will not be asked to act until the monies are deposited (Rule 35.15(6)).

CHAPTER 22
PART 36—OFFERS TO SETTLE AND PAYMENTS INTO COURT

Introduction

Part 36 is very much part of the Woolf landscape in that it supports the process by which parties are encouraged to settle claims or part of claims without the necessity of proceeding to trial. RSC Order 22 and CCR Order 11 were the relevant provisions under the old rules. These related, however, solely to payments into court and were quite restrictive in their scope.

Alongside this formal regulation of payments into court a body of law developed concerning offers to settle. These were referred to as "Calderbank" offers, following a decision in relation to family proceedings in which a payment into court was inappropriate, *Calderbank v Calderbank* [1975] 3 All ER 333, [1975] 3 WLR 586, CA. A "Calderbank" offer was an offer made "without prejudice save as to costs". This made it clear that the offer would become open for consideration by the court when the court came to deal with the question of costs. This was to be differentiated from a "without prejudice" offer which could not be referred to in relation to costs since there was no condition applied to the privilege attaching to it.

The issue of offers to settle was addressed by Lord Woolf in the Interim Report (Chapter 24). His suggestions for change were—

- The system of payments into court should be replaced by a system of offers.
- Any party, the claimant as well as the defendant, should be able to make an offer to settle.
- Offers should be in respect of the whole case or of individual issues (including liability) of claims.
- Offers could be made before the start of proceedings.
- There should be financial incentives to encourage claimants, in particular, to make offers.
- Where an offer has been made, the court should exercise a wider discretion in respect of costs and interest than it habitually does at present.

In the Final Report, Lord Woolf debated the question of whether payments in should be required to support offers to settle. In furtherance of the Interim Report, Lord Woolf made recommendations in his Final Report—

- To be effective, an offer would not have to be supported by a payment in.

- A party may withdraw an offer but an offer which is open for less than 21 days should be disregarded by the court for costs purposes.
- Additional interest on awards should be payable to a claimant who makes an offer which is not accepted and the claimant matches or exceeds the offer at trial.
- Extra interest will normally run from the date of the offer but the court may order a different start date where appropriate.
- A party who recovers at trial the amount which he claimed should be treated as if he had made an offer for that amount, and be entitled to extra interest.

Part 36, from its Brown Book origination which flowed from the Interim and Final Reports, has undergone much change. In many respects the result still follows Lord Woolf's recommendations. One of the main departures, however, is that often in relation to money claims must be supported by a payment in.

The broad picture of Part 36 is—

- Either party can take advantage of the provisions of Part 36. A claimant can make an offer at any time in relation to both money claims and non-money claims. The defendant can make an offer prior to the commencement of proceedings in relation to both a money claim and a non-money claim. After the proceedings have commenced, a defendant can make an offer to settle a non-money claim but must make a payment in in relation to a money claim in order to take advantage of Part 36.
- An offer made prior to the commencement of proceedings in accordance with Part 36 may enjoy the benefits of Part 36. If it relates to a money claim, however, it must be supported by a payment into court within 14 days of the commencement of proceedings.
- In order to secure the automatic benefits of Part 36 an offer, whether made before or after the commencement of proceedings, must follow in form and content Rule 36.5. Similarly, a payment in must be made in accordance with the procedure set out in Rule 36.6.
- A Part 36 offer is made when **received** by the offeree. A Part 36 payment is made when notice of the payment into court is **served** on the other party.
- A party receiving an offer or notice of payment in may seek clarification of it.
- Offers and payments in under Part 36 must remain open for acceptance for 21 days.
- An offer can be withdrawn without the court's permission but that permission is required if the payment in is to be withdrawn.
- If an offer or payment in is accepted, the claimant will be entitled to costs up to the date of serving notice of acceptance.
- If at trial the claimant fails to beat a Part 36 payment or a defendant's Part 36 offer, the claimant will be liable for costs after the period for which the offer or payment in was open for acceptance.
- If the claimant does better than a Part 36 offer, he may be awarded additional costs and interest.

- Part 36 is excluded from small claims track claims after allocation, although will be a matter for consideration for any period during which the claim is on one of the other tracks (Rule 36.2(5)).

Part 36 must be considered with the costs rules which make specific reference to attempts to settle proceedings (see below). Further, Part 36 sits with some recent developments in which the court has been willing to penalise parties who do not make a reasonable attempt to negotiate a settlement prior to the commencement of proceedings—see, for example, *Butcher v Wolfe* (1998) Times, 9 November. The interplay between the costs rules and developments within the authorities increases the discretion of the court but at the expense of certainty to the parties. Just because an offer to settle or a payment in does not comply with Part 36, does not mean that a party can simply ignore it. The discretion of the court is emphasised time and again throughout the Rules. Under the CPR the court will always have to have in mind its obligation to deal with cases justly under Part 1 of the overriding objective and, for instance, to ensure that the parties are on an equal footing.

The form of a Part 36 offer

A Part 36 offer must be in writing (Rule 36.5(1)). Often negotiations take place orally or in general "without prejudice" correspondence. An offer made in that fashion, however, does not become a Part 36 offer until it is converted into writing and otherwise complies with Rule 36.5 and the Practice Direction.

A Part 36 offer is treated as though it were labelled "without prejudice except as to costs" (Rule 36.19(1)) and cannot be referred to in front of the **trial judge** until after liability and generally quantum (but see Rule 36.19(3)(c)) have been decided (Rule 36.19(2)). Although the Part 36 offer does not have to be labelled as "without prejudice except as to costs", it is suggested that all Part 36 offers should specifically state in writing that they are made "without prejudice except as to costs". Without that label in writing, confusion may abound.

The Part 36 offer **must**—

- State that it is a Part 36 offer (Paragraph 5.1(1), Practice Direction to Part 36).
- State whether it relates to the whole of the claim or to part of it or to an issue that arises in it and, if so, identify that Part or issue (Rule 36.5(3)(a)).
- State whether it takes into account any counterclaims (Rule 36.19(3)).
- State whether interest is excluded from the offer. If it is, then the offer must state—
    - whether interest is offered; and
    - if so, the amount offered, the rate or rates offered and the period or periods for which it is offered (Rule 36.22(2)). In accordance with Rule 36.22.(1), if nothing is said about interest then the offer will be treated as inclusive of all interest up to the final date on which it may be accepted, i.e. usually 21 days after the offer is made.

It is suggested that the interest element of any offer should be detailed. If it is not detailed, a party may seek clarification of this element of the offer under Rule 36.9.

- If a Part 36 offer is made not less than 21 days before the start of the trial, it must be expressed to remain open for acceptance for 21 days from the date it is made. It must also state that after 21 days the offeree may only accept it if—
  - the parties agree the liability for costs; or
  - the court gives permission.

  (Rule 36.6)
- If a Part 36 offer is made less than 21 days before the start of the trial then it must state that the offeree may only accept it if—
  - the parties agree the liability for costs; or
  - the court gives permission

  (Rule 36.5(7)).
- The offer must be signed by the offeror or his legal representative (Paragraph 5.1, Practice Direction to Part 36). Under Paragraph 5.5, if the offer is made by a company or other corporation then a person holding a senior position in the company or corporation may sign the offer on the offeror's behalf but must state the position he holds. The definition of whether a person holds a senior position is repeated on occasions throughout the Rules—
  (1) in respect of a registered company or corporation, a director, the treasurer, the secretary, chief executive, manager or other officer of the company or corporation; and
  (2) in respect of a corporation which is not a registered company, in addition to those persons set out in (1), the mayor, chairman, president, town clerk or similar officer of the corporation (Paragraph 5.6, Practice Direction to Part 36).

  The definition in relation to a registered company or corporation is somewhat circular since the reference to a manager or other officer presumably means a manager or other officer holding a relatively senior position. It does not mean an officer for the purposes of the Companies Acts.

Time

A Part 36 offer is made when it is received by the offeree (Rule 36.8(1)). Whether or not it is received might be the subject of debate before the court. The offeror would have to prove receipt by the offeree. He may do this by providing evidence of posting or delivery which will give rise to a rebuttable presumption. The defendant would then be obliged to rebut that presumption by evidence that he did not receive the offer. It is suggested that as a matter of good practice the parties should communicate with each other following the making of an offer to determine the date of receipt so that the period for which the offer is open for acceptance can be determined without further debate.

A Part 36 offer is accepted when notice of its acceptance is received by the offeror. Again this might be a matter of debate which would have to be determined in the same way. Note that in either case if the party is legally represented, any Part 36 offer or notice of acceptance must be served on the legal representative. For these purposes a person is legally represented if they have instructed a legal representative (a term defined in Rule 2.3(1)) to act for them in relation to a claim.

Periods of time must be measured in accordance with Rule 2.8. Thus reference to periods in Part 36 such as 21, 14 or 7 days refers to "clear days" which means that in computing the number of days, the day on which the period begins is not included. Generally in Part 36 the end of the period is not defined by reference to an event. If it were then the day on which that event occurs is also not included.

Offers prior to commencement of proceedings

Rule 36.10 makes general provision in relation to the application of Part 36 to offers which are made before proceedings are commenced. As noted above, it is not only pre-action offers that comply with Rule 36.10 which can be taken into account by the court when making any order as to costs. Rule 44.3 allows the court when considering an order for costs to take into account—

- conduct before as well as during the proceedings; and
- any payment into court or admissible offer to settle made by a party which is drawn to the court's attention (whether or not made in accordance with Part 36).

This reflects the court's wide discretion under Rule 44.3(1). A recent example of the exercise of that discretion taking into account conduct and admissible offers was given in *Butcher v Wolfe* (1998) Times, 9 November in which the usual costs rule was reversed because the plaintiff, having received a pre-action offer to settle, refused it without negotiation.

Subject to the court's general discretion, it is suggested that nothing is lost by a party making an offer strictly in accordance with Rule 36 prior to the commencement of proceedings if any offer is then to be made. For a defendant's offer to be effective after proceedings have commenced in relation to a money claim, the defendant must make a payment into court (see below).

The limitations of Rule 36.10 should be noted. Debate in the Civil Procedure Rules Committee surrounded the automatic nature of Part 36 applying to pre-action offers. The result is that the consequences of a failure to accept a Part 36 offer made prior to the commencement of proceedings are not automatic. Under Rule 36.10(1) the only requirement of the court is that it will take the offer into account when making any order as to costs. Subject to this obligation to take it into account thereafter, the matter remains within the discretion of the court.

The matter the Court may take into consideration would include the extent of disclosure of the claimant's case prior to the offer being made. The offer may, however, also be considered under the general costs provisions (Rules 44.3 and 44.5).

Further, that discretion only relates to costs and not the other consequences that could flow from a failure to accept an offer, particularly a claimant's offer, as provided in Rule 36.21, for example, additional interest. If advantage is to be taken of the automatic provisions of Rule 36.20 or the powers of the court under Rule 36.21, parties must comply with the general provisions of Part 36 insofar as they relate to offers or payments in after the commencement of proceedings.

The remainder of 36.10 deals with the mechanics of the offer, its effect and the acceptance.

As above, an offer complying with Rule 36.10 must also comply with Rule 36.5 as to the form and content of a Part 36 offer. As to the period for which the offer must remain open, Rule 36.10(2)(a) does not expressly tie the period to exactly 21 days. It simply says that the offer must be expressed to be open for at least 21 days after the date it was made. In accordance with Rule 36.5(3)(c) the offer will be deemed to include interest.

If the offer is made by a defendant then they must offer to pay the costs of the offeree up to the date 21 days after the offer is made.

If the offer relates to a money claim then if proceedings are commenced and the offer has been made by the defendant, the defendant must make a payment into court within 14 days of service of the claim form. (Note that the trigger here is not service of the particulars of claim as with many other provisions within the Rules.) The payment in must be no less than the sum offered in the offer before the proceedings began (Rule 36.10(3)).

If an offer has been made in accordance with Rule 36.10 but it is not accepted and proceedings are started, neither the offer nor the Part 36 payment made in accordance with Rule 36.10(3) can be accepted without the permission of the court.

An offer made in accordance with Rule 36.10 may be withdrawn at any time. It is no more than an offer to enter into a contract and like any offer can be withdrawn at the instance of the offeror. It may seem somewhat at odds with the contractual nature of a Part 36 offer that the Court can give permission for acceptance notwithstanding that the period for acceptance has expired and is in contractual terms the offer has lapsed.

As above there are no automatic consequences flowing from an offer made under Rule 36.10 save the obligation of the court to take it into account when dealing with costs, accordingly nothing automatically flows from acceptance of the Part 36 offer save as provided within it. It is for this reason that where a defendant makes an offer under Rule 36.10 it must include an offer to pay the costs up to 21 days after the date it is made. Accordingly, upon acceptance, liability for those costs will arise as a matter of contract. Thus if the claimant is making the offer they should include within the offer provisions as to costs.

A Rule 36.10 offer should not be confused with a tender of money due leading to a defence of tender to any claim subsequently issued. For a defence of tender, a payment into court must be made following the commencement of proceedings.

Rule 36.10 and the pre-action protocols

As above, Rule 36.10 must be seen within the context of the encouragement by Lord Woolf to settle claims before proceedings are issued, i.e. to avoid litigation wherever possible. The pre-action protocols set out the procedure to be followed in relation to proceedings covered by them (currently limited to personal injury and clinical disputes). Those procedures include the exchange of information and documents allowing parties to understand the other party's case with a view to evaluating the claim, defence and any counterclaim for the purposes of attempting to achieve a settlement.

The protocols have the further purpose that if settlement is not possible, the claim and any counterclaim can proceed as quickly as possible under the procedures provided by the CPR. The practice direction to the protocols (Paragraph 4) specifically requires parties involved in potential proceedings not covered by approved pre-action protocols to follow the spirit of the protocols in relation to the exchange of information and documents.

These matters bear directly on offers made under Rule 36.10 to this effect. When the court takes into account an offer made under Rule 36.10 in relation to the order for costs it will consider what information was available to the offeree at the time to determine whether they acted reasonably in not accepting the offer (see page 280 and following. Accordingly, if an offeror wishes to take the full benefit of Rule 36.10 they must enable the offeree to make a proper value judgment of the offer. Certainly solicitors will be extremely wary of accepting offers made, whether before or after the proceedings have been commenced, in relation to which they do not have the full picture.

Rule 36.10 offers and clarification under Rule 36.9

The simple picture is that Rule 36.9 has no application to Rule 36.10. Rule 36.9 is limited to Part 36 offers and an offer made under Rule 36.10 is not such an offer. The more complex picture, however, is that clearly, as above, the principles rather than the letter of Rule 36.9 apply to Rule 36.10. Thus when an offer is received the offeree should ask the offeror to explain any provision within the offer which is not clear. A refusal to provide that clarification would undoubtedly be taken into account by the court when it comes to consider the question of costs and the offer made under Rule 36.10.

Part 36 payment

A Part 36 payment can only be made after proceedings have been commenced. In relation to a money claim, the automatic consequences of Part 36 will only flow if a Part 36 payment is made in accordance with Rule 36.6 (Rule 36.3(1)).

There are a couple of exceptions—

(1) If there has been an interim payment in relation to which the defendant wishes to make a Part 36 offer, the offer can be made by reference to the interim payment and no payment into court is required (Rule 36.5).

(2) Under Rule 36.23 the defendant need not make a Part 36 payment and in the alternative can make an offer to settle the claim if—

- at the time he makes the offer he has applied for, but not received, a certificate of recoverable benefits under the Social Security (Recovery of Benefits) Act 1997; and
- he makes a Part 36 payment not more than seven days after he receives the certificate.

If a claim consists of both a money claim and a non-money claim, if the defendant wishes to settle the money claim by a payment, a Part 36 payment must be made for that part of the claim (Rule 36.4).

Making a Part 36 payment

A Part 36 payment is made when written notice of the payment into court is served on the offeree (Rule 36.8(2)). The timing of when the payment is made (i.e. the notice is served) is the trigger for the commencement of the period of 21 days for which the payment remains open for acceptance under Rule 36.11(1)). Accordingly it is entirely logical that the 21 days should start from the time when the claimant is served with the notice.

Service only has to be effected on the offeree. It does not have to be effected on any other parties to the action. The notice may be in Form N242A or otherwise as long as it contains the requisite information.

Either the party can effect service or the court will. Rule 36.6(3) as amended provides that, unless the offeror informs the court when the money is paid into court that he has served the notice, the court will do so.

Part 6 deals with service. If the court is to serve then the offeror will have to lodge with the court the notice and sufficient additional copies for each party to be served (Rule 6.3(3)). Rule 6.7 provides for the periods after which service will be deemed to have taken place. For instance, if the notice is posted first class it will be deemed to be served the second day after it was posted. If sent by fax before 4.00 p.m., it will be deemed to be served the same day. If at 4.00 p.m. or later, service is deemed on the business day after the day on which it was transmitted.

If the court serves, the offeror will be notified when service was effected.

If the offeror serves then he must file a certificate of service. Rule 6.10 provides for the contents of that certificate which will be in Form N215.

Rule 36.6(2) sets out what must be included in the Part 36 payment notice (Form N242A)—

- the amount of the payment;
- whether the payment relates to the whole or part of the claim or to any issue that arises in it and, if so, to which part or issue;

- whether it takes into account any counterclaim;
- whether it takes into account any interim payment that has been made; and
- if the notice stipulates that interest is not included in the payment (it does not have to state whether interest is included), the notice must state whether interest is offered and, if so, the amount offered, the rate or rates offered and the period or periods for which it is offered (Rule 36.22(2)).

In relation to the latter point it would be a matter of good practice for the notice to specify if interest is included. Even if it is included, details should be proffered of how much interest is included in the payment, the rate of interest and the period for which payment is made. Otherwise the offeror may be met with a request for clarification under Rule 36.9.

If the claim is both a money claim and a non-money claim and a Part 36 offer is made in relation to the non-money claim, the payment notice must—

- identify the document which sets out the terms of the Part 36 offer; and
- state that if the claimant gives notice of acceptance of the Part 36 payment he will be treated as also accepting the Part 36 offer (Rule 36.4(3)).

There are special provisions in relation to provisional damages (Rule 36.7). These also dictate what should be included in the payment notice. If a claim includes a claim for provisional damages, the Part 36 payment notice must specify whether or not the defendant is offering to agree to the making of an award of provisional damages.

Rule 36.23 deals with the particular circumstances arising under the Social Security (Recovery of Benefits) Act 1997. Rule 36.23(3) dictates what should be included in the Part 36 payment notice if, following acceptance of the payment into court, the resulting payment would be a compensation payment as defined in Section 1 of the Social Security (Recovery of Benefits) Act 1997. The notice must state—

- the amount of gross compensation;
- the name and amount of any benefit by which that gross amount is reduced in accordance with Section 8 and Schedule 2 to the 1997 Act; and
- that the sum paid in is the net amount after deduction of the amount of benefit.

In addition to these provisions, the Practice Direction to Part 36 (Paragraph 5.1) provides that the payment notice must—

- state that the payment into court is a Part 36 payment; and
- be signed by the offeror or his legal representative.

The practical logistics of making a payment in differ between a County Court/District Registry and the RCJ. In the former the offeror will tender to the court the payment notice and a cheque made payable to Her Majesty's Paymaster General. In the RCJ the notice should be accompanied by—

- a cheque made payable to the Accountant General of the Supreme Court;
- a sealed copy of the claim form; and
- the Court Funds Office Form 100.

(Paragraph 4.1, Practice Direction to Part 36)

Mixed Claims

If a claim consists of non-money claims and money claims an offeror has three options—

- An offer for the whole which would not include an offer of payment, for example, an offer of an undertaking, settlement of a claim for an injunction and damages.
- A payment in for the whole claim, for example, taking the example above, making no offer of an injunction but paying in a sum against the damages.
- An offer and a payment in.

Amendment to or withdrawal of a Part 36 offer or Part 36 payment

There was much debate in the Civil Procedure Rules Committee as to whether a party should be entitled to withdraw a Part 36 offer during the period for which it was stated to be open, i.e. usually 21 days. The competing principles are to equate a Part 36 offer with a Part 36 payment (which cannot be withdrawn without the court's permission) or, alternatively, to equate it with a normal offer in contractual terms which can be withdrawn at any time before acceptance. The latter principle won through.

A Part 36 offer, although stated to be open for acceptance for 21 days, may be withdrawn at any time prior to acceptance. This only has effect for the period for which the offer is open for acceptance (usually 21 days after it was received by the offeree). Thereafter the offer may only be accepted if the parties agree liability for costs or the court gives permission (Rule 36.5(6)).

A Part 36 payment is very different. The whole or part of it may only be withdrawn with the permission of the court.

A Part 36 offer can be amended at any time. The effect of such an amendment would be the withdrawal of the original offer and its replacement either with a reduced or an improved offer. Under Rule 36.8(3) an improvement to a Part 36 offer is effective when details of it are received by the offeree. No mention is made of a reduction in the offer although it is suggested that similarly a fresh Part 36 offer on reduced terms will be effective when its details are received by the offeree.

Rule 36.5(8) provides that if a Part 36 offer is withdrawn it will not have the consequences flowing from the fact that it was a Part 36 offer even for the period for which it was open for acceptance. This contradicts the old authority of *Garner v Cleggs* [1983] 1 WLR 862 when the Court of Appeal considered that a withdrawn payment into court could still be of relevance in relation to the cost for the period between the date of payment in and the date the court gives permission to withdraw the payment. It must be remembered, however, that costs are always in the discretion of the court and the court may take into account an offer that is withdrawn as it feels appropriate, in the examination of conduct in relation to costs under either Rule 44.3 or 44.5.

As above, a Part 36 payment can only be withdrawn with the permission of the court. Thus any reduction in the payment would require the same permission.

An increase in a Part 36 payment does not require permission. A party wishing to make an increase in the Part 36 payment should follow the same procedure as when the payment is made save that the documentation will be limited to the amount of the increase. The increase is effective when notice of the increase is served on the offeree (Rule 36.8(4).

Neither for the improvement to a Part 36 offer or an increase in a Part 36 payment is there a set form. Rule 36.8(3) in relation to an improvement to a Part 36 offer refers to the communication of its details to the offeree. Rule 36.8(4) provides that the increase in a Part 36 payment is effective when notice of the increase is served on the offeree. It is suggested that in either case parties would be best advised to follow the usual procedure for making a Part 36 offer or Part 36 payment.

Clarification of a Part 36 offer or a Part 36 payment notice

Rule 36.9 provides a mechanism by which an offeree can seek clarification either of a Part 36 offer or of a Part 36 payment notice. Within seven days of receiving a Part 36 offer or service of a notice of payment into court, the offeree may ask the offeror to clarify any aspect of the offer or payment notice (Rule 36.9(1)). By way of example, if the question of interest is not noted on the notice of payment into court, the payment in will be taken to include interest. An offeree may wish to have some clarification of the interest element; the date from which it runs and the rate.

This initial period of seven days to respond to a request is specifically short so that the offeree has time to consider the offer or payment in within the usual period of 21 days. As with all time periods, the court has the power to extend it under Rule 3.1(2)(a). The parties can also agree to vary by written agreement under Rule 2.11. Applying Rule 36.9(1) strictly, the request should be made and received by the offeror within the seven days. In applying these types of time limits, however, the parties should bear in mind their obligations to co-operate in order to assist the court in achieving the overriding objective. The party making a request outside the seven days will have in mind the 21 day period for acceptance of the offer or payment in and any necessity to extend it.

If clarification is not forthcoming within seven days of the receipt of the request, the offeree may make an application to the court seeking an order that the clarification be given by the offeror. Such an application is made in accordance with Part 23. Accordingly the application notice must comply with Rule 23.6, i.e. state the order that is being sought and briefly why the applicant is seeking the order. Paragraph 6.3 of the Practice Direction to Part 36 also provides that the notice should state the respects in which the terms of the Part 36 offer or Part 36 payment notice are said to need clarification.

Unless the court is to make special arrangements, it is quite likely that such an application will be heard some considerable time after the period of 21 days for acceptance has expired. Accordingly it is suggested that the application should also include an application to extend the time for acceptance of the offer or payment in. Rule 36.9(3) provides that if the court makes an order for clarification, it must then specify the date when the Part 36 offer or Part 36 payment is treated as having been made. There is no like provision if the court does not make an order and therefore the offeree will need an extension of the 21 days or permission to accept the offer or payment in out of time.

Acceptance of Part 36 Offer or Part 36 payment

As above, Rule 36.8(1) and (2) provides for when a payment in or an offer is made for the purposes of the Rules. This is the trigger date for the period for acceptance of an offer or payment in.

Defendant's Part 36 offer or Part 36 payment (Rule 36.11)

Offer or payment in made more than 21 days before trial

The claimant may accept either an offer or a payment in within 21 days (Rule 36.11(1)). Acceptance is effected by the "giving" of a written notice of acceptance to the offeror. Acceptance is effective, however, only upon receipt of it by the offeror (Rule 36.8(5)). The notice must also be filed with the court (Paragraph 7.6, Practice Direction to Part 36). The notice of acceptance must contain—

- the claim number;
- the title of the proceedings;
- identification of the Part 36 offer or Part 36 payment; and
- the signature either of the offeree or his legal representative

(Paragraph 7.7, Practice Direction to Part 36).

The notice of acceptance of payment in is in Form N243.

Acceptance outside the 21 day period or if the offer or payment in is made less than 21 days before the start of trial

In either case the parties can either agree liability as to costs or the claimant must seek the permission of the court to accept. As above the parties are obliged to co-operate as to the appropriate terms. If agreement is not possible, however, the claimant must make an application under Part 23. Depending upon the court arrangements, if the trial is impending then the application may need to be made to the trial judge at any time prior to the commencement of the trial. Upon this application the offer or payment in will have to be disclosed to the court contrary to the general provisions about non-disclosure. The judge will have to decide whether his position in the trial will be compromised by such disclosure. Clearly the primary issue will be the question of where the liability for costs falls. The parties will have in mind the usual consequences of acceptance of a defendant's offer or payment in under Rule 36.13. In relation to a payment in, the court will make consequential orders as to a payment out and the payment of interest on any monies held in court.

Claimant's Part 36 offer or Part 36 payment

As with a defendant's offer or payment in, the regime in relation to a claimant's Part 36 offer differs between an offer that is made 21 days or more before the trial and one that is made less than 21 days before the trial.

Offer made 21 days or more before the trial

The usual rules apply that the offer may be accepted no more than 21 days after it was made (as to the time when it is made see above) (Rule 36.12(1)). There is no specified form for acceptance, which, for the avoidance of doubt, be done in writing.

Offer made less than 21 days before trial or accepted out of time

Unless the parties agree the liability as to costs, application must be made by the defendant to accept an offer made less than 21 days before the trial or if the defendant wishes to accept the offer outside the period of 21 days under Rule 36.12(1). The empowerment of the court to give permission to accept an offer which has effectively lapsed, in contrast, does not sit happily with the concept that the offer is a normal contractual offer. Presumably, however, the court will protect the claimant upon such an application particularly in relation to costs. In any event prior to acceptance this offer can always be withdrawn. The application must be made in accordance with Part 23. Upon the application the court will determine where costs fall. The court will have in mind the usual cost consequences under Rule 36.14.

Co-Defendants

Rule 36.17 provides for the particular circumstances in which there is more than one defendant but the Part 36 offer or Part 36 payment is made by only one or more of those defendants. There are two differing circumstances provided for in the Rule—

(1) The defendants are sued jointly; or, in the alternative.

(2) The defendants are sued on the basis that they have a several liability.

Joint or alternative liability

Rule 36.17(2) allows the claimant to accept an offer or payment in by one or more of a number of defendants as long as the claimant discontinues the claim against the defendants that have not made the offer or payment in and those other defendants consent to the acceptance. Clearly this gives those other defendants the opportunity to take up with the court the question of the liability for costs either of the claimant or of a fellow defendant if, for instance, a contribution or indemnity notice has been served in accordance with Rule 20.6 (Rule 36.17(2)). Otherwise the claimant must make an application to the court for its permission to accept the offer or payment in.

Several liability

If it is alleged by the claimant that one or more of the defendants has several liability from the others then the claimant may accept the offer or payment in and if he is entitled in law to do so continue against the other defendants who it is alleged have that several liability.

Other cases requiring the court's permission

Some of the circumstances in which the court's permission is required for the acceptance of a Part 36 offer or Part 36 payment are summarised above. Rule 36.18 provides for some other circumstances. For instance, Rule 36.18(1) in combination with Rule 21.10 provides that when a litigation friend acting on behalf of a child or patient wishes to accept a Part 36 offer or Part 36 payment, they must seek the permission of the court. On the hearing of that application under Part 23 the court will make appropriate orders bearing in mind the interests of the child or patient. In particular, the court might wish to consider exactly the result of any acceptance bearing in mind any conditional fee agreement that has been entered into on behalf of the child or patient with the solicitor prosecuting the claim.

Payment out

Normally payment out is made upon a request for payment in a standard form (Form N243). The request should detail to where the payment is to be made. If payment can be made into a bank account then the name of the bank, the sort code number, the title of the account and the account number should be given. If not, then the request should state that a payment by cheque is required. If the party making the request is legally represented then they should give the main business address and reference of the legal representative. If not, then they should give their own name and address. In the Royal Courts of Justice a Form 201 (Court Funds Office Forms) is also required to accompany the request (Paragraph 8, Practice Direction to Part 36).

Payment will usually be made in accordance with the request. If, however, a party is not legally represented but is or has been in receipt of legal aid, the payment will be made to the Legal Aid Board rather than that party so that the Legal Aid Board can have a first call on those monies in accordance with the Legal Aid Charge. Additionally, an appropriate court order will be required to secure payment out if the proceedings involve a child or patient and the acceptance of the offer or payment in relates to the claim by, on behalf of or against the child or patient.

Further, if the court's permission is required to accept an offer or payment in, the court will make an order on the same occasion about payment out.

Finally, if a defendant puts forward a defence of tender before claim and makes a payment in after proceedings have commenced to support that claim under Rule 37.3, the money can only be paid out to the accepting claimant upon appropriate order of the court (see tender at page 285).

Consequences of acceptance

Costs

There are two differing regimes for the costs consequences of acceptance dependent on whether the offeror is the defendant or the claimant.

Acceptance of a claimant's Part 36 offer

Under Rule 36.14 the costs consequences of acceptance of a claimant's Part 36 offer are that the claimant is entitled to his costs up until service of the notice of acceptance is effected (for the provisions relating to service see Part 6 and above).

If a court order is required to enable the defendant to accept the Part 36 offer, the court will make an appropriate order for costs. The parties should try and agree the cost consequences. It would be quite usual for the defendant to pay the costs up until agreement can be reached about the costs consequences. If agreement cannot be reached, the court may apportion blame for the failure to settle. The consequence may be, for instance, that the court will make an order for costs in favour of the claimant only up until the time that he should have accepted a reasonable offer by the defendant to pay costs consequent upon the acceptance of the offer out of time.

Defendant's Part 36 offer or Part 36 payment

Rule 36.13(1) provides that in usual circumstances where acceptance of the offer does not require the permission of the court, the claimant is entitled to the cost of the proceedings up to the date of serving notice of acceptance (as to service see Part 6 and as to the notice see above).

If the Part 36 offer or Part 36 payment relates to part only of the claim, the claimant can abandon the remainder. In that event Rule 36.13(2) provides that the claimant will be entitled to the cost of the proceedings up to the date of serving notice of acceptance unless the court orders otherwise. Rule 36.15(3) provides, however, that in such a case whilst the claim will be stayed, the liability for costs should be determined by the court unless the parties can agree them. This allows the defendant to seek the court's assistance in relation to costs where it would be unfair for the defendant to pay all of the costs of the claim bearing in mind the proportion of the claim which has been abandoned and the importance of the issues arising in it.

Under Rules 36.5 and 36.6 the offer or payment notice respectively must state whether they take into account any counterclaim by the defendant. If they do then the acceptance by the claimant carries with it any costs attributable to the counterclaim.

Other costs consequences

The order for costs that arises upon acceptance either of an offer or payment in is deemed to have been made on the standard basis unless agreement is reached to the contrary (Rule 36.13(4) and Rule 44.12(1)(b) and (c)). The three month time limit for the commencement of assessment proceedings provided for under Part 47 runs from the date that the notice of acceptance is served or the date of the court order if the permission of the court was required (Rule 47.7).

If a party to the proceedings is a child or patient and the money is ordered or agreed to be paid to or for the benefit of that party, or money is ordered to be paid by him or on his behalf, there must be a detailed costs assessment of the solicitor and own client costs between that child or patient and the solicitor. Only the amount that follows from that detailed assessment is then payable between the child/patient and the solicitor (Rule 48.5). The court need not order the assessment of costs, however, if—

- there is in the court's opinion no need to do so to protect the interest of the child or patient or his estate;
- another party has agreed to pay a specified sum in respect of the costs and the solicitor acting for the child or patient accepts that sum in full and final satisfaction of their own costs;
- the costs are summarily assessed and again the solicitor waives any further claim over and above that summary assessment; or
- there is an insurer or other persons liable and able to pay the costs of the solicitor without any call upon the child or patient

(Paragraph 1.2, Practice Direction to Part 48).

In addition to costs, there are various other consequences of acceptance of either a Part 36 offer or a Part 36 payment—

- Under Rule 36.15(1) if the offer or payment in relates to the whole of the claim then the claim is stayed upon acceptance. This stay, however, does not affect the ability of the appropriate party to pursue the question of costs nor, if there is a payment in, an application for payment out (Rule 36.15(5)). The Court's assistance may further be required for some parts of the settlement such as the recording of an undertaking.
- If the Part 36 payment is paid in settlement either of the whole of the claim (whether or not that includes a non-money claim) or in settlement of the money part of a claim (which payment in was accompanied by a Part 36 offer for the non-money part of the claim), the acceptance of the payment in is deemed to be acceptance in settlement of the whole of the claim including the money and non-money parts of it (Rule 36.4(4) and Paragraph 7.11, Practice Direction to Part 36).
- If acceptance is made of a Part 36 offer, the effect is as if a Tomlin Order had been made in accordance with the Part 36 offer. This has the effect of making a contract between the offeree and offeror upon the terms of the offer which has been accepted. As with a Tomlin Order, the proceedings will be stayed save for the purpose of enforcing the terms of the contractual agreement. Although a breach by one party of the terms would entitle the other to seek a remedy for breach of contract, fresh proceedings are not necessary. The party may apply to the court seeking a remedy as a result of the breach. That application would be made in the proceedings which were the subject of the stay. The application would be made in accordance with Part 23 and therefore the requirements of that Part would need to be satisfied particularly as relates to the contents of the application notice and the evidence in support of the application (Rule 36.15(2), (5)(a) and (6)).

Cost consequences that may follow from non-acceptance of the offer or payment

Claimant fails to do better than a Defendant's Part 36 offer or Part 36 payment (Rule 36.20)

Rule 36.20 is causing a little controversy. Taken strictly it makes provision for the cost consequences if a claimant fails to do better than a Part 36 offer whichever party (i.e. claimant or defendant) makes the offer. The writer's understanding is that the Vice Chancellor has made it clear that this was not intended and that Rule 36.20 only applies to either a defendant's Part 36 offer or a Part 36 payment. Following from that, if a claimant fails to do better than a defendant's Part 36 offer or a Part 36 payment, the court will order the claimant to pay any costs incurred by the defendant after the latest day on which the payment or offer could have been accepted without needing the permission of the court (Rule 36.20(2)). Accordingly this will usually mean that in this event the claimant will pay the defendant's costs incurred after the 21 day period for which the offer or payment in was open for acceptance under Rule 36.11.

In relation to a Part 36 payment, Rule 36.20(1)(a) refers to a claimant failing to do better than a Part 36 payment. Some debate may ensue as to the measure of how much better the claimant has done. On the face of it, one penny more than a payment in will mean that the claimant has beaten the Part 36 payment. It must be remembered, however, that Rule 44.3(4)(c) provides that when the court exercises its discretion as to costs, it will take into account any payment into court or admissible offer to settle made by a party which is drawn to the court's attention (whether or not made in accordance with Part 36). This provides the court with a degree of discretion in relation to an offer or payment in made under Part 36 which either does not quite comply with the procedural requirements or which, whilst beaten by the claimant, is not beaten by much (relatively). Accordingly the court could take into account the payment in or offer whether the claimant has just beaten it or just failed to beat it. This discretion of the court, however, is somewhat tempered by the provisions of Rule 36.20(2) since the usual order in favour of the defendant should follow unless the court considers it unjust to do so (Rule 36.20(2)).

Rule 36.20(1)(b) deals with a Part 36 offer. Specifically, if a claimant fails to obtain judgment which is more advantageous than a defendant's Part 36 offer, the usual order as to costs under Rule 36.20(2) will follow. What is more advantageous is a matter for the court's discretion. The circumstances in which the court may have to decide these issues could, for instance, be in relation to the seeking of injunctive relief in which certain undertakings are offered by the claimant. The court will have to consider whether those undertakings were less or more advantageous than the injunctive relief sought.

Rule 36.20 only applies when there is a trial. Accordingly it has no application to an application for summary judgment. Upon such an application, the court would have an open discretion unhindered by Rule 36.20.

Rule 36.21—Claimant does better than he proposed in his Part 36 offer

The provisions of Rule 36.21 remain much debated. They follow Lord Woolf's recommendations and the debates in the Civil Procedure Rule Committee as to how to compensate the claimant when he does better than his own Part 36 offer. The simple award of costs gives no benefit since this would follow in any event. Accordingly the Committee concluded various additional awards that the claimant may be able to obtain upon doing better than his own Part 36 offer. For the purposes of Rule 36.21 "better" means that at trial, the defendant is held liable for more than the offer, or the judgment against the defendant is more advantageous to the claimant than his offer. The additional awards are—

- Interest on the whole or part of any sum of money (excluding interest) awarded to the claimant at a rate not exceeding 10% above base rate for some or all of the period starting with the latest date on which the defendant could have accepted the offer without needing the permission of the court (usually the 21 days under Rule 36.12(1)). This interest is in addition to the interest that may be claimed and awarded in the claim itself such as interest under Section 35A of the Supreme Court Act 1981 or Section 69 of the County Courts Act 1984.
- Costs on an indemnity basis from the latest date when the defendant could have accepted the offer without needing the permission of the court.
- Interest on those costs at a rate not exceeding 10% above base rate.

The court "will" make these additional awards unless it would be unjust to do so (Rule 36.21(4)). In that consideration under Rule 36.21(5) the court must take into account all the circumstances of the case including—

- the terms of any Part 36 offer;
- the state in the proceedings when any Part 36 offer or Part 36 payment was made;
- the information available to the parties at the time when the Part 36 offer or Part 36 payment was made; and
- the conduct of the parties with regard to the giving or refusing to give information for the purposes of enabling the offer or payment into court to be made or evaluated.

The question that may arise often is whether or not the defendant was in a position to evaluate the nature of the claimant's claim and an appropriate settlement of it at the time that the Part 36 offer is made. This will be important particularly when an offer is made prior to the commencement of proceedings. Rule 36.9 which provides for the seeking and obtaining of clarification of a Part 36 offer has no application prior to the commencement of proceedings. Notwithstanding its absence, clearly a party making a Part 36 offer must provide the offeree with sufficient information for them to gauge that offer against the claim that is being made. If the offeror appears unco-operative or simply does not provide the necessary information then the court will take that into account when considering the appropriate order for costs.

One factor that the court may look at is whether there has been compliance with a pre-action protocol and particularly any requirement to disclose the substance of the claim and give disclosure of appropriate documents prior to the commencement of proceedings.

Even if the Court concludes that it would not be unjust to make the orders, it must then exercise the wider discretion as to the rate of interest and the period for which it will apply. As with the defendant's offer, if the claimant does better than his own offer but only marginally, the Court can have regard to the offer under Rule 44.3(4)(c) in relation to the costs but as a matter of principle it would seem unlikely to alter the costs outcome.

Deduction of Social Security benefits

Rule 36.63 and the Practice Direction to Part 36, Paragraph 10 provide the mechanism, for the deduction from a payment in, of benefits which the payer is liable to pay direct to the Compensation Recovery Unit. The regime is generally governed by the Social Security (Recovery of Benefits) Act 1997. The Rules fit into this regime by providing that the payer receives from the Secretary of State a certificate of recoverable benefits, and then files it with the Part 36 payment notice, which itself is in a modified form. The notice sets out the gross amount before deduction, which is the "payment in" for the purposes of the consequences of payment in and the net amount after deductions, details of which are given.

If a defendant wants to make a Part 36 payment in and applies for a certificate of deductions, he can make a Part 36 offer to cover the period whilst waiting for the certificate, as long as payment in is made within 7 days of receipt of the certificate (Paragraph 10.2, Practice Direction to Part 36).

Part 37—Miscellaneous provisions about payments into court

Part 37 simply deals with three particular circumstances in relation to payments into court generally.

The first of those provides the opportunity for a defendant to convert a payment into court made under a court order into a Part 36 payment. Rule 37.2 decrees that when a defendant makes a payment into court following an order made under Rule 3.1(3) (the general power of the court to make an order for payment in) or Rule 3.1(5) (the power of the court to make an order for payment in following a failure to comply with a pre-action protocol), the defendant can choose to treat the whole or any part of the money paid into court as a Part 36 payment. He does that by filing a Part 36 payment notice which must also be served in accordance with Part 36 either by the court or by the defendant (as to the contents and service of the notice, see above). From the time that the notice is served, the money to which the notice relates is treated as a Part 36 payment.

Accordingly that money may be accepted by the claimant in satisfaction of the claim or the part of it to which the payment relates (see Part 36 generally) either with or without the court's permission. That permission will be necessary in accordance with Part 36 but if it is not then permission is not required simply because the payment in was not originally made under Part 36.

Defence of tender

If a defendant relies upon the defence of tender before claim, the amount that he says he tendered must be paid into court. Until that payment in, he cannot rely upon the defence of tender before claim (Rule 37.3). When the payment into court is made, the defendant can choose to treat the whole or any part of the money as a Part 36 payment. As with Rule 37.2, the conversion is done by the filing and service of a Part 36 payment notice.

Proceedings under the Fatal Accidents Act 1976 and the Law Reform (Miscellaneous Provisions) Act 1934

Rule 37.4 provides for the apportionment by the court of monies paid into court and accepted in satisfaction of claims under the Fatal Accidents Act 1976 and the Law Reform (Miscellaneous Provisions) Act 1934.

CHAPTER 23
PART 23—APPLICATIONS FOR COURT ORDERS

Introduction

The methods of application for orders under the RSC and the CCR caused much confusion amongst litigants and practitioners. As with other parts of the Rules, the aim of the revisions was to produce a uniform and easily understood system, firstly for starting proceedings and secondly for making applications both before and after issue of the claim. Order 32 of the RSC and Order 13 Rule 1 of the CCR provided the old rules for applications. The general scheme of things under Part 23 is—

- A party sets out in a form known as an application notice the order that they are seeking and briefly the grounds upon which the application is made.
- The evidence in support of the application can be included in the application notice as long as the facts are verified by a statement of truth.
- The application is issued by the Court upon payment of the appropriate fee. The applicant is informed of the date given by the Court for the hearing.
- The application notice may be served by the Court or the applicant. Any written evidence in support must be served with the application notice.
- No less than three days notice must be given of the hearing.
- Usually the hearing will be in public.
- The Court will make an appropriate order and will usually deal with costs immediately after the order is made.

The Rules

An application to the Court under Part 23 is usually made for some form of interim relief. An order for final relief should be sought by way of a claim either under Part 7 or Part 8. This general rule is breached by applications, for instance, for final relief prior to the commencement of proceedings, particularly for pre-action disclosure under Rule 31.16. All applications made prior to the commencement of a claim should be made under Part 23 and thus comply with the requirements established by it (Paragraph 5, Practice Direction to Part 23). Thus the application notice must state what order the applicant is seeking and briefly why the applicant is seeking the order under Rule 23.6.

Prior to the commencement of proceedings, applications under Part 23—

> **must be made to the Court where it is likely that the claim to which the application relates will be started unless there is good reason to make the application to a different Court.**

Paragraph 2 of the Practice Direction to Part 7 sets out some general guidance as to where to start proceedings. Reference should also be made to the High Court and County Courts Jurisdiction Order 1991. The restrictions on where proceedings can be started are relatively limited. Examples of restrictions might be—

- An application for pre-action disclosure in relation to either a claim for £15,000 or less or in a personal injury action less than £50,000 should not be made to the High Court (see Paragraphs 2.1 and 2.2, Practice Direction to Part 7).
- An application for, by way of example, a freezing order prior to the commencement of proceedings where the claim exceeds £30,000 and relates to Chancery business in which the Court's jurisdiction in equity is being used should only be sought in the High Court (Paragraph 2.5, Practice Direction to Part 7; Section 23 of the County Courts Act 1984 and the County Courts Jurisdiction Order 1981).
- An injunction in relation to a mortgage claim for a dwelling house outside Greater London should be made in the appropriate County Court.
- An application for pre-action disclosure or an injunction relating to a claim for damages for libel or slander should be issued in the High Court.

If an application is made after the commencement of proceedings then generally it should be made to the Court in which the case is proceeding (Rule 23.2(1) and (2)).

The Court could determine that all or part of a case should be heard at some different venue such as a Civil Trial Centre. Notwithstanding that direction, any application in the proceedings until the parties are notified of a date fixed for the trial would be made to the Court administering the claim. Under Rule 23.2(3) once a fixed date is notified to the parties then the application must be made to the Court where the trial is to take place. It is likely that we will see the establishment of more Civil Trial Centres around the country in the near future.

The question of where to make an application often arises in relation to the transfer of proceedings. In accordance with the general rule, when an order is made for a transfer, any subsequent application should be made to the Court to which the proceedings have been transferred. Part 30 (Transfer), however, makes one exception. If an application is made to set aside the order for transfer in accordance with, for instance, Rule 23.10, the application should be made to the Court which made the transfer order (see Paragraph 6.1, Practice Direction to Part 30). Otherwise an appeal from the District Judge in relation to the order for transfer should be made to the Circuit Judge in the Court to which the case has been transferred as a result of the order. (As to appeals in relation to transfers, see Paragraph 5.1, Practice Direction to Part 30.)

By Rule 23.2(5) when proceedings to enforce a judgment have "begun", any application must be made to the Court which is dealing with the enforcement of the judgment unless the Rules or practice directions provide to the contrary. The usual manner in which this will come into play is when an application is made to set aside a judgment entered in default. Part 13 provides for such an application. In accordance with Rule 23.2(5) generally the application will be made to the Court where enforcement is proceeding. Thus, for example, where a warrant of execution is issued in the enforcement of a judgment, the execution will take place under the auspices of the bailiff in the Court for the district in which execution is to take place. Under Rule 13.4 where an application is made to set aside a default judgment the Court will transfer the application to the defendant's home court in the circumstances as set out in Rule 13.4(1)(a)–(d). As to the definition of "home court", see page 150

Generally the process of making an application to the Court will be commenced by the completion and issuing of an application notice. There will be some rare circumstances in which an application notice is not required (Rule 23.3).

If time limits have been set for the issue of an application, any limits will be met not by the date of issue but by the date when the application notice is received by the Court (Rule 23.5).

The combination of Rule 23.6 and Paragraphs 2.1–2.10 of the Practice Direction to Part 23 provides for what should be included in the piece of paper known as the application notice. There is a prescribed form. It should be used but is not obligatory as long as any notice contains—

- The title of the claim.
- The reference number of the claim.
- The full name of the applicant.
- Where the applicant is not already a party, his address for service.
- Either a request for a hearing or a request that the application be dealt with without a hearing (see below).
- If the application is to be made to a Judge, the application notice should so state (Paragraph 2.6, Practice Direction to Part 23).
- What order the applicant is seeking.
- Briefly why the applicant is seeking the order.

The fee payable to the Court on an application notice is £50.

Parties are obliged to make an application as soon as it becomes apparent that it is desirable or necessary to make it (Paragraph 2.7, Practice Direction to Part 23).

Applications should be issued so that they can be dealt with at hearings that have already been fixed. The parties are under an obligation to assist the Court to achieve the overriding objective. One of the Court's obligations under Rule 1.4(2) is to deal with as many aspects of the case as it can on the same occasion. There are some specific examples in the Rules and otherwise. In the Commercial Court Guide parties are encouraged to consider the question of disclosure prior to the case management conference. If specific disclosure under Rule 31.12 is necessary then it may be appropriate to make an application to that effect returnable on the date of the case management conference. Similarly, in other proceedings, the case management conference should be used to dispose of any applications the parties consider necessary for the just disposal of the proceedings. As will be seen in relation to Part 26, if the allocation questionnaire states that one of the parties proposes to make an application for summary judgment, the Court will fix a date for a hearing. This still requires, however, the applicant to issue an application notice returnable on the date given by the Court.

Application without a Hearing

As detailed above, on the application notice the applicant can either request a date for a hearing or request that the application be dealt with without a hearing. In the latter case the notice and the file will be passed to a Master or District Judge to decide whether the application is suitable for consideration without a hearing (Paragraph 2.3, Practice Direction to Part 23). It will only deal with the matter without a hearing—

- if the parties agree as to the terms of the order;
- if the parties agree that the Court should dispose of the application without a hearing; or
- if the Court does not consider that a hearing would be appropriate.

This latter provision requires a positive step by the Court to decide that a hearing would **not be appropriate** although the Practice Direction uses the phrase "suitable for consideration without a hearing". One circumstance that may lead to an order being made without a hearing would be upon application for sanctions following a failure to comply with case management directions although question whether there may be a problem under the European Convention for the Protection of Human Rights (Article 6) and the Human Rights Act 1998.

Rule 40.6 sets out the circumstances where an agreed judgment or order may be made by consent. A slight problem might arise where a consent order is sought in relation to an application to which the applicant and the respondent are not all of the parties to the proceedings. Rule 40.6(1) provides that the Rule (40.6) applies where **all the parties agree the terms of an order**. Paragraph 10.2 of the Practice Direction to Part 23 refers, however, to **all parties affected by an order** rather than all parties to the action. Bearing in mind the close definition of the applicant and the respondent under Part 23, it seems sensible that where a consent order is sought, only those persons who would have to be served with it should have to consent to it, and that the reference to parties in Rule 40.6(1) is limited to them.

Rule 40.6 generally deals with the division of empowerment of Court officers and judges in relation to the making of consent orders. The Rule sets out those orders and the circumstances in which a Court officer can enter a consent order. Alternatively, a judge must make the consent order although this can be done without a hearing (Rule 40.6(6)).

The mechanics for obtaining a consent order are that the draft order should accompany the application. The draft order should be signed by the legal representative acting for each of the parties to whom the order relates or by the party if he is a litigant in person (Rule 40.6(7)). In the alternative, each of the parties affected by the order can write to the Court consenting to the making of it (Paragraph 10.2, Practice Direction to Part 23).

Fixing a Hearing

Upon issuing the application notice the Court will provide a date for the hearing (unless a hearing is not to take place). This will be notified to the parties on Form 244A. The application notice itself does not have a space for the time, date and place of hearing.

Service

Generally a copy (not the original) of the application notice must be served on each respondent to it (Rule 23.4(1)). The emphasis is service on the respondent to the application and not the parties to the proceedings themselves. There may well be applications where there is more than one claimant or defendant in which the application only relates to less than all of the parties such as an application for specific disclosure under Rule 31.12 against a particular claimant or defendant.

An application by a solicitor for an order that he has ceased to be the solicitor acting for a party is made by application under Part 23 but the application notice is only served on the solicitor's client and not on the other parties to the proceedings—although the order will be.

There may be circumstances in which an application notice should not be served at all. This may be provided within the Rules themselves or at the discretion of the Court. Within the Rules, for example, Rule 31.19 allows a person to apply, without notice, for an order permitting him to withhold disclosure of a document on the ground that disclosure would damage the public interest. Paragraph 3 of the Practice Direction to Part 23 sets out specific circumstances in which an application may be made without serving an application notice—

- Where there is exceptional urgency.
- Where the overriding objective is best furthered by doing so.
- By consent of all parties.
- With the permission of the Court.
- Where a date for hearing has been fixed and there is not enough time to serve an application notice in order to make an application at the hearing.
- Where a court order, Rule or practice direction permits (as in Rule 23.4(2)).

Whilst dealing with Part 23, readers are reminded of the Court's power to make an order of its own initiative under Rule 3.3. Whilst the general rule is that where a court proposes to make an order of its own initiative, it should give a person likely to be affected by the order an opportunity to make representations, specifying the time by and the manner in which the representations must be made (Rule 3.3(2)). The Court does not have to hear the parties or give them an opportunity to make representations (Rule 3.3(4)) but where it does, it should give them three days notice of a hearing. If no hearing is held then a party affected by the order may apply to have it set aside, varied or stayed (Rule 3.3(5)).

The copy of the application notice can be served by either the Court or the applicant (Rule 6.3). If the applicant is to effect service then the Court must be notified. If the Court is to effect service then any written evidence in support of the application must be filed with the application notice itself. Sufficient copies will also be required for service itself (Rule 23.7(2)).

Whoever serves the applicant notice, it must be served as soon as practicable after it is filed and generally must be served at least three days before the Court is to deal with the application (Rule 23.7(1)). There are, however, some exceptions in the Rules as to that period of notice. For instance, 14 days notice has to be given of an application under Part 24 (summary judgment). The measurement of periods of time is dealt with in Rule 2.8. The period of three days means three clear days. Accordingly the day of service is not included and neither is the day of the hearing. Thus if an application is to be heard on a Friday then the last day for service is the preceding Monday. If service is effected by post or document exchange the letter would have to be posted on the previous Thursday (Rule 6.7). Within that period of three days, weekends, bank holidays, Christmas Day and Good Friday are excluded (Rule 2.8(4)).

The Court has a power to abridge times under Rule 3.1(2)(a). Rule 23.7(4) drives home this point by providing specifically that the Court can determine that even where notice is short, sufficient notice has been given in the circumstances of the case. This is likely to apply most often in "time applications".

The parties can also agree in writing to vary the time in accordance with Rule 2.11.

If there is not sufficient time to give the appropriate notice then Paragraph 4.2 of the Practice Direction to Part 23 encourages the applicant to give informal notification of the application. Part 6 deals with service and particularly deemed service in Rule 6.7. Applying that Rule, if, as above, the application notice must be served on Monday for hearing on Friday, if it is served by first class post then the last day of posting is the previous Thursday before 5.00pm since the deemed day of service is the second business day after posting. If service is effected by fax then it can be effected on the Monday as long as it is effected before 4.00pm.

In addition to the application notice, it must be accompanied by a copy of any written evidence in support and a copy of any draft order which the applicant has attached to the application (Rule 23.7(3)).

The Hearing

If the hearing does not take place in front of the Judge at the Court, it may take place either by telephone or video conferencing. Paragraphs 6.1, 6.2 and 6.3, of the Practice Direction to Part 23 set out the rather detailed provisions in relation to telephone hearings. The much shorter provisions relating to video conferencing are contained within Paragraph 7 of the Practice Direction.

At the hearing the court may review the management of the case entirely and parties must be prepared to deal with any matters raised (Paragraph 2.9, Practice Direction to Part 23).

If an applicant or respondent fails to attend the hearing then the Court may proceed in its absence (Rule 23.11).

Upon the hearing of the application the Court can require legal representatives and the parties to attend under Rule 3.1(2)(c) although this power is likely to be exercised for hearings significant in the case management process under Part 26 or one of the three tracks.

Evidence

Peppered throughout the Rules are examples of applications that must be supported by evidence. As above, the application for an order that a solicitor has ceased to act must be supported by evidence under Rule 42.3(2)(b). Similarly, although not an absolute requirement, an application for summary judgment under Part 24 will usually be supported by evidence. Paragraph 9.1 of the Practice Direction to Part 23 reminds applicants that—

> **as a practical matter, the Court will often need to be satisfied by evidence of the facts that are relied on in support of or for opposing the application.**

Under Rule 32.2(1) generally evidence upon the hearing of applications should be in writing only. The Court does have the power to make an order for the cross examination of witnesses upon an application under Rule 32.7. If an order for cross examination is made but the party does not attend then the evidence may not be used unless the Court gives permission (Rule 32.7(2)).

Evidence in writing may be given by—

- the statement of case;
- the application notice; or
- a witness statement.

In each case, the evidence must be verified by a statement of truth in accordance with Part 22. Rule 32.14 provides for the consequences if a person makes or causes to be made, a false statement in a document verified by a statement of truth without an honest belief in its truth. In those circumstances proceedings for contempt of Court may be brought although only by the Attorney General or with the permission of the Court.

In addition to the three methods of giving evidence above, a party may give evidence by affidavit under Rule 32.15 but will generally not be allowed to recover the additional cost of making the affidavit.

The formalities for a witness statement are set out in the Practice Direction to Part 32 and particularly under Paragraphs 17–22 (Practice Direction to Part 32). As to the method of exhibiting documents to a witness statement, reference should be made to Paragraphs 11–15 of the Practice Direction to Part 32. The Practice Direction also deals with affidavits at Paragraphs 2–10.

There are no like provisions as to the evidence contained in a statement of case or the application notice itself but it is suggested that it would be for the best to follow the practice directions relating to, for instance, witness statements. Thus in accordance with Paragraph 18.1 of the Practice Direction to Part 32, the statement of case or the application notice being used as evidence should state—

- the full name of the witness;
- his place of residence;
- his occupation; and
- the fact that he is a party to the proceedings or is the employee of such a party if it be the case.

It should be remembered that when documents are to be relied upon at the hearing of the application they should be exhibited, verified and identified in the statement of case or the application notice if either or both of them are to be used for the purposes of the evidence at the hearing of the application.

Whilst the evidence for the application should be filed with the Court, the exhibits do not have to be filed unless the Court otherwise directs (Paragraph 9.6, Practice Direction to Part 23), but they do have to be available to the court on the hearing.

Summary assessment

The parties should be in a position to deal with summary assessment of costs on the hearing of the application after any order is made. The requirements in relation to summary assessment are set out in Paragraphs 4.3–4.10 of the Practice Direction to Part 44.

Generally the Court will only effect a summary assessment of costs for a hearing that lasts less than one day. If the hearing is to last more than one day then summary assessment may be inappropriate but the Court may make an order for a payment on account of costs under Rule 44.3(8). Accordingly parties should be prepared to deal with such an application at the end of the hearing.

If the hearing lasts less than a day then the Court will generally summarily assess costs there and then. In preparation for this, each party who intends to claim costs must prepare a written statement of the costs generally along the lines of Costs Form 1, Statement of Costs (Summary Assessment). That statement must be filed at the Court and served on any respondent to the application no less than 24 hours before the date fixed for hearing. If a party fails to comply with that obligation, that default will be taken into account in relation to the summary assessment.

It may be appropriate for the parties to try and agree the level of costs to be claimed by either of them on summary assessment prior to the hearing. In relation to such an agreement it is suggested that two important matters should be considered—

- Instructions should be obtained from the client before agreeing any figures for summary assessment.
- Any agreement should be stated to be without prejudice to a party's position on hourly rates and time spent in any subsequent detailed costs assessment although that costs assessment will not include the items summarily assessed.

The summary assessment only relates to the costs of the application and not any general costs which will fall to be determined after the hearing or trial, either by summary or detailed costs assessment.

If an order is made by consent, the parties should agree a figure for costs to be inserted in the consent order or agree that there should be no order for costs. Whilst the parties may wish to agree that costs will be "costs in the case", i.e. decided at a later stage, the Court may not agree and may make an order for costs with immediate summary assessment. If thc parties cannot agree costs, attendance on the appointment will be necessary but unless good reason can be shown for the failure to deal with costs by agreement, no costs will be allowed for the attendance (Paragraph 4.4(3), Practice Direction to Part 44).

Whilst the system of "certificates for counsel" has gone it is replaced by the court expressing an opinion as to whether a hearing was fit for one or two counsel (Paragraph 2.6, Practice Direction to Part 44). In the absence of an opinion to this effect counsel's fees are still allowable but in cases of doubt an "opinion" should be requested.

The Order

The form and drawing of orders made by the Courts on applications is set out in Part 40. Generally the order will be drawn up by the Court usually on the basis of the draft order accompanying the application unless—

- the Court orders a party to draw it up;
- a party, with the permission of the Court, agrees to draw it up;
- the Court dispenses with the need to draw it up; or
- it is a consent order made under Rule 40.6 (Rule 40.3(1)).

If the order is drawn up by the party then it must be filed no later than seven days after the date on which the Court allowed the party to draw it up. If it is not filed within that period then any other party may draw up the order and file it (Rule 40.3(3)).

The order will be sealed by the Court and must bear the date on which it is given or made (Rule 40.2(2)).

Service will usually be effected by the Court under Rule 6.3 although as well as drawing up the order a party can seek to serve it. If the Court is to serve then sufficient copies must be provided to the Court so that it may effect service. When the Court seals it, it will then serve it on **each party to the proceedings** (Rule 40.4(1)). On the face of it this may mean that service of the order is not only effected upon the applicant and the respondent but also all the other parties to the proceedings. Rule 40.4(2) provides that any order must be served on—

- the applicant and the respondent; and
- any other person on whom the Court orders it to be served.

This would seem to differentiate between a Court service (in which case the order must be served on all parties) and a party serving in which case it must be served only on the applicant and the respondent.

RSC Order 44 provides some supplementary rules in relation to service of certain orders made in the Chancery Division.

An order generally takes effect from the day when it is given or made, or such later date as the Court may specify (Rule 40.7). If the order is for the payment of an amount of money then the party must comply with that order within 14 days of the date of the order unless the Court or the Rules specify otherwise (Rule 40.11).

Under Rule 23.9, if no notice of the application has been given, when the Court makes an order a copy of the application notice and any evidence in support must, unless the Court orders otherwise, be served with the order on any person against whom the order was made and against whom the order was sought. This could have quite a substantial effect in relation to applications for freezing or searching orders under Part 25. If the application is unsuccessful, unless the Court otherwise orders the order dismissing the application and the evidence in support must be served on the respondent who has been given no notice of the application. Practitioners, therefore, should ensure that they seek an order from the Court relieving them of this obligation if appropriate.

Under Rule 23.10 a person served with an order made on an application but on whom the application notice was not served, may apply to the Court for the order to be set aside or varied. In any event, under Rule 40.9, any person who is not a party to proceedings but who is directly affected by an order may apply to have the judgment or order set aside or varied. Under Rule 23.10 such an application must be made within seven days after the date on which the order is served but there is no like limitation under Rule 40.9.

As dealt with previously under Rule 3.3 if the Court makes an order of its own initiative a party affected by the order may apply to have it set aside, varied or stayed.

If the application notice has been served and the applicant or respondent simply fails to attend the hearing then the Court may proceed in his absence (Rule 23.11). If an order is made at the hearing then the Court may, on application or of its own initiative, re-list the application so that the absent applicant or respondent can be heard. Upon such a re-listing there is no automatic stay on the order itself which will have full effect unless the Court orders otherwise until such time as it is dealt with on the re-hearing.

Appeals

Detailed consideration of the provision of the CPR in relation to appeals falls outside the scope of this work. Briefly, the old appeal provisions under the RSC and CCR have been re-codified into the dovetailed provisions of Schedule 1and Schedule 2 of the CPR.

In the High Court—

- RSC Order 55 makes general provisions in relation to appeals to the High Court from a court, tribunal or person.
- RSC Order 56 makes general provisions in relation to appeals to the High Court by way of case stated.
- RSC Order 57 deals with divisional court proceedings.
- RSC Order 58 provides from Master, Registrars, Referees and Judges.
- RSC Order 59 deals with appeals to the Court of Appeal (note that there are extensive practice directions in relation to the business of the Court of Appeal).
- RSC Order 60 provides for appeals to the Court of Appeal from the Restrictive Practices Court.
- RSC Order 61 deals with appeals from tribunals to the Court of Appeal by way of case stated.

In the CCR—

- Order 37 Rule 6 provides for appeals from a District Judge.
- The CCR enjoins with the RSC in relation to other appeals and particularly RSC Order 59 for appeals to the Court of Appeal.

Hearings

For the other applicable rules relating to hearings under Part 23, the reader is referred to Part 39 at page 319.

CHAPTER 24
PARTS 32, 33—EVIDENCE (INCLUDING HEARSAY)

Introduction

There are two Parts of the CPR which deal generally with evidence although Rules in other Parts of the CPR also deal with aspects of evidence such as those provisions relating to statements of case or the disclosure and inspection of documents (Part 31) or applications (Part 23).

One aspect of evidence received especial attention from Lord Woolf in his Interim and Final Reports—witness statements. It became commonplace and eventually obligatory that in order to call a witness at trial a written statement of their evidence had to be provided to the other parties. A practice direction by the Lord Chief Justice and the Vice Chancellor of January 1995 provided that such witness statements should stand as evidence in chief of the relevant witness.

Whilst Lord Woolf welcomed the development of witness statements over the years as the "cards on the table" approach to litigation, he was critical of the manner in which the process of witness statements had become somewhat abused. He suggested that witness statements had "... ceased to be the authentic account of the lay witness; instead they have become an elaborate costly branch of legal drafting". Lord Woolf put this development down to a number of factors. One of them derived, he suggested, from the inflexibility of the witness statement standing as the evidence in chief. Lord Woolf suggested that witnesses should be able to expand on their witness statements at trial partly to let them "bed in" to the very trying process of giving evidence rather than go straight into cross examination without an opportunity of giving any oral evidence under first examination.

He also recommended that the content and form of witness statements should—

- as far as possible be in the witness's own words;
- not discuss legal propositions;
- not comment on documents;
- conclude with a statement, signed by the witness, that the evidence is a true statement and that it is in his own words.

Lord Woolf suggested that with the inception of the Civil Evidence Act 1995 and the reduction in formalities in relation to hearsay evidence, drafting of witness statements should become much easier. In future it should reflect more closely the process of preparing affidavits in which reference may be made to matters beyond the direct knowledge or observation of the witness whilst indicating the source of knowledge, belief or information on which the witness is relying.

The general lie of the land provided by Parts 32 and 33 is—

- In interim applications evidence (other than expert evidence; for which see Part 35) will usually be in writing by witness statement. At trial, evidence will be oral.
- If a witness is to give evidence at trial, a witness statement must be served in advance.
- At trial the witness statement will stand as evidence in chief although the witness may be able to amplify the witness statement or in certain circumstances give additional evidence.
- If hearsay evidence is to be relied upon at trial, notice to that effect may be given either by the service of a witness statement in appropriate circumstances or by service of a notice under the Civil Evidence Act 1995. No notice, however, is required for hearings other than trial.
- The Court can require a witness to attend at a hearing other than trial to be cross examined.
- The form of witness statement is regulated by practice direction.
- If a witness is unco-operative and a party cannot obtain a statement, then a witness summary can be served in place of a witness statement.
- Facts in witness statements will be verified by a statement of truth. If a witness provides a false statement without an honest belief in its truth, that could be the subject of proceedings for contempt of Court.
- Whilst witness statements in interim applications replace affidavits, a witness can choose to swear an affidavit as that evidence.
- Affidavits are obligatory in certain instances e.g. applications for search orders (suggesting some qualitative difference between witness statements and affidavits).

The Rules

Part 32 starts with a common principle running throughout the CPR. The emphasis in Rule 32.1 is that the Court is in control of the evidence to be produced in the course of proceedings. In the initial drafts of Rule 32.1, it was an obligation of the Court to control the evidence. The final version, however, simply allows the Court to control the evidence but does not go so far as to make it an obligation (although see the comments below). The control of the Court is exercised by giving directions as to—

- the issues on which the Court requires evidence;
- the nature of the evidence which it requires to decide those issues; and
- the way in which the evidence is to be placed before the Court.

This empowerment reflects both obligations arising under Part 1 (the overriding objective) and its discretion to manage cases under Part 3.

In exercising any discretion including the controlling of evidence the Court will have regard to Rule 1.1 and its obligation to deal with cases justly. Thus evidence might be limited to save expense under Rule 1.1(2)(b) or to ensure that the case is dealt with in ways which are proportionate to the financial position of each party under Rule 1.1(2)(c)(iv).

Rule 32.1(1) refers in particular to the identification of issues and the evidence required to resolve them. Under Rule 1.4 the Court has an obligation to identify the issues at an early stage, decide promptly which issues need full investigation and trial and decide the order in which issues are to be resolved.

Similarly, under its case management powers in Rule 3.1, the Court may decide the order in which issues are to be tried and exclude an issue from consideration (Rule 3.1(2)(j) and (k)).

Rule 32.1(2) provides the Court with an explicit power to exclude evidence that would otherwise be admissible. Similarly, Rule 32.1(3) provides that the Court can limit cross examination.

These issues will become particularly important in Fast Track cases in which the parties will have a very limited time in which to present their evidence to the Court (about 90 minutes). In its management of a Fast Track trial, the Court will have to work with the parties to ensure that the necessary evidence is obtained in that 90 minute period.

In exercising any of its powers to control the evidence, the Court will have in mind the requirements of Article 6(1) of the European Convention for the Protection of Human Rights which requires that a trial should be fair. Subject to reasonable limitations, the Court will be wary of for example, excluding cross examination altogether since this might be determined to be in breach of Article 6(1).

Rule 32.2 provides the general rule that evidence at trial will be given orally and at any other hearing in writing.

In relation to hearings other than trial, the evidence may be provided by—

- a witness statement;
- a statement of case;
- an application notice.

All of these have to be verified by a statement of truth (see Part 22). The statement of truth reads—

> **"I believe that the facts stated in this witness statement/statement of case/application notice are true."**

In the event that a witness makes a false statement in a document verified by a statement of truth without an honest belief in its truth, he may be subject to proceedings for contempt of Court (Rule 32.14). These may only be brought, however, by the Attorney General or with the permission of the Court (see below).

Under Rule 32.7, the Court does have the power to require upon the hearing of an application, for instance, a witness to attend the hearing for cross examination. If that person does not then attend, the evidence may not be used unless the Court gives permission.

A witness giving evidence in writing for a hearing other than trial may give that evidence by way of affidavit if he so chooses, although the additional cost of making the affidavit will be irrecoverable (Rule 32.15). In certain instances evidence for applications must be by sworn affidavit; applications for—

- Search orders (Part 25)
- Freezing injunctions (Part 25)
- Contempt proceedings (RSC Order 52)

The detail of the form of witness statements and affidavits is set out in the Practice Direction—witness statements Paragraphs 17.1–19.2 (see below); affidavits Paragraphs 3.1–6.2.

There is no set form for the manner in which evidence is to be given within a statement of case or an application notice. It is suggested that the evidence contained within either a statement of case or an application notice should follow the format set out in Paragraphs 18.1–19.2 of the Practice Direction. It must be remembered particularly that documents to be proffered in evidence should be exhibited, verified and identified by the witness. The regulation of exhibits is set out in Paragraphs 11.1–15.4 of the Practice Direction to Part 32.

Witness statements for use at Trial

There is no general requirement for witness statements to be provided in relation to a hearing in the Small Claims Track. The Court could require witness statements but it does not form part of the standard directions contained within the Practice Direction to Part 27. In the Fast Track and Multi Track it will be a standard direction for witness statements to be exchanged at some point prior to trial.

The witness statement should contain all of the evidence that that witness proposes to give at trial in relation to any issues of fact to be decided (Rule 32.4(2)). The witness statement should be in the witness's own words, expressed in the first person and set out—

- the witness's full name;
- the witness's residential address or, in certain cases, his place of work;
- the witness's occupation or description; and
- the fact that he is a party or an employee of a party to the proceedings (Paragraph 18.1, Practice Direction to Part 32).

The witness statement must indicate the facts known to the witness directly or those of which he has been informed or of which he believes. The witness statement should set out the source of any relevant information or belief (as to hearsay evidence see below).

The witness statement will stand as evidence in chief subject to any order to the contrary. Reflecting Lord Woolf's suggestion, however, the Court may give permission for a witness to amplify the witness statement and give evidence in relation to any new matters which have arisen since the witness statement was served on the other parties (Rule 32.5(3)). Insofar as there is time, this might allow the judge "… to hear the witness give evidence in his or her own words before coming under the pressure of cross examination" (Paragraph 56,

Chapter 12, page 129, Final Report). It may also assist to allow the witness to "bed in" to giving evidence before the rigours of cross examination. It is unlikely, however, that time will allow such luxury in the Fast Track bearing in mind the limited period for each party to present the evidence. In any event under Rule 32.5(4) there is a specific restriction that the Court will only give permission for amplification or fresh evidence if"... there is good reason not to confine the evidence of the witness to the contents of his witness statement".

If without an appropriate order (see below) a witness is not called to give oral evidence and the statement has not been put in as hearsay evidence by the party presenting the evidence, the other party may put the witness statement in as hearsay evidence (Rule 32.5(5)).

An application may be made to the court for an order that a witness statement may be presented in evidence without calling the witness to give evidence. An application and an order to this effect may be appropriate if:

- there is no dispute as to facts or there is unlikely to be such a dispute;
- the only or main issue is the meaning of a document or statutory provision;
- the only or main issue is a question of law; or
- a defence has not been filed.

An application under Part 23 would have to be made providing the other party an opportunity to object.

Witness Summaries

As an alternative to a witness statement a party may serve a witness summary if the party is unable to obtain a witness statement from the witness. This does, however, require the permission of the Court. Application should be made in accordance with Part 23 but no notice of the application is required.

A witness summary could be a witness statement endorsed with a statement of truth which the witness has refused to sign a summary of the evidence which the party believes a witness will give or simply the questions to be put to the witness. Insofar as possible a witness summary should follow the format of a witness statement. It should contain a summary of—

- the evidence, if known, which would otherwise be included in the witness statement; or
- if the evidence is not known, the matters about which the party serving the witness summary proposes to question the witness (Rule 32.9(2)).

The witness statement should also include the name and address of the intended witness (Rule 32.9(3)).

Content

Rule 32.14 provides that anyone making a false statement in a document verified by a statement of truth without an honest belief in its truth may be liable to proceedings for contempt brought either by the Attorney General or by a party with permission of the Court. This covers the statements of case and witness statements and could include application notices if so verified. This is dealt with in the chapter dealing with statements of truth (Part 22). Reference should also be made to RSC Order 52 (committal) in CPR Schedule 1.

Service of witness statements

If a witness statement or a witness summary for use at the trial is not served in accordance with any order of the Court, the witness may not be called to give oral evidence unless the Court gives permission (Rule 32.10). Whilst emphasising the need to serve witness statements in accordance with the order of the Court, it also highlights that if a witness summons is served on a witness to require their attendance at the trial, the party seeking their attendance must serve a witness summary in respect of the intended witness. If a witness summary is not served, they may not be able to call the witness even though he responds to the witness summons. (As to witness summonses, see Part 34 below.)

As with documents disclosed during the course of proceedings (see Part 31), witness statements may only be used for the purpose of the proceedings in which they are served unless—

- the witness gives consent in writing;
- the Court gives permission; or
- the witness statement is put in evidence at a hearing held in public

(Rule 32.12).

If a witness statement stands as evidence in chief then anyone may inspect it unless there is a direction to the contrary arising from the—

- interests of justice;
- public interest;
- nature of any expert medical evidence in the statement;
- nature of any confidential information in the statement; or
- need to protect the interests of any child or patient

(Rule 32.13).

Costs

In relation to written evidence generally, some reference should be made to the costs Rules. During the consultation process in relation to this Part, concern was expressed that practitioners are drafting over lengthy witness statements. It was proposed to correct what was seen as an abuse by providing specifically within this Part for penalties in costs. In the event there is no express provision within Part 32 but under Rule 44.3 or 44.5, the Court could disallow costs in relation to all or parts of a witness statement which had little or no bearing on the issues to be decided by the Court.

Inspection of documents

Before passing from the provisions relating to witness statements, readers are reminded that under Rule 31.14 a party may inspect a document mentioned in a statement of case, a witness statement, a witness summary or an affidavit.

There is no like provision for inspection of a document mentioned in an application notice even if it be verified by a statement of truth.

Notices to admit facts and to admit or produce documents

These two provisions from the old Rules have been retained subject to certain amendments.

Rule 32.18 provides in short that one party can ask another to admit facts or "...part of the case..." by service of a notice specifying the facts or part of the case. There is no longer a requirement to respond to a notice to admit facts within a specified period, nor an express provision of the cost consequences of not making an admission. Clearly, however, in exercising the Court's discretion in relation to costs, the cost of proving the facts included in the notice and anything arising from them are likely to be ordered in appropriate circumstances against the Respondent to the notice.

Rule 32.18(3) provides importantly (like the old Rules) that the admission in response to a notice may only be used in the proceedings in which the notice to admit is served and by the party who served the notice. This makes inadmissible in any subsequent litigation proof of such admissions. This is to encourage parties to admit facts for the purpose of proceedings in order to try and limit the issues and if possible achieve settlement.

Rule 32.19 (notice to admit or produce documents) like Rule 32.18 above (notice to admit facts) is a consolidation of the old Rules. The provisions in relation to notices to admit or produce documents are often overlooked by litigators. The specific provision that a party is deemed to admit the authenticity of a document without the notice is often missed. The time limit on service of the notice should be noted. Thus the notice must be served—

- by the latest date for serving witness statements; or
- within seven days of disclosure of the document;

whichever is the later. Disclosure under Rule 31.2 takes place when a party states that the document exists or has existed.

Hearsay Evidence—Part 33

Warning: The timing of Civil Evidence Act 1995 has changed and requires earlier consideration of hearsay evidence.

The regime in relation to hearsay evidence was overhauled by the Civil Evidence Act 1995. Part 1 of the Civil Evidence Act 1968 was thereby repealed but on the face of it the 1995 Act does not apply to proceedings which were commenced before 31 January 1997. The new Rules are very much built around the 1995 Act—no reference being made to the 1968 Act. The Practice Direction of May 1999 now extends the 1995 Act to proceedings commenced before 31 January 1997.

The definition of hearsay is set out in Rule 33.1. Defining hearsay evidence is not an easy task and the Rules simply lift the definition from Section 1(2) of the Civil Evidence Act 1995—

> "...a statement made otherwise than by a person while giving oral evidence in proceedings, which is tendered as evidence of the matters stated..."

The regime in Part 33 relates only to evidence given at trial. Hearsay evidence given at other hearings is generally admissible as long as the witness differentiates between the evidence which is gained from his own knowledge and that of which he was informed or he believes. If the evidence is based on information or belief then the source of it must be given (see Paragraph 18.2, Practice Direction to Part 32).

Part 33 follows the provisions of the Civil Evidence Act 1995 by providing the machinery for notice to be given under the Act of an intention to rely upon hearsay evidence and the service of counter notices where the credibility of a witness is to be attacked.

The Rules

The basic tenet of the Civil Evidence Act 1995 is that a party can rely on hearsay evidence but to do so he must give appropriate notice to the other side. Section 2 of the Civil Evidence Act 1995 provides—

(1) A party proposing to adduce hearsay evidence in civil proceedings shall, subject to the following provisions of this section, give to the other party or parties to the proceedings—

(a) such notice (if any) of that fact, and

(b) on request, such particulars of or relating to the evidence,

as is reasonable and practicable in the circumstances for the purpose of enabling him or them to deal with any matters arising from its being hearsay.

(2) Provision may be made by rules of court—

(a) specifying classes of proceedings or evidence in relation to which subsection (1) does not apply, and

(b) as to the manner in which (including the time within which) the duties imposed by that subsection are to be complied with in the cases where it does apply.

(3) Subsection (1) may also be excluded by agreement of the parties; and compliance with the duty to give notice may in any case be waived by the person to whom notice is required to be given.

(4) A failure to comply with subsection (1), or with rules under subsection (2)(b), does not affect the admissibility of the evidence but may be taken into account by the court—

(a) in considering the exercise of its powers with respect to the course of proceedings and costs, and

(b) as a matter adversely affecting the weight to be given to the evidence in accordance with section 4

Rule 33.2 deals with the mechanics of giving notice and timing (see below). Under Rule 33.3, notice is not required for—

- evidence at hearings other than trials (see above);
- an affidavit or witness statement which does not contain hearsay evidence;

- a statement which a party to a probate action wishes to put in evidence and which is alleged to have been made by the person who is stated the subject of the proceedings; or
- where the requirement is excluded by practice direction.

Under the CCR, service of notice relating to hearsay evidence was not required if no defence or answer was filed. There is no like provision under the new Rules.

Part 33 has no application to proceedings in the small claims track being excluded along with "the strict rules of evidence" under Rules 27.2(1)(d) and 27.8(3).

The Rules in relation to hearsay evidence have no direct application to experts reports. If hearsay evidence is included in an expert's report, notice of it will, in any event, be given by the service of the report in a like manner to Rule 33.2 (below).

Rule 33.2 sets out the machinery for the giving of notice under the Civil Evidence Act 1995 and the timing of it.

Notice can be given in one of two ways: either by the service of a witness statement in accordance with appropriate directions given by the Court on allocation or subsequently, or by an appropriate formal notice.

If a party intends to rely on hearsay evidence at trial and either—

- evidence is to be given by a witness giving oral evidence; or
- evidence is contained in a witness statement of a person who is not being called to give oral evidence;

notice is given for the purposes of the Act by the service of the witness statement in accordance with the Court's earlier order.

If the evidence is contained in a witness statement and the witness has not been called to give evidence, then in addition to the witness statement the person relying upon the evidence should inform the other parties that the witness is not being called to give oral evidence, giving reasons why.

In all other cases, i.e. when hearsay evidence is not contained within a witness statement, under Rule 33.2(3) notice must be given which—

- identifies the hearsay evidence;
- states that the party serving the notice proposes to rely on hearsay evidence at trial; and
- gives the reason why the witness will not be called.

Witness statements may not be served without an order of the Court.

The time limit for serving both the witness statement acting as a notice under the Civil Evidence Act 1995 and a separate notice in other cases is the date for serving witness statements in accordance with the order of the Court (Rules 33.2(1)) and 33.2(4)).

In addition to the notice under Rule 33.2(3), if the hearsay evidence is contained in a document the party relying upon it must supply a copy of that document to any party upon request (Rule 33.2(4)).

As with all time limits, they may be varied by the parties by agreement in writing (Rule 2.11) subject to the restriction of interference with certain dates under Parts 28 (Fast Track) and 29 (Multi Track). Further, the Court has the power to abridge or extend time under Rule 3.1(2)(a).

The fundamental change to the time limits under the new Rules should be noted. Previously under RSC Order 38 Rule 21(4) the time limit for service of a Civil Evidence Act notice was 28 days after setting down or, if not set down, 28 days after obtaining a hearing date. Under CCR Order 20 Rule 15 the time limit was 28 days before trial. Usually under the CPR, witness statements follow the completion of disclosure and inspection. Thus exchange of witness statements and the necessity to comply with Rule 33.2 in relation to hearsay evidence will take place at an early stage in the process. In the Fast Track witness statements will usually be exchanged some 20 weeks before the trial.

Power to call witnesses for cross examination on hearsay evidence

Section 3 of the Civil Evidence Act 1995 stipulates—

> *Rules of court may provide that where a party to civil proceedings adduces hearsay evidence of a statement made by a person and does not call that person as a witness, any other party to the proceedings may, with the leave of the court, call that person as a witness and cross-examine him on the statement as if he had been called by the first-mentioned party and as if the hearsay statement were his evidence in chief.*

Rule 33.4 provides the mechanics within the Rules to put Section 3 into effect. Following service of notice under Rule 33.2 that a party intends to rely upon hearsay evidence, the party upon whom the notice is served may make application to the Court to call the maker of **the original statement** to be cross examined on the contents of the statement. Although the words "**the original statement**" are not defined within the Rules, the Civil Evidence Act 1995 defines it as—

> **the underlying statement (if any) by—**
>
> **(a) in the case of evidence of fact, a person having personal knowledge of that fact; or**
>
> **(b) in the case of evidence of opinion, the person whose opinion it is.**

(Section 13 of the Civil Evidence Act 1995)

The word "statement" is also defined in the Act (Section 13) and means any representation of fact or opinion, however made.

For the Rules relating to service the reader is referred to Part 6.

The application for permission will have to be made in accordance with Part 23.

If permission for cross examination is given, the witness who is called is treated in accordance with Section 3 as a witness of the party giving notice under Rule 33.2 and the hearsay statement will stand as that witness's evidence in chief. It is outside the scope of this work to discuss whether a witness called in this fashion may amplify the witness statement and give evidence in relation to new matters which have arisen since the hearsay statement was made under Rule 32.5(3).

Credibility

Rule 33.5 puts into effect Section 5(2) of the Civil Evidence Act 1995. That section provides—

(2) Where in civil proceedings hearsay evidence is adduced and the maker of the original statement, or of any statement relied upon to prove another statement, is not called as a witness—

(a) evidence which if he had been so called would be admissible for the purpose of attacking or supporting his credibility as a witness is admissible for that purpose in the proceedings; and

(b) evidence tending to prove that, whether before or after he made the statement, he made any other statement inconsistent with it is admissible for the purpose of showing that he had contradicted himself.

Provided that evidence may not be given of any matter of which, if he had been called as a witness and had denied that matter in cross-examination, evidence could not have been adduced by the cross-examining party

Under Rule 33.5 a party wishing to attack the credibility of the person making the original statement (see the definition above) must give notice to the party that serves the original notice under Rule 33.2 that evidence will be called to attack the credibility of the person who made the original statement. That notice must be given no more than 14 days after the day on which the original hearsay notice was served under Rule 33.2.

If notice is given by the other party in accordance with Rule 33.5 of an intention to call evidence to attack the credibility of the person making the original statement, a witness statement of any person giving such evidence at trial ("in relation to any issues of fact to be decided at the trial" (Rule 32.4(2)) will need to be served in accordance with Rule 32.4. Since notice of an intention to call hearsay evidence is given when witness statements are served, permission of the Court will be required in order to serve any further witness statements after that time has expired.

Similarly, having received a notice under Rule 33.5, if the party decides to call the maker of the original statement, a witness statement will have to be prepared and served in accordance with Rule 32.4. Permission to serve a witness statement out of time will be required.

Use of plans, photographs and models as evidence

Rule 33.6 regulates the use of evidence which is not—

- contained in a witness statement, affidavit or expert's report;
- to be given orally at trial;
- evidence of which prior notice must be given under Rule 33.2; or
- evidence which may be received without further proof under Section 9 of

the Civil Evidence Act 1995 (proof of records of business or public authority).

The Rule itself gives examples of such evidence over and above that provided for under Section 9 of the Civil Evidence Act 1995 as plans, photographs or models.

In order to use such evidence at trial the party intending to use it must give appropriate notice. There are four separate time limits for the giving of such a notice—

- Generally notice must be given no later than the latest date for serving witness statements (Rule 33.6(4)).
- If there are to be no witness statements or the evidence which is to be used is intended solely for the purpose of disproving an allegation made in a witness statement, notice must be given at least 21 days before the hearing at which the evidence is to be used.
- If the evidence is not being put in as part of factual or expert evidence, notice must be given 21 days before the hearing at which it will be used.
- If the evidence forms part of an expert's report then the notice must be served when the expert's report itself is served.

Having given notice, the party is obliged to give every other party an opportunity to inspect it (Rule 33.6(8)). Following that inspection the parties should attempt to agree the admission of the evidence without further proof. If agreement cannot be reached then an appropriate application may be made to the Court although having given notice the party giving it may introduce the evidence at trial.

Evidence of finding on question on foreign law

Although evidence is largely regulated by the Civil Evidence Act 1995, there are some remaining provisions of the Civil Evidence Act 1972 that have not been repealed by the 1995 Act. These include evidence of foreign law. Rule 33.7 puts in place the machinery for the use in evidence of findings in relation to foreign law in accordance with Section 4(2) of the Civil Evidence Act 1972.

In brief the sub-section provides that where any question as to the law of any jurisdiction outside England and Wales has been decided in any proceedings in that jurisdiction then generally the finding if reported or "recorded in citable form" will be admissible in the proceedings within the jurisdiction.

Under Section 4(3) a party cannot adduce that evidence unless they have given appropriate notice provided for in the Rules. As the Rule records (33.7(3)) the notice should be served with the witness statements if there are any. If not then notice must be served no less than 21 days before the hearing at which the finding will be put in as evidence. Under Rule 33.7(4) notice must—

- specify the question on which the finding was made; and
- enclose a copy of a document where the finding is reported or recorded.

CHAPTER 25
PART 34—DEPOSITION AND COURT ATTENDANCE BY WITNESSES

Introduction

Part 34 contains the Rules relating to the procedure to be followed to require a witness to attend a hearing or trial and the taking of evidence at a place and time other than the hearing. The Part combines at the same time one piece of plain English and another of legalese. Witness summonses have for some time served as subpoenae in the County Court. The High Court, however, has retained up to now subpoenae. Under the CPR the process of enforcing the attendance of a witness at Court is now referred to as a witness summons in both the High Court and County Court. On the other hand the evidence given by a witness under examination other than at a hearing or trial before the Court remains a "deposition" with the witness being referred to as a deponent and presumably the examination being referred to as a deposition hearing.

The regulation of witness summonses and depositions needs to be considered in conjunction with various other Rules.

- Instead of ordering a deposition hearing under Rule 34.8 the Court could adjourn the proceedings to a private address to enable a witness to give evidence under its power to specify the place where the trial or other hearing shall take place (Rule 30.6).
- The Court may transfer the whole or part of the proceedings in accordance with its powers of transfer under Part 30 taking into account particularly Rule 30.3(2)(b) (transfer of hearing/trial to another court).
- As an alternative to a witness summons, the Court may make an order under Rule 31.17 for disclosure against a person who is not a party to the proceedings (see below).

Witness Summonses

The Rules relating to witness summonses were contained in RSC Order 38 Rules 13–19 and CCR Order 20 Rule 12. Practice differed between the two Courts although as with much else, the CPR now provide a uniform system for requiring a witness to attend Court to give evidence or produce documents to the Court.

As above, comparison needs to be made with Rule 31.17, which with the statutory support of Section 34 of the Supreme Court Act 1981 and Section 53 of the County Courts Act 1984, allows the Court to order that disclosure be given by a person who is not a party to the proceedings. Whilst Rule 31.17 does not introduce a new principle to the Rules, it opens completely the scope of proceedings in which such an order may be made. Previously it could only be made in proceedings involving personal injury or death. As commented in Chapter 20 it will be interesting to see the extent to which the Court exercises the power under Rule 31.17. In certain circumstances the formality of the procedure of disclosure under Rule 31.17 might be appropriate but it is suggested that married with the ability of the Court to specify a date when documents should be produced to the Court, a witness summons under Part 34 may offer a cheaper and speedier process than making application under Rule 31.17.

A witness summons is in the form N20. The person seeking the issue of the summons must complete the section of it as to whether the witness is required to give evidence or to produce documents or both (Rule 34.2(1) and Paragraph 1.1, Practice Direction to Part 34). If the witness is required to produce documents then details of the documents must be set out on the witness summons. Although there is no direction in relation to what details are required, clearly they must be sufficient for the witness to identify the documents in order to respond to the summons.

Two copies of the witness summons must be lodged with the Court for issue and sealing. A party will receive one back if they have indicated to the Court that they propose to serve. Otherwise the other copy will be used for Court service (see below) (Paragraph 1.2, Practice Direction to Part 34).

A witness summons which requires the production of documents may require a witness to produce documents to the Court on a date other than a date fixed for hearing. This provision (Rule 34.2(4)) has been welcomed by commentators because of the difficulty that has arisen in the past in relation to the production of documents under a subpoena or witness summons. Previously a subpoena or witness summons was only returnable at a hearing. Accordingly the witness would produce the documents at the hearing itself. This could lead to much wasted time and expense. Accordingly a practice had developed by which the Court were setting notional hearing dates so that witnesses would produce documents some time in advance of the real hearing or trial. Rule 34.2(4) makes this unnecessary and the Court will provide a date for the production of the documents. In order to issue a summons for the production of documents at a date other than the hearing date, permission is required under Rule 34.3(2). As detailed below, there is no specific provision within the Rule or the practice direction as to whether an application for permission needs to be made with or without notice. Generally permission of the Court for any step should be sought in accordance with Part 23, i.e. by the issue of an application notice. Following from that, the general rule under Part 23 is that notice has to be given of a hearing unless a Rule, practice direction or Court order provides to the contrary. It is suggested that the application will not have to be served since there is no respondent to it.

The witness summons is returnable before the Court and thus where it provides for the production of documents, the obligation is to produce them to the

Court, not to the party requesting them by way of witness summons. As a matter of practice, however, if in response to a witness summons a party agrees to provide the original or copies of the documents requested to the party seeking them, it is presumed that the party seeking the documents may vacate the date set by the Court for production notwithstanding that the precise obligation under the witness summons is to produce the documents to the Court.

The witness summons must be issued under Rule 34.3(3) in the court where the case is proceeding or the court where the hearing in question will be held. Under Part 30 the Court can transfer proceedings. Until it does so, the case is proceeding in the court of issue. If an order for transfer is made it has effect on the date when it is made (Paragraph 3, Practice Direction to Part 30). Under Rule 30.6 the Court may determine that a hearing should be held at a place other than the court where the case is proceeding. In that event, under Rule 34.3(3)(b) it is only the court where the hearing is to take place that can issue a witness summons in relation to that hearing. Readers are reminded that in the Practice Direction to Part 29 (Multi Track) it is stated that most trials in multi track will normally take place at a civil trial centre.

Permission

Generally if a witness summons is returnable at the trial of a claim, permission is not required to issue a witness summons whether it be a summons for a witness to give evidence or produce documents or both. Under Rule 34.3(2), however, there are three exceptions—

- if the witness summons is issued less then seven days before the date of the trial;
- if a witness is to attend Court to give evidence or produce documents on any date except the date fixed for trial (as above); or
- the hearing at which attendance or production is required is not the trial.

As commented on above, it is presumed that no notice of an application for permission will be required and may not require the filing of an application notice. The practice under the CCR for leave to issue a witness summons for a directions hearing was that the application for that leave was made "ex parte" (CCR Order 20 Rule 12(8)). If the filing and service of an application notice were to be a prerequisite, there may be a slight logistical difficulty since such an application would have to be issued in the court in which the case is proceeding under Rule 23.2 subject to the exception that where the parties have been notified of a fixed date for trial, the application must be made to the court where the trial is to take place (Rule 23.2(3)).

If the summons is to be issued less than 7 days prior to the trial, consideration will have to be given not only to the question of the sufficiency of the notice to the witness but also the service of a witness statement or witness summary. Permission may be required to serve a statement or summary out of time. Such an application would involve the other party to the proceedings requiring the issue and service of an application notice under Part 23.

Service

The Rules as to service under the RSC and CCR differed in that a subpoena had to be served personally whilst a witness summons could be served by post. Prior to 26 April 1999 service of a subpoena had to be effected by the party or their legal representative whilst in the County Court service could be effected by the Court. Under the CPR both the High Court and the County Court now have obligations to serve documents in accordance with Part 6 and various service provisions scattered amongst the Rules, subject to anything to the contrary in the relevant court guides such as the Commercial Court Guide.

Rule 34.6 provides that the Court will serve the witness summons unless the party seeking its issue informs the Court at the time of issue that he will effect service.

Service may be effected by first class post under Rule 6.2(1)(b). It may also be effected, however, by other methods set out in Rule 6.2(1) subject to the tender of money in accordance with Rule 34.7 (below). Thus solicitors will often wish to effect personal service of the witness summons to ensure that there is absolute certainty as to its receipt. The Court will usually effect service by post in which event the deemed day of service is the second day after it was posted (Rule 6.7(1)).

At the time of service the witness must be offered or paid money to cover his expenses in travelling **to and from** the Court and compensation for loss of time (Rule 34.7). If the Court is to effect service then this money must be lodged with the Court when the witness summons is lodged for issue. If payment to the Court is made by cheque there may be some delay to allow clearance of the cheque before the Court will draw its own cheque and effect service. The amount payable by way of compensation for the loss of time derived from the amount payable to witnesses in the Crown Court under the Prosecution of Offences Act 1995 and Costs in Criminal Cases General Regulations 1986 (Paragraph 3.3, Practice Direction to Part 34).

The witness summons together with the monies payable under Rule 34.7 must be served no less than seven days before the date on which the witness is required to attend. As with all measurements of time, the seven days is "clear" days thus excluding the day of service and the day on which attendance is required.

As above, if the Court is asked to issue a summons less than seven days before the date of the trial or for any hearing other than the trial, the witness summons will not be issued without express permission from the Court. If that permission is forthcoming, a direction is also required under Rule 34.5(2) that a witness summons should be binding although it is going to be served less than seven days before the date on which attendance is required. Although there is nothing in the Rule to this effect, presumably when the Court gives the direction it may also direct by when service has to be effected for the witness summons to be binding under Rule 34.5(2). As above, permission may also be required to serve a witness statement or summary out of time.

Rule 34.5(2) appears only to cater for the circumstances where it is clear that upon issue of the witness summons it will be served less than seven days before the date on which attendance is required. If a witness summons is issued in good time but the party is unable to serve it less than seven days before the return date, the Court could nonetheless determine that the summons is binding by shortening the time under Rule 3.1(2)(a).

Amending, setting aside or varying the Witness Summons

Under Paragraph 1.3 of the Practice Direction to Part 34, if a mistake is made in the name or address of a person named in a witness summons then it may be corrected as long as the summons has not been served. Presumably, other amendments can be made prior to service with the endorsement of the Court such as the addition or exclusion of documents listed within the summons. If corrections are made to the summons then it must be re-sealed by the Court and marked "Amended and Re-sealed" (Paragraph 1.4, Practice Direction to Part 34).

The witness may apply to set aside or vary a witness summons. An application would be required in accordance with Part 23. Accordingly the application notice must state briefly why the applicant is seeking to set aside or vary the witness summons and it must be served no less than three clear days before the hearing date unless the witness summons was issued in aid of an inferior court or tribunal in which case only two days notice is required (Paragraph 2.4, Practice Direction to Part 34).

Although there is no specific practice direction on the point, it is suggested that akin to Paragraphs 2.2 and 2.3 of the Practice Direction to Part 34, the application to set aside or vary should be made to the court that issues the summons and that that application would be heard by a Master at the Royal Courts of Justice or a District Judge in the District Registry or County Court. This might cause some difficulties for the witness. The court of issue may be highly inconvenient. In appropriate circumstances the Court would have the power to determine that the hearing to set aside or vary should take place in a more convenient County Court for the witness in question although whether this will be really practicable might be in some doubt.

Witness Summons in aid of inferior Court or Tribunal

Rule 34.4(3) defines an "inferior court or tribunal" as one that does not have the power to issue a witness summons in relation to the proceedings before it. Examples of such a court or tribunal would be proceedings under the Arbitration Act 1996 or proceedings before the Inland Revenue Commissioners.

Under the old rules the jurisdiction to issue such a witness summons was restricted to the High Court. RSC Order 38 Rule 19 set out the procedure under which application had to be made to the Crown Office for a writ of subpoena. That writ then had to be served personally.

This restriction has been removed under the CPR and both the High Court and County Courts have jurisdiction to issue witness summonses in aid of inferior courts or tribunals. There is no geographical restriction on the appropriate court. It is suggested that a court convenient to the witness might be the appropriate court of issue. If an application is subsequently made to set aside, it would seem reasonable that such an application ought to be heard in a court convenient to the witness rather than to the tribunal or the parties.

Whichever court the witness summons be issued out of, there are no different rules thereafter in relation to the witness summons save as highlighted above.

- Under Rule 34.4(2) application to set aside should be made to the court that issued the witness summons.
- Under Paragraph 2.3 of the Practice Direction to Part 34 the application to set aside the witness summons will be heard in the High Court by a Master of the Royal Courts of Justice or otherwise by a District Judge.
- Under Paragraph 2.4 of the Practice Direction to Part 34 the notice of the application to set aside is two days rather than the normal three days.

Evidence by Deposition

Introduction

The taking of evidence by deposition was previously regulated under RSC Order 39 and CCR Order 20 Rule 13. As editorial comment to those two rules suggests, this Part of the Rules is primarily directed at witnesses who are unable to attend at Court because of, for instance, illness. As commented above, the Court does have the power to alter the location of a hearing or part of it to enable a witness to give evidence. It may be directed, for instance, that a witness's evidence should be taken at their home. This change of location of the trial or hearing occurs during the course of it. The purpose of the Rules relating to taking evidence by deposition, however, is to allow evidence to be taken before a hearing or trial takes place. Thus in the case of terminal illness the evidence of a witness who may not survive until the trial may be taken by deposition under Rule 34.8.

Some commentators on the new Rules have seen within Rule 34.8 the opportunity, however, to expand the circumstances in which deposition hearings are held. A deposition hearing might be appropriate for the evidence of expert witnesses whose availability for the actual trial of the claim might cause some difficulties. Thus a deposition hearing might be set at which the expert or experts make themselves available for examination and cross examination at a convenient time. Practitioners will be a little nervous, however, of carrying out an examination and cross examination of a witness in front of a person other than the trial judge. Subject to it appearing appropriate, however, the judge who will hear the trial could preside over the deposition hearing.

It remains to be seen the extent to which the Court uses the provisions of Rule 34.8 for these extended purposes. Certainly there is no limitation upon the Court's discretion within the Rules but it is suggested that it is unlikely that the Court will go marching down the road of full deposition hearings as in the American model. In any event in the USA the taking of depositions and deposition hearings are part of the discovery process. Rule 34.8 is not part of the discovery process within this jurisdiction.

The Rules

The Rules within Part 34 relate to the taking of depositions either in England and Wales or abroad for use as evidence in proceedings before the courts in England and Wales. There is a separate provision (RSC Order 70) for the taking of depositions in England and Wales for use as evidence in proceedings before courts abroad pursuant to letters of request. Although this separate provision is contained within Schedule 1 of the CPR, the Practice Direction to it appears with the Practice Directions relating to Part 34.

Under Rule 34.8(1) the Court has general jurisdiction to make an order for a person to be examined before the hearing takes place. As above, there are no limitations to the grounds upon which an order can be made. In exercising its discretion, however, the Court is bound to take into account the overriding objective and particularly Rule 1.1(2).

The application for an order will be made in accordance with Part 23 and it is suggested should be supported by written evidence.

The application can seek and the order can provide that the examination shall take place on oath before—

- a judge;
- an examiner of the court; or
- such other person as the court appoints.

Previous practice was that an examination before a judge would only be ordered in exceptional circumstances.

Examiners are appointed by the Lord Chancellor but allocated to an examination by the Senior Master of the Queen's Bench Division. The allocation process is conducted through the Foreign Process Section of the Masters Secretaries Department of the Royal Courts of Justice. Accordingly if an order is made for examinations by an examiner of the Court, application should be made to the Foreign Process Section for the allocation of a particular examiner (Paragraph 4.2(1), Practice Direction to Part 34). The order for examination must state the date, time and place of the examination. As above, it might be appropriate for the examination to be conducted at a place convenient to the witness in which event a local examiner might be allocated.

The order may also provide that a witness statement or witness summary relating to the evidence to be given by the witness should be served prior to the examination taking place.

The order may also require the production of necessary documents for the purposes of the examination.

The order for examination should be served in the usual way. As with a witness summons, however, it must be accompanied by monies to cover the expenses of travelling to and from the place of examination and compensation for loss of time. There is no specific practice direction for examinations relating to compensation for loss of time. Presumably reliance is made on the appropriate figures for witness summonses as provided in Paragraphs 3.2 and 3.3, Practice Direction to Part 34 (see above).

Under Rule 34.9 the examination is to be conducted as if the witness were giving evidence at trial. If the examiner considers it appropriate the examination may be conducted in private. In exercising that discretion the examiner should have reference to the practice direction to Part 39 in relation to the holding of hearings in public and private.

- The Practice Direction to Part 34 sets out in some detail the regulation of the examination, the recording of evidence and procedures for enforcing the attendance of the witness at the examination (see Rules 34.9 and 34.10 and Paragraphs 4.3–4.11, Practice Direction to Part 34). The examination can be recorded on audio tape or video tape. If the use of examination grows in the manner mentioned above, it is likely that there will be increasing use of video tape to record the proceedings. Whether or not the examination is recorded on audio tape or video tape, the deposition must always be recorded in writing either by the examiner or by a shorthand writer or stenographer.

The deposition so recorded may then be used in evidence at a hearing under Rule 34.11(1). If, however, a party intends to put in a deposition at a hearing they must give 21 days notice of that intention before the day fixed for the hearing (Rule 34.11(2) and (3)). The Court may still require the deponent to attend the hearing and give the evidence orally (Rule 34.11(4)).

Examination of a person out of the Jurisdiction

Unlike examination of a person within the jurisdiction, the process to obtain an order for examination out of the jurisdiction can only be effected through the High Court.

Application is made in the High Court for the issue of a letter of request to the judicial authorities of the country in which the proposed deponent is (Paragraph 5.1, Practice Direction to Part 34). The application is made in accordance with Part 23 if it is made within existing proceedings. Otherwise it is made by issuing a claim form under Part 8 (Paragraph 5.2, Practice Direction to Part 34). Paragraph 5.3 of the Practice Direction sets out the documents that must accompany the application notice or claim form. These include a draft letter of request to the appropriate judicial authorities, the form of which is set out in Annexe A to the Practice Direction. The examination abroad has to follow the same course as that taking place within the jurisdiction and Paragraphs 4.1–4.12 of the Practice Direction to Part 34 apply to it equally.

CHAPTER 26
PART 39—HEARINGS AND TRIALS

Introduction

Rules and Practice Directions relating to the trial of an action and hearings during the course of proceedings appear in various parts throughout the Rules. Part 23 provides generally for applications before and during the course of proceedings. Parts 27, 28 and 29 make specific provisions for the hearing or trials in the small claims track, the fast track and the multi track respectively. The reader is referred to the relevant chapters dealing with Parts 23, 27, 28 and 29.

Part 39 sweeps up the general Rules in relation to all hearings including trials.

Hearings in public

The concept of hearings in chambers, in camera or open Court has been replaced by a simpler categorisation under the CPR. In future hearings are either in public or in private. Although in future there may still be reference to hearings in chambers or in Court this is a reference to the type and size of room rather than whether or not the public may be admitted.

This alteration has been driven by the provisions of the European Convention for the Protection of Human Rights which by Article 6 (1) provides that Court hearings should generally be held in public unless the hearing falls within the exceptions to article 6 (1). Those exceptions are—

Right to a fair trial

1. In the determination of his civil rights and obligations or of any criminal charge against him, everyone is entitled to a fair and public hearing within a reasonable time by an independent and impartial tribunal established by law. Judgment shall be pronounced publicly but the press and public may be excluded from all or part of the trial in the interest of morals, public order or national security in a democratic society, where the interests of juveniles or the protection of the private life of the parties so require, or to the extent strictly necessary in the opinion of the court in special circumstances where publicity would prejudice the interests of justice.

For this reason Rule 39.2 (1) provides that hearings should take place in public unless they fall within the exceptions under Rule 39.2 (3). Those exceptions are—

- Publicity would defeat the object of the hearing.
- The hearing involves matters relating to national security.

- Publicity would damage any confidential information to be referred to at the hearing.
- A private hearing is necessary to protect the interests of any child or patient. This would include the approval of a compromise or settlement on behalf of a child or patient or an application for the payment of money out of Court to such person (Paragraph 1.6, Practice Direction to Part 39).
- The application has been made without notice and it would be unjust to the Respondent for the hearing to be in public.
- The hearing involved uncontentious matters arising in the administration of trust or a deceased persons estate.
- The Court considers that the hearing should be in private in the interests of justice.

The Practice Direction to Part 27 provides special directions in relation to a small claims hearing. A Judge hearing a claim in the Small Claims Track can hold it in private if the parties agree. There is no like provision for either the Fast Track or the Multi Track. A hearing held in public may still be held "in chambers" in the sense that it could be held in the Judge's private room but members of the public will be entitled to attend. Clearly there may be some practical difficulties. If a larger room or a Court is available it may be appropriate for the hearing to be adjourned into it so that members of the public can attend.

Whether or not a hearing or trial takes place in private the right of the public or press to obtain copies of the claim form under Rule 5.4 (2) (a) is unaffected. If the hearing takes place in public then a member of the public is entitled to a copy of the judgment or order (Rule 5.4 (2) (b)) and to a transcript of any judgment. This is not the case, however, if the hearing is in private. In that case the Court would have to give permission before these documents would be released (Paragraphs 1.11 and 1.12, Practice Direction to Part 39).

There is no like differentiation, however, in relation to the availability of witness statements. Under Rule 32.13 a witness statement which stands as evidence in chief may be inspected unless the Court makes a positive order to the contrary. The grounds for that order are set out in Rule 32.13 (3)—

- It is in the interest of justice.
- It is in the public interest.
- Any expert medical evidence in the statement should not be made available.
- There is confidential information contained in the statement which should not be open to inspection.
- It is in the interests of a child of patient that the witness statement should not be available to inspection.
- Instead of determining that the whole of a witness statement should not be open to public inspection the Court may exclude words or passages from it (Rule 32.13 (4)).

Right of audience

The change of language and the principle that hearings and trials should take place in public is intended to have no consequential effect upon the rights of audience of either legal or lay representatives. The rights of audience of lay representatives arise from the Lay Representative (Rights or Audience) Order 1992. A lay representative may only represent a party in a case proceeding in the Small Claims Track.

The statutory basis for other rights of audience is set out in Section 27 of the Courts and Legal Services Act 1990. That section and regulations arising from it often differentiate between hearings in chambers and hearings in open Court. For instance Section 27 (2)(e) provides that a person employed by a qualified litigator has a right of audience in chambers in the High Court or County Court. Paragraph 1.14 Practice Direction to Part 39 provides specifically that any rights of audience which existed prior to 26 April are unaffected by the new terminology and general principle. So that the fact that a hearing now takes place in public whereas previously it was held in private (i.e. in chambers) does not mean that an employee or a qualified litigator no longer has a right of audience. To a certain degree reference will have to be made to previous practice to determine whether or not a right of audience exists.

Presumably the same applies to Court dress so that if what was previously a chambers application is now in public will not mean that a Barrister has to wear a wig and gown in order to make representations. Why advocates should still be required to dress up in bizarre 18th century costume in the 21st century remains a mystery particularly bearing in mind that one of the tenets of the new Rules is that the Court system should be administered so that it no longer remains an alien world to the person in the street.

This alien world is also continued, unfortunately, in the Practice Direction to Part 39 which deals with Court sittings in the High Court and Court of Appeal. The year continues to be divided into four periods bearing titles such as Michaelmas, Hilary and Trinity. It is suggested, with all due respect, that in a unified modern system the Courts should simply be open for business throughout the year subject to appropriate holiday periods.

Attendance at Trial

As with hearings under Part 23 the Court may proceed with the trial in the absence of a party (Rule 39.3 (1)). This has no application to the claim in the small claims track which has its own Rules under Rule 27.9.

If none of the parties attend the trial the Court will usually strike out the whole of the proceedings which would include both the claim and any counterclaim (Rule 39.3 (1) (a)). Where it does strike out the proceedings or any part of them it may subsequently restore them usually following application of one of the parties although it could restore them of its own initiative under Rule 3.3. As with any application for effective relief against a sanction imposed the Court will take into account all the circumstances under Rule 3.9 (1); for instance whether the application has been made promptly. Rule 39.3 (5) sets out specific limitations on the Courts' discretion to restore the proceedings in that it will only do so if the Applicant—

- acted promptly when he found out that the Court had exercised its power to strike out;
- had a good reason for not attending the trial; and
- has a reasonable prospect of success at the trial.

It is to be noted that test under Rule 39.3 (5)(c) is as to **reasonable prospect of success rather than a real prospect** as is required under Parts 13 (setting aside the default judgment) and 24 (summary judgment). It is suggested, however, that in these circumstances the test under Rule 39.3 (5)(c) equates directly with the test of real prospect.

An application for restoration is made in accordance with Part 23 (Paragraph 2.3, Practice Direction to Part 39) and that must comply with the provisions of that Part. It must be supported by evidence which explains why the Applicant failed to attend the Court and when he found out about the order made in his absence. If it is the Claimant that does not attend at the trial then the Court may strike out the claim and any defence to a counterclaim. It is not, however, obliged to do so and in accordance with the general rule it may proceed with the trial in the absence of the claim and insofar as it is able to do so. Whatever order is made the Claimant may apply for it to be set aside. Again the Court will consider all of the matters set out in Rule 3.9 but also those particularly set out in Rule 39.3 (5) as above. The application must be made in accordance with Part 23 supported by evidence giving reasons for failure to attend and stating when the Claimant found out about the order made in his absence.

If it is the Defendant that does not attend then the Court may strike out the defence and/or any counterclaim. The Court is not obliged to take that course and may allow the Claimant to prove the claim and obtain judgment on the claim plus costs. The absent Defendant can make application to set aside the judgment order made in his absence. Once again he must make application in accordance with Part 23 supported by the evidence referred to above. The Court will take into account the factors referred to previously.

In addition to the factors under Rule 3.9 and Rule 39.3 (5) the Court will have regard to the overriding objective when exercising its discretion (Rule 1.2). In particular the Court will have regard to those matters set out in Rule 1.1(2) including that under which the Court must allot to a set of proceedings an appropriate share of the Courts resources.

In making an order under Rule 39.3 the Court could attach conditions to it such as requiring a party to make a payment into Court generally or payment on account of costs which have been wasted by the non attendance to the party that did attend.

Trial bundle

Rule 39.5 and Paragraph 3.1–3.10 seek to regulate the bundles of documents to be prepared and submitted to the Court for either a hearing or a trial. This question of bundles has long vexed Judges who often blame parties, particularly solicitors for submitting large bundles of documents the contents of which are largely irrelevant to the matters to be decided at the hearing or the trial. Out of this perceived problem has grown a practice of producing core bundles containing the important documents to which repeated reference will be made during the course of the trial.

There is no regulation of bundles for hearings other than trials within the Rules or Practice Directions. Reference should be made, however, to the various Court guides that are being produced by the Courts as to documents to be provided on an application. Further it is suggested that the parties have regard to the items set out in Paragraph 3.2 of the Practice Direction to Part 39 insofar as relevant in preparation of the bundle for an application whether made under Part 23 or otherwise.

As far as the trial is concerned Rule 39.5 (2) provides that the Claimant must file the trial bundle not more than 7 days and not less than 3 days before the start of the trial. It is likely that in giving appropriate directions at the case management stage, listing or pre-trial review the Court will also provide directions as to the lodging of trial bundles with the Court. The standard directions contained in the Practice Direction to Part 28 (fast track) provides directions concerning trial bundles. Similarly Paragraph 9.2 of the Practice Direction to Part 29 provides that directions on listing should include provision about the preparation of the trial bundle.

The parties are under a duty to co-operate and this co-operation extends naturally to the preparation of the trial bundle. The trial bundle is the responsibility of those acting for the Claimant (Paragraph 3.4, Practice Direction to Part 39). Accordingly it should be prepared initially by the Claimant's representatives and submitted to the other parties. Their representatives should attempt to agree the contents. Paragraph 3.9 of the Practice Direction to Part 39 encourages the parties to agree in particular—

- That the documents in the bundle are authentic.
- That the documents in the bundle may be treated as evidence of the facts stated in them even if a notice under section 2 of the Civil Evidence Act 1995 (notice of proposal to adduce hearsay evidence) has not been served in accordance with that section.

It may not of course be possible to agree the contents of the bundle. There is often argument about the inclusion of documents for which there is a claim of privilege. Ultimate responsibility for the trial bundle lies with the Claimant and his legal representatives. Insofar as other parties do not agree parts of the bundle, those documents in question, if included at all, should be drawn to the Courts attention as not agreed and a summary of the reasons why agreement has not been reached should be included in the bundle (Paragraph 3.9, Practice

Direction to Part 39). As a matter of practice the preparation of the bundles is often delegated to junior members of staff. The Practice Direction (Paragraph 3.4) reminds legal representatives that ultimately it is they (presumably the most senior of them) who takes responsibility for the trial bundles. Accordingly it is suggested that those taking responsibility ensure that the examination and use of the trial bundle by the Judge does not cause embarrassment and criticism.

Paragraph 3.10 of the Practice Direction to Part 39 provides that the party filing the trial bundle should also supply identical bundles to all the parties. There is no explicit provision in relation to costs of that production but presumably it would be acceptable to charge a reasonable fee for that production as is current practice. The Practice Direction, however, drives home the point that the Claimant must ensure that everyone in front of the Court is working from the same bundle.

In relation to trial bundles reference should also be made to the Practice Directions to the specialist proceedings under Part 49 and the various Court guides which at the time of writing or in the course of preparation including the Commercial Court Guide and the Guides for the Chancery and Queen's Bench Division of the High Court. In addition the Court of Appeal Practice Direction has its own provisions relating to bundles for hearing (Section 7 of the Practice Direction to RSC Order 59).

Settlement or discontinuance after the trial date is fixed

The Practice Direction to Part 39 (Paragraph 4) reminds parties as specifically provided in Part 27, 28 and 29 that if settlement is reached the Court should be notified immediately and if a date has been fixed for trial the listing officer should specifically be notified upon settlement or discontinuance of proceedings.

Representation at trial of companies or other corporation

Rule 39.6 provides specifically for the identity of a representative at trial of companies or other corporations. As dealt with previously a company or other corporation can act as a litigant in person in both the High Court and County Court. Certain other parts of the Rules detail who can sign Court documents on behalf of a company or other corporation including the Statement of Truth or the Statement of Case. In that latter example the person signing has to hold a senior position in the company or other corporation as defined in, for example, Paragraph 3.5, Practice Direction to Part 22. Rule 39.6 stipulates that a company or other corporation may be represented at trial simply by an employee. That employee, however, must have been formally authorised to represent the company or corporation. At the trial the representative must provide a written statement which details—

- The full name of the company or corporation as stated in its certificate or registration.
- The registered number of the company or corporation.

- The position or office in the company or corporation held by the employee.
- The date on and manner in which the representative was authorised to act for the company or corporation (Paragraph 5.2, Practice Direction to Part 39). The authority to act could be given by an appropriate officer of the company or by the board itself. Whichever it is the party must make clear the derivation of the authority.

The entitlement of an employee to represent a company or other corporation is subject to the Courts discretion and requires the positive permission of the Court (Rule 39.6 (b)).

The corollary to Rule 39.6 is that a company or other corporation cannot be represented by anyone other than an employee or an authorised litigator with right of audience or, in the small claims track only, a lay representative. This would appear to overturn the decision in *Kinnell v Harding Wace* [1918] 1 KB 405.

CHAPTER 27
PART 40—JUDGMENTS AND ORDERS

Introduction

Part 40 is one of the sweep-up provisions of the CPR which deals with the general subject of judgments and orders, their—

- form;
- drawing up;
- service; and
- effect.

Under the old Rules, RSC Order 42 and CCR Order 22 made like provisions for the High Court and County Court respectively. Practice differed between the two Courts. It also differed between the Divisions of the High Court—Queen's Bench and Chancery.

The CPR sets out a generally uniform system in relation to the aspects of judgments and orders set out above. The general picture is—

- Judgments or orders will generally be drawn up by the Court unless it is a consent order or arrangements are made with the Court that a party will draw it up.
- Unless provided otherwise, generally a judgment does not need to be served and neither does an order made at trial. Any other order must be served.
- The Court will usually effect service unless arrangements are made with the Court to the contrary. The parties may agree the terms of a judgment or an order. In certain cases a Court officer may seal the agreed judgment or order as an administrative act but otherwise the sealing requires a judicial act upon application.
- A judgment or order takes effect on the day that it is given or made.
- Money judgments must be discharged within 14 days but interest runs from the day that judgment is given.

At the time of writing there are two Court guides, the Commercial Court Guide and the Chancery Guide. The Queen's Bench Guide is in prospect. Readers should be aware that these Guides may make special provisions in relation to the courts to which they relate. In addition there may be practice directions that relate specifically to such courts, for instance, Chancery Division Practice Direction No 8 deals with drafting orders and consent orders.

Further, the practice directions to Part 40 make special provisions in relation to certain types of orders such as accounts and inquiries and structured settlement.

In addition to Part 40, references to judgments and orders are scattered throughout the other Parts and practice directions. The main ones include—

- Part 3—The Court's case management powers
- Part 4—Forms
- Part 5—Court documents
- Part 6—Service of documents
- Part 12—Default judgment
- Part 13—Setting aside a default judgment
- Part 14—Admissions
- Part 21—Children and patients
- Part 23—General rules about applications for Court orders
- Part 24—Summary judgment
- Part 25—Interim remedies
- Part 26—Case management
- Part 27—Small Claims Track
- Part 28—Fast Track
- Part 29—Multi Track
- Part 36—Offers to settle and payments into Court
- Part 38—Discontinuance
- Part 42—Change of solicitor
- Part 44—General rules about costs
- Part 45—Fixed costs
- Part 49—Specialist proceedings
- RSC Order 44 (Procceedings under Judgments and Orders: Chancery Division, which applies also in the county court (Section 2, Practice Direction to Part 40)
- The enforcement provisions of the RSC and CCR

Because of this scattering amongst the Rules of other provisions, Rule 40.1 provides that Part 40 is subject to any other Rules that make a different provision in relation to judgments and orders.

The Rules

Rule 40.2 prescribes that generally a judgment or order must—

- state the name and judicial title of the person who made it;
- bear the date on which it was given or made; and
- be sealed by the Court.

The sealing, however, does not affect when the judgment or order has effect. Under Rule 40.7 the judgment or order has effect on the day that it is made unless the Court specifies some other day or it is a judgment against a State. Until, however, a judgment is drawn up and sealed by the Court, it cannot be enforced and money cannot be taken out of Court. On the other hand, interest on the judgment begins to run on the date that judgment is given (Rule 40.8).

If judgment is reserved, the judge may provide copies of his judgment in advance to advocates. That judgment, however, does not have effect until is it formally delivered in Court.

For certain types of judgments and orders there are prescribed forms in the Practice Direction to Part 4. That Practice Direction consists of three tables. The first is for forms that apply in both the High Court and County Court ("N" forms). The second contains High Court forms confusingly divided into four sub-categories. The third sets out the forms that have to be used in the County Court (again rather confusingly referred to as "N" forms).

There is a general blank form of order or judgment (N24). Otherwise there are forms of judgment and order for specific circumstances such as default judgment or judgment on admission (both CPR "N" forms), an order for time (a practice form in Table 2 of the Practice Direction) and an order for possession under CCR Order 24 (a County Court "N" form).

Part 4 and its practice direction are slightly confusing as to whether or not the prescribed forms have to be used. Rule 4(1) says that the forms "shall" be used but the Practice Direction on occasion says that they "may" be used. It is suggested that insofar as possible the forms should be used but if circumstances dictate, the form may be used as the basis for, in this case, the judgment or order as long as any information or guidance which appears in the form under Part 4 is included in the judgment or order that is finally produced.

In addition to Part 4, regard must be had to Part 25 and its Practice Direction which prescribe what must be included in an order for an injunction. The practice direction sets out as annexes examples of both freezing injunctions and search orders.

Drawing up and filing of Judgments and Orders

Under Part 23 a draft order should accompany the application notice making the drawing and sealing of the order quicker and easier.

Rule 40.3 and the practice direction set out the general position that judgments and orders will be drawn up by the Court. This was the practice in the County Court and Chancery Division of the High Court but not in the Queen's Bench Division. Rule 40.3, however, carries on the previous practice that the Court may require or give permission to one of the parties to draw up the order (meaning preparing the form of order and arranging for it to be sealed by the Court). In appropriate circumstances the Court could dispense with the need to draw up the order (Rule 40.3(1)(c)). If the order is made by consent under Rule 40.6 (see below), the parties will draw up the order to be sealed by the Court.

If the Court does order or give permission to a party to draw up an order then it must be filed with the Court within seven days of that order or permission (Rule 40.3(3)(a)). If that party does not do so then any other party may immediately draw up the order and file it (Rule 40.3(3)(b)). Under the old Rules, a party that did not have "carriage" of the order required permission to draw up the order. This restriction no longer applies and no permission is required. This might lead to some confusion and the Court will have to exercise some care that it is not sealing two or more different forms of order submitted by the parties.

Often the Court will direct that a statement of the terms of the order should be agreed by the parties (previously referred to as a "minute of order") and on occasions signed by the parties' advocates. If such a direction is made then the parties must file the agreed statement no later than seven days after the direction was made (Paragraph 1.4, Practice Direction to Part 40). An agreed statement should contain the full heading of the case since it may well be simply adopted by the Court as the order and sealed as such. The body of the order should be confined to setting out the decision of the Court and the directions required to give effect to it.

Where the Court is drawing up an order to be agreed by the parties the Court may direct—

- that a draft of the order is endorsed by each of the parties signifying their agreement to it and returned to the Court before the order is sealed; or
- that the parties attend before the Court to signify their agreement to the draft order (Paragraph 1.5, Practice Direction to Part 40).

The Practice Direction to Part 40 prescribes certain matters that should be included in the order.

- Paragraph 5 prescribes the contents where damages include payments made by a defendant for recoverable benefits under the Social Security (Recovery of Benefits) Act 1997.
- Paragraph 6 sets out what should be included in a final judgment where an interim payment has already been made which is either more or less than the total amount awarded in the judgment.
- A party may require the Court to include in any judgment the place at and manner in which the claim form has been served. Such a statement may be important for enforcement purposes, particularly abroad. If the judge allows a statement to be included (although it would be rarely refused) then Paragraph 7 of the Practice Direction provides that the statement would be included in a preamble to the judgment.
- The Court is empowered to give judgment for a sum of money in a foreign currency whether the claim is in tort or in contract. Such foreign currency presumably now includes the Euro. Paragraph 10 of the Practice Direction provides the form of order—

  It is ordered that the defendant pay the claimant (state the sum in the foreign currency) or the Sterling equivalent at the time of payment.
- If the judgment or order requires the preparation and/or execution of a deed or document the order must include detail of who will prepare and/or approve the document (Paragraph 2.1, Practice Direction to Part 40).
- If the order requires an act to be done the order should state the time by which it must be done and if appropriate the consequence of not doing it e.g. an "unless" order (Paragraph 8.1, 8.2, Practice direction to Part 40).
- If the judgment is payable by instalments it should set out: the total; the amount of each instalment; the date payment falls due, and to whom it should be paid.

The Practice Direction draws attention to the costs rules and in particular that if an order makes no mention of costs then none are payable under Rule 43.5(5). If the Court does make an order for costs and summarily assesses them then the order will provide a single figure which must then be paid within 14 days.

Consent Orders

Rule 40.6 divides consent orders into two types. There are those that may be made simply by a Court officer as an administrative act and those that must be made by a judge as a judicial act. Rule 40.6(3) sets out the types of order that may be entered in the Court records and sealed by a Court officer. The Court officer may not enter and seal any order, however, if a party is a litigant in person or if the approval of the Court is required by the CPR or any statute. An example of such a restriction would be when the claimant is a child or patient and a structured settlement is proposed—in that event there must be a hearing under Rule 21.10 and the Practice Direction to Part 40.

Subject to these limitations, the Court officer may take the administrative step of entering and sealing a judgment or order for—

- the payment of an amount of money (whether then quantified or to be decided subsequently by the Court); or
- the delivery up of goods.

In addition the officer can enter and seal an order for—

- the dismissal of proceedings in whole or in part;
- the stay of proceedings on agreed terms which dispose of the proceedings entirely (see the reference to Tomlin Orders below);
- the stay of enforcement of a judgment;
- setting aside a default judgment which has not been satisfied;
- the payment out of money which has been paid into Court;
- the discharge from liability of any party; and
- the payment, assessment or waiver of cost.

In these circumstances, where the officer does enter and seal the order it will be made on the date of entry and seal for all other purposes. A consent order made by a Court officer will not bear the name and judicial title of the person who makes it (Rule 40.2(1)(c)).

Responsibility for ensuring that the proposed order is one that may be made by a Court officer lies primarily with the officer himself. He may, however, refer the matter to a judge under Rule 3.2.

If the Court officer exceeded his powers under Rule 40.6 in part then at least that part of the order would be invalid. Similarly, if one of the parties is a litigant in person or approval of the Court is required, the whole of the order would be invalid.

If a form of proposed consent order falls outside those that may be entered and sealed by a Court officer, application must be made in accordance with Part 23 for a judgment or order in the agreed terms. The application notice should be accompanied by the draft judgment or order to be entered or sealed. The Court will often use that draft as the judgment or order that will be sealed by the Court. Accordingly the draft should, as a matter of practice, comply with Rule 40.6(7) and Paragraph 3.4 of the Practice Direction. It should have on it the words "by consent" and should be signed by the legal representative acting for each of the parties to whom the order relates or by a party when he is acting as a litigant in person. The practice direction refers to the consent judgment or order being signed by solicitors or counsel whilst the Rule refers to "legal representative" which is a defined term under Rule 2.3(1) and includes a solicitor's employee or other authorised litigator instructed to act for a party in relation to a claim. The Rule should prevail.

In accordance with Paragraph 3(3) an application for a consent judgment or order will usually be dealt with by the Court without the necessity for the serving of the application notice. Similarly a hearing will usually not be required (Rule 23.8(a)).

Paragraphs 10.1–10.5 of the Practice Direction to Part 23 make other provisions in relation to consent judgments or orders—

- Where all the parties affected by an order have written to the Court consenting to the making of the order, a draft of which has been filed with the Court, the Court will treat the draft as having been signed by all those parties.
- The parties to an application for a consent order must ensure that they provide the Court with any material it needs in order to be satisfied that it is appropriate to make the order. For these purposes a letter will generally be acceptable.
- Where a judgment or order has been agreed in respect of an application or claim where a hearing date has been fixed, the parties are obliged to inform the Court immediately that agreement is reached.
- The form of consent order that is submitted to the Court must comply with Rule 40.2. Thus space should be left for the insertion of the name and judicial title of the person making the judgment or order and for the date on which it is given or made.
- Consent orders are encouraged for the case management directions to be given upon allocation under Part 26 or on a case management conference for Parts 27 (Small Claims Track), 28 (Fast Track) and 29 (Multi Track). The Practice Directions to each of those Parts set out standard directions that parties should try and agree at the time of submitting the allocation questionnaire.
- If the parties agree to vary the directions subsequently, they can do so by written agreement under Rule 2.11 or (in relation to disclosure) under Rule 31.5, 31.10(8) or 31.13. No order is required and the written agreement does not have to be filed with the Court. There are, as previously dealt with (page ___), certain parts of the case management directions that may not be altered by the parties (see Rule 28.4 and 29.5). To alter the directions in relation to the matters listed in those Rules, a consent order is required. The application for the order must be supported by an agreed statement of the reasons why the variation is sought (see

Paragraphs 4.5(2), Practice Direction to Part 28 and 6.5(2), Practice Direction to Part 29).

The fee payable on an application by consent is £25 in both the High Court and county Court (Supreme Court Fees Order 1999 and the County Court Fees Order 1999).

In relation to an agreed order the parties should also agree the order that needs to be made in relation to costs. As mentioned above, under Rule 43.5(5) if nothing is said in relation to costs then none are payable under that order. Such agreement in relation to costs should also deal with agreement as to their quantification under the powers of the Court to make a summary assessment (Rule 44.7(a) and Paragraphs 4.3–4.10, Practice Direction to Part 44). If agreement cannot be reached in relation to the quantification of the costs then the parties will have to attend to argue the point.

Even if an order is submitted as agreed between the parties, the Court is not obliged to make the order as asked. Indeed under its obligation to actively mange cases under Rule 1.4, the Court is required to give positive thought to whether the agreed order is appropriate bearing in mind all of the obligations of the Court under the CPR, particularly the overriding objective. For instance, the parties may agree that the case management conference or some subsequent hearing such as a pre-trial review should be adjourned. The Court will usually be loathe to agree to such an adjournment without some good reasons.

In similar fashion the parties may agree that costs should be "in the case" (i.e. determined at the end of the case and in accordance with its outcome) but with a view to making a summary assessment of those costs the Court may consider it appropriate to make an order against one of the parties and then to summarily assess those costs in accordance with Part 44 and its Practice Direction. It remains to be seen how far the Courts press summary assessment with this effect.

Often in dealing with an application before the Court the applicant will ask the Court to make a consent order relying on a letter of consent from the respondent or his solicitors or a draft statement of agreed terms of order signed by the respondent's solicitors. No difficulty arises if the remedy sought by the applicant falls wholly within the remedy or remedies claimed in the application notice. If, however, the order sought goes outside the remedy or remedies mentioned in the application notice or, for that matter, the claim form, or if undertakings are to be given by the respondent, practice varies from court to court. The Chancery Guide under the Chancery Practice Direction Number 8 suggests the adoption of a uniform procedure in the Chancery Division and perhaps a procedure to be adopted universally. It is suggested that, subject to the usual discretion of the Court, no order will normally be made in those circumstances unless there is a consent of the respondent—

- Where solicitors are on the record a written consent signed by those solicitors on their headed notepaper.
- Where solicitors are acting but "not on the record" (presumably, i.e. not "acting" for the purposes of the Rules) a written consent signed by those solicitors on their headed notepaper as long as there is a certificate from

them that they have fully explained to the respondent the effect of the order and that the respondent appeared to understand it.

- A written consent signed by a respondent acting in person but only if the Court is satisfied that the respondent understands the effect of the order (usually meaning that there is a full letter explaining it to him in simple language to which he responds).
- The respondent's undertaking will only be accepted if—
    - the letter or other document offering the undertaking is signed by the respondent personally;
    - solicitors certify on their headed notepaper that the signature is the signature of the respondent; and
    - the solicitors certify that there has been a full explanation to the respondent of the consequences of giving the undertaking and that the respondent appeared to understand the explanation.

Warning: The Court may consider any matter relating to case management on any occasion when the case is in front of the Court. If a hearing takes place upon an application the order for which has been agreed between the parties the Court could consider other matters of case management. Those attending should be prepared for that possibility.

Tomlin Order

The Tomlin Order will undoubtedly be as popular under the new Rules as it has grown to be under the old rules. Indeed, to a certain extent the Tomlin Order has been recognised within the new Rules when a settlement is achieved under Part 36. Under Rule 36.15, if a Part 36 offer relating to the whole of the claim is accepted, the claim is stayed upon the terms of the offer and either party may apply to enforce those terms without the need for a new claim (Rule 36.15(2)).

The Rules do not otherwise make specific provision for Tomlin Orders. Accordingly the wording of such an order will follow that of previous practice. Chancery Division Practice Direction Number 8 in the Chancery Guide suggests short wording for a Tomlin Order—

> **and the claimant and the defendant having agreed to the terms set forth in the schedule hereto, it is ordered that all further proceedings in this claim be stayed, except for the purpose of carrying such terms into effect. Liberty to apply as to carrying such terms into effect.**

It has become increasingly popular to maintain a degree of secrecy about the agreement by not scheduling the terms of the agreement but by referring to it in a separate document retained by the parties. This keeps the agreement from public access to Court records under Rule 5.4.

If secrecy is desired, t is suggested that the above short version might be changed to—

> **and the claimant and the defendant having agreed to terms of settlement set forth in the document headed ______________**

and signed by the parties, the original of which is retained by ____________________ and a copy of which is retained by ____________________, it is ordered that all further proceedings in this claim should be stayed except for the purpose of carrying such terms into effect. Liberty to apply as to carrying such terms into effect.

Service

Under Rule 40.4 orders other than those made at trial must be served on the applicant and the respondent and any other person that the Court directs. Such other person is likely to be someone who is affected by the order in some fashion. Indeed, under Rule 40.9 such a person is entitled to apply to the Court to have an order set aside or varied. If an application has been made without service of a copy of the application notice, the order must be served whether or not the application has been granted or dismissed. The order must contain a statement of the right to make an application to set it aside or vary it. The order must be accompanied by a copy of the application notice and any evidence in support (Rule 23.9).

Generally judgments do not have to be served, subject to the Court making an order to the contrary. RSC Order 44 Rule 2 deals specifically with the service of judgments in claims for—

- the administration of the estate of a deceased person;
- the execution of a trust; and
- the sale of any property.

Under Rule 6.3 the Court will serve the order (or judgment if appropriate) unless the Court provides to the contrary either by order or permission. If service is to be effected by the Court then under Rule 40.4(1) sufficient copies must be provided to the Court for service (including one for the Court file). Rule 40.4(1)(b) suggests that the order once sealed must be served on each party to the proceedings. Service of an order following an application has to be served only on the applicant and the respondent to the application (Rule 40.4(2)(a)).

Service is not a prerequisite to an order taking effect. Under Rule 40.7 the judgment or order takes effect from the day when it is given or made. The Court may specify a later date but not an earlier date. In similar fashion, interest on the judgment under Section 17 of the Judgments Act 1838 or Section 74 of the County Courts Act 1984 generally runs from the date that the judgment is given (Rule 40.8).

There remains a differentiation between the High Court and the County Court in relation to interest on judgments. In the High Court, the Judgments Act 1838 provides that interest is payable on all judgments. In the County Court, however, the position is regulated by Section 74 of the County Courts Act 1984 and the County Courts (Interest on Judgment Debts) Order 1991 (as amended). Under the Order, interest is payable at the judgment rate (currently 8%) on judgments for £5,000 or more. If judgment provides for payment by instalments, interest runs on instalments as they fall due (Article 3).

Rule 40.8(2) provides that interest can be determined to run from a date before the date that judgment is given. Whilst it is normal to claim interest in the High Court under Section 35A of the Supreme Court Act 1981 and in the County Court under Section 69 of the County Courts Act 1984, a party may claim interest under a contractual provision which is more advantageous.

The power of the Court to determine that interest runs on the judgment from a date prior to the date that judgment is given is unlikely to have significant effect in relation to ordinary claims in which interest forms part of the claim as above, particularly bearing in mind the limitations on interest in the County Court under the 1991 Order. Importantly, however, interest on any costs order or certificate can be determined by the Court to run from a date prior to the giving of that order or certificate.

Just as service is not a prerequisite to the taking of effect of the judgment or order, similarly payment of an amount of money under the judgment or order is required generally to be made within 14 days of the date of the judgment or order under Rule 40.11 save for some judgments entered under Parts 12 (default) or 14 (on admission).

Judgment on Claim and Counterclaim

Rule 40.13 provides what may happen when judgment is given for specified amounts in favour of both the claimant on the claim and the "defendant" on the counterclaim. The general provision is that the Court will order that the balance payable taking into account the claim and counterclaim should be paid from one party to the other. The Court may make separate orders as to costs under Rule 40.13(3) although it is suggested that in practice the Court may make an order under Rule 44.3(6)(a) under which a proportion of one party's costs is paid by the other.

Correction of errors in Judgments or Orders

Under Rule 40.12, the Court has the power to correct accidental slips and omissions. This power to amend is, however, limited in its scope and does not extend, for instance, to additional relief pleaded but singly forgotten by the Court and the parties. The Court does, however, have an inherent power to vary orders to make the meaning and intention of the Court clear (Paragraph 4.5, Practice Direction to Part 40).

Registration of Judgments

The registration of judgments is regulated by the Registration of County Court Judgments Regulations 1985. High Court judgments are not subject to registration, nor are Tomlin Orders (see above). In the county court the court must send to the keeper of the register details of every money judgment with certain exceptions. This would include some orders for costs on summary assessment. The regulations have, however, been amended by the Register of County Court Judgments (Amendment) Regulations 1999 specifically excluding summary costs orders. The amendments otherwise make some consequential changes flowing from the CPR.

Enforcement

The provisions relating to enforcement of judgments and orders are contained in the Schedules to the CPR. Detailed consideration is outside the scope of this work. Generally there have been no alterations of substance. The whole of the enforcement process is under review. It is likely that changes will be effected in 2001.

Although committal for contempt is also included in the Scheduled Rules (RSC Order 52), the Practice Direction to Part 40 (Paragraphs 9.1–9.4) reminds parties that to enforce an order by contempt proceedings, the order must be endorsed with a "penal notice".

CHAPTER 28
PART 38—DISCONTINUANCE

As originally conceived in the Brown Book, a party was relatively free to discontinue a claim or part of a claim at any stage of the proceedings. Lord Woolf was keen to encourage and facilitate parties abandoning hopeless claims or parts of claims at as early a stage as possible. During the process of consultation and consideration by the Committee, concerns were expressed that this could lead to abuse by parties by which claims may be discontinued at a late stage to be followed by fresh proceedings either within or outside the jurisdiction.

Accordingly, in its final product, Part 38 gives a measure of control to the Court over a party wishing to discontinue all or part of a claim.

Part 38 has equal application to Part 20 (counterclaim and other third party claims) following from the provisions of Rule 20.3 It has no application, however, to other statements of case such as a defence. A defendant can admit the truth of the whole or any part of another party's case at any stage of the proceedings and the claimant can make an application for judgment based on that admission (see Rules 14.1 and 14.3).

Part 38 has no application where the claimant abandons one of more than one remedy and continues in relation to the remaining remedy (Rule 38.1(2)). In those circumstances the party abandoning such a remedy should seek to amend the claim form and/or particulars of claim in accordance with Part 17.

Withdrawal and discontinuance under the RSC were dealt with in Order 21. In the CCR it was dealt with in Order 18. The latter gave more scope for a claimant to discontinue a claim than the RSC. Under the RSC the Court's leave to discontinue was necessary unless the action or a particular claim within it was discontinued no later than 14 days after service of the defence. RSC Order 21 also made provision for the withdrawal of the defence or part of it but this forms no part of Part 38 as above.

The general order of events under Part 38 is as follows—

- A party may discontinue all or part of a claim at any time without permission (Rule 38.2(1)) save where permission is required because there is an undertaking, injunction or interim payment (Rule 38.2(2)).
- The discontinuing party is liable for the costs of the other party although the Court may make an alternative order (Rule 38.6).
- The defendant may apply for the discontinuance to be set aside up to 28 days after the notice of discontinuance is served upon him (Rule 38.4);

- The claimant needs permission to issue new proceedings based on the same or similar facts if he discontinues after the defence has been served (Rule 38.7).
- Where only part of a claim has been discontinued, the claimant is liable for the costs relating to that part which will usually be assessed at the conclusion of the remainder of proceedings. If, however, they are assessed and payable immediately, the remainder of the proceedings may be stayed if the assessed costs are not paid (Rules 38.6(2) and 38.8).

The preliminary step for a claimant seeking to discontinue where the claimant has received an interim payment is to seek and secure the consent in writing of the defendant who made the interim payment.

If that consent is not forthcoming, the claimant will require the Court's permission to discontinue. If there is more than one claimant, the claimant seeking to discontinue should seek the consent in writing of the other claimants. Again, if this is not forthcoming, the claimant seeking to discontinue will require the permission of the Court to do so (Rule 38.2(2)).

There is no like provision where there is more than one defendant. The claimant is quite free to discontinue against one or more of the defendants without the Court's permission (Rule 38.2(3)).

The only other circumstance in which permission from the Court is required before discontinuance can be effected is if there has been an interim injunction or any party has given an undertaking to the Court (Rule 38.2(2)(a)).

In order to seek the Court's permission, an application will have to be made in accordance with Part 23. Accordingly, under Rule 23.6, the application notice must state what order the applicant is seeking and briefly why the applicant is seeking the order. The rationale behind seeking the Court's permission is so that the Court can give appropriate directions. In relation to an injunction or an undertaking the Court may wish to consider the discharge of the injunction or the undertaking and the question of damages arising from the restrictions following from the injunction or undertaking. In relation to an interim payment, the Court will wish to consider whether it should be repaid in part or whole under Rule 25.8(2) and whether interest should be paid in accordance with Rule 25.8(5).

Finally, where there is more than one claimant the Court will have to consider whether the claimant wishing to discontinue is a necessary party to the claim. If he is then it may be appropriate to strike him out as a claimant and add him as a defendant on appropriate terms.

Unless the Court orders otherwise, the application for permission would have to be made on notice to each respondent to the application (Rule 23.4(1)). Evidence would not necessarily be required to support such an application but if there is written evidence in support then it should be served with the application notice (Rule 23.7(3)). Service must be effected at least three days before the Court is to deal with the application (Rule 23.7(1)(b)).

Where application is made for the Court's permission and it is given, the Court will give appropriate directions.

Subject to those directions, or if permission was not necessary, the claimant may proceed to discontinue the claim or part of a claim by filing a notice of discontinuance (Form N279). It is not obligatory to use the form but would be usual. If the form is not used then it must be headed with the Court in which it is proceeding, the names of the parties and their status. In addition, in the body of the notice the claimant must state that he has served notices on every other party to the proceedings. Where there is more than one defendant, he must also identify against which defendants the claim is discontinued (Rule 38.3(4)).

Upon giving permission, the Court will give direction as to from when the discontinuance is effective. If permission is not necessary, discontinuance is effective from the date of service (Rule 38.5(1)) and if discontinuance relates to the whole of the claim against a particular defendant, then the proceedings are brought to an end as against him on that date of service (Rule 38.5(2)).

This does not affect the defendant's entitlement to deal with any question as to costs. In the first instance, however, he may wish to seek to set aside the notice of discontinuance in accordance with Rule 38.4(1). If so, he must make an application within 28 days after service of the notice for discontinuance. He can make such application whether or not he has consented to the discontinuance or the Court has given permission. He may wish to make such an application if there are good reasons why the matter should proceed to trial and be dealt with finally by the Court. Any such application would have to be made in accordance with Part 23 with its requirements as to what should be contained in the application notice and its service together with any evidence in support (see page 289).

The claimant who discontinues is generally liable for the costs of the defendant against whom he discontinues up to the time that the notice of discontinuance takes effect. The Court may, however, order otherwise if circumstances make it appropriate.

In accordance with Rule 44.12(d), a costs order will be deemed to have been made on the standard basis on the date that the discontinuance takes effect. It is that date which starts the period for the commencement of detailed assessment proceedings under Part 47. Accordingly those proceedings must be commenced within three months of the date that the discontinuance takes effect (Rule 47.7). If the defendant has made an application to set the notice of discontinuance aside, which application has been dismissed, the three month period under Part 47 starts from the date of the dismissal of the application (Rule 47.7). If points of dispute in the assessment are served and the matter has to go forward to a hearing, the notice of discontinuance is one of those documents that must be filed with the Court.

If the claimant discontinues only in relation to part of a claim then he will be liable for the costs relating only to that part of the proceedings which he is discontinuing (Rule 38.6(2)(a)). Generally those costs should not be assessed until the conclusion of the remainder of the proceedings, although the Court does have a discretion to order otherwise. An alternative would be for the Court to make an order under Rule 44.3(8) that there should be some form of payment on account of the costs. This will very much depend on how much of the whole claim has been discontinued and the effect that that is likely to have on the ultimate liability for costs. If the Court does make an order that the assessment of costs should not wait until the conclusion of the proceedings, it could summarily assess those costs or pass them to be assessed by detailed costs assessment.

Whatever method of assessment is chosen when those costs become payable and the claimant fails to pay them within 21 days of the date on which the parties agreed the sum payable by the claimant or the date on which the Court ordered that the costs be paid, the Court may stay the remainder of the proceedings until those costs are paid (Rule 38.8).

CHAPTER 29
PARTS 43-48—COSTS

Introduction

The general costs rules of the CPR are Parts 43, 44, 45, 46, 47 and 48.

- Part 43 provides a general introduction and definitions. The Practice Direction to it, however, provides some important detail particularly in relation to estimates of costs.
- Part 44 forms the core of the costs rules for the principles upon which orders for costs are made and the quantification of costs so ordered.
- Part 45 provides the rules in relation to fixed costs.
- Part 46 deals with fast track trial costs.
- Part 47 sets out the procedure for the detailed costs assessment formerly known as taxation.
- Part 48 provides for particular types of costs including those between solicitors and clients and litigants in person.

Reference shall also be made to Part 27 which regulates costs on the Small Claims Track.

The Interim and Final Report

In the chapter on costs in the Interim Report, Lord Woolf said that—

> **The problem of costs is the most serious problem besetting our litigation system.**

Lord Woolf set about analysing the problems with the system and some of the cures. This writer believes that the result of the reforms in relation to costs, which include some suggestions of Lord Woolf but also other important changes, are likely to have a very dramatic effect upon the conduct of litigation in the future, particularly in lower value claims. Even in higher value claims the provision of estimates under the new rules and summary assessment are likely to have a substantial effect upon the manner in which costs are incurred during the course of litigation.

The changes to the rules relating to costs have been enjoined in a general campaign to reduce costs of litigation or at least to make them more proportionate and predictable. At the time of writing, further changes are proposed to the Rules in order to regulate the relationship between solicitor and client as far as costs are concerned and to bring to an end the indemnity principle (see below). In addition, at the time of writing the Access to Justice

Bill is being considered by Parliament. The provisions of this Bill and the eventual statute are likely to have a dramatic effect upon the costs regime. Legal Aid will be reduced. It is intended that the gap thereby created will be filled by conditional fee agreements and appropriate insurance schemes to protect the litigant in relation to their own costs and any adverse costs.

The flavour of changes has been stated by the Lord Chancellor reflecting some of the views of Lord Woolf—

> **Civil justice today is too expensive and too exclusive. The very rich and the very poor have access but middle income Britain is left out in the cold—and middle income Britain is the overwhelming majority of people in this country. They cannot litigate because the lawyer's fees are so high and because they cannot afford the risk of losing and having to pay their opponent's lawyer's fees as well.**
>
> **Not only is civil justice far too expensive for people to afford because of the scale of the costs: they are deterred from pursuing good cases because they cannot make any rational assessment of how much it will cost them in the end. These and the level of costs are the biggest bars to access to justice.**
>
> **Lord Irvine of Lairg, October 1997**

Lord Woolf in his Final Report set out three particular significant problems with the costs regime existing prior to 26 April 1999—

- Litigation is so expensive that the majority of the public cannot afford it unless they receive financial assistance.
- The costs incurred in the course of litigation are out of proportion to the issues involved.
- The costs are uncertain in amount so that the parties have difficulty in predicting what their ultimate liability might be if the action is lost.

Lord Woolf recommended as follows—

- Orders for costs need to reflect more precisely the obligations the new Rules place on the parties.
- The Court should have power to deal with the question of costs even where all other issues have been resolved without litigation.
- Where one of the parties is unable to afford a particular procedure, the Court, if it decides that that procedure is to be followed, should be entitled to make its order conditional upon the other side meeting the difference in the cost of the weaker party, whatever the outcome.
- The Court should be able to order payment of interim costs in cases where the opponent has substantially greater resources where there is a reasonable likelihood that the weaker party will be entitled to costs at the end of the case.
- Benchmark costs should be established by the Court for the assistance of user groups for multi track proceedings with a limited and fairly constant procedure.
- The new standard basis of taxation should be based on the wording of the Solicitors (Non-Contentious Business) Remuneration Order 1994: that

the amount allowed should be what is "reasonable to both parties to the taxation". The indemnity basis should remain as it is.

- There should be a review of the Rules on the costs recoverable by a litigant in person with a view to simplification.

Lord Woolf identified within these recommendations that the changes would—

- Reduce the scale of costs by controlling what is required of the parties in the conduct of proceedings.
- Make the amount of costs more predictable.
- Make costs more proportionate to the nature of the dispute.
- Make the Court's powers to make orders as to costs a more effective incentive for responsible behaviour and a more compelling deterrent against unreasonable behaviour.
- Provide litigants with more information as to costs so that they can exercise greater control over the expenses incurred by their lawyers on their behalf.

In prospect these goals have partly been achieved by the recommendations of Lord Woolf, but also by further provisions which have found their way into the new Rules during the course of drafting and finalisation.

Outside the costs rules themselves, the extension of the small claims track to claims of £5,000 or less and the fixed costs regime of the fast track are intended to reduce the level of costs required to bring a matter to trial. A simplified procedure for lower value multi track claims is intended to achieve the same objective.

The exercise by the Court of the overriding objective is also intended to reduce the cost of litigating. In particular the regulation by the Court of procedure under its obligations to actively manage cases (Rule 1.4) and the overriding principle of proportionality under Rule 1.1(2) are intended to drive down the costs that have to be incurred in the resolution of the dispute.

Within the costs rules themselves the application of proportionality and the examination of the conduct of parties is also intended to serve the purpose of reducing the level of costs, particularly in lower value claims. The costs rules, however, also serve a further purpose in imposing sanctions on parties in the event that the Court concludes that they have acted unreasonably or have failed to comply with a Court orders, pre-action protocols, the Rules or the Practice Directions. No doubt the stick is somewhat more prominent in the Rules than the carrot.

The Rules

Scope of costs Rules and definitions

Part 43 and its Practice Direction provide definitions of certain phrases and words used during the course of the costs rules. Practitioners will become familiar with the new terminology.

- "Taxation" goes and is replaced by either "summary assessment" or "detailed assessment";

- "Taxing Masters" become "Costs Judges"; and
- "Supreme Court Taxing Office" becomes "Supreme Court Costs Office".

Other definitions will arise in the examination of the remaining Rules.

The Practice Direction to Part 43 largely deals with the form of the bill of costs to which reference is made below at page 373, VAT on bills of costs and estimates of costs.

Estimates of costs

Section 4 of the Practice Direction to Part 43 covers the provision of estimates of costs. This section was included relatively late in the day in the preparation of the Rules and emanates from an issues paper that was discussed at the Civil Procedure Rule Committee. In its suggestions the paper went a good deal further than the resulting Section 4 within the Practice Direction. The suggested regime included not only the provision of estimates for the purpose of the Court and other parties but also as between the solicitor and client. It was intended that consultation would take place prior to the new Rules coming into effect on 26 April 1999 on all of the suggested aspects. This did not happen. For this reason Section 4 as currently written is limited to the provision of estimates of costs to the Court and the other parties. At the time of writing a consultation paper has been issued, "Controlling Costs" CP4/99, which makes the following recommendations—

- In all cases—
    - solicitors will be required to provide evidence to the Court (at allocation stage) that they have informed the client of the basis on which they propose to charge and, where relevant, their hourly rate; and
    - solicitors will be required to provide an inclusive charging basis, thereby abolishing the uplift for care and conduct element claimed in the bill of costs.
- Additionally, in fast track cases—
    - solicitors will be required to file a final estimate of costs at the listing stage, which will set the maximum recoverable costs both for between the parties costs and solicitor and own client costs.
- The paper also addresses the question of whether the indemnity principle for costs should be retained (see below).

The period for consultation on this paper is extremely short and it is likely that there will be early changes to the Rules covering at least some of the items included in the consultation paper.

In the meantime Section 4 of the Practice Direction to Part 43 regulates the provision of estimates to the Court and to the other parties.

The provision of estimates under Section 4 is for recoverable costs and not those as between solicitor and client although it seems likely that parties will use the costs payable by the party to their solicitor as the basis for the estimate. It is suggested in any event that in providing that estimate, no account need be taken of the application of the principle of proportionality under Rule 44.5 since this is such an unknown quantity. Clearly comment may be made by the Court when viewing the estimate as to the likely recoverability bearing in mind the principle of proportionality, and recoverability of costs goes to the very heart of litigation but the solicitor is not obliged to introduce it into the estimate.

Under Paragraph 4.2 of the Practice Direction to Part 43 the estimate is divided into two parts—

(1) an estimate as to the costs incurred to the date of the provision of the estimate;

(2) an estimate of the costs that will be incurred in taking the matter to trial

Section 4 of the Practice Direction to Part 43 stipulates two specific occasions when the estimate must be provided, namely—

- upon the filing of the allocation questionnaire but only if the value of the claim is outside the financial scope of the small claims track; and
- upon the filing of the listing questionnaire.

In relation to Part 8 (alternative procedure) there is no allocation questionnaire because the claim is treated as allocated to the multi track (Rule 8.9(c)). Accordingly no allocation questionnaire is served by the Court. It is possible, however, that when giving directions the Court could direct any party to file an estimate of costs under Paragraph 4.3, Practice Direction to Part 43 (see below).

The allocation questionnaire has a specific section dealing with estimates of costs (Section I). The figures are inserted in the boxes provided. In addition, the Practice Direction at Paragraphs 4.4 and 4.5(1) indicates that a separate estimate of costs should be provided in the form of a statement of costs, an example of which is given in the schedule of costs forms—Form 1. (As to the completion of that form, see the section dealing with summary assessment below.) Two separate statements or two columns on the same statement need to be provided dealing with the costs incurred to date and the future costs.

On filing the estimate of costs with the allocation questionnaire, a party must serve a copy of the estimate of costs on every other party unless the Court otherwise directs (Paragraph 4.5(1), Practice Direction to Part 43). It should be remembered that there is no like obligation in relation to the completed allocation questionnaire itself which will be served by the Court after allocation under Rule 26.9.

The listing questionnaire as drafted at the time of writing does not contain space for the estimate of costs. Parties are still obliged, however, to draw up a statement of costs in the form mentioned above and file it with the listing questionnaire and at the same time serve a copy of it on every other party unless the Court otherwise directs (Paragraph 4.5(2), Practice Direction to Part 43). The estimate with the listing questionnaire has to be divided as above between costs already incurred and those to be incurred if the matter goes to trial (Paragraph 4.5(3), Practice Direction to Part 43).

In addition to these two specific occasions upon which estimates of costs have to be provided, the Court can require a party at any stage to file an estimate of costs and serve copies of it on all the other parties (Paragraph 4.3, Practice Direction to Part 43). Unless the Court orders otherwise, the estimate must be filed and served within 28 days of such an order (Paragraph 4.3). Where it is intended that this provision of an estimate should be used is where a step is proposed in the proceedings which may have substantial cost consequences. The Court may direct that comparative estimates of costs should be provided comparing the cost of taking that step and not taking it. The Court will then take into account those estimates as one of the factors in the exercise of its discretion. The example given in Paragraph 4.3 is of a direction for a split trial or for the trial of a preliminary issue.

How binding are the estimates?

The proposals in the consultation paper mentioned above include one to the effect that estimates provided in the fast track at the listing questionnaire stage will be binding upon the parties. Until the changes (if made) are effected following the consultation paper, the estimates are not in any way binding upon the parties. The provision of estimates in litigation is difficult because the process of litigation is often reactive and develops in ways which cannot necessarily be predicted. Notwithstanding these problems and whilst estimates are not binding, no doubt they will be used by a paying party in appropriate circumstances as a ground for challenging the eventual claim for costs or elements within it. Clearly estimates should be realistic but practitioners may be tempted to inflate them to ensure that they take into account every possible development that might occur. A party may eventually claim more than the estimates on proving that time has been expended and steps taken in support of the final claim. This will become more difficult the later the estimate is provided.

The Rules do not currently provide for the regulation of the relationship between the solicitor and client as to the provisions of costs estimates. The consultation paper proposes, however, some regulation of that relationship. At the time of writing there is little purpose in speculating on the outcome of that consultation. The Law Society, however, has already agreed changes to the solicitor's practice rules to regulate more closely the relationship between the solicitor and client in relation to costs. A new Rule 15 of the Solicitors Practice Rules 1990 has been agreed by the Council of the Law Society and will be effective from 3 September 1999 (Solicitors Practice (Costs Information and Client Care) Amendment Rule 1999). As a consequence a new costs information and client care code has been agreed (Solicitors Costs Information and Client Care Code 1999) which requires, amongst other matters, that—

- the solicitor should give the client the best information possible about the likely overall costs, including a breakdown between fees, VAT and disbursements;
- the solicitor should discuss with the client whether the likely outcome in a matter will justify the expense or risk involved including, if relevant, the risk of having to bear an opponent's costs; and
- the solicitor should keep the client properly informed about costs as the matter progresses.

The combination of the CPR and the new practice rules and code bring a dramatic change to the regulation of the relationship between the solicitor and client in relation to costs. Any further discussion of that subject is outside the scope of this work.

Part 44—General rules about costs

Part 44 of the CPR contains the most important core rules of the costs provisions relating to—

- the exercise of the Court's discretion when making an order for costs;
- the exercise of the discretion when quantifying those costs;
- the bases of assessment, namely standard and indemnity;
- the two procedures for assessment, namely summary assessment and detailed assessment; and
- costs provisions following "misconduct".

Costs in the Small Claims Track

There is an important provision in relation to costs outside the general rules for costs. Part 27 provides the rules in relation to claims which have been allocated to the small claims track (see Chapter 16 pages 173–186 for a full discussion of those provisions). As detailed there, the costs regime under Part 27 does not apply until allocation to the small claims track. Upon first allocation (and not re-allocation) the small claims track regime in relation to costs has retrospective effect and it applies to work done before as well as after allocation save to the extent (if any) that an order for costs in respect of that work was made before allocation (see Paragraph 5.1, Practice Direction to Part 44). Any costs that are payable under Part 27 will be subject to the general costs rules subject to anything to the contrary contained within Part 27.

It will be remembered that there are two particular provisions relating to costs in the small claims track for claims that might have been allocated to the fast track—

- If the parties agree to allocation to the small claims track for a claim which would normally be allocated to the fast track, the fast track costs regime applies to the costs of the claim save that the trial costs are in the discretion of the Court (Rule 27.14(5)).
- If the claim is one which would be allocated to the fast track but for the admission of part of the claim by the defendant which reduces the amount in dispute to a sum a claim for which would normally be allocated to the small claims track, the Court may, on entering judgment for the admitted part of the claim, allow costs in respect of the proceedings down to that date (Paragraph 5.1(3)(ii), Practice Direction to Part 44).

Costs following allocation and re-allocation

In accordance with Rule 44.11, Rule 27.15 and Paragraphs 6.1–6.3, Practice Direction to Part 44, the Rules in relation to costs that flow from the allocation to a particular track apply to the proceedings only so long as the claim remains within the track. Thus upon re-allocation the costs rules applying to the relevant track following re-allocation apply to the proceedings from the date of re-allocation. If the re-allocation is from the small claims track, the Court must decide upon re-allocation whether any party is to pay the costs to any other party down to the date of the order to re-allocate in accordance with Part 27 (Paragraph 6.2, Practice Direction to Part 44). If an order for costs is made then the Court should assess those costs in accordance with the procedure for summary assessment (Paragraph 6.3, Practice Direction to Part 44).

Solicitors duty to notify client of an adverse costs order—Rule 44.2

Rule 44.2 provides (somewhat out of place) that a solicitor is obliged to notify their client of an adverse order for costs within seven days of the order. There is no policing provision to this Rule. Policing provisions were stipulated in earlier drafts of the Rules but these have been abandoned. Initially it was intended that if the solicitor breached this Rule they would be personally liable for the adverse costs. This was considered likely to lead to satellite litigation. Accordingly the proposal was dropped. The next suggestion was that upon breach of the Rule the solicitor would be liable to indemnify the client for the adverse costs. This was also dropped upon consideration by the Committee. The result is that there is no policing provision.

The draft of Rule 44.2 preceded the introduction of the Rules in relation to summary assessment. In a manner those Rules have overridden the effect of Rule 44.2. In the event that a solicitor does not inform a client of an adverse order for costs within seven days, it is highly probable that they will have informed the client within 14 days because by combination of Rules 44.7 and 44.8, summary assessment will usually follow an adverse costs order during the course of proceedings and the amount assessed will have to be paid within 14 days of the order itself.

The lack of a policing provision is addressed in the Practice Direction—

1.1 For the purposes of rule 44.2 "client" includes a party for whom a solicitor is acting and any other person (for example an insurer or a trade union) who has instructed the solicitor to act or who is liable to pay his fees.

1.2 Where a solicitor notifies a client of an order under that rule, he must also explain why the order came to be made.

1.3 Although rule 44.2 does not specify any sanctions for breach of the rule the court may, either in the order for costs itself or in a subsequent order, require the solicitor to produce to the court evidence showing that he took reasonable steps to comply with the rule.

(Practice Direction to Part 44)

Matters to be taken into account when making an order for costs

The discretion of the Court in relation to costs derives from Section 51 of the Supreme Court Act 1981 (as substituted by Section 4 of the Courts & Legal Services Act 1990).

Costs in civil division of Court of Appeal and High Court

(1) Subject to the provisions of this or any other Act and to rules of court, the costs of and incidental to all proceedings in the civil division of the Court of Appeal and in the High Court, including the administration of estates and trusts, shall be in the discretion of the court, and the court shall have full power to determine by whom and to what extent the costs are to be paid.

(2) Nothing in subsection (1) shall alter the practice in any criminal cause or matter, or in bankruptcy.

(3) Provision may be made by rules of court for regulating any matters relating to the costs of proceedings in the civil division of the Court of Appeal or in the High Court, including the administration of estates and trusts.

This discretion was carried on into the Rules of the Supreme Court and by application into the County Court.

The discretion has been repeated within the CPR at Rule 44.3(1). On the face of it the Rule is somewhat more limiting than Section 51, repeating that the Court has a discretion as to—

- whether costs are payable by one party to another;
- the amount of those costs; and
- when they are paid.

No mention is made here of costs being payable by or to a non-party. The Court retains the power under Section 51 to make an order for costs against the non-party (see *Aiden Shipping Ltd v Interbulk Ltd* [1986] AC 967, [1986] 2 All ER 409). If the Court is contemplating making an order for costs against a non-party, Rule 48.2 sets out the considerations that the Court should have unless the Court is considering whether to make an order against the Legal Aid Board or a wasted costs order (see Rule 48.7) or against a respondent to a pre-action application (see Rule 48.1).

Costs follow the event

Although the Court has a general discretion as to costs, Rule 44.3(2) repeats the position under the old Rules that generally an unsuccessful party will be ordered to pay the costs of the successful party.

This provision was added to the Rules at a fairly late stage following further consultation on the draft Rules. Initially the question of success was simply one of the factors to be taken into account when the Court exercised its discretion as to the order for costs. The intention was that the discretion of the Court to take into account all the circumstances was to be emphasised as overriding the former rule that the successful party should recover their costs. Following consultation, the status of success was raised by the introduction of Rule 44.3(2). The Rule, however, should be seen in context. It specifically states at Rule 44.3(2)(b) that the Court can make a different order. Certainly the emphasis of the other considerations that the Court has to take into account has been heightened in comparison to the old rules. Under Rule 44.3(4) the

Court is obliged to take into account "all the circumstances". Some of those circumstances are then specified—

- the conduct of all the parties;
- whether a party has succeeded on part of his case, even if he has now been wholly successful; and
- any payment into Court or admissible offer to settle made by a party which is drawn to the Court's attention (whether or not made in accordance with Part 36).

Conduct

Rule 44.3(5) goes on to specify what "conduct" as above includes—

> **Conduct before, as well as during, the proceedings and in particular the extent to which the parties followed any relevant pre-action protocol.**

This ability of the Court to examine conduct before as well as during the proceedings follows very much Lord Woolf's recommendations as to sanctions to be imposed by the Court to strengthen its case management role (see Chapters 6 and 7 of the Final Report). In accordance with the approved pre-action protocols and in all other cases (see Paragraph 4, Practice Direction to the pre-action protocols), parties are obliged to co-operate in the exchange of information and documents in relation to a potential claim before proceedings are commenced. Their failure to do so may be the subject of cost sanctions under Rule 44.3(5)(a). This is not the only sanction. It will be remembered that a failure to follow a pre-action protocol may lead to an order for payment into Court of a sum of money under Rule 3.1(5).

Rule 44.3(5(a) is wide in its scope. It goes beyond simply an examination of whether a pre-action protocol has been followed and allows the Court to impose sanctions on any type of "misconduct". Attempts by the Court to impose sanctions have not always been successful—for instance, the debacle over Order 17 Rule 11(9), a provision which has found no home in the CPR and is repealed completely on and after 26 April 1999. In recent years, however, the Courts have been willing to undertake a closer examination of the circumstances of a case and more expansively to make an alternative order for costs "... when it appears to the Court that in the circumstances of the case some other order (than costs follow the event) should be made as to the whole or any part of the costs" (RSC Order 62 Rule 3(3)).

Three recent cases have highlighted the exercise of the discretion of the Court—

- *Butcher v Wolf* (1998) Times, 9 November
- *Burrows v Vauxhall Motors Ltd* [1998] PIQR
- *Oksuzoglu v Kay* [1998] 2 All ER 361

All these cases followed a similar line in that the Court imposed a sanction on the successful party for a failure to attempt to settle the case when settlement might have reduced the costs of the proceedings. The first mentioned is the most dramatic in that the plaintiff refused to consider further an alternative to the defendant's offer to settle. Eventually the case was compromised at trial on similar terms to the defendant's original offer. The plaintiff was ordered to pay the costs of the defendant on the basis of—

> **the overall reasonableness of each party's position and whether the dispute could and should have been settled, or at least more cheaply resolved.**

With the increasing emphasis on avoiding litigation wherever possible or at least limiting the issues to be resolved by the Court, we may expect to see this type of proactive approach by the Court to costs to increase.

- **Whether it was reasonable for a party to raise, pursue or contest an allegation or issue.**

The possible sanction against this type of conduct follows the principles established by the Final Report and the CPR that parties should consider at an early stage, including before proceedings are started, whether a particular allegation should be raised or contested. The issues in relation to a claim which require determination by the Court should be identified at an early stage and only those issues are pursued to trial if necessary.

- **The manner in which a party has pursued or defended his case or a particular allegation or issue.**

In consideration of the "manner" in which a case has been pursued or defended, the Court will bear in mind the concept of proportionality under the overriding objective and whether or not the pursuit or defence has been proportional to either the case as a whole or a particular allegation or issue. Thus if, for instance, a party acts oppressively, they may be deprived of their costs notwithstanding success at trial.

- **Whether a claimant who has succeeded in his claim in whole or in part exaggerated his claim.**

This goes somewhat wider than the principle that a claimant recovering only nominal damages should be deprived of the usual order for costs. The term "exaggeration" does, however, impart the flavour of both a positive and knowing exaggeration and an exaggeration as to something of substance in relation to the claim as a whole.

There are some further points to be made about conduct within the CPR.

- The conduct under Rule 44.3 is the conduct of the parties and not a non-party. Under Rule 48.2(1)(a) where the Court is considering an order in favour of or against a non-party, that non-party must be added as a party to the proceedings in which case conduct would fall to be considered under Rule 44.3 (see the discussion in relation to Rule 48.2 below).

- The conduct of the legal representative of a party and any consequent liability of that legal representative for costs may be considered under Rule 44.14 and Rule 48.7 (see below).
- If the Court falls short of altering the general rule as to costs notwithstanding some failing in the conduct of a party, the Court may alternatively make a direction upon the making of the order for costs so that when the costs come to be assessed, the attention of the costs judge is brought to that particular conduct when quantifying the costs in accordance with Rule 44.5.
- Conduct can also be taken into account under Part 27. As mentioned in relation to that Part, the Court can take into account "unreasonable behaviour" on the part of a party in exercising the discretion as to costs under Part 27 (Rule 27.14(2)(d)).
- In the fast track the trial costs may be increased or decreased if a party has behaved unreasonably or improperly (Rule 46.3(7) and (8)).

Part 36 offers

As above, one of the circumstances which the Court can take into account when deciding what order to make about costs is any payment into Court or admissible offer to settle whether or not made in accordance with Part 36.

Under Part 36 an offer can be made before proceedings are commenced. Rule 36.10(1) provides that the Court will take the offer into account when making any order as to costs provided that the offer complies with Rule 36.10. The Court is obliged to take such offer "into account" but it is not obliged, for instance, to award costs against a claimant that failed to beat such an offer although this may be the consequence. The position is somewhat different if a Part 36 offer or a Part 36 payment is made after the proceedings have commenced. Rules 36.20 and 36.21 provide specifically for the costs consequences where a claimant fails to beat a Part 36 offer or a Part 36 payment or does better than his own Part 36 offer. The costs consequences flowing from Rule 36.20 and Rule 36.21 apply automatically unless the Court considers it unjust that they should do so. (Part 36 is dealt with in Chapter 6).

Rule 44.3(4)(c) contemplates at least two slightly different circumstances in which the Court would take into account a payment into Court or an admissible offer outside the framework of Part 36.

- If a claimant only narrowly beats a Part 36 payment or offer or narrowly fails to beat his own offer, he may seek that the Court should take it into account in some fashion in any event. Under the old rules the Court did this in *Charm Maritime Inc v Elborne Mitchell* [1997] CAT 1363, [1997] CLY 555. The Court may be willing to exercise the discretion under Rule 44.3(4)(c), particularly if substantial costs have been incurred in achieving a small increase on the offer that has been made. It is suggested, however, that the Courts will be hesitant to avoid the strictures of Part 36 other than in clearly appropriate circumstances.

- It may well be that there are particular circumstances in which the defendant finds it difficult to make a Part 36 payment because of, for instance, lack of resources. The defendant may only be able to afford to make an offer in settlement including payment of an agreed sum by instalments. The Court might be persuaded that in those circumstances the offer, which should have been backed up by a Part 36 payment, will be taken into account notwithstanding the absence of a Part 36 payment.

The reference to "admissible offer" means an offer which is stated to be "without prejudice save as to costs". An offer which is stated to be simply "without prejudice" would not be admissible at this stage of the proceedings although it would be admissible when the Court comes to assess the costs.

Types of costs orders—Rule 44.3(6))

Rule 44.3(6) sets out the types of orders that the Court may make. The Rule has to be read in conjunction with Rule 44.3(7). This promotes in the absence of an order for all of the costs that one party pays a proportion of the other party's costs or the costs from or until a certain date only. What the Court should positively attempt to avoid is directing that one party should pay the costs in relation to a particular issue. Such an order is difficult to work out upon assessment because an exercise of dividing the general costs has to be undertaken which is not an easy task. Better that as above the Court simply orders that one party pay a proportion of the other party's costs or costs from or until a certain date only.

Paragraph 2.4 of the Practice Direction to Part 44 sets out commonly made costs orders and their effect—

2.4 There are certain costs orders which the court will commonly make in proceedings before trial. The following table sets out the general effect of these orders. The table is not an exhaustive list of the orders which the court may make.

Term	*Effect*
• Costs • Costs in any event	The party in whose favour the order is made is entitled to the costs in respect of the part of the proceedings to which the order relates, whatever other costs orders are made in the proceedings.
• Costs in the case • Costs in the application	The party in whose favour the court makes an order for costs at the end of the proceedings is entitled to his costs of the part of the proceedings to which the order relates.
• Costs reserved	The decision about costs is deferred to a later occasion, but if no later order is made the costs will be costs in the case.

Term	*Effect*
• Claimant's/ Defendant's costs in the case/ application.	If the party in whose favour the costs order is made is awarded costs at the end of the proceedings, that party is entitled to his costs of the part of the proceedings to which the order relates. If any other party is awarded costs at the end of the proceedings, the party in whose favour the final costs order is made is not liable to pay the costs of any other party in respect of the part of the proceedings to which the order relates.
• Costs thrown away	Where, for example, a judgment or order is set aside, the party in whose favour the costs order is made is entitled to the costs which have been incurred as a consequence. This includes the costs of— (a) preparing for and attending any hearing at which the judgment or order which has been set aside was made; (b) preparing for and attending any hearing to set aside the judgment or order in question; (c) preparing for and attending any hearing at which the court orders the proceedings or the part in question to be adjourned; (d) any steps taken to enforce a judgment or order which has subsequently been set aside.
• Costs of and caused by	Where, for example, the court makes this order on an application to amend a statement of case, the party in whose favour the costs order is made is entitled to the costs of preparing for and attending the application and the costs of any consequential amendment to his own statement of case.

Term	*Effect*
• Costs here and below	The party in whose favour the costs order is made is entitled not only to his costs in respect of the proceedings in which the court makes the order but also to his costs of the proceedings in any lower court. In the case of an appeal from a Divisional Court the party is not entitled to any costs incurred in any court below the Divisional Court.
• No order as to costs • Each party to pay his own costs	Each party is to bear his own costs of the part of the proceedings to which the order relates whatever costs order the court makes at the end of the proceedings.

There are two other important provisions within Rule 44.3(6).

- The Court is empowered under the Rule to make an order in relation to costs incurred before proceedings have begun. This is an encodification of the principles reviewed by Megarry V-C in *Re Gibsons Settlement Trusts* [1981] CH 179, [1981] 1 All ER 233. In that case the Court confirmed that costs arising from the dispute relevant to the proceedings as issued should be recoverable. Presumably that principle stands whether or not an order is made by the Court under Rule 44.3(6)(d). It is suggested, however, that if substantial costs have been incurred before proceedings have begun, an order should be sought to make the position clear. This becomes particularly important under the principles established by the Final Report and the CPR under which encouragement is given to "avoid litigation wherever possible" by attempting to settle a claim before an action is issued. In that process substantial costs may be incurred.
- This question of costs incurred before proceedings have begun is likely to be of some concern to parties wishing to have a degree of certainty as to exactly if and when costs are payable. It must be remembered that if a Part 36 offer made before the commencement of proceedings makes no mention of costs, no costs will be payable if it is accepted. The usual course in negotiations prior to commencement is that the costs become part of the package for settlement. If costs cannot be agreed, the matter is not settled and proceedings may be commenced. The difficulty for parties is if there is a difference as to the quantification of any costs payable. Before commencing proceedings a claimant will have to consider whether the offer for costs is reasonable bearing in mind the new costs rules and particularly issues such as conduct and proportionality.
- Under Rule 44.3(6)(g) the Court can award interest on costs from or until a certain date including a date before judgment. This is a change under the new Rules effected also by the Civil Procedure (Modification of Enactments) Order 1998 which amends the Judgments Act 1838 to allow

the Court to order interest to run from a date before judgment. Under the old rules, interest ran on costs from the date judgment was pronounced (*Hunt v R M Douglas (Roofing)* [1988] 3 WLR 975, [1988] 3 All ER 823 HL).

Part of the rationale for this change is to reflect the fact that parties incur costs during the whole process of the litigation. The awarding of interest prior to the giving of judgment may compensate for that outgoing from the time when it was made.

Payment of costs on account—Rule 44.3(8)

Under Rule 44.3(8) when the Court makes an order for costs it may order that an amount be paid on account before the costs are assessed. This will generally only happen if an order for costs is made in favour of one party against another. The Court should have in front of it sufficient detail in relation to costs to deal with an application for payment on account. If the costs order was made upon an application, the Court will generally have in front of it the statement of costs prepared for summary assessment. If the order for costs is made at trial, the Court will either have a statement of costs for the purpose of summary assessment or the estimates of the parties that were provided upon the filing of the listing questionnaire. It is suggested, however, that parties should have more detailed and up to date figures for costs for the purpose of the trial and an application under Rule 44.3(8).

The Court may use its power to order an amount to be paid on account as an alternative to summary assessment.

The power to make an order for payment on account reflects again the concept that where a party is the beneficiary of an order for costs, they should be immediately compensated in appropriate circumstances for all or part of their outgoings relating to the matter for which they had the benefit of the order for costs.

If the Court does make an order for a payment on account, the payment must be made within 14 days of the order, either under Rule 44.8 or Rule 40.11.

It is suggested that one of the factors that the Court may wish to take into account when considering whether to make an order for payment on account is the possible outcome of the proceedings as a whole. Although a party may have the benefit of an order for costs in relation to a particular issue, if the payment of costs awaits the outcome of the proceedings, there may be appropriate set-off between the parties leading to a balancing payment by one party to the other. Payment on account may cause some problems for a party because that payment eventually has to be recovered as a result of the outcome of the proceedings as a whole.

Costs set-off—Rule 44.3(9)

Rule 44.3(9) regulates for the set-off of costs where each party has the benefit of a costs order. As encouraged by Rules 44.3(6) and 44.3(7) this situation should be avoided wherever possible by the making of an order by which one party pays to the other a proportion of costs taking into account, say, success by the claimant on the claim and by the defendant on the counterclaim. If, however, the court does make orders for costs in favour of both the claimant and defendant , the court can eventually order a set–off of the two resulting certificates with payment of the balance from one to the other, or delay the issue of a certificate to one party until the other party is paid what is due under the certificate issued in their favour.

Miscellaneous points arising under Rule 44.3

- Certificates for Counsel no longer apply although the old system is replaced by a similar system under Paragraph 2.6 of the Practice Direction to Part 44. This provides that where the Court makes an order for costs, it may state its opinion as to whether or not the hearing was fit for the attendance of one or more Counsel. If it does so then that opinion will be taken into account on assessment.
- An order which is silent about costs is an order that there is "no order as to costs" (Rule 44.13(1)).
- Naturally, when exercising its discretion in relation to costs, the Court is obliged to take into account the overriding objective under Part 1.

Basis of assessment

Rule 44.4 introduces phrases which are familiar to practitioners. Under Rule 44.4(1) costs are assessed either on the standard basis or on the indemnity basis. The difference between the two is dealt with below. Rule 44.4(1) goes on to repeat another familiar concept that **the Court will not allow costs which have been unreasonably incurred or are unreasonable in amount**. This repeats language included in RSC Order 62 Rule 12(2). That rule dealt with "taxation on the indemnity basis" and provided that "all costs shall be allowed except insofar as they are of an unreasonable amount or have been unreasonably incurred".

The marked difference between Rule 44.4(1) and Order 62 Rule 12 comes in the assessment under the standard basis. Under Order 62 Rule 12(1) the receiving party had to overcome not one but two hurdles in relation to the recovery of costs. This rule provided that when costs were taxed on a standard basis "... there shall be allowed a reasonable amount in respect of all costs reasonably incurred". Accordingly, not only did the costs have to be reasonably incurred but the receiving party only received a reasonable amount in respect of those costs. That reasonable amount was measured by what the Court thought it unreasonable for the paying party to pay. The twin hurdles have been removed under the new Rules but a new one placed in front of the receiving party on the standard basis—the test of proportionality (see below).

The difference between the tests of "reasonableness" and "proportionality" may be of some importance. Indeed the two concepts become somewhat mixed. In deciding to disallow costs under Rule 44.4(1) on the basis that they have been unreasonably incurred or are unreasonable in amount, the court is likely to include a consideration of the test of proportionality. Costs may be unreasonable simply because they are "disproportionate".

It should be noted that the reference to the indemnity basis within Part 44 is to be differentiated from the principle of indemnity under *Gundry v Sainsbury* [1910] 1 KB 645. Under that principle, a party can only recover costs actually incurred in bringing or defending the proceedings. This is the indemnity principle and not the indemnity basis for the purpose of Part 44. The two are easily confused. The consultation paper referred to above proffers the idea of abandoning the *Gundry v Sainsbury* indemnity principle.

Standard basis of assessment

Rule 44.4(2) provides that where costs are to be assessed on the standard basis, the Court will only allow costs which are proportionate to the matters in issue. Any doubt which the Court has as to whether costs are reasonably incurred or reasonable and proportionate in amount is found in favour of the paying party.

This is not the only place in which the question of proportionality arises. We have seen that it gains prominence in Part 1 under which it forms the most important basis for the exercise of the Court's discretion under the CPR. Proportionality also comes into account in the Rules relating to disclosure and inspection (Part 31).

The concept of proportionality is causing considerable concern amongst practitioners. This is largely because it places in the hands of the Court a considerable discretion and until some standards are established, the application of the principle is an unknown quantity. Anecdotal tales about the application of the principle abound. One of those was that certain courts were applying a fixed percentage of the claim as a ceiling for recoverable costs on a standard basis. Anecdotal or not, those reports led the Civil Procedure Rule Committee to attempt some guidance which is included in Paragraphs, 3.1, 3.2 and 3.3 of the Practice Direction to Part 44.

3.1 In applying the test of proportionality the court will have regard to rule 1.1(2)(c). The relationship between the total of the costs incurred and the financial value of the claim may not be a reliable guide. A fixed percentage cannot be applied in all cases to the value of the claim in order to ascertain whether or not the costs are proportionate.

3.2 In any proceedings there will be costs which will inevitably be incurred and which are necessary for the successful conduct of the case. Solicitors are not required to conduct litigation at rates which are uneconomic. Thus in a modest claim the proportion of costs is likely to be higher than in a large claim, and may even equal or possibly exceed the amount in dispute.

3.3 Where a trial takes place, the time taken by the court in dealing with a particular issue may not be an accurate guide to the amount of time properly spent by the legal or other representatives in preparation for the trial of that issue.

It is suggested that the final sentence in Paragraph 3.1 does not necessarily convey the overall intention that establishing fixed percentages as a ceiling for recoverable costs is inappropriate in all cases as an unnecessary predetermining fetter on the Court's discretion in relation to the case before it. Concern remains that the Court will use the principle of proportionality, particularly in summary assessment, as a quick easy but harsh tool for the assessment process.

Factors in assessment

Rule 44.5 sets out the factors which the Court has to take into account in deciding the amount of costs. Firstly, under Rule 44.5(2) the Court must give effect to any orders which have been made in the course of the proceedings and presumably any directions of the Court has given accompanying such orders. As above, the Court may direct that the costs judge considers particular steps taken in the proceedings in relation to the assessment.

Other than orders the Court has to have regard to "all the circumstances". By Rule 44.5(3) those circumstances include—

- **The conduct of all the parties including in particular**—
  - conduct before, as well as during, the proceedings; and
  - the efforts made (if any) before and during the proceedings in order to try to resolve the dispute.

By repeating in part the provisions in relation to conduct already contained within Rule 44.3, the Rules might appear to give rise to a degree of double jeopardy for the receiving party whose conduct has already been examined by the Court when it considered making the order for costs. The difference in the assessment procedure is that the Court has available to it both the time and evidence in relation to conduct, having as it does, the documents of the receiving party filed in support of the bill of costs claimed. It is to be noted, however, that the question of conduct does not just relate to that of the receiving party but to that of "all of the parties".

In an examination of conduct both here and under Rule 44.3 it is presumed that the Court will follow the principle established in *Francis v Francis and Dickerson* [1956] P 87, [1955] 3 All ER 836 to the effect that the reasonableness of the conduct will be measured by what a reasonable solicitor would have done at the time that the course of conduct was followed in the interests of his client, i.e. the Court will not look at the matter in hindsight and measure the conduct against subsequent events.

The Court's power to look at attempts to settle claims before and during the proceedings under the assessment procedure is much wider than that when the Court considers making an order for costs. Under the latter the Court looks at payments in and admissible offers. In the assessment procedure the Court can look at any attempts to settle and indeed, most importantly, the absence of them.

Once again the Court can impose sanctions for failure to "avoid litigation wherever possible", failure to narrow the issues and any oppressive action by a party.

The amount or value of any money or property involved

This provision reflects the general approach of the Court that reasonableness and proportionality are measured against the matters in issue.

- **The importance of the matter to all the parties.**
- **The particular complexity of the matter or the difficulty or novelty of the questions raised.**
- **The skill, effort, specialised knowledge and responsibility involved.**
- **The time spent on the case.**

Practitioners will be somewhat surprised to see this element of the costs claim so low down in the criteria to which the Court is to have regard. Under the system prior to 26 April 1999, the time spent on the case and the skill, effort, specialised knowledge and responsibility involved were almost the first items to be considered upon a taxation. This was reflected in the so called "Seven Pillars of Wisdom" in Appendix 2 to RSC Order 62 and in the Practice Direction No 2 of 1992 issued by the Supreme Court Taxing Office in November 1992. Despite the position in which these two elements are found within Rule 44.5(3), they still dominate the scene in relation at least to the mechanics of assessment since they form the basis for the drawing of both the statement of costs for summary assessment and estimates and the bill of costs for detailed assessment. As will be seen from those forms, the sum total of the costs is derived from time spent on the case and the level of fee earner employed to undertake the work. Accordingly it is suggested that the assessment exercise will follow a course under which the Court has before it the total of the costs claimed. Each item will then be examined to assess whether it was proportionately and reasonably incurred and proportionate and reasonable in amount. In that exercise, conduct in relation to a particular item might be considered, for example, whether or not a particular issue has been pursued oppressively. This should give a total. That total may then be subject to consideration in relation to its proportionality to the matters in issue and its quantification in light of the party's overall conduct including attempts to settle the proceedings or particular issues, an exercise which, clearly, could take some time. Accordingly it is an exercise which is likely to be undertaken in detailed costs assessment rather than summary assessment. The time available to the Court on summary assessment of costs is extremely limited. In a fast track case the Court may only have a few minutes to carry out this exercise.

One element of the breakdown of costs which has been the matter of debate during the course of the preparation of the Civil Procedure Rules is the hourly charge. Prior to 26 April 1999, in accordance with the Practice Direction (No 2 of 1992) (see above), each chargeable item was divided into two parts—the first representing the direct cost of the work and the second the appropriate allowance for care and conduct. These two factors are referred to as "A" and "B". A is an assessment of the direct cost of running a case. It did not necessarily equate with the actual costs to the individual practice. Two recent cases have referred to broad average direct costs (*Johnson & Others v Reed Corrugated Cases* [1997] Core CLR 180) and comparable direct costs (*L v L (Legal Aid taxation)*

[1997] 1 Costs LR 9). Over recent years the Courts have developed a practice of assessing factor A on the basis of surveys conducted by local law societies about costs in their particular area. This has largely replaced the former practice of simple reliance upon the taxing officer's knowledge combined with an expensive time affidavit. The B element covers matters which cannot be assessed on an hourly rate such as supervision, indirect expenses reflecting the complexity of the case and the degree of skill and responsibility required in pursuing it, and the solicitor's profit element. The B factor is expressed as a percentage of the direct costs figure. Thus the direct costs figure may be £75 per hour to which the B factor is then applied as a percentage of, say 50%, producing a resultant hourly charge of £112.50.

During the course of the drafting of the Rules there have been moves to encourage solicitors to claim and quote to the client an all-inclusive hourly charge. This has in any event become more common practice amongst solicitors although the consultation paper, "Controlling Costs", refers to a residual resistance to follow the encouragement. The new position was reflected in the costs Practice Direction issued by the Chief Taxing Master (Supreme Court Taxing Office Practice Note 2/98). This said—

> **Wherever possible ... party and party assessment of costs should be based on an hourly charging rate inclusive of care and conduct.**

The Practice Direction was aimed only at summary assessment but is likely to be of wider significance. It only regulated the position up to 26 April 1999 whereupon the Rules and practice directions took over.

The Practice Direction issued by the Chief Taxing Master was supported by guideline figures for hourly rates across the country for four grades of fee earner. This guideline did cause some problems since there appeared to be differing applications of it throughout the country.

At the time of writing the interested parties are working on establishing a new system to apply under the CPR and the practice directions. Work is being undertaken around the country to determine appropriate rates for hourly charges inclusive of mark-up. In replacement of the four grades of fee earners included in the Chief Taxing Master's Practice Direction referred to above, there are now three grades, namely—

- solicitors with over four years post qualification experience;
- other solicitors and legal executives and fee earners of equivalent experience; and
- trainee solicitors and fee earners of equivalent experience.

A short timescale has been set so that by Autumn 1999 the Senior Costs Judge (as he now is) will issue guidance for hourly rates throughout the country.

Within this whole process the calculation of Counsel's fees, which can often be a very substantial part of the claim for costs, remains an anomaly. The process by which Counsel's fees are agreed with a solicitor remains much the same as it has for very many years. The solicitor negotiates a fee with Counsel's clerk. This ad hoc system is becoming increasingly difficult to defend. The practice has developed over the past few years by which solicitors will ask for an hourly rate and agree a fee based on an assessment of the time involved. Some Chambers issue fee notes with notification of time involved for the purpose of taxation. The practice, however, is not widespread. The anomalous nature of the system is being highlighted by summary assessment of costs under which Counsel are required to justify for the first time their own fees having previously enjoyed the luxury of delegating that task to solicitors and Counsels' clerks. Any further discussion of the point is outside the scope of this work but the writer predicts that there will have to be further changes in the quantification and transparency of Counsel's fees.

- **The place where and the circumstances in which work or any part of it was done**

This is the final matter to which the Court is to have regard under Rule 44.5(3). It reflects one of the factors which was taken into account under the old Rules (RSC Order 62 Appendix 2).

Procedure for assessing costs

Summary assessment

Summary assessment of costs under Rule 44.7 is one of the central developments of the new Rules emphasising the "pay as you go" flavour of the cost rules. It is intended to ensure that parties are compensated at an appropriate stage of the proceedings and in appropriate circumstances for money expended by them. Further, it increases the transparency of the costs regime so that a party can determine likely liability and recoverability of costs at as early a stage as possible. The dramatic effect of summary assessment arises from a combination of Rules 44.7 and 44.8. Under the old regime prior to 26 April 1999 the general rule was that costs would only be taxed and payable at the conclusion of the proceedings. The Court could, but rarely did provide, that costs should be "taxed and paid forthwith". The combination of taxation and payment was important because although the Court could order under RSC Order 62 Rule 8 that costs be taxed forthwith, it did not follow automatically that they were payable forthwith. This needed to be the subject of a separate order.

Under the new regime, if costs are summarily assessed, they are automatically payable "forthwith"—within 14 days (Rule 44.8). Accordingly, if payment is not to be made, the Court must positively extend the time under Rule 44.8. It has the power to do so under Rule 3.1(2)(a). Indeed it may be said that the Court has an obligation to consider whether to extend the time for payment in accordance with the overriding objective. An over harsh application of Rules 44.7 and 44.8 could lead to unfairness in that a party may be locked out of proceedings simply because they are unable to meet the costs order within 14 days. If, as planned, the conditional fee agreements become the more usual method of funding litigation, an increasing number of litigants will simply be unable to afford to meet the costs order on summary assessment. The sanction for non-payment would be either a stay of the proceedings or the liability to normal methods of execution of an order including insolvency proceedings.

The alternative view is that if a party undertakes litigation they must be aware of the consequences. If the Court has ordered that one party pay the costs of the other, it may be said that there is no reason why the receiving party should not be compensated immediately for money which they have had to expend. All these factors go into the melting pot for consideration by the Court.

Conditional fee and "Thai Trading" agreements raise a further problem with summary assessment. In both cases the quantification of a solicitor's fees (if any) is determined by the outcome of the litigation. Very often such agreements are entered into because a party cannot afford to fund representation. In that event it is unlikely that such a party will be able to fund any costs that are ordered against them as a result of summary assessment. This will undoubtedly cause difficulties. The receiving party would question the rationale that summary assessment should be refused because of the paying party's funding arrangements. If the liability is insured then call may be made upon the insurance company. At the time of writing, however, few insurance companies have addressed the problem and under current standard wording for such policies, the liability arising from summary assessment is not covered. The market will have to develop quickly to meet this gap.

Summary and Assessment Procedure

The Practice Direction (Paragraphs 4.3–4.10) sets out the procedure for summary assessment and some of the limitations.

Dealing with the limitations first, the Court can only summarily assess costs where it makes an order for costs in a party's favour. Thus the Court is not entitled to make a summary assessment of costs where it orders "costs in case"; "costs in the application"; or "costs reserved".

In addition, the Court is not entitled to make a summary assessment of costs of a receiving party who is an assisted person under the Legal Aid Act 1988 (Paragraph 4.9(1), Practice Direction to Part 44). Further, it is not entitled to make a summary assessment of the costs of a receiving party who is a child or patient under Part 21 unless the solicitor acting for the child or patient has waived the right to further costs (Paragraph 4.9(3), Practice Direction to Part 44).

On the other hand the Court may make a summary assessment of costs where the paying party is an assisted person under the Legal Aid Act 1988 although those costs are not payable under Rule 44.8 within 14 days. In similar fashion the Court may make a summary assessment of costs payable by a child or patient although clearly the question of ability to meet the consequent order will be a factor to be taken into account when the Court exercises its discretion as to the timing of payment.

Prior to a hearing at which a party intends to make application for an order for costs, the party intending to claim costs must prepare a written statement of the costs he intends to claim. An example of the manner in which a statement should be set out appears at Form 1 of the schedule of costs forms. The requirement is to break down the costs showing separately—

- number of hours to be claimed;
- the hourly rate to be claimed;
- the grade of fee earner;
- the amount and nature of any disbursement to be claimed, other than Counsel's fees for appearing at the hearing;
- the amount of solicitor's costs to be claimed for attending or appearing at the hearing;
- the fees of Counsel to be claimed in respect of the hearing; and
- any VAT to be claimed on these amounts (see Paragraph 4.5(2), Practice Direction to Part 44).

The hourly rate should be in accordance with the composite hourly guideline rates referred to above.

The statement must be filed with the Court and served as soon as possible and in any event not less than 24 hours before the date fixed for the hearing (Paragraph 4.5(4), Practice Direction to Part 44). If a party fails to file and serve in accordance with the Practice Direction, the Court may impose some form of penalty, particularly if an adjournment is necessary as a result of the non or late service.

The general rule (repeated in Paragraph 4.4(1), Practice Direction to Part 44) is that a summary assessment will follow—

- the trial in a fast track claim; and
- any other hearing which has lasted **less** than one day.

Clearly the costs that are dealt with at the end of a trial are those for the whole of the proceedings (subject to any earlier summary assessment). The costs following any other hearing will simply relate to that hearing.

Whether or not there is a summary assessment remains in the discretion of the Court subject to the guidance of the Practice Direction. The Court may simply not have time to effect a summary assessment. The Court could in those circumstances take one of three courses—

- Order detailed costs assessment to take place in the usual way at the end of the proceedings.
- Adjourn the summary assessment to a later date although the summary assessment cannot be undertaken by a costs judge, a district judge or an authorised court officer (Paragraph 4.8, Practice Direction to Part 44).
- Order detailed costs assessment in the usual way but make an order that there should be a payment on account of the costs in accordance with Rule 44.3(8).

As above, when the Court is exercising its discretion it must have regard to the overriding objective which includes the requirement to ensure that the parties are on an equal footing and deal with claims expeditiously and fairly.

If a summary assessment is made, the Court will simply specify the amount payable as a global figure which includes all items including VAT (Paragraph 4.7, Practice Direction to Part 44).

If the parties agree the order that is to be made by the Court so that an order by consent can be made without attendance, the parties are obliged to agree a figure for costs or that there should be no order for costs. If agreement cannot be reached, the parties will have to attend (Paragraph 4.4(3), Practice Direction to Part 44). The Practice Direction goes on to say that unless good reason can be shown for the failure to deal with costs by agreement, no costs will be allowed for that attendance. Presumably, however, the exercise of the Court's discretion is dependent upon at whose door failure to agree lies.

Detailed costs assessment

The procedure for detailed costs assessment is set out at length in Part 47 (see below).

Costs in the Small Claims Track and Fast Track

The Rules relating to costs on these tracks were dealt with in the parts of this work dealing with the relevant Rules, namely Part 27 (small claims) see page 183 and Part 46 (fast track) see page 198.

Deemed costs orders

There are various situations provided for in the CPR under which an order for costs is made automatically upon some event. These provisions are divided into those which provide for automatic fixed costs under Part 45 and those that provide for costs to be assessed on the standard basis in accordance with the general costs rules. Of the latter there are four instances in the Rules which are repeated in Rule 44.12. These four are—

- Rule 3.7 (defendant's right to costs where claim struck out for non-payment of fees);
- Rule 36.13(1) (claimant's right to costs where he accepts defendant's Part 36 offer or Part 36 payment);
- Rule 36.14 (claimant's right to costs where defendant accepts the claimant's Part 36 offer); or
- Rule 38.6 (defendant's right to costs where claimant discontinues.

Under Part 36 if the Court's permission is required for acceptance, the Court will make an appropriate order for costs (Rule 36.11(3)). For further discussion of Part 36, see Chapter 22 page 267.

Rule 44.12(2) provides that interest on the costs deemed to have been made in accordance with Rule 44.12 begins to run from the date on which the event giving rise to the entitlement to costs occurred.

Misconduct

There are various ways in which misconduct on the part of a party or a legal representative can be punished under the CPR. In various ways sanctions can be imposed including those sanctions available to the Court under Rules 44.3

and 44.5. Whilst these sanctions are generally aimed at the parties, there are two specific Rules within the costs rules under which a legal representative can be made personally liable for costs. The first of these is under Rule 44.14. The second is under Rule 48.7. This latter provision is dealt with under Part 48.

Rule 44.14 reflects a summary of part of the former provisions contained within RSC Order 62 Rule 10, Rule 11 and Rule 28. Those provisions of the RSC which related to misconduct on the part of a party recognised by the Court outside the assessment proceedings are effectively dealt with under Rule 44.3.

The provisions of Rule 44.14 should be also read with Rule 44.5 since on assessment the Court can use its powers under that Rule to examine the conduct of any parties. Misconduct could be punished under Rule 44.5 without the necessity of resort to Rule 44.14.

Insofar as Rule 44.14 provides for sanctions against the legal representative, it reflects very much Rule 48.7. Both derive from the powers given by Section 51(6) Supreme Court Act 1981.

> **In any proceedings mentioned in sub-section (1), the Court may disallow, or (as the case may be) order the legal or other representative concerned to meet the whole of any wasted costs or such part of them as may be determined in accordance with the Rules of Court.**

Sub-section 7 provides a definition of wasted costs.

> **Wasted costs means any cost incurred by a party—**
>
> **(a) as a result of any improper, unreasonable or negligent act or omission on the part of any legal or other representative or any employee of such a representative; or**
>
> **(b) which, in the light of any such act of omission occurring after they were incurred, the Court considers it unreasonable to expect that party to pay.**

Rule 44.14 is specifically dealing with the power of the Court during the assessment process only. This may indeed be the only occasion on which the Court has the opportunity to consider misconduct if, for instance, a deemed order for costs is made under Part 36.

The power of the Court is to be invoked in two separate situations.

- If the assessment proceedings have not been conducted in accordance with Part 47 or any direction of the Court as a result of a failure of a party or his legal representative; or
- a party or legal representative is guilty of conduct which was unreasonable or improper before or during the proceedings which gave rise to the assessment proceeding (Rule 44.14(1)).

Paragraph 7.2, Practice Direction to Part 44 gives an example of the conduct which may be punished under Rule 44.14—if a party or legal representative takes steps which are calculated to prevent or inhibit the Court from furthering the overriding objective. Presumably this would include interfering with the Court's obligation to deal with a case expeditiously and fairly or in a manner to ensure that the parties are on an equal footing.

Although the Court has the power to make an order under Rule 44.14 of its own initiative, it will usually only do so upon application generally by the paying party. If the paying party proposes to make such an application, it may not be sufficient to mention it simply in the points of dispute. It is suggested that following the practice under the RSC, the appropriate course is to issue an application under Part 23 supported by evidence. The respondent to that application may be either or both of the party and his legal representative.

Upon the hearing of the application the Court may under Rule 44.14(2)—

- disallow all or part of the costs which are being assessed; or
- order the party at fault or his legal representative to pay costs which he has caused any other party to incur.

In relation to this latter provision, proof of causation and damage is required and would have to be the subject of evidence presented to the Court.

The Court does have subsidiary power to punish a party that has failed to follow the procedures under Part 47. This is provided under Rule 47.8. The Court may disallow all or part of the interest otherwise payable to the receiving party (see below).

Reflecting the provisions of Rule 44.2, Rule 44.14(3) provides that if an order is made under the Rule against a legally represented party and the party is not present when the order is made, the party's solicitor (not "legal representative") must notify the client in writing of the order no later than seven days after the solicitor receives notice of the order. As with Rule 44.2, there is no policing provision to this but the Practice Direction to Part 44 (Paragraph 7.3) provides that the Court may require the solicitor to produce to the Court evidence that he took reasonable steps to comply with the obligation.

Part 45—Fixed costs

The fixed costs regime under the CPR results from a combination of Appendix 3 to RSC Order 62 and Appendix B to CCR Order 38. The fixed costs regime under Part 45 applies automatically unless the Court otherwise orders. Thus in an application under Order 24 for summary judgment for a specified sum of money where judgment is given, the recoverable costs will be limited to the fixed costs under Part 45 unless the Court otherwise orders. Accordingly, if such an application incurs considerable costs, it should be remembered that application must be made to avoid the fixed costs regime.

The application of Part 45 and the fixed costs regime is limited to specific circumstances. Generally it will only apply if the claim is for a specified sum of money. This is to be differentiated from a claim for an unspecified sum of money. The former will generally be a claim for a debt which can be specified. The latter would include a claim for damages for personal injury.

In a claim for a specified sum of money the fixed cost regime applies automatically to—

- Judgment in default under Rule 12.4(1). Such a judgment is obtained by filing a request in the appropriate practice form which is N205A (Notice of Issue (Specified Amount) and Request for Judgment) or N225 (Request for Judgment and Reply to Admission (specified amount) (see below for the completion of the form in relation to costs).

- Judgment on an admission which is obtained under Rule 14.4(3). This Rule only applies where the whole of the claim is admitted. That admission can be made in the relevant practice form (N9A) (Form of Admission and Statement of Means to accompany Form N1). The request for judgment is made in Form N225 (Request for Judgment and Reply to Admission (Specified Amount)). As to the completion of the latter form in relation to costs, see below.
- Judgment on an admission of part of the claim under Rule 14.5(6). Again the admission can be made on Form N9A. When a part admission is made, the Court sends out a notice in Form N225A which is then completed by the claimant. The claimant may accept the amount admitted in satisfaction of the whole claim. It is only in those circumstances that the fixed costs regime applies.
- Summary judgment under Part 24. As above, following the hearing of an application, unless the Court otherwise orders, the fixed costs regime applies. Parties should be careful to ensure that an application to override the fixed costs regime is made in appropriate circumstances.
- The Court makes an order to strike out the defence under Rule 3.4(2)(a) as disclosing no reasonable grounds for defending the claim. Such an order may be made of the Court's own initiative under Rule 3.3 or upon application. Once again, if application is made, parties should be careful to ensure that if the fixed costs regime does not provide sufficient recompense for costs for the making of the application, the claimant must seek from the Court an order overriding Part 45. Rule 3.4(2)(a) applies not only to the whole of the defence but to part of it. It is suggested that under Rule 45.1(2)(a)(iv) the reference to the defence means the whole of it and not simply part of it. It is to be noted that the fixed cost regime does not apply to any other instance of strike out such as striking out for abuse.
- The defendant pays the money claimed within 14 days after service of particulars of claim on him, together with the fixed commencement costs stated in the claim form.
- The claimant accepts payment into Court in satisfaction of the whole of the claim, such payment having been made within 14 days after service of the particulars of claim as long as the payment in includes fixed costs as stated in the claim form (see Rule 45.3(2)). This provision needs to be seen in the light of Rule 36.10 which provides that where an offer to settle is made before proceedings are commenced followed by a payment in within 14 days of the claim form being served, the payment in cannot be accepted without the permission of the Court. The payment in, however, following an offer to settle before the commencement of proceedings, would not need to include the fixed costs stated in the claim form. The position is similar if the payment in is made following commencement of proceedings but within 14 days after service of the particulars of claim.

If the claim is not for a specified amount, the only circumstances in which the fixed cost regime applies is if the Court gave a fixed date for the hearing when it issued the claim and judgment is given for the delivery of goods (see the Practice Direction relating to Consumer Credit Act claims supplementing CPR Rule 7.9).

The costs concerned are the solicitor's charges. In addition to those, the Court fees may also be recovered.

The claim form (N1) has upon its face a box on the bottom right hand corner setting out, amongst other things, the solicitor's costs. In this box there should be inserted one of the figures set out in Table 1 of Part 45 under Rule 45.2. Those figures may be supplemented by further claims for solicitors' costs in relation to items set out in Table 3 of Part 45 under Rule 45.5. These figures are then repeated in the request for judgment. In addition on the request for judgment a figure is entered on the space available for the costs on entry of judgment. Those costs are set out in Table 2 to Part 45 under Rule 45.4.

Tables 1 and 3 are reproduced at pages 45, 46.

In addition to Part 45, the retained part of RSC Order 62 and CCR Order 38 in the Schedule to the CPR include provisions for fixed costs where the claim is for possession of land (RSC Order 62) or the claim is for recovery of property, including land, with or without a claim for a sum of money or in proceedings for the enforcement of a tribunal or other award (CCR Order 38).

Under Rule 27.14 (small claims track), the recoverable costs include those payable under Part 45 attributable to issuing the claim. Paragraph 1.2 of the Practice Direction to Part 45 provides that those recoverable fixed costs are the sum of the fixed commencement costs provided in Table 1 of Rule 45.2 and the appropriate court fee or fees paid by the claimant. This would apply after allocation to the small claims track and does not affect the position where judgment is entered before allocation.

Part 46—Fast Track Trial costs

This subject has been dealt with extensively in the section of this work dealing with the fast track.

Part 47—Procedure for detailed assessment of costs and default provisions

The new provisions replacing taxation procedure under Order 62 codify developments in practice over the past few years.

The general order of things is as follows—

- Unless cost are to be summarily assessed in accordance with Rule 44.7, costs to be assessed by the detailed procedure will only be assessed at the conclusion of the proceedings (Rule 47.1).
- The assessment procedure is commenced by the service of a notice of commencement and a copy of the bill of costs (Rule 47.6).

- Detailed assessment procedure must be commenced within three months of the date of the judgment (Rule 47.7).
- If the paying party wishes to object to all or part of the bill of costs, points of dispute must be served within 21 days (Rule 47.9).
- If points of dispute are not served, the receiving party may obtain a default costs certificate (Rule 47.11).
- If only part of the bill is disputed, the receiving party may make application for an interim costs certificate (Rule 47.15).
- As to the matters in dispute, the receiving party must file a request for a detailed assessment hearing within three months of the expiry period before commencing detailed assessment proceedings as above (Rule 47.14).
- The sanction for failure to meet the time limit set by Part 47 is the disallowance of interest on the costs.
- Following assessment a final costs certificate will be issued (Rule 47.16).
- The Court can order that interest on costs shall run prior to the date of judgment.
- The costs are payable within 14 days of any certificate of costs (Rule 44.8). Costs can be appealed but usually the Court's permission is required. A pre-condition is that a request has been made to the Court seeking reasons for the decision (Rules 47.23 and 47.24).

The Rules

General rules about detailed assessment

Part 47 opens with some general matters relating to detailed assessment. The first of these specifies the time when detailed assessment may be carried out (Rule 47.1). This reflects the former rules that generally detailed assessment will only be carried out at the conclusion of the proceedings. The Practice Direction (Paragraph 1.1, Practice Direction to Part 47) sets out what is meant by the conclusion of proceedings, namely—

> **when the Court has finally determined the matters in issue in the claim, whether or not there is an appeal.**

This combined with Rule 47.2 means that detailed costs assessment does not have to await the outcome of an appeal unless the Court directs otherwise. If such a direction is sought, application must be made either to the Court making the order or to the Court to which the appeal against that order is being made.

If a paying party served with a notice of commencement believes that the detailed costs assessment has been commenced too early, he can make application to the Court for an order to that effect, effectively setting aside the notice of commencement (Paragraph 1.1(3), Practice Direction to Part 47).

On the other hand under Paragraph 1.1(4), the costs judge or district judge can allow cost assessment proceedings where "... there is no reasonable prospect of the claim continuing."

Rule 47.3 limits the powers of an "authorised court officer". Such an officer is to be distinguished from a costs judge as defined in Part 43. A court officer is authorised to deal with claims for costs not exceeding £17,500 (excluding VAT) in the case of senior executive officers and £35,000 (excluding VAT) in the case of principal officers (Paragraph 1.3, Practice Direction to Part 47). The Practice Direction also allows the parties to agree that a court officer should not deal with an assessment or, in the absence of an agreement, for one party to make an application to that effect.

Generally the assessment proceedings will take place in the Court in which the case has proceeded or judgment has been given. The Court does have the power either to transfer proceedings for the purpose of assessment (Rule 30.3) or, alternatively, to simply direct that the assessment should take place in another County Court or in the Supreme Court Costs Office without the necessity for a full transfer of the proceedings (Rule 47.4(2), (3) and (4)).

Stage 1—Commencement

The process is commenced under Rule 47.6 by the receiving party serving on the paying party—

- a notice of commencement in the relevant practice form (Costs Forms: Form 5); and
- a copy of the bill of costs.

The notice in Form 5 must be completed to show as separate items—

- the total amount of the bill of costs as drawn; and
- the additional amounts which will be payable by way of fixed costs and court fees if a default cost certificate is obtained (Paragraph 2.3, Practice Direction to Part 47).

The fixed costs are £80 (Paragraph 2.3(3), Practice Direction to Part 47). The court fee is £40 in accordance with the Supreme Court Fees Order 1999 and the County Court Fees Order 1999.

The bill of costs should follow Form 2 of the Schedule of Costs forms taking in also, where appropriate, the certificates set out in Form 4. If a party wishes to depart from Form 2 then he should include in the background information of the bill an explanation justifying the departure (Paragraph 1.7, Practice Direction to Part 43).

The form and contents of the bill of costs are set out in Section 2 of the Practice Direction to Part 43. Section 3 of the same Practice Direction sets out the regulation of the VAT element within the bill of costs. Detailed discussion as to the contents of the bill of costs is outside the scope of this work. It will be noted, however, that there is no requirement to show separately the expense of time plus uplift (A+B) and the precedent in Form 5 simply refers to a solicitor's charges by a composite global rate save in relation to a claim on the Legal Aid Fund. Included in the bill should be a claim for the "reasonable" costs of preparing and checking the bill of costs (Paragraph 2.16, Practice Direction to Part 43).

The bill should be signed by the party or solicitor giving the appropriate certificates as in Form 4. The most important is the certification that the indemnity principle has not been breached i.e. the receiving party is not asking to recover more from the paying party is paying his solicitor. In accordance with *General of Berne Insurance Co v Jardine Insurance Management* [1998] 2 All ER 301, CA, and *Bailey v IBC Vehicles* [1998] 3 All ER 570, CA, the indemnity principle applies item by item.

The notice and bill of costs have to be served in accordance with Part 6. Service is, however, not effected by the Court since the Court has no involvement in this initial stage of the process. Under Paragraph 2.2, Practice Direction to Part 47, in addition to the notice and the bill of costs, the receiving party must serve—

- copies of the fee notes of Counsel and of any expert in respect of fees claimed in the bill;
- written evidence as to any other disbursement which is claimed and which exceeds £250; and
- a statement giving the name and address for service of any person upon whom the receiving party intends to serve a notice of commencement.

Service must be effected on the paying party but also other "relevant persons". These persons are defined by Paragraph 2.5, Practice Direction to Part 47 as—

- any person who has taken part in the proceedings which gave rise to the assessment and who is directly liable under an order for costs made against him;
- any person who has given to the receiving party notice in writing that he has a financial interest in the outcome of the assessment and wishes to be a party accordingly; and
- any other person whom the Court orders to be treated as such which will usually require an application by that other person to be joined as a party to the assessment proceedings in accordance with Part 19.

The party serving the notice will have inserted a date in the notice by which the paying party must serve the points of dispute (the date being no less than 21 days from the date of service of the notice). If the notice is to be served outside the jurisdiction then the date to be inserted must reflect the provisions of RSC Order 11 as if the notice were a claim form and the points of dispute a defence (Paragraph 2.4, Practice Direction to Part 47). Service of the notice of commencement and the bill of costs together with the supporting documents must be effected generally within three months of the event which gives rise to the right to detailed assessment—usually the giving of a judgment (taking effect on the day that it is made under Rule 40.7) (Rule 47.7).

If the paying party fails to commence the detailed assessment proceedings by service of the appropriate documents, the paying party may apply to the Court for an order requiring the receiving party to take the appropriate steps to commence the detailed assessment proceedings. The order made may be subject to an "unless" condition, the breach of which may lead to a reduction in the costs that can be claimed or to their complete disallowance (Rule 47.8).

The application will be made in accordance with Part 23 subject to the provision in Paragraph 2.11(2) of the Practice Direction to Part 47 that the application notice must be served at least seven days before the hearing. Upon hearing the application the Court could make an unless order that if the order is breached, either all or part of the costs will be disallowed. A Court might impose a sanction under 44.14 ordering costs of the application either against the party at fault or his legal representative.

Whether or not there is an application under Rule 47.8(2), the Court can impose sanctions against the receiving party for commencing the assessment proceedings late. Those sanctions are set out in Rule 47.8(3) as a disallowance of all or part of the interest otherwise payable to the receiving party upon the costs awarded. The Court may also impose a sanction under Rule 44.14 disallowing all or part of the costs which are being assessed.

Any of the time limits under Part 47 may be extended by the parties by agreement under Rule 2.11. If agreement on an extension cannot be reached, a party may apply to the Court extending time under Rule 3.1(2)(a).

Points of dispute

In order to participate in the costs assessment procedure, the paying party must serve points of dispute in relation to any item in the bill of costs to which they object. An example of the manner in which points of dispute should be set out appears at Form 6 of the Schedule of Costs Forms. This consists of three columns, two of which are obligatory under Paragraph 2.14, Practice Direction to Part 47. Those two are—

- identification of each item in the bill of costs which is disputed; and
- a concise statement of the nature and grounds of dispute.

It is suggested in the same Paragraph that the paying party should put forward an alternative figure to be allowed for each item in respect of which a reduction is sought.

The final suggested column is space to allow the claimant to put in their comments on the same form. It would be useful therefore if the paying party also provided a computer disk containing the points of dispute so that the receiving party can insert their comments upon it. If a disk is not served and the points of dispute are capable of being copied onto a computer disk, the receiving party may request a disk copy of them within 14 days of the receipt of the points of dispute. The paying party must then supply that disk free of charge within seven days of the request (Paragraph 2.17, Practice Direction to Part 47).

The points of dispute must be signed either by the party or by the legal representative (Paragraph 2.14, Practice Direction to Part 47).

The points of dispute must be served within 21 days of the service of the notice of commencement (Rule 47.9(2)). That period can be extended either by agreement or by the Court under Rule 2.11 or Rule 3.1(2)(a) respectively.

If points of dispute are not served within the time limit, there are two consequences—

- The receiving party may apply for a default costs certificate. This application is made by a request in Form 7 of the Schedule of Costs Forms. A fee is payable upon request (£40 in both the High Court and County Court—Supreme Court Fees Order 1999 and County Court Fees Order 1999).

Upon filing the Court will issue a default costs certificate which will either be in Schedule of Costs Forms, Form 9 (County Court) or Form 10 (High Court). The certificate will include the amount of the bill plus the Court fee of £40 plus the fixed costs allowable under Part 45 being £80 (Rule 47.11(3) and Paragraph 2.1, Practice Direction to Part 45).

Under Rule 47.12 the Court must set aside a default costs certificate if the receiving party was not entitled to it. Similarly, if the receiving party finds out that the notice of commencement did not reach the paying party at least 21 days before the default costs certificate was issued, the receiving party must apply to set aside the certificate. Alternatively, if the certificate is proper, the paying party may apply to set it aside under Rule 47.12(2). An application would have to be made in accordance with Part 23 and must be supported by evidence (Paragraph 3.9(1), Practice Direction to Part 47). The application should also be accompanied by a draft of the points of dispute it is proposed to serve if the application is granted (Paragraph 3.9(3), Practice Direction to Part 47).

The paying party in default must show good reason for the Court to set aside the default costs certificate. One of the matters which it may take into account will be whether the application is made promptly (Paragraph 3.9, Practice Direction to Part 47). In addition, the Court will have regard to the overriding objective under Part 1 and the provisions of Rule 3.9 (Relief from Sanctions). In making an order the Court may make it subject to conditions including a condition that a payment on account be made in accordance with Rule 44.3(8) (Paragraph 3.10, Practice Direction to Part 47).

If a default costs certificate is set aside, the Court will give appropriate directions for the assessment proceedings (Paragraph 3.11, Practice Direction to Part 47).

- The other consequence of not filing points of dispute within the time limit set by Rule 47.5(2) (subject to any extension), is that the paying party may not be heard further in the detailed assessment proceedings unless the Court gives permission.

Costs payable under a default costs certificate must be paid within 14 days of the date of the certificate (Rule 44.8).

Agreeing costs

At any time, whether before or after points of dispute are served, the parties may agree the amount of costs. If agreement is reached, application for the costs certificate should be made under Rule 40.6 (Consent Judgments and Orders) for an order that a certificate be issued in the terms set out in the application.

Thus on the face of it an application has to be issued (with the fee) for a consent order to be made. In accordance with Rule 40.6(7) the order must be drawn up in the terms agreed. It must be expressed as being "by consent". It must also be signed by the parties acting in person or by the legal representative. The Court officer can deal with the application and issue the consequent certificate (Paragraph 2.18, Practice Direction to Part 47).

Under Rule 47.10(2) the application for a certificate consequent upon an agreement must be made to the Court which gave the judgment or order if the right to detailed assessment arises from that judgment or order (unless the proceedings have since been transferred). Otherwise the application has to be made to the venue for the detailed assessment proceedings under Rule 47.4.

If the receiving party asserts that the paying party has agreed to pay the costs but he refuses to pay or accede to a consent order, the receiving party may apply to the Court for an appropriate certificate on the basis of a compromise (Paragraph 2.19, Practice Direction to Part 47). Such an application must be supported by evidence and will be heard by the Costs Judge or a District Judge. The application must be made in accordance with Part 23. Thus the application notice and the evidence in support must be served no later than three days before the application is to be heard. Under Paragraph 2.20 of the Practice Direction to Part 47, the respondent to the application must file and serve any evidence he relies upon at least two days before the hearing date. The two time limits do not sit well together.

If agreement has been reached, the assessment proceedings may be discontinued in accordance with Part 38, although unless a detailed assessment hearing has been requested, there seems little purpose in involving the Court in the discontinuance. Application may, however, be made consequent upon the agreement for a costs certificate to be issued. If an assessment hearing has been requested, the receiving party is not entitled to discontinue the detailed assessment proceedings unless the Court gives permission (Paragraph 2.22(3), Practice Direction to Part 47).

Steps consequent upon service of points of dispute

If points of dispute are served that do not seek to dispute all parts of the bill of costs, the receiving party may make an application under Rule 47.15 for an interim costs certificate. Such an application must be made in accordance with Part 23 (Paragraph 5.1, Practice Direction to Part 47). It is, however, a pre-condition of such an application that the receiving party makes an application for an assessment hearing in accordance with Rule 47.14 and pays the court fee for detailed assessment (see below).

Upon receipt of points of dispute, the receiving party does have the option to serve a reply. It will be remembered that the points of dispute in Form 6 referred to above may contain a column allowing for the receiving party's comments in relation to the points of dispute. There is no obligation to serve a reply but if one is served then service must be effected within 21 days of service of the points of dispute (Rule 47.13).

Subject to an application for an interim costs certificate or the service of a reply, the normal course will be for the paying party to request simply a detailed assessment hearing under Rule 47.14. That request must be filed with the Court within three months of the expiry of the period for commencing the assessment proceedings, that is, usually three months after the judgment or order giving rise to the entitlement to costs.

The request for hearing must be made in Form 8 of the Schedule of Costs Forms (otherwise Form N258). The form sets out the items that must accompany it which are also detailed in Paragraphs 4.3, 4.4 and 4.5, Practice Direction to Part 47. A fee of £160 is payable in the High Court; £120 in the county court.

If a hearing date is not requested by the receiving party within the three month time limit, the consequences are similar to those following from a failure to commence the proceedings within the first three month time limit. Thus the paying party may make application for an order requiring the receiving party to file the request. That application would be made in accordance with Part 23. Upon the hearing the Court is likely to make an unless order so that if the terms of the order are breached, all or part of the costs to which the receiving party would otherwise be entitled will be disallowed (Rule 47.14(4)). Such an application may not be made after a request for a detailed assessment hearing has been made, albeit out of time. In those circumstances, upon hearing the detailed assessment the Court may disallow interest which would otherwise be payable on all or part of the costs awarded (Rule 47.14(5)) or impose the sanctions under Rule 44.14 by disallowing all or part of the costs that would otherwise have been awarded.

The three month time limit set by Rule 47.14(2) can be extended by the parties in accordance with Rule 2.11 or by order of the Court in accordance with Rule 3.1(2)(a).

The Hearing

On receipt of the request for the hearing the Court will usually fix a date. In particularly complex bills the Court may give directions for the management of the assessment or fix a date for a preliminary appointment (Paragraph 4.6, Practice Direction to Part 46).

Subject to that, the Court will give at least 14 days notice of the time and place where the hearing will take place (Paragraph 4.7(1), Practice Direction to Part 47).

No less than seven days and no more than 14 days before the date for the hearing, the receiving party must file with the Court the papers in support of the bill (Paragraph 4.12, Practice Direction to Part 47). Details of those papers are set out in Paragraph 4.13, Practice Direction to Part 47).

If after the date has been set the proceedings are settled, the Court must be notified immediately (Paragraph 4.10(2), Practice Direction to Part 47).

Parties are free to vary the bill of costs, points of dispute or reply at any time prior to the hearing. A document showing the changes must be filed at the Court and copies of it must be served (Paragraph 4.11(1), Practice Direction to Part 47). Upon the hearing the Court is entitled to disallow any changes or to allow them subject to conditions including that any costs wasted by the variation are paid (Paragraph 4.11(2), Practice Direction to Part 47).

The detailed assessment hearing will be conducted in much the same way as previously subject to the changes in the criteria for determining the costs under Part 44. As with previous practice, any disallowance or reduction will be shown on the original bill by the costs officer. The original will then be passed back to the receiving party duly marked. The bill of costs must then be completed by entering in the fourth and fifth columns of the standard form of bill (Form 2 Schedule of Costs Forms) the figures allowed. The sum of the bill must be recalculated and completed. The completed bill of costs must then be filed with the Court no later than 14 days after the detailed assessment hearing (Paragraph 5.4, Practice Direction to Part 47). Together with the bill of costs the receiving party must produce receipted fee notes and accounts in respect of all disbursements exceeding £500. Those of £500 or less are covered by the certificate that they have been discharged which is included in the bill of costs itself (see above). For this purpose disbursements does not include Counsel's fees. The receipted fee notes for these must be produced to the Court (Paragraph 5.9, Practice Direction to Part 47).

A final costs certificate will not be issued until all the Court fees have been paid.

The final costs certificate will then be issued under Rule 47.16(3) and served under that Rule on the parties. It will show—

- the amount of any costs which have been agreed between the parties or which have been allowed on detailed assessment; and
- where applicable, the amount agreed or allowed in respect of VAT on the costs agreed or allowed (Paragraph 5.8, Practice Direction to Part 47).

A model form of an interim costs certificate is at Form 11 Schedule of Costs Forms. Draft final costs certificates appear as Forms 12 and 13 of the Schedule of Costs Forms.

The certificate will include a figure for costs of the assessment which have been allowed to the receiving party upon the assessment. The presumption under Rule 47.18 is that the receiving party will be awarded costs although the Court does have the power to make some other order. In considering whether to make such other order the Court must take into account all the circumstances including—

- the conduct of all the parties;
- the amount, if any, by which the bill of costs has been reduced; and
- whether it was reasonable for a party to claim the costs of a particular item or to dispute that item (Rule 47.18(2)).

Offer to settle

In order to protect themselves against the almost inevitable order for costs, a paying party can make a written offer to settle the costs of the proceedings set out in the bill of costs. In the normal way such an offer would be expressed to be without prejudice save as to the costs of the detailed assessment proceedings (Rule 47.19(1)). No time limits for offers to settle are set out in the Rule. Paragraphs 7.4–7.6 of the Practice Direction, however, provides some regulation. The paying party's offer to settle should be made within 14 days of service of the notice of commencement. The offer by the receiving party should be made within 14 days of service of the notice of commencement. The offer by the receiving party should be made within 14 days of service of points of dispute. The costs officer must not be told about the offer or the fact that one has been made until he comes to deal with the question of costs of the assessment proceedings. At that point the offer can be produced and the Court will take it into account. Rule 47.19 stipulates that the receiving party can also make an offer to settle although there are no specific provisions as there are in Part 36 for the effect of such an offer if the receiving party beats it.

In any event Rule 47.19 does not apply if the receiving party is an assisted person.

Legal Aid

The claim on the Legal Aid Fund in a bill which includes a claim against another party should be shown separately in the bill (and see Paragraphs 9.1–9.7 to the Practice Direction below).

Generally the assessment procedure in making a claim solely against the Legal Aid Fund is much the same as the party and party procedure as though the Legal Aid Fund is the paying party. Rule 47.17, however, provides a slightly different procedure for commencement. The proceedings are commenced by filing with the Court a request in Form 8 of the Schedule of Costs Forms. In addition to the request, other documents must be lodged with the Court—

- a copy of the bill of costs (the form of which appears on Form 3 Schedule of Costs Forms);
- the document giving the right to detailed assessment (see further Paragraph 4.5, Practice Direction to Part 47);
- a copy of all orders made by the Court relating to the costs which are to be assessed;
- copies of any fee notes of Counsel and any expert in respect of fees claimed in the bill;
- written evidence as to any other disbursement which is claimed and which exceeds £250 (not £500 as above);
- the Legal Aid Certificates, any amendments to them, any authorities and any certificates of discharge or revocation of Legal Aid;
- the file with the relevant papers in support of the bill; and
- a statement signed by the solicitor giving appropriate details (see Paragraph 6.3, Practice Direction to Part 47).

A fee of £120 is payable in the High Court and £80 in the county court.

The request must be filed within three months after the date when the right to detailed assessment arose (Rule 47.17(2)).

If notice of the assisted person's interest has been given to the Court, the solicitor must also serve a copy of the request on the assisted person, in accordance with Regulation 119 of the Legal Aid (General) Regulations 1989. If the assisted person then wishes to attend the assessment hearing, a date will be fixed. Otherwise the Court will provisionally assess the costs without the attendance of a solicitor unless it believes it appropriate to hold a hearing. After provisional assessment the bill will be returned to the solicitor together with a notice in Form 14 of the Schedule of Costs Forms. That notice indicates the amount of costs which the Court proposes to allow (Paragraph 6.5, Practice Direction to Part 47).

If the solicitor is dissatisfied with the provisional assessment he may ask the Court to fix a date for the hearing within 14 days after receiving the notice in Form 14 as above. The Court will then fix a date and give at least 14 days notice of it (Paragraph 6.7, Practice Direction to Part 47).

If the provisional assessment is accepted, the solicitor will complete the bill as above and return it to the Court.

There are special provisions within the Practice Direction (Paragraphs 9.1-9.7) in relation to a claim on the Legal Aid Fund where there is also a claim against another party. If the claim upon the Legal Fund is restricted to Legal Aid prescribed rates, upon requesting the detailed assessment hearing, amongst the documents filed is a schedule which sets out all the items in the bill which are claimed against other parties calculated at the Legal Aid prescribed rate (see Paragraph 4.3(l)(iv) Form 3 Schedule of Costs Forms).

As reference to Form 3 will indicate, the schedule sets out the items which may be claimed out of the Legal Aid Fund only upon the Legal Aid prescribed rates. Whilst in the main bill claimed against the other party they will be shown at party and party rates, in the schedule they are shown in the Legal Aid prescribed rates. The schedule is divided into two parts, namely those costs which are payable by the paying party and those costs which are payable only out of the Legal Aid fund. Generally the Legal Aid assessment will follow immediately the party and party assessment.

Appeals

The position in relation to appeals against assessment is different between detailed assessment and summary assessment. Summary assessment is subject to the normal appeal rules contained within the dovetailed provisions in the schedules to the CPR. The procedure for appeals in detailed assessment is set out within Part 47 (Rules 47.20–47.26).

There are two pre-conditions to the making of an appeal. Firstly, the prospective appellant must seek written reasons for the decision in accordance with Rule 47.23. If the party seeking reasons is the receiving party then the request for reasons must be filed with the completed bill of costs under Rule 47.16 (that is, 14 days after the detailed assessment hearing). If it is the paying party seeking the reasons then the request must be filed within seven days after the end of the detailed assessment hearing (Rule 47.23(3)). The request will have to be made in writing since it must clearly identify the particular part of the decision for which reasons are requested (Paragraph 8.3, Practice Direction to Part 47). The Court is not obliged to give written reasons and Paragraphs 8.4–8.8, Practice Direction to Part 47 set out the grounds for refusal.

If written reasons are given by the Court, copies will be served on the parties.

The second pre-condition to appealing is that the Court's permission (where necessary) must be given (Rule 47.21(1)). Permission is not necessary if the appeal is against—

- a decision of an authorised court officer; or
- a decision of a Costs Judge or a District Judge to impose a sanction on a legal representative under Rule 44.14 (Powers in Relation to Misconduct) or Rule 48.7 (Wasted Costs Order).

The permission to appeal must be sought within 14 days after receiving the written reasons under Rule 47.23 or, if the Court directs that reasons do not need to be obtained, within seven days after the date of the direction (Rule 47.24(4)).

The request for permission can be made simply by letter delivered to the Court and copied to the other parties. It must set out the title of the action and the Court reference. It must also set out the basis upon which permission is sought (Paragraph 8.10, Practice Direction to Part 47).

The usual procedure will be that the Court will firstly give written reasons and then consider the request for permission to appeal. In considering the request the Court will take into account—

- whether the ground of appeal has a reasonable prospect of success;
- whether the costs of the appeal are likely to be disproportionate; and
- if the appeal is against a case management decision (remember that the procedure applies to any decision made in detailed costs assessment proceedings), whether an appeal at that stage in the proceedings is appropriate (Paragraph 8.14, Practice Direction to Part 47).

If permission is refused, the request can be renewed in front of a High Court Judge or Circuit Judge (Paragraph 8.17, Practice Direction to Part 47). If the Judge grants permission upon that application, he will generally extend the time for appealing. If he does not do so then the time for appealing is seven days after his decision (Paragraph 8.17(4), Practice Direction to Part 47).

Having overcome these hurdles, the appellant may commence the appeal proceedings by serving a notice of appeal (Form 16 Schedule of Costs Forms). Within that notice each item appealed must be detailed together with the grounds upon which the appeal is made in relation to that item.

If the appeal is against a decision of an authorised Court officer, the appeal is to a District Judge or, additionally in the High Court, a Costs Judge. In this instance the notice of appeal must be filed within 14 days after service of the Court officer's reasons or, if the Court has directed that reasons need not be obtained, within seven days after the date of that direction (Rule 47.25(2)).

If the appeal is against an order of a Costs Judge or a District Judge then it is made either to a High Court Judge or to a Circuit Judge in the County Court (Rule 47.22(2)). In that case the notice (Form 16 Schedule of Costs Forms) setting out the grounds for appeal must be filed within 14 days after permission to appeal is given (Rule 47.25(3)). If the appeal to the High Court Judge or Circuit Judge follows an appeal from an authorised Court officer to a Costs Judge or District Judge, the appellant must prepare a note of the decision given by the Costs Judge or District Judge, agree it with the other parties and seek the approval of it by the Court. The approved note must then be filed.

Upon receipt of the notice the Court will fix a date and serve a copy of the notice on all the other parties (Rule 47.25(4)).

Powers of the Court on Appeal

If the appeal is from an authorised Court officer, the appeal is by way of re-hearing.

In any appeal, if the Court is satisfied that the appeal should be allowed, it may make any order and give such directions as it considers appropriate (Rule 47.26(1) and(2)).

The Court hearing an appeal from a Costs Judge or District Judge will usually sit with two assessors, one of whom must be a District Judge or a Costs Judge and the other a practising barrister or solicitor.

Part 48—Costs—Special cases

Part 48 is a sweep-up provision that provides for costs in particular cases. These cases are—

- Costs payable by or to non parties.
- Costs payable pursuant to a contract.
- Costs in favour of a trustee or personal representative.
- Costs where money is payable by or to a child or patient.
- Costs of a litigant in person.
- Wasted costs orders.
- Assessment of solicitor and client costs including those under conditional fee agreements.

Pre-Commencement disclosure and disclosure by a non-party

Rule 48.1 regulates the costs regime in relation to pre-action disclosure under Rule 31.16 and disclosure by a non-party under Rule 31.17. The relevant statutory provisions are Sections 33 and 34 of the Supreme Court Act 1981 and Sections 52 and 53 County Courts Act 1984. The Rule repeats the general provision that normally the applicant will pay the costs of the party against whom disclosure is sought but the Court may make a different order having regard to all the circumstances including—

- the extent to which it was reasonable for the person against whom the order was sought to oppose the application; and
- whether the parties to the application have complied with any relevant pre-action protocol.

Both the pre-action protocols and the practice direction to them promote potential parties to litigation to exchange information and documents which would be disclosed during the course of proceedings if they were to be started. As already covered, there are sanctions available to the Court for a failure to do so. When considering making an order for costs, Rule 48.1(3) repeats the principle that the Court will look at all the circumstances in exercising its discretion. The Court must also have regard to the overriding objective. If a party to an application has refused to provide documents in accordance with either the letter or spirit of a pre-action protocol, the Court might impose a sanction on them by at least not giving them the benefit of an order for costs.

If an order for costs is made following an application that lasted no more than a day, the Court is likely to assess those costs summarily in accordance with Rule 44.7. This may cause some slight difficulties because the award of costs includes future costs in that under Rule 48.1(2)(b) the award includes the costs of complying with any order made on the application. Bearing in mind the speculative nature of those costs, the Court might adjourn the summary assessment until the order has been complied with. It could make an order for payment on account in accordance with Rule 44.3(8).

Costs orders in favour of or against non-parties—Rule 48.2

As previously dealt with, Section 51 of the Supreme Court Act 1981 gives a wide discretion to the Court repeated in Rule 44.3(1), as to whether costs are payable by one party to another, the amount of those costs and when they are to be paid. The discretion extends to making costs orders against non-parties. Rule 48.2 provides that where the Court is considering making an order in favour of or against a person who is not a party to the proceedings, the person must be joined to the proceedings simply for the purpose of those costs and given an opportunity to make representations to the Court at a hearing. The Court of Appeal set out the considerations for orders for costs against non-parties in *Symphony Group Plc v Hodgson (1993) 4 All ER 143*. The Rule does not apply, however, in relation to orders against the Legal Aid Board, potential wasted costs orders or orders covered by Rule 48.1 above since these three are regulated elsewhere.

Costs payable pursuant to contract

Rule 48.3 provides simply that if costs are payable pursuant to contract, the costs are presumed to have been reasonably incurred and are reasonable in amount. This repeats the basis upon which costs are assessed on the indemnity basis. It is still the case that where costs are assessed pursuant to contract, the

Court will not allow costs which have been unreasonably incurred or are unreasonable in amount. On the indemnity basis under Rule 44.4(3), any doubt concerning reasonableness is found in favour of the receiving party. Where costs are payable pursuant to the contract, the paying party has a similar burden but it is not a burden that cannot be overthrown and the costs remain within the discretion of the Court.

Mortgagee's costs

Rule 48.3 appears to be causing some unnecessary problems in relation to the recovery of costs by mortgagees. Although the evidence is anecdotal, it appears to be the case that some are assuming that the position in relation to mortgagees' costs has been substantially changed by the CPR and mortgagees' costs are always subject to assessment by the Court. This simply is not the case. Any lengthy discussion is outside the scope of this book but the general position is as follows—

- Mortgagees' costs are recoverable pursuant to contract.
- In order to effect recovery of costs, the mortgagees do not need an order for costs in their favour.
- If contrary to this principle an order is sought and obtained, the Court does have a proactive role in the assessment of those costs and they will be subject to Rule 48.3.
- If no order for costs is sought and no order made, the mortgagee is still entitled to recover the costs notwithstanding Rule 44.13(1) simply as a matter of equity and contract.
- Notwithstanding that the mortgagee seeks to recover costs simply pursuant to the contract, the Court still has some control over those costs—
    - the Court has jurisdiction to determine the terms of redemption including the quantification of costs;
    - the mortgagor has the right to apply for assessment under Sections 70 and 71 of the Solicitors Act 1974.

The leading case is *Gomba Holdings v Minories Finance Ltd [1993] CH 171*. The CPR do not change the principles established in that case.

Mortgagees' costs could be subject to summary assessment but only if an order for costs is sought and made. Summary assessment would have to be undertaken on the basis of Rule 48.3.

Rule 48.3 does not regulate the position between solicitor and client which is subject to a separate regime referred to below.

Costs of a trustee or personal representative

Rule 48.4 is simply a repeat of RSC Order 62 Rule 14 save in one respect. The Rule repeats therefore the general principle that a trustee or personal representative is entitled to be paid his costs out of the estate unless he "... has acted for a benefit other than that of the fund". The words in quotes replace the former provision that costs would be presumed unreasonably incurred (and thus disallowed) if they were incurred contrary to the duty of the trustee or personal representative. It is outside the scope of this work to discuss the difference between the two.

The costs are assessed on the indemnity basis. Thus proportionality has no application and any doubt as to reasonableness will be found in favour of the trustee or personal representative.

Costs of a trustee are often subject to contract. If that is the case then Rule 48.4 has no application and the regime under Rule 48.3 applies, although the principles of the two provisions are alike. If the trustee is a solicitor trustee, however, neither Rule 48.3 nor 48.4 may have application and the position may be regulated under Rule 48.8 (see below).

Costs payable by or to a child or patient

Part 21 regulates proceedings where a child or patient is one of the parties.

The general rule under Rule 48.5 is that costs payable by a child or patient to his solicitor (albeit through a litigation friend) must be subject to an order for detailed assessment. That assessment will take place on the indemnity basis in accordance with Rule 48.8. If a conditional fee agreement has been made between the child or patient and the solicitor, this will be subject to assessment under Rule 48.9. That Rule provides that the client may apply for assessment of the base costs or of a percentage increase or of both (Rule 48.9(3)). It is presumed that assessment of both will take place automatically under Rule 48.5 if the conditional fee agreement is between a child or patient and a solicitor.

There are exceptions to Rule 48.5 set out in the Practice Direction (Paragraph 1.2). They are as follows—

- Where the Court believes that an assessment is not necessary to protect the interest of the child or patient or his estate.
- Where the solicitor acting for the child or patient waives rights to claim any further costs than those agreed to be paid by another party or determined by the Court by way of summary assessment.
- Where someone else including an insurer is liable to discharge the solicitor's costs and the Court is satisfied that that other person is financially able to discharge those costs.

Litigants in person

The recoverable costs of litigants in person are regulated primarily by the Litigants in Person (Costs and Expenses) Act 1975. As a result of that Act, the RSC was amended under Order 62 Rule 18. The CCR was amended under CCR Order 38 Rule 17. Those provisions are repeated broadly in Rule 48.6. There is still no definition of a "litigant in person". The term is neither defined in Rule 2.3 nor in the glossary. Rule 48.6(6) does, however, provide two examples of a "litigant in person". It provides that the term includes—

- a company or other corporation which is acting with out a legal representative; and

- a barrister, solicitor, solicitor's employee or other authorised litigator who is acting for himself.

As to the first category, the position prior to 26 April 1999 was that in the High Court a company had to be represented by a solicitor. In the County Court a company could act in person. Under the CPR there is no restriction on a company acting in person.

The second example given of a litigant in person needs to be considered in light of Paragraph 1.7, Practice Direction to Part 48. The distinction is drawn somewhat artificially between a solicitor who is acting for himself and a solicitor who, although acting for himself, does so in his firm's name. This was a matter of some debate in the Committee. The result is that a solicitor represented by his firm or by himself in his firm's name is not, by the Practice Direction, a litigant in person. A solicitor using his firm's name is not bound by the restrictions of Rule 48.6. If the firm's name is not used then the provisions of Rule 48.6 apply.

The general picture under Rule 48.6 is that a litigant in person is entitled to recover costs—

- as would have been allowed if the work had been done or the disbursements made by a legal representative on the litigant in person's behalf;
- the payments reasonably made by him for legal services relating to conduct of the proceedings; and
- the cost of obtaining expert assistance in connection with assessing the claim for costs (Rule 48.6(3)).

Save for disbursements, the costs allowed, however, may not exceed two-thirds of the amount which would have been allowed if the litigant in person had been represented by a legal representative (Rule 48.6(2)). Even then the litigant in person must prove financial loss (Rule 48.6(4)). Otherwise the recoverable costs are limited to £9.25 per hour for the time spent reasonably doing the work to which the costs relate (Paragraph 1.6, Practice Direction to Part 48 and Rule 48.6(4)).

In order to prove financial loss, the litigant in person must produce to Court written evidence of the loss. That evidence must be served on the parties to the assessment at least 24 hours before the assessment hearing (Paragraph 1.4, Practice Direction to Part 48). If the litigant in person is commencing detailed assessment proceedings then the written evidence should be served with the notice of commencement (Paragraph 1.5, Practice Direction to Part 48).

Wasted costs orders

Rule 48.7 deals with wasted costs orders. This Rule needs to be considered with Rule 44.14 which provides for the Court's powers in relation to misconduct. Under that Rule also, orders may be made against a legal representative. Rule 44.14 and Rule 48.7 are based upon the very wide powers contained in Section 51 of the Supreme Court Act 1981 and particularly Section 51(6) which allows the Court to order a legal representative to meet "wasted costs". Rule 44.14 applies during the assessment procedure whereas Rule 48.7 applies during the course of the proceedings generally.

Section 51(6) Supreme Court Act 1981 is somewhat wider than Rule 48.7(1) since it applies not only to legal representatives but also to "other representatives". That term includes "any person exercising a right of audience or a right to conduct litigation". This would catch lay representatives who have a right of audience under the Lay Representatives (Rights of Audience) Order 1992.

A wasted costs order means an order requiring a legal representative to make a payment and an order that the costs of a legal representative should be disallowed in whole or in part (Rule 48.7(1)).

The application for a wasted costs order can be made at any time although the recommendation in Paragraph 2.1 of the Practice Direction to Part 48 is that applications for wasted costs should be left until after the end of the trial.

The legal representative must be given a reasonable opportunity to attend a hearing to give reasons why the Court should not make a wasted costs order (Rule 48.7(2)). Accordingly, if a party is intending to apply for a wasted costs order, they must give at least three days notice in writing to the legal representative indicating—

- what it is alleged the legal representative has done or failed to do; and
- the costs that are sought against him (Paragraph 2.3, Practice Direction to Part 48).

Upon an application the Court may give directions as to the serving of the notice or any consequent order upon the client to the legal representative in question (Rule 48.7(5)).

Paragraph 2.6, Practice Direction to Part 48 sets out the procedural approach of the Court to making a wasted costs order. The Court should deal with the matter in two stages. Firstly, the Court must be satisfied—

- that there is evidence or other material which, if unanswered, would be likely to lead to a wasted costs order being made; and
- that the wasted cost proceedings are justified notwithstanding the likely costs involved.

One of the problems that has arisen in recent years in relation to "wasted costs" is that much satellite litigation has developed, the cost of which becomes disproportionate to the costs involved. The new provisions allow the Court to apply some control over the process to ensure that the pursuit of wasted costs is proportionate and reasonable bearing in mind the costs that might be involved in doing so.

If the Court is satisfied that the wasted costs "proceedings" should go forward, the Court will give the legal representative an opportunity to be heard and then make a decision.

Following from the Court of Appeal decision in *Thidehalgh v Horsefield* (1994) 3 All ER 848, an order for wasted costs will only be made if—

- he has acted improperly, unreasonably or negligently;
- his conduct has caused a party to incur unnecessary costs; and

- it is just in all the circumstances to order him to compensate that party for the whole or part of those costs.

These criteria are cumulative—all must be proved to the satisfaction of the Court.

In considering whether to make an order, the Court is entitled to require that privileged documents are disclosed to the Court and, subject to the Court's discretion, to the other party to the application for an order (Rule 48.7(3)).

Privilege is one of those terms included in the glossary. The meaning provided there is—

> **The right of a party to refuse to disclose a document or produce a document or to refuse to answer questions on the ground of some special interest recognised by law.**

As made clear, privilege is a right of a party and not a legal representative. Accordingly a party can waive the privilege. The solicitor is not entitled to waive the privilege. Rule 48.7(3) was intended to overcome the perceived potential injustice for a legal representative in not being able to produce documents which might prove, for example, that the fault lay not with the legal representative but with the client. It would be said, however, on the part of the legal representative, that under the old rules he was entitled to the benefit of the doubt arising from his inability to produce documents without waiver of privilege by the client.

Some doubt has been raised as to the propriety of the ability of the Court to override privilege under Rule 48.7(3). The relationship between solicitor and client and the privilege that attaches is regarded by many as sacrosanct—breaches of it have the potential to fall foul of the European Convention on Human Rights.

Instead of making a decision on the evidence before the Court, the Court could direct that a Costs Judge or District Judge investigate the matter and report to the Court. Alternatively the Court could refer the whole matter to the Costs Judge or District Judge (Rule 48.7(6) and (7)).

Detailed assessment of solicitor and own client costs

The general regime in relation to solicitor and own client costs is that they are assessed on the indemnity basis. The definition of the indemnity basis is provided in Rule 44.4. Firstly, the Court will not allow costs which have been unreasonably incurred or are unreasonable in amount (Rule 44.4(1)). Under Rule 44.4(3) any doubt as to whether costs were reasonably incurred or reasonable in amount is found in favour of the receiving party, that is, under Rule 48.8, the solicitor.

Not only is the solicitor entitled to the benefit of the doubt but also, under Rule 48.8(2), there is a presumption that as between solicitor and client, the costs—

- have been reasonably incurred if they were incurred with the express or implied approval of the client;

- are reasonable in amount if their amount was expressly or impliedly approved by the client; but
- have been unreasonably incurred if—
  - they are of an unusual nature or amount; and
  - the solicitor did not tell his client that as a result he might not recover all of them from the other party.

These provisions reflect those of Order 62 Rule 15.

In the winter of 1998 much debate was had within the Committee and between the Law Society and the Committee as to the provisions of Section 74(3) of the Solicitors Act 1974. This provides:

(3) The amount which may be allowed on the taxation of any costs or bill of costs in respect of any item relating to proceedings in a county court shall not, except insofar as rules of court may otherwise provide, exceed the amount which could have been allowed in respect of that item as between party and party in those proceedings, having regard to the nature of the proceedings and the amount of the claim and of any counterclaim.

A solicitor and own client bill relating wholly or partly to contentious business can only be assessed in the County Court if it does not exceed £5,000 (Section 69(3) Solicitors Act 1974). Otherwise the bill must be assessed in the High Court. In that event Section 74(3) has no application. Thus, although much has been made of Section 74(3), it is of limited effect. Where it is believed it will have effect is in the fast track, particularly on the application of a fixed costs regime.

In any event the effect of Section 74(3) can be negated if the solicitor and client have entered into a written agreement which expressly permits payment to the solicitor of an amount of costs greater than those which the client could have recovered from another party to the proceedings (Rule 48.8(1A)). The Law Society guidance on Rule 48.8 (see Gazette 96/16, 21 April 1999) said that the client care letter must be signed by the client. Failure to do so will result in the costs being limited by Section 74(3). Whilst this must clearly accord with good practice, it is suggested that the signature of the client is not necessary for there to be a written agreement under Rule 48.8(1A).

As previously mentioned, the Solicitors Practice Rules are being changed with effect from 3 September 1999. In particular there is a new Rule 15 which provides for information to be provided to the client concerning costs and other matters and the complaints handling procedure.

Conditional fees

At the time of writing the prospect is that the uplift under a conditional fee agreement will be recoverable from another party to the proceedings under the Access to Justice legislation due to become law in autumn 1999. In the meantime the conditional fee uplift may only be recovered from the client.

Conditional fees are relatively new on the litigation scene having been legalised by Section 58 of the Courts and Legal Services Act 1990. Conditional fees should be differentiated from contingency fees which allow the representative to take a share in the award. Contingency fees are allowed in non-contentious work which includes claims in front of employment tribunals. Contingency fees remain unlawful for contentious business which includes work done before proceedings are begun provided the work is carried out "with a view to the proceedings being begun and that they are begun".

The essential element of a conditional fee is that there is no fee payable if the claim is lost but if the claim is won, the solicitor's hourly rate may be enhanced by up to 100% as a success fee. Accordingly a conditional fee consists of a base cost (the normal hourly charge) and a percentage increase (being the increase agreed under the conditional fee agreement).

On a solicitor and client assessment of costs arising from a conditional fee agreement, the client may apply for assessment of the base costs or of the percentage increase or of both (Rule 48.9(3)).

The base costs are assessed in the normal way on the indemnity basis (Rule 48.9(4)) i.e. burden of proof on the client and no application of the principle of proportionality.

The assessment of the percentage increase, however, takes into account proportionality (Rule 48.9(5)). In assessing the percentage increase, however, the Court is obliged to consider the position as the solicitor or Counsel saw the claim at the time that the increase was agreed. This encodifies the principle established in *Francis v Francis & Dickerson [1956] P 87*. For this purpose it is suggested that solicitors should have some record of the reasons behind assessing the risk at the time that it was assessed and why a particular percentage increase was suggested and agreed.

The Practice Direction sets out some factors relevant to assessing the percentage increase (Paragraph 2.15, Practice Direction to Part 48)—

- The risk that the circumstances in which the fees would be payable might not occur.
- The disadvantages relating to the absence of payment on account.
- Whether the amount which might be payable under the conditional fee agreement is limited to a set proportion of any damages recovered by the client.
- Whether there is a conditional fee agreement between solicitor and Counsel.
- The solicitor's liability for any disbursements.

If the client is making application to reduce the percentage increase then the client must set out in the application notice—

- the reasons why the percentage increase should be reduced; and
- what the percentage increase should be (Paragraph 2.14, Practice Direction to Part 48).

Solicitor and client assessment procedure

Rule 48.10 sets out the special procedure for the assessment of costs between solicitor and client.

Application for assessment is made by the claim form under Part 8. It may follow, however, an action by the solicitor for recovery of costs. That claim would have been issued under Part 7.

Reference should also be made to RSC Order 106 (in Schedule 1 CPR) which provides rules concerning proceedings relating to solicitors under the Solicitors Act 1974. If an order is made for assessment then the solicitor must serve a breakdown of costs within 28 days of that order (Rule 48.10(2)). The breakdown consists of details of the work done under the bill of costs being assessed and, in applications under Section 70 of the Solicitors Act 1974, a cash account (Paragraph 2.21, Practice Direction to Part 48).

An example of a breakdown is included in the Schedule of Costs Forms at Form 20.

Copies of fee notes of Counsel and of any expert must accompany the breakdown together with written evidence as to any other disbursement exceeding £250.

The client must serve points of dispute within 14 days after service of the breakdown (Rule 48.10(3)). If the client fails to do so, the solicitor is not entitled to obtain a default costs certificate but the Court does have the power to issue an interim certificate under Rule 47.15. In any event a client who does not serve points of dispute is not entitled to be heard on the assessment unless the Court gives permission (Paragraph 2.29, Practice Direction to Part 48).

The solicitor may serve a reply but is not obliged to do so. If he does so then it must be served within 14 days of service of the points of dispute.

Either party may file a request for a hearing date after the points of dispute have been served (Rule 48.10(5)). The request must be no later than three months after the date of the order for costs to be assessed (Rule 48.10(5)). The request must be in Form 21 of the Schedule of Costs Forms. It must be accompanied with the documents and information set out in Paragraph 2.26 of the Practice Direction to Part 48. An estimate of the length of time the detailed assessment hearing will take must also be provided. The Court will set a date and give the parties at least 14 days notice of it.

Under Rule 47.16 the solicitor must file the completed bill within 14 days after the assessment hearing unless the Court disposes with that requirement.

After the detailed assessment hearing is concluded the Court will—

- complete the Court copy of the bill so as to show the amount allowed;
- determine the result of the cash account;
- award the costs of the detailed assessment hearing in accordance with Section 70(8) Solicitors Act 1974; and
- issue a final costs certificate showing the amount due following the detailed assessment hearing.

The provisions relating to appeal under Part 47 apply to a solicitor and client assessment.

CHAPTER 30
PART 42—CHANGE OF SOLICITOR

Introduction

The special place for the solicitor in litigation is to some extent retained in Part 42 which deals with the mechanics of establishing when a solicitor acts for a party. This is differentiated from the words "legal representative" which appear throughout the Rules. Under Rule 2.3(1) a—

> **legal representative means a barrister or a solicitor, solicitor's employee or other authorised litigator (as defined in the Courts & Legal Services Act 1990) who has been instructed to act for a party in relation to a claim.**

Part 42 must be read on conjunction with Part 6 and particularly Rule 6.5. That Rule provides for the establishment of an address for service of a party. Rule 6.5(2) provides that the address for service must be within the jurisdiction. Subject to that requirement the party has two choices for the address for service. They can either give the business address of their solicitor as the address for service or the address of their residence or place of business.

In relation to a claim form, this general rule is repeated in Rule 6.13 which provides that the claim form must include the defendant's address for service which may be the business address of the defendant's solicitor if he is authorised to accept service on the defendant's behalf.

Rule 6.5(5) deals with the address for service in all situations save in relation to the service of the claim form. The difference between the two is that for everything other than the claim form, the address for service of a party is the business address of his solicitor as long as the solicitor is acting for the party to be served. There is no requirement that the solicitor must be authorised to accept service.

The question then arises as to when is a solicitor acting for the party to be served. The answer is provided in Part 42 which is primarily aimed at establishing exactly when a solicitor is acting for a party and accordingly when the solicitor's business address is the address for service. As well as determining the address for service, which depended previously on whether the solicitor was "on the record", the question of a solicitor being "on the record" affected the recoverability of costs. Both under the old Rules and the CPR, questions arise as to exactly when is a party to the proceedings a "litigant in person" for the costs rules and particularly Rule 48.6. Previous commentaries have suggested that there is no definition of a "litigant in person". It is suggested that the common view under the old rules was that a party was a "litigant in person" unless they had a solicitor "on the record".

As above, under Parts 6 and 42 the solicitor still enjoys a unique position if only in relation to their ability to proffer their business address as the address for service of a party. Whilst, for instance, a barrister is included within the definition of a "legal representative", he cannot proffer his address as an address for service in relation to someone who has a residence or business address within the jurisdiction.

The CPR do not define what is a litigant in person. It may be considered that a litigant in person is a party for whom a solicitor is not acting. The difficulty, however, is that there is no definition of exactly when a solicitor is "acting for a party". Rule 42.1 provides that where the address for service of a party is the business address of a solicitor, the solicitor will be considered to be acting for that party until there is a formal change of solicitor in accordance with the remainder of Part 42. This, however, is only a deeming provision for the purpose of establishing an address for service under Rule 6.5(5). Thus the Rules do not assist in establishing when a solicitor is acting for a party to differentiate with a litigant in person although generally this should not cause a difficulty.

The Rules

Part 42 is the result of unification of the provisions of RSC Order 67 and CCR Order 50 Rule 5.

Rule 42.1 deals with the general rule that—

> **where the address for service of a party is the business address of his solicitor, the solicitor will be considered to be acting for that party until the provisions of this Part have been complied with.**

As above, this is a deeming provision to maintain some uniformity about the address for service of a party. Although a party may use the legal services provided by a solicitor, there is no obligation on the party to give the solicitor's business address as the address for service. If that address is given, however, the solicitor's business address will remain the address for service until a notice of change is filed at the Court and served on every other party in accordance with Rule. 42.2(2) or the Court makes an order under Rule 42.3.

Rule 42.2. provides the mechanics for changing the address for service upon the appointment or change of solicitor. Thus, if—

- a party for whom a solicitor is acting wants to change its solicitor;
- a party, after having acted in person (which in these circumstances equates with having given their residence or business address as the address for service) appoints a solicitor to act on his behalf (again "act" is equated with the solicitor giving their business address as the address for service); or
- a party, after having conducted its claim by a solicitor (having the same meaning as above) intends to act in person;

the party or his solicitor must—

- file a notice of the change of address for service; and
- serve the notice on every other party and, where appropriate, on the former solicitor.

The practice form is N434. It must state the party's new address for service and (in the version filed at Court) state that the notice has been served on every other party and, where appropriate, on the former solicitor.

The CPR do not change the general rule that co-claimants must be represented by the same solicitor. Accordingly a notice under Rule 42.2 may be ineffective insofar as it purports to provide that co-claimants are represented by different solicitors: *Black King Shipping Corporation v Massi, The Litsion Pride [1985] 1 Lloyds Rep 437.*

In the particular circumstances in which a party wants to change solicitor or to act in person in succession to a solicitor, Rule 42.2(5) is a deeming provision to the effect that although the contractual arrangements may have been terminated between the solicitor and client, the former solicitor will still be considered to be the party's solicitor for the purposes of the address for service unless and until notice is served on all other parties (and the former solicitor).

Unlike documents which are issued or prepared by the Court, a notice of change has to be served by the party. As above, under Rule 42.2(4) when the party files the notice of change it must state that they have served it.

Legal Aid

Rule 42.2(6) deals with the mechanics of changing solicitor upon the discharge or revocation of a Legal Aid Certificate. Under the legal aid legislation, Part X of the Civil Legal Aid (General) Regulations 1989 provides for revocation and discharge to follow certain events and the effect thereafter of that revocation or discharge. In general terms the discharge of a certificate means that the legal aid certificate comes to an end on the date of discharge although the Area Director does have discretion as to the date of discharge. Revocation, on the other hand, means that the assisted person is deemed never to have had legal aid save for the purposes of Section 18 of the Legal Aid Act 1988 (Regulation 74, Civil Legal Aid (General) Regulations 1989). Regulation 83 provides that the retainer of a solicitor and Counsel selected by or acting on behalf of the assisted person determines forthwith (subject to appeal) on the receipt by the assisted person of a notice of revocation or discharge of a certificate. In those circumstances Rule 42.2(6)(a) provides that at the same time as the notice of revocation or discharge is served, the solicitor shall cease to be the solicitor acting in the case for the purposes of Part 42.

In those circumstances the solicitor can still be retained privately by the party but in that case a notice of change has to be filed as though the party had previously acted in person and the solicitor was being appointed for the first time. If the party wishes to act in person he can do so but he must give an address for service. That address must be in compliance with Rule 6.5(2) and (3).

Solicitor ceasing to act

The remaining provisions of Part 42 deal with the circumstances in which a solicitor voluntarily or involuntarily ceases to act for a party. If the decision is voluntary and no notice of change is served by the party, the solicitor must make an application to the Court for a declaration that he has indeed ceased to be the solicitor acting for the party. That application would be made in accordance with Part 23 and must comply with the requirements of that Part. The party must be given notice of the application (although the Court can direct otherwise) and the application must be supported by evidence. That evidence could be provided either on the application notice verified by a statement of truth or by a separate witness statement (Rule 42.3(2)). Notice of the application does not have to be given to any other party to the proceedings and they have no part to play in the application.

If the order is made by the Court then a copy of it must be served on every party to the proceedings (Paragraph 3.3, Practice Direction to Part 42). Unless the Court serves it, a certificate of service must be filed by either the party or the solicitor serving it. The solicitor will be entitled to be paid for the costs of the application simply under their contractual retainer by the client since the application is incidental to the litigation.

Rule 42.4 deals with the involuntary cessation of acting for a party. If a solicitor who has acted for a party—

- has died;
- gone bankrupt;
- ceased to practise; or
- cannot be found;

any party to the proceedings may apply for an order declaring that the solicitor has ceased to be the solicitor acting for the other party in the case in the event that the party for whom that solicitor acted has not given appropriate notice of change or intention to act in person.

The application will have to be made under Part 23. Notice of it must be given to the party for whom the solicitor acted although presumably the address for service remains that of the solicitor and it is unclear whether the notice here (Rule 42.4(2)) is required to be actual notice rather than effectively deemed notice by the provisions of Part 6.

If an order is made, a copy of it must be served on every other party to the proceedings and if the applicant serves it then the applicant must file a certificate of service (Form N215) (Rule 42.4(3)). Again there is a slight difficulty as to the appropriate address for service of the party whose solicitor was the subject of the application. This difficulty might become a little more acute if the party concerned is out of the jurisdiction.

In the event of the Court making the order, the party for whom the solicitor acted would be obliged to give an address for service within the jurisdiction (Rule 6.5(2)). If that party has a residence or place of business within the jurisdiction then that address must be given unless a new solicitor is appointed and the business address of the solicitor is given as the address for service.

INDEX

£45.00 CL335 25.9.07

97

1380 ff

+ £45.00